Foundations for Teaching Technical Communication: Theory, Practice, and Program Design

ATTW Contemporary Studies in Technical Communication

M. Jimmie Killingsworth, Series Editor

Published in cooperation with the Association of Teachers of Technical Writing

Volume 1:
Foundations for Teaching Technical Communication: Theory, Practice, and Program Design
edited by Katherine Staples and Cezar M. Ornatowski, 1997

In preparation:

Volume 2:
Writing at Good Hope: A Study of Negotiated Composition in a Community of Nurses
by Jennie Dautermann

Volume 3:
Computers and Technical Communication: Pedagogical and Programmatic Perspectives
edited by Stuart A. Selber

Volume 4:
The Practice of Technical and Scientific Communication: Writing in Professional Contexts
edited by Jean A. Lutz and C. Gilbert Storms

Foundations for Teaching Technical Communication: Theory, Practice, and Program Design

edited by

Katherine Staples
Austin Community College

and

Cezar Ornatowski
San Diego State University

Volume 1 in ATTW Contemporary Studies in Technical Communication

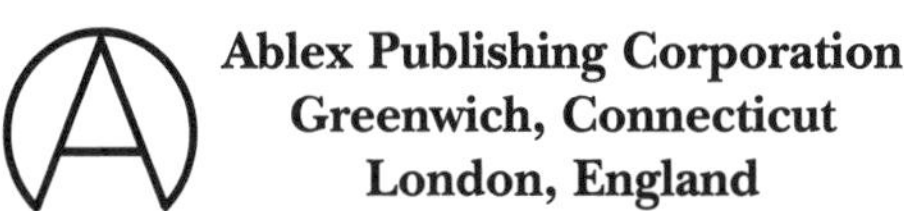

Ablex Publishing Corporation
Greenwich, Connecticut
London, England

Second Printing 1998

Printed in the United States of America

Library of Congress Cataloging-in-Publication Data

Staples, Katherine.
Foundations for teaching technical communication : theory, practice, and program design / Katherine Staples and Cezar M. Ornatowski.
p. cm.—(ATTW contemporary studies in technical communication)
Includes bibliographical references and index.
ISBN 1-56750-320-9 (cloth).—ISBN 1-56750-321-7 (paper)
1. Communication of technical information—Study and teaching. I. Ornatowski, Cezar M. II. Title. III. Series.
T10.5.S75 1997 97-19136
CIP

Ablex Publishing Corporation
55 Old Post Road #2
P.O. Box 5297
Greenwich, CT 06830

Published in the U.K. and Europe by:.
JAI Press Ltd.
38 Tavistock Street
Covent Garden
London WC2E 7PB
England

CONTENTS

Part IV Program Design

PREFACE

This collection is an attempt to map the key elements in an emerging discipline. However, the notion of mapping is misleading here because it implies the existence of a fixed terrain and established roadways. The present collection, on the contrary, seeks to chart the outlines of a dynamic, growing, and expanding field: an emerging and fast-changing landscape with few fixed paths and many possibilities for exploration.

In a recent collection of research essays on writing in the workplace, Rachel Spilka has noted that "before the discipline can mature any further, it needs to determine where it has been and where it needs to go next" (*Writing in the Workplace: New Research Perspectives.* Carbondale and Edwardsville: Southern Illinois UP, 1993, p.vii). We would add that the discipline should also attempt to determine where it is. That is the purpose of the present collection. It attempts to answer the question of where we are today, not in order to limit possibilities or define boundaries but to serve as a marker on the way, an orientation point, an invitation to the journey ahead. In this sense, the collection follows in the footsteps of other landmark anthologies that have charted the course of technical communication at earlier stages of its growth, collections such as Anderson, Brockmann, and Miller's *New Essays in Scientific and Technical Communication* (1983), Odell and Goswami's *Writing in Nonacademic Settings* (1985), and Fearing and Sparrow's *Technical Writing: Theory and Practice* (1989).

The idea for this book grew from our work on a special issue of *Technical Communication Quarterly* (Summer 1993), which brought us together as collaborators to confront and synthesize our different but overlapping perspectives of technical communication as scholars, teachers, program administrators, and consultants. This book reflects our shared view of this diverse field and our sense of its unique potential for synthesis of theory and practice, research and application, teaching and learning, the academy and the workplace. The book is a celebration of this potential.

In the course of our work on this project, we have also come to appreciate the different and overlapping professional communities that inhabit the terrain of technical communication. These communities—ATTW, STC, CPTSC, IEEE, CCCC, MLA—reflect both the profession's, and our own, diverse interests, perspectives, and needs. Our membership in these diverse communities has been a source of inspiration as well as of creative tension.

We wish to acknowledge the communities and individuals that helped us on our collaborative journey. Billie Wahlstrom and Mary Lay, editors of *Technical Communication Quarterly*, first brought us together as collaborators. We appreciate the support of M. Jimmie Killingsworth, Sherry Little, and ATTW in establishing the new ATTW series in technical and professional communication and in encouraging us to contribute to it.

We also want to acknowledge the help and support of many individuals whose work on this and other projects contributed directly and indirectly to our vision and our work. We can mention here only a few of the many colleagues who have become friends and friends who have also become colleagues: David McMurrey, Stephen Bernhardt, Norm Colbath, Roger Grice, Kenneth Rainey, and Karen Schriver. We also want to acknowledge the example and intellectual achievement of our parents, and the forbearance and support of our loved ones, Merrie Sasaki and Tomasz Kot.

Katherine Staples
Cezar Ornatowski

INTRODUCTION

Katherine Staples & Cezar Ornatowski

TECHNICAL COMMUNICATION IN THE 1990s

In the last decade, technical communication—as an academic discipline and professional field—has grown and changed dramatically.

For one, technical communication has developed a sophisticated and growing body of theory and research. Technical communication scholars, teachers, and practicing professionals have drawn on a wide variety of disciplines, practices, and technologies—new theories of rhetoric, new views of organizational behavior, new techniques of inquiry, new media, and new conceptions of education and learning—to chart the outlines of a new multidisciplinary field.

The growth in disciplinary knowledge has been paralleled by the growing diversity and sophistication of the technical communication profession. Whether as writers, editors, or visual communicators, technical communicators occupy increasingly expert and critical roles in the organizations they serve. Constantly evolving, these roles have expanded in scope and complexity as in responsibility and prestige.

In response to these developments, technical communication courses and programs have grown both in number and in sophistication. By bringing together theory and practice, the ideals of the academy and the demands of the workplace, these courses and programs have created a new education space common to academic knowledge and professional practice. Thus, they have the potential to redefine the nature of teaching, learning, and expertise. In this sense, technical communication education has become an important component in the debates that are shaping the present and future of American education.

This collection provides a review of the theoretical and practical knowledge—the theories, issues, developments, and practices (both professional and educational)—that are shaping the discipline of technical communication today. In bringing together the different aspects of this diverse and changing field, the collection provides an opportunity to assess the current scope and status of technical communication. It therefore represents a self-reflection that is a necessary step for further growth of the field.

However, the book not only reflects disciplinary growth; it also reflects shared perceptions of disciplinary tensions. These tensions—between the humanities and technology, university and workplace, theory and practice, fine arts and applied ones, education and training—are implicit in the entire history of technical communication and continue to underlie many of the issues raised by the following essays. These same tensions also underlie many important issues in American education and American life. We believe that, by its very nature, technical communication, as both a discipline and a profession, inevitably highlights these tensions and also has the potential to address them. By bringing together the different aspects of the field—theory and practice, workplace and education—this collection hopes to support a continuing dialogue that can contribute to the creation of what Billie Wahlstrom (in this volume) calls a "unified vision of the discipline."

In this vision, the technical communicator emerges as an educated decision maker whose professional decisions are informed by critical thinking skills, theory, application, ethics, communication ability, and knowledge of and about technology. As a discipline, technical communication defines a new community of practice and research as well as a new education space characterized by shifting roles, evolution and change, diversity and integration. The contributors to this volume represent the distinctive voices and views that characterize the diversity and inclusiveness of technical communication.

DESIGN OF THE BOOK

The collection is divided into four major sections: "Theoretical Foundations," "Practical Foundations," "Professional Roles for Technical Communicators", and "Program Design." This organization reflects our belief that technical communication is at once founded in theory and oriented toward practice (pedagogical as well as workplace) and that these dual foundations are reflected in technical communication education and program design.

Theoretical Foundations

The section on "Theoretical Foundations" discusses the major theories that have helped to redefine the nature of technical communication and that have begun to reshape technical communication education. Drawing on the advances in organizational theory, rhetorical theory, social constructionism, and cognitive psychology, the essays in this section extend and complicate our understanding of communication dynamics and of the ways in which knowledge is constructed and perceived in social contexts. At the same time, the essays present potentially conflicting views, exploring the tensions between the individual and society, between writer and audience, between individual cognition and social context.

The section opens with Mary Coney's overview of the impact of recent theory on technical communication. Coney notes that much has changed since Anderson, Brockmann, and Miller, in their landmark 1983 collection of essays, found theory to be the "least healthy" component of the field. In her assessment of the growth and current status of theory in technical communication, Coney focuses on three areas of concern she considers central to technical communication: audience, process, and style. Of these, she finds that audience has received the most theoretical attention. She discusses the contribution to technical communication of three major orientations in audience analysis (reader-response, cognitivist, and ethnographic) and suggests that increasingly complex representations of audience in technical communication are emerging from recent work, representations that are challenging established paradigms of document design. In reviewing recent research on the writing process in relation to technical communication, Coney finds that a reorientation has taken place, from a predominantly cognitive to a predominantly social view of writing. While the former has contributed to a significant improvement in the quality of technical documentation, the latter has helped scholars understand the complex nature and positioning of workplace writing. Finally, in her review of the work on style in technical communication, Coney notes the gradual departure from the positivistic view of language and from the tenets of "plain style" toward a rhetorical perspective that sees the technical writer as commanding a variety of styles and approaches appropriate to accomplishing different rhetorical purposes. Coney suggests that the recent growth of theory in technical communication has served to deepen and complicate, rather than explain, the fundamental problems and questions of the discipline.

Teresa Harrison and Susan Katz urge teachers and students of technical communication to take organizations seriously and to develop an appreciation for the kind of social context that organizations provide in order to enhance their performance as technical communicators. Critical to this appreciation is the acknowledgment of organizations as cultures and as communities of knowledge and practice that, to a significant extent, both shape, and are shaped by, communicative activities. Organizations as systems of shared norms and as communities of knowledge, as well as systems of power and authority, exert powerful pressures on members and provide models of thought and action. Teachers and students of technical communication need to be aware of these pressures and systems to be able to critically reflect on their own professional practice, on the organizational worlds they inhabit, and on the wider social implications of their practice. Only such an awareness can contribute to better organizational citizenship. Taking organizations seriously, therefore, Harrison and Katz suggest, also involves appreciating the ethical implications of communicating in organizations.

Cezar Ornatowski's discussion of the rhetorical dimensions of technical communication extends the discussion of the relationship between technical communication and its social and institutional context. Drawing on social constructionism, studies of writing in professional contexts, rhetoric of science, and philosophy and sociology of science and technology, Ornatowski argues that technical communication is fundamentally rhetorical; it represents a specific deployment of symbols in areas of culture that deal with organized productive activity and with the human relationship to technology and its products. A rhetoric of technical communication theorizes the characteristic dimensions and mechanisms of that deployment, as well as its effects.

In his discussion of the implications of social constructionist theory for technical communication, Mahalingam Subbiah suggests that social constructionist theory provides an alternative vision of knowledge making in business, industrial, and government organizations, a vision that enables technical communicators to become more critical and responsible members of organizations and more responsible citizens of the larger social community. Subbiah insists that the social constructionist perspective as applied to technical communication must place issues of power, authority, negotiation, and argument, in addition to collaboration and consensus, in the foreground as central to the way knowledge is constructed in communities of discourse. In addition, technical communicators must recognize the interconnection between knowledge and language and the centrality of language in communal knowledge-making processes. Such foregrounding of language and argument helps make technical communicators aware of their central role in organizational knowledge-making and of the professional and ethical implications of that role.

Janice Redish explains the contributions of cognitive psychology to technical communication, showing how the findings of cognitive research can help technical communicators to best reach readers, to design more readable documents, to better understand their own writing and perceptual processes, as well as to better teach students of technical communication. Although cognitive psychology was traditionally oriented toward individual cognition, Redish emphasizes that recent research has included considerations of context and culture to arrive at a richer description of how people interpret both discourse and their world.

Practical Foundations

The "Practical Foundations" section deals both with broad professional and pedagogical issues—such as ethics, gender, collaboration, multiculturalism, new technologies, and media design—and with the expanding and overlapping professional roles that technical communicators occupy. The essays in this section provide the intellectual tools for understanding and for appropriate action in social contexts specific to technical communication. In these contexts, professional communicators experience tension between, on the one hand, the tools, tasks, and roles they must continually master and, on the other, the complex situations in which they must act and the implications of their choices for action.

In their opening statement, Paul Meyer and Stephen Bernhardt redefine workplace literacy by evaluating it in the context of the changing demands of the workplace and of the information society that technical communicators serve. These demands include responsibility and accountability; self-motivation for continual learning; adaptability to change; strong interpersonal communication, negotiation, and cooperation skills; and adaptive reading and computer skills. Although Meyer and Bernhardt acknowledge that education goes beyond merely workplace preparation, they argue that emerging conceptions of workplace literacy challenge the traditional technical communication curriculum.

The section on current issues in technical communication continues with Scott Sanders's review of the recent debates on ethics in technical communication. Sanders identifies three major approaches to ethical analysis: practical, philosophical, and rhetorical. The progression from practical to rhetorical conceptions of ethics marks out, Sanders notes, a major shift in the focus of analytical concern in discussions of ethics, from the product of ethical deliberation (the document or action itself) toward the processes that influence the decision to act and the practices of the community in which the action occurs. Following this shift, the fundamental notion of what it means to be an ethical technical communicator has changed as well, from rule-based exhortations to be ethical toward complex considerations of rhetorical ethos-based probing of the manifold relationships between writers, readers, documents, and contexts. Such "postmodern rhetorical" conceptions of ethics, Sanders points out, are antifoundational, deriving ethical guidelines not from fundamental principles but from a process of inquiry inherent in the dynamics of composing and communicating in social contexts.

Linda LaDuc argues for the recognition of the centrality of gender as a salient organizing principle in technical communication. She shows that both scholarship and teaching regarding gender issues have recently become more sophisticated, conceptually and methodologically, progressing from uncovering how gender politics limit and oppress women to investigating how gender, as a complex of social, cultural, and psychological phenomena, affects us all. The implication for technical communicators is that gender, far from being merely one variable among many, is a basic and enduring constituent of human identity and human action and affects all acts of communication.

In their discussion of collaboration in technical communication, Rebecca Burnett, Christianna White, and Ann Hill Duin examine the nature of face-to-face and computer-mediated collaboration in relation to issues of culture, authority, conflict, and gender. They suggest that the basic conditions of collaborative interaction are intentionality and purposefulness. They point out that research in collaboration has moved from describing where and how collaboration occurs to an examination of issues that affect collaboration, such as authority, conflict, and gender. Along the way, they suggest that conflict is preferable to consensus in collaboration, provided it concerns substantive issues, because it facilitates creative problem resolution.

Emily Thrush discusses the implications for technical communication of the increasing internationalization of business and the increasingly multicultural workforce. She sets up a preliminary framework—based on concepts from linguistics, anthropology, sociology, history, political science, and economics—to help technical communicators become aware of the dimensions of communication relevant to cultural and linguistic diversity. Thrush suggests that technical communicators need to learn much more about the impact of cultural differences on communication, about the implications of those differences for what are taken to be the basic principles of document design, and for the teaching of technical communication in an increasingly multicultural and international context.

Henrietta Nickels Shirk undertakes the task of making sense out of the new computer technologies that have been changing the work of technical communicators. She classifies the myriad available communication tools in terms of the metaphors that best describe the dominant roles in which they serve technical communicators: as pens, links, webs, or minds. She examines how the new technologies changed the professional work of technical communicators and the challenges they present to practitioners and educators. Among these challenges are responding appropriately to the abundance of electronic tools for creating communication products; developing appropriate technical, design, and rhetorical skills to deal with the new tools (for instance, addressing multiple levels of audience in hypermedia); and dealing with the changes in work patterns and work space design brought about by the new tools (for instance, electronic networking or telecommuting). The new electronic tools, Shirk notes, not only provide new perspectives on the nature and structure of texts, but also redefine the creative process itself by forcing a shift from the one-dimensionality of print-based textuality and toward the multidimensionality of the electronic communication spaces. What is especially interesting is that the metaphors Shirk uses to explain the working of new communication technologies are taken from the humanities; the metaphors thus serve to rhetorically bridge the apparent gap between technology and the humanities.

The discussion of new communication technologies is continued in Stuart Selber's analysis of the principles of media design—a new and fast-emerging frontier in technical communication. Selber notes that media design is informed by interdisciplinary practice and presents serious challenges to technical communication practice, theory, and education. Media design requires technical communicators to perform the tasks of architects, cartographers, and rhetoricians, combining highly developed technical skills with expertise in such disparate areas as film, animation, theater, cognitive and learning psychology, linguistics, and software development, besides the more traditional education in English, writing, organizational theory, and technical expertise—an intersection of disciplines that challenges current models of technical communication. Most significantly, Selber emphasizes that computer technologies and interfaces are value-laden and both are shaped by and shape humans and human activities; therefore, media design involves not merely extensive technical expertise but also important ethical dimensions, dimensions that remain to be explored and that present additional challenges to researchers and educators. Technical communication, Selber concludes, must provide critical perspectives on the dominant ideologies that influence the development of design tools.

Professional Roles for Technical Communicators

The essays in the section on professional roles for technical communicators discuss three evolving professional and social roles: technical writer, technical editor, and visual communicator. The essays show that the roles of technical communicators are becoming simultaneously more specialized and broader, as technical communicators are required to master a growing array of technical tools and to demonstrate specialized technical knowledge while they assume responsibilities in areas beyond their traditional purview: project development and management, technology design, marketing, and others. The essays discuss both the evolving roles for technical communicators as well as their implications for professional practice and teaching.

Roger Grice shows that a career that once involved mainly "writing" now involves far more extensive and sophisticated participation in a series of iterative processes that comprise product development and publication development and review. Such participation increasingly requires not only language and writing skills but an adaptive ability to acquire, apply, and mediate technical knowledge through collaboration with diverse experts. Grice proposes a technical communication curriculum without "right answers," one in which students, like technical communicators in the workplace, are accountable for making, evaluating, and thoughtfully reviewing a variety of communication products and interpreting their consequences.

Elizabeth Turpin and Judith Gunn Bronson review the traditional editing process from substantive to copy edits. They describe new technical tools available to technical editors, showing that these can create substantial risks for document quality when they encourage communicators to bypass or abbreviate the editing process. They also describe the expansion of the technical editor's role into the areas of quality control, usability testing, and collaboration. They advocate the development of technical editing courses and programs with substantive, often specialized, technical content and with emphasis on the expanded roles for technical editors.

Kenneth Rainey demonstrates that new information delivery systems have made the role of the visual communicator integral to effective on-the-job communication. Visual communicators must understand new media, their uses, the ways in which users learn from them, and their implications.

Program Design

The essays in the "Program Design" section discuss the special design considerations for different kinds of technical communication programs and courses. The essays describe the ways in which technical communication education has been defined, structured, and presented at different types of institutions and at different educational levels. The essays show how programmatic activity strives to achieve a series of fluid, necessary balances—between theory and practice, between technology and the humanities, between workplace and the academy—to assess, redefine, and strengthen the nature of postsecondary professional education. Along the way, the essays define a new education space, calling for a new model of technical communication education at every level and redefining research and teaching, teachers and learners, and academic and workplace educational settings and stakeholders.

In the opening essay, M. Jimmie Killingsworth argues in favor of technical communication's lack of concrete disciplinary definition, openness, and programmatic diversity. He shows that the dual character of technical communication as both an academic discipline and a profession creates an evolving "space of work" that defies consistency but allows for autonomy in pedagogy, curriculum, and research methodology.

Sam Geonetta describes the social, economic, and disciplinary rationale for designing a bachelor's level technical communication program. Geonetta shows that along with the compelling arguments for such programs come risks in the form of lack of disciplinary identity and of a curriculum that must balance a wide range of increasingly specialized communication and technical courses. He argues in favor of a dynamic, flexible, and evolving undergraduate curriculum to address the professional and social responsibilities of future technical communicators.

Katherine Staples shows that although two-year colleges are ideally suited to provide an advanced and flexible curriculum to meet the needs of a changing workplace, two-year college technical communication programs (despite some documented successes in associate, certificate, and non-credit instruction) too often develop in isolation from the wider disciplinary community. While two-year college academic programs are designed to serve the needs of their regions, Staples argues that the development of technical communication as a discipline and a profession requires two-year college program faculty and administrators to become active members of the national professional and disciplinary communities. Only in this way can two-year college technical communication programs contribute to the development of the discipline and profit from the support and curricular models of programs at other levels.

Sherry Burgus Little traces the remarkable growth of certificate programs in technical communication. She shows the diversity in the length, level, and emphases of existing certificate programs. This diversity reflects the continuing debate over the relationship between the theoretical and the practical—a debate that shows that technical communication is still experiencing uneasiness about its own identity, an uneasiness centered in what Little calls "the stigma of vocationalism."

In her discussion of the evolution of the technical communication service course, Nell Ann Pickett argues that the service course's ability to adapt to a wide range of curricula and to incorporate the findings of a growing body of technical communication research and theory, while retaining its character as a comprehensive communication offering typically combining written, spoken, and visual communication, assures its continuing importance, and perhaps centrality, in the undergraduate curriculum. She provides practical guidelines for designing and proposing such a course, outlining the major curricular and pedagogical concerns.

Billie Wahlstrom defines the current state of technical communication research, showing that such research includes a range of different methodologies tied to the development of the profession and broadly included under the term "rhetoric." Wahlstrom argues that the widely differing methodologies thus included can be nonetheless rigorous. She outlines the types of questions that technical communication research can usefully address and the institutional needs for a research program in technical communication.

Meg Morgan concludes the section by arguing for the importance of program evaluation in an emerging and changing discipline such as technical communication. She describes an innovative evaluation model based on Total Quality Management (TQM) principles. The model provides for an evaluation of the individual features of each program, as well as for identifying the program's "stakeholders," the unique set of academic and workplace partners involved in each program, and for evaluating how successfully the program meets the needs of all its stakeholders.

TECHNICAL COMMUNICATION COMES OF AGE

The essays in this volume underscore the richness and breadth of technical communication today, as they define a new theoretical, professional, and educational space, a space marked by multiplicity and change. The essays also highlight emerging trends and issues that characterize technical communication today. Practically all of the essays acknowledge a major reorientation in the discipline, a reorientation that includes the following:

- A shift away from a view of technical communication as a transaction between writer and audience and toward a social and contextual view of technical communication.
- A shift away from a focus on the communication product or action and toward the consideration of the underlying deliberative processes and professional practices of the community.
- A shift away from the view of language as a reflection of external reality and toward a rhetorical perspective that recognizes the epistemic function of language and of communicative practices.
- A shift away from the representation of the technical communicator as conduit and presenter of information and toward a recognition of the complex positioning of the technical communicator, whose activities are central to collective decision and knowledge making, who helps sustain, but also has the capacity to change, organizational culture, and who mediates between human aspirations and the imperatives of technology, industry, and business.

This reorientation challenges deeply held disciplinary assumptions and values and has major professional and educational implications.

The essays also note major changes in the technical communication workplace and in the nature of professional expertise. They note a need for more specialized technical knowledge, along with a blurring of distinctions and specializations and a general increase in responsibility.

But they also note a need for knowledge and skills beyond the technical: collaboration, responsible action and behavior, decision making, cross-cultural literacy, knowing how to learn—skills that traditionally belong to the humanities and social sciences. Technical communicators teach as well as learn, and they are partners as well as consumers in research projects. Technical communication—as a discipline and a profession—redefines the nature of expertise socratically. If the university and the college are to retain their roles as sites of inquiry and source of knowledge, then the situatedness of education and research needs to be redefined. Perhaps technical communication as a discipline has the potential to reshape the way academics see themselves and knowledge. As Meg Morgan shows in her essay, evaluation of programs in technical communication involves a wide range of concerned shareholders, and effective evaluation makes them aware of and respectful of one another. And although all this mutability results in a certain uneasiness about disciplinary and professional identity, it also signals technical communication's coming of age.

THEORETICAL FOUNDATIONS

1

TECHNICAL COMMUNICATION THEORY: AN OVERVIEW

Mary B. Coney

University of Washington

INTRODUCTION

It is now over a decade since the publication of *New Essays in Technical and Scientific Communication*, a collection of essays intended to set a new standard for the three subdisciplines in the field: research, practice, and theory. In their introduction, the editors find the theoretical stem to be "the least healthy" and argue that "until very recently, it would have been an exaggeration even to talk about a theoretical subdiscipline" (Anderson, Brockmann, & Miller, 1983, p. 7,9). In their diagnosis for this state of affairs, they cite "an environment [in the pedagogical and professional subdisciplines] inhospitable to the speculation and skepticism that scholarly research requires" (p. 9). As one goal of this essay is to assess the current state of theory in our profession, these earlier opinions are worth revisiting. It would, I think, be difficult to find many in our field who would disagree with the editors then and equally difficult to find many who would agree with them now.

Partly because of this 1983 collection, which became a kind of intellectual line in the dust for scholars, the situation has changed dramatically, particularly for the theoretical stem. As the field has gained a more respectable academic foothold (see Killingsworth, this collection), it has attracted more technical communicators into theory work and the results are impressive by any variety of measures: the number of articles devoted to theory not only in technical communication journals but in "mainstream" journals such as *Rhetoric Review, College English, Written Communication,* and *College Composition and Communication* as well as the professional journals such as IEEE *Transactions in Professional Communication* and *Technical Communication*; the number of theory-rich collections such as Selzer's (1993) *Understanding Scientific Prose,* Killingsworth and Gilbertson's (1992) *Signs, Genres, & Communities,* and Bazerman and Paradis's (1991) *Textual Dynamics of the Professions*; the number of sessions on theory held at the Modern Language Association, College Conference on Composition and Communication, and even the professional meetings of International Professional Communication Conference and the Society for Technical Communication Annual Conference. In the annual bibliography published each fall by *Technical Communication Quarterly* (whose recent change of name from *The Technical Writing Teacher* adds another kind of proof of the general intellectualizing of the field), there are currently enough theory entries to require separate sections, entitled "Theory and Philosophy" and "Rhetoric of Science." Even technical communication textbooks, those easy targets of scholars, have begun to respond to this theory work by revising many of their bedrock lessons about the nature and practice of technical communication.

Such an impressive sampling can testify only indirectly, however, to the nature and quality of the theory work produced by and about technical communication. Because it would be o'er-reaching of me to attempt any comprehensive evaluation of this work in the last 11 years, I will focus on only three areas of study that seem to me most central to technical communication—audience, the writing process, and style. I will describe what I see as the prevailing theoretical positions, characterize the challenges to these positions, and suggest what's at stake for the field of technical communication.

AUDIENCE

Of all the topics to be discussed, audience has probably received the most theoretical attention, even in the early period of the 1940s and 1950s, when most of the attention was on pedagogy and practice. For most scholars entering technical communication from a language-based background, especially English and especially as it was traditionally taught, questions about the intended readers of a document and their influence on the shaping of that document were new and exciting considerations. Schooled in the constraints of New Critical theory, where concern for readers was considered a fallacious move, scholars who taught technical communication were freed to analyze, teach, and theorize about texts in a whole new way—from seeing them as hermetically sealed works isolated from readers' everyday lives to dynamic documents that act directly on those lives.

Audience analysis was developed in the pioneer textbooks (Mathes and Stevenson, 1976; Pearsall, 1969; Souther and White, 1977) and, with little change, is carried as a staple chapter in most contemporary textbooks. Typically, the content on audience is taught as a two-part process: (1) discover as much as possible about the intended readers of a document, including their educational level, working habits, informational needs, and professional responsibilities; (2) determine as precisely as possible how the document would be used by those readers and under what conditions, for instance, as a repair manual on an oil rig, a reference chart in a laboratory, or a research article archived in the library. The assumption is that, armed with all this information, technical writers can produce a document that meets the audience's needs and thereby can accomplish their own purposes with a high degree of predictability. Underlying this interest in the reader is a belief in the author's ability to control meaning by creating a stable text whose content will be understood with as little ambiguity as possible.

This belief, as well as the value of audience analysis, has been challenged by reader response theorists on several theoretical fronts. Some rhetoricians argue that analysis alone is not a sufficient guide for writers, that in addition a mock, or pretend, reader needs to be imbedded in the text as a rhetorical companion to the persona put forth by the author. It is the quality of communication, or "fit," between these two figures that determines the success of a document (Booth, 1961; Burke, 1969; Coney, 1987; Gibson, 1950). If the writer has created an appealing enough mock reader, the actual intended readers will take on the role during the reading process, absorb the information, and return to their individual selves, enlightened and ready to make use of the information. Others argue that even that rhetorical model is too simplistic. Walter Ong (1975) denies any relation between the mock reader and actual readers who choose to pick up a text. For him, the audience for a text is always a fiction, created by the author but drawn from a long tradition of audiences for earlier, similar texts. And while Ong uses literary sources to demonstrate his thesis, he holds that it applies "ceteris paribus" to all texts, including scientific and technical (p. 17). For a thorough investigation of Ong's hypothesis, see Selzer's collection; for fuller articulations of reader-response theories, see the Suleiman and Crosman (1980), and Tompkins (1980) collections.

Unlike Ong, cognitive psychologists who specialize in reading comprehension build their theories on *actual* readers rather than on fictional constructs. Yet, while they acknowledge that each individual brings to a text prior knowledge that affects the reading of a particular text, they, like Ong, are finally more interested in aggregating individual readers into groups, unified by shared characteristics, about whom hypotheses can be formulated and predictions made. By their experimental methodologies, cognitivists are bringing scientific rigor to the study of many of the untested precepts in technical communication, such as use of headings, passive voice, and embedded clauses, and their effects on readers. (For a summary of this research, see Spyridakis and Wenger, 1992.)

Although their methods differ from those of the cognitivists (and often from each others'), ethnographers in composition studies hold the same basic assumption about audience as the cognitivists—that while individual members of an audience bring individual histories and expectations to the reading of a text, the audience can be led to make similar interpretations of that text (Kleine, 1990; North, 1987). One example of applied research in technical communication that is based on this assumption is usability testing. Employing such ethnographic methods as videotaping and stimulated recall, researchers are studying readers closely in naturally occurring work situations as they attempt to extract information from or interact with texts (including on-line texts). Research findings are attracting widespread industry support, encouraging researchers to extend their findings to include subjects as users of products in addition to texts (Ramey, 1989; Schriver, 1989).

Speaking from both a post-modern and psychoanalytic perspective, Norman Holland (1992) questions a number of these approaches to audience—particularly, the validity of generalizing about readers and the attempts to create an unambiguous text. In his studies, he found that individual readers bring strong identity themes to their reading that prevent any unified response:

> We can account for the wide differences in their readings only by saying they were governed by widely different personal needs and defenses. The days of "the" reader are over—at least for those of us who have looked at actual readers. . . . As a result. . . we could no longer sustain the traditional literary idea of a stable text with a determinate "meaning." Rather, readers make meaning. (p. 87; italics added)

And while Holland uses literary examples (like many of the theorists discussed), his findings cannot be easily dismissed in theory work in technical communication. All technical communication teachers have experienced the failure of trying to write a class assignment or set of instructions that is understood by each reader in the way intended. Research recently conducted at the University of Washington would seem to confirm Holland's conclusions that readers bring quite personal and unpredictable agendas to the act of reading. Subjects selected for their similarities (graduate students in the Department of Technical Communication) were videotaped reading several technical documents. The purpose was to develop a scheme for tracking rhetorical roles as they were assumed, changed, or rejected by the subjects. The findings were that the individual readers brought widely different cognitive and emotional responses to their reading, responses that dramatically affected their rhetorical role playing and their interpretation of the texts (Thompson & Coney, 1995). Perspectives coming from gender and feminist studies and reader response theories are giving further reason to doubt the possibility for identifying a uniform reader (Lay, 1991; Allen, 1991; Dragga, 1993; Tompkins, 1980).

Even theorists are not immune from their own personal history. Holland puts it well:

> We were not explorers discovering features of a text "out there" with "real" boundaries and meaning. What we were describing as facts stemmed from our own critical activity. In getting at meaning, we would share some professional maneuvers, but each of us interpreted differently—and was bound to. We had different backgrounds, different genders, different bodies, different wishes, fears, defenses, and identities. And they matter. (p. 87)

If any generalization is possible at this point, it is that for technical communicators, nothing matters *more* than audience. Are the writers and readers in technical communication any less complex than Holland and his readers? Are technical texts any less subject to differing interpretations than literary texts? Are there ways to control responses to achieve a predetermined goal? Is that always good? And if so, what are the textual and rhetorical features that serve to guide readers into a common reading? Finding answers to these questions is critical if technical communicators are to continue their commitment to understanding their readers—both real and rhetorical.

THE WRITING PROCESS

A second truism long and widely held in technical communication—in addition to the importance of audience—is that writing is best done and taught as a logical process. Although the most influential study of this process was conducted by Linda Flower and John Hayes, a rhetorical scholar and a psychologist, technical communicators had already developed their own theoretical model, which drew on two very different sources: the engineering design process, with its emphasis on linear stages, and the rhetorical tradition, with its emphasis on purpose and audience as primary considerations (Souther & White, 1977; Perrin, 1950).

The model-based approach, which preceded process, has proven unsatisfactory on several fronts (Winkler, 1983). Despite its appeal to students and new employees who want examples to follow, there are no perfect models that can be taught in preparation for writing in the workplace: Formats change from company to company and different disciplines require different kinds of documentation. Although word processing programs provide a variety of structural models, they rarely match the demands of a particular situation. And, as Victoria Winkler points out, "Although the structural models for teaching writing suggest the *kinds* of information writers need for a particular discourse type, they do not provide writers with the means of generating that information" (p. 115). With the growing use of electronic mail for information exchange in the workplace, the formalities of traditional forms of documentation are giving way to a more informal discourse, more akin to speech than formal writing.

Certainly, another reason for the dominance of writing as process is the flurry of empirical research spawned by Flower and Hayes. Cognitive psychologists are continuing to bring their experimental methodologies to bear on the writing habits of beginning and expert writers to establish a more scientific basis on which to develop course materials, teaching strategies, and measurements and standards for mastery (Butterfield, 1994; Bereiter & Scardamalia, 1983). This writing-as-cognition approach has obvious value for an academic field such as ours that intersects with science and engineering: It brings the writing class closer to the laboratory in both its terminology and its procedures.

But this very "scientizing" of writing, with its focus on subjects who, one by one, perform writing tasks in isolated, experimental settings, makes it vulnerable to attack from social constructionists. Kenneth Bruffee (1981) argues that "writing is not an inherently private act but is a displaced social act we perform in private for the sake of convenience" (p. 745). Marilyn Cooper (1989), in "The Ecology of Writing," takes the argument even further:

> Increasingly, writing researchers have found that "elegant" [experimental] methods of studying writing are reductive, producing results that have no bearing on what writers—either beginning or expert—do. The common view of the natural science paradigm of research—the bracketing of variables so that a single one can be studied in isolation—is fundamentally inapplicable in the human sciences. No variables in human behavior are isolable." (p. viii)

For Cooper, "writing is not fundamentally a cognitive process, though of course thinking is involved. Writing is a way of interacting with others." Thus, to understand writing "we must first and primarily understand its place in the social process" (p. x).

Admittedly, this argument makes for a much messier, less controlled approach to studying writing. Yet it is not without its own methodologies that can yield insights not possible within the experimental framework. The ecological model that Cooper and Holzman (1989) develop in their book *Writing as Social Action* postulates a series of dynamic interlocking systems that writers affect and are affected by: systems of ideas, purposes, interpersonal interactions, cultural norms, and textual forms. Together, these form a web in which one act affects the whole. Not surprisingly, this model leads Cooper and Holzman into issues such as literacy education, gender, community, and bureaucratic structures that can promote or deny human development and expression.

Given the constant changes in the workplace environment for technical writers, the increasingly electronic forms of technical documentation, and the political and economic consequences of technological change, technical communicators need to consider theories that provide an inclusive research program, one that incorporates both the quantitative and the qualitative data about writers as they work individually to produce text, *and* as they are affected by and affect these external forces (Brandt, 1992). The point here is that scholars in technical communication can hardly afford to join sides. While each scholar might choose to do theory work in the social, rhetorical, or cognitive tradition, they should at least be cognizant of the complex nature of writing and of the range of theories dedicated to understanding it.

STYLE

To find the major influence on the prevailing model of style in scientific and technical communication, one needs to go back to the 16th and 17th centuries when modern science was first beginning to define its philosophical position (Whitburn with Davis, Higgins, Oates, & Spurgeon, 1978). Calling for a language that adequately served their demands for observation and description, reformers such as Francis Bacon, John Wilkins, and John Webster decried the stylistic excesses of the period, best exemplified by John Lyly's *Euphues: An Anatomy of Wit.* Ignoring the fact that Lyly's exaggerated rhetorical flourishes were themselves a parody of contemporary courtly prose, these writers called for a style "plain and naturall, not being darkened with . . . Rhetoricall flourishes. [Just as] Obscurity in the discourse is an argument of ignorance in the mind, The greatest learning is to be seen in the greatest plainnesse . . ." (quoted in Jones, 1951, p. 78).

What is remarkable, despite the changes science itself has undergone in the last three centuries, is that this early position on style has remained largely unchanged. Except for the modernized spelling, almost identical arguments appear in the majority of current texts in our field: "Literary tricks, metaphors and the like, divert attention from the substance to the style. They should be used rarely, if at all, in scientific writing" (Day, 1988, p. 3); the best technical style is no style at all (Markel, 1992). Whitburn et al. (1978), who has traced the history of the plain language movement, finds that the "stylistic ideal of plainness ought not to continue as unchallenged as in the past. Revolutions are typically reactions against excesses, and the reactions are often as excessive as the original abuses" (p. 52). Changes in the knowledge and practice of science and technology and what he calls the "writing crisis we now confront" should lead us to reconsider the value of plain language as an adequate pedagogical or professional model. For one thing, it tends to focus too heavily on the finding and correcting of mechanical error, and, for another, it limits unduly the range of linguistic and rhetorical expression available to communicate ideas effectively for modern audiences. For students, writing too often becomes a defensive maneuver to avoid mistakes rather than a creative way to engage with others.

In a 1979 landmark essay that introduced many already teaching in technical communication to the ideas and consequences of post-modern theory, Carolyn Miller expanded Whitburn's position by attacking the philosophical tradition informing the plain language ideal—positivism, the belief in the existence of a reality separate from human perception and emotion. Calling it the "windowpane theory of language," she summarized the positivist supposition about language that has prevailed in technical communication, as well as in the sciences and engineering:

> [It] provides a view out onto the real world, a view which may be clear or obfuscated. If language is clear, then we see reality accurately; if language is highly decorative or opaque, then we see what is not really there or we see it with difficulty. (p. 611–12)

Miller then cites philosophers who represent the "new epistemology," such as Kuhn, Ziman, and Bronowski, who argue against the objective/subjective dichotomy and the privileging of science as having special claims to truth. Instead, she concludes, "Science is, through and through, a rhetorical endeavor" (p. 616).

In a spirited critique of contemporary prose style, Richard Lanham (1974) puts forth many of the same arguments. His analysis of the CBS theory of writing recalls Miller's windowpane view of language:

> We may call this conception, building on its three central values of clarity, brevity, and sincerity, the "C-B-S" theory [which] . . . . argues that prose ought to be maximally transparent and minimally self-conscious, never seen and never noticed . . . . "Rhetoric" in such a view very naturally becomes a dirty word, pointing to superficial ornament on the one hand and duplicity on the other. It becomes, that is, everything which interferes with the natural and efficient communication of ideas. "Rhetoric" is what we should get rid of in prose, not what we should analyze. (Lanham, 1983, p. 2)

And in one of the few books on style per se, Lanham extends the logic of his argument to the teaching of composition. Because the textbooks hold up as ideal a prose style that has essentially one goal, to disappear, they have literally "argued their subject out of existence. They do not teach style, they abolish it." And to fill the vacuum created by the nontopic of style, the "Books" indulge in "the American fetish for correctness, the agony over those droll Victorian antimacassars 'usage' and 'abusage'" (1974, p. 17).

A well-known answer to Lanham's indictment is Joseph Williams's book *Style: Ten Lessons in Clarity and Grace* (1994). It not only deals with such substantive stylistic issues as cohesion and emphasis but also applies linguistic and cognitive scholarship to his lessons. For example, while he does affirm the ideal of clarity, he defends it on the strength of the psychological findings that readers can most easily take in and remember information if characters and actions are matched with the subject and verbs of sentences. Yet even here, the emphasis is on correction rather than invention, on economy rather than situation: The exercises consist mainly of revising appalling examples of prose rather than encouraging students to find a stylistic solution for a particular rhetorical effect. Williams's treatment of the topic is much more sophisticated than it is in most textbooks, but the lessons are still more coercive than creative. They do not adequately respond to Lanham's position that "successful prose styles vary as widely as the earth." Lanham continues,

> People seldom write simply to be clear. They have designs on their fellow men. Pure prose is as rare as pure virtue, and for the same reasons. The classical discussions of style concern themselves less with clarity than with more common human purposes, with advantage and pleasure. (1974, p. 17)

Are these purposes, these arguments, germane to technical communication? Are "advantage and pleasure" appropriate goals to teach technical communication students? I think so, if "purpose and satisfaction" are understood in the sense of fulfilling needs, both writers' and readers'.

The paradox I find so puzzling in the upholding of the plain language model by so many technical communication textbooks is that most scholars in the field—who are, after all, also the writers of textbooks and teachers—have largely rejected the philosophy on which the plain language model is based: positivism. Influenced by such philosophers as Richard Rorty and Stanley Fish and technical communication theorists such as Miller and Whitburn, scholars have embraced the social constructionist view of knowledge. A belief in facts objectively obtained and authority of texts has yielded to a belief in communal assent and power of readers to determine meaning (Dombrowski, 1995; also see the Ornatowski and Subbiah chapters in this section). Yet a concomitant theory of style to achieve assent and empower readers has yet to be written for technical communication.

A promising beginning is the recently published *Technical Communication* (Lay et al., 1995). Described by its authors as a "third-generation" textbook, "it focuses on the social construction of knowledge that situates communicative acts in a meaningful context" (*Instructor's Resource Guide,* 1). Their credo is spelled out forcefully (dare I say *clearly*?) in the preface:

> We don't believe that either communication or technology is an isolated phenomenon; instead, we believe that they occur in a rich setting that is shaped by economics, ethics, legal considerations, and social and cultural forces. Therefore, the examples, assignments, and exercises we offer here assume that the technology is created and used by people with various values, interests, and needs—and that technical communicators can and should help audiences understand and use technology, make decisions about technology, and solve problems with technology. (Lay et al., p. ix)

Their chapter on style reflects these beliefs in that it teaches that a variety of styles are available for the technical writer and that appropriateness is determined more by the immediate situation than by an abstract standard of correctness. However, their exercises fall short of their promise in that they, like Williams, focus more on revision of a garbled piece of prose than on the production of an effective message. For example, they call for editing of an appraisal performance, which "must be clearly written," and exhort students to "revise [by] reducing it significantly and organizing it logically" (p. 303). How much more consistent would it have been if the exercise had set up a particular rhetorical situation and asked students to write an appraisal in a style suiting that situation. Think of the learning—not to mention pleasure—that could have come from peer readings!

A text that *does* practice a much more supple, situational, even playful approach to style is not really a text at all (in the sense of textbook), nor was it originally written in English (perhaps the most telling point of all). It is *Exercises in Style* by Raymond Queneau (1981), translated from French by Barbara Wright. Absent of theory, this delightful little book takes an unexceptional event—equivalent to what Queneau calls a "rather slight theme" from a Bach fugue—and expresses it in 99 stylistic variations. The facts are minimal: A long-necked young man gets on a crowded bus and eventually finds a seat. Later he is observed at a bus station with a friend who comments on his outfit. Yet by the time readers get through even half of the hilarious versions, the book demonstrates two serious points: (1) that there are almost an endless variety of styles available to express even the most factual set of circumstances, and (2) that each new stylistic version calls into question the "factuality" of previous tellings. In short, Queneau produces by his "exercises in style," first published in 1947, a post-modern demonstration of the instability of text and the power of language to create reality. If technical communication is to have a theory of style consistent with current theories about the nature of text, language, and reality, then surely this little French "trifle" would seem to point the way better than even the most recent treatments of style in well-received technical communication textbooks. A theory of style that allows for a full range of rhetorical choices would not only serve students and professional practice; it would also confirm the experiences of research scientists. In a study of the role metaphor plays in conceptualization and abstraction, Liliane Papin (1990) cites famous instances of metaphorical leaps into new insights, such as Archimedes' displaced bathwater allowing him to figure out how to calculate the volume of irregular shapes. Less known is evidence that "the failure to explore certain metaphors has slowed down the development of science." Papin cites the studies of historians Bohm and Peat, who speculate that the edge is given to those who exhibit "an extremely perceptive state of intense passion and high energy" that allows scientists to see beyond appearances (p. 1259). Bohm and Peat hypothesize that through metaphorical play, incommensurables can coexist and the disorder created by the "either-or model of conventional science" can be lessened (p. 1261).

In the same spirit of conciliation, I would conclude that any fully articulated theory of style for scientific and technical prose needs to accommodate the richness and complexity of thought expressed by that prose. No one style, plain or any other, is sufficient for the demands of technical communication.

OBSERVATIONS

A few observations rather than conclusions seem appropriate, except for the obvious conclusion that theory work, once begun, is never settled, never complete. And it should not be expected to be. The controversies that this essay has attempted to chart speak to the health of theory in technical communication; they attest to the "speculation and skepticism" that Anderson et al. found lacking a decade ago. The controversies also speak to the state of the field itself, which some theorists argue is marked more by fragmentation than agreement. Accordingly, they urge technical communicators "to entertain a 'rhetoric of dissensus' as part of our understanding of how human knowledge gets constructed and deconstructed" (Van Pelt, 1994).

Theory, in other words, reflects and deepens—rather than explains away—the complexities inherent in any field of study, no less so in technical communication, which must take into account the immediacies of the workplace, the classroom, the laboratory, as well as the work of scholars, both in and out of the field. The process of doing theory requires tolerance as well as curiosity, introspection as well as exploration. This aspect of theory work is best described by Eagleton (1990) in *The Ideology of the Aesthetic:* "Theory is just a kind of catching ourselves in the act of being subjects, a deeper appropriation of what we already are" (p. 129). And like all subjects we are always in flux, never fixed.

Another observation is that there is a tendency to borrow theories from other fields and graft them onto technical communication. While one might argue that some theories "take" less well than others (and each theorist has a favorite candidate), this trend is good for a number of reasons, and there's no reason for (or sign of) change. This borrowing keeps technical communication in tune with the larger world of scholarly research and keeps fresh ideas flowing into the field; it provides insights not always evident from a practical point of view and suggests methodologies by which these insights can be tested; and most important, it is in keeping with the interdisciplinary nature of technical communication. It is through the work technical communicators do, both tangible and theoretical, that they come to learn more about themselves as well as about others.

REFERENCES

Allen, J. (1991). Gender issues in technical communication studies. *Journal of Business and Technical Communication, 5*, 371–392.

Anderson, P.V., Brockmann, R.J. & Miller, C.R. (Eds.). (1983). *New essays in technical and scientific communication: Research, theory, practice.* Farmingdale, NY: Baywood.

Barthes, R. (1975). *The pleasure of the text.* (R. Miller, Trans.). New York: Hill and Wang.

Bazerman, C. & Paradis, J. (Eds.). (1991). *Textual dynamics of the professions: Historical and contemporary studies of writing in professional communities.* Madison, WI: University of Wisconsin Press.

Bereiter, C. & Scardamalia, M. (1983). Levels of inquiry in writing research. In P. Mosenthal, L. Tamor, & S.H. Walmsley (Eds.), *Research in writing: Principles and methods.* New York: Longman.

Booth, W.C. (1961). *The rhetoric of fiction.* Chicago, IL: University of Chicago Press.

Brandt, D. (1992). The cognitive as the social. *Written Communication, 9,* 315–355.

Bruffee, K. (1981). Collaborative learning. *College English, 43,* 745–747.

Burke, K. (1969). *The rhetoric of motives.* Berkeley, CA: University of California Press.

Butterfield, E.C. (Ed.). (1994). *Children's writing: Toward a process theory of the development of skilled writing.* Greenwich, CT: JAI.

Coney, M.B. (1984). The implied author in technical discourse. *Journal of Advanced Composition* (1984): 163–172.

Coney, M.B. (1987). Contemporary views of audience: A rhetorical perspective. *Technical Writing Teacher, 14,* 319–338.

Cooper, M.M. (1989). The ecology of writing. In M. M. Cooper & M. Holzman (Eds.), *Writing as social action.* Portsmouth, NH: Boynton/Cook.

Cooper, M.M. & Holzman, M. (Eds.). (1989). *Writing as social action.* Portsmouth, NH: Boynton/Cook.

Day, R.A. (1988). *How to write & publish a scientific paper* (3rd Ed.). New York: Oryx.

Dombrowski, P.M. (1995). Post-modernism as the resurgence of humanism in technical communication studies. *Technical Communication Quarterly, 4,* 165–185.

Dragga, S. (1993). Women and the profession of technical writing: social and economic influences and implications. *Journal of Business and Technical Communication, 1,* 312–321.

Eagleton, T. (1990). *The ideology of the aesthetic.* Oxford: Basil Blackwell.

Flower, L. & Hayes, J. (1981). A cognitive process theory of writing. *College Composition and Communication, 32,* 365–387.

Gibson, W. (1950). Authors, speakers, readers, and mock readers. *College English, 11,* 265–269

Holland, N.N. (1992). *The critical I.* New York: Columbia University Press.

Jones, R.F. (Ed.). (1951). *The seventeenth century : studies in the history of English thought and literature from Bacon to Pope.* Stanford, CA: Stanford University Press.

Killingsworth, M.J. & Gilbertson, M. (1992). *Signs, genres, and communities in technical communication.* Amityville, NY: Baywood.

Kleine, M. (1990). Beyond triangulation: Ethnography, writing, and rhetoric. *Journal of Advanced Composition,* 117–125.

Lanham, R.A. (1974). *Style: An anti-textbook.* New Haven, CT: Yale University Press.

Lanham, R.A. (1983). *Analyzing prose.* New York: Scribner's.

Lay, M.M. (1991). Feminist theory and the redefinition of technical communication. *Journal of Business and Technical Communication,* 348–370.

Lay, M.M., Wahlstrom, B.J., Duin, A.H., Little, C.L., Selfe, C.L., Selzer, J., Rude, C.D., & Doheny–Farina, S. (1995). *Technical communication.* Chicago: Irwin.

Markel, M.H. (1992). *Technical writing: situations and strategies.* (3rd Ed.). New York: St. Martin's.

Mathes, J.C. & Stevenson, D.W. (1976). *Designing technical reports: Writing for audiences in organizations.* Indianapolis, IN: Bobbs–Merrill.

Miller, C.R. (1979). A humanistic rationale for technical writing. *College English, 40,* 610–617.

Ong, W.S.J. (1975). The writer's audience is always a fiction. *PMLA, 90,* 9–21.

North, S.M. (1987). *The making of knowledge in composition: Portrait of an emerging field.* Portsmouth, NH: Boynton/Cook.

Papin, L. (1990). This is not a universe: Metaphor, language, and representation. *PMLA, 107,* 1253–1265.

Pearsall, T.E. (1969). *Audience analysis for technical writing.* Beverly Hills, CA: Macmillan.

Perrin, P.G. (1950). *Writer's guide and index to English.* (Rev. Ed.) New York: Scott, Foresman.

Queneau, R. (1981). *Exercises in Style.* (B. Wright, Trans.). New York: New Directions.

Ramey, J.R. (1989). Usability evaluation and its relationship to traditional approaches in research and design. *IEEE Transactions on Professional Communication, 32,* 207–209.

Schriver, K.A. (1989). Evaluating text quality: the continuum from test-focused to reader-focused methods. *IEEE Transactions on Professional Communication, 32,* 238–255.

Selzer, J. (1993). *Understanding scientific prose.* Madison, WI: University of Wisconsin Press.

Souther, J.W. & White, M.L. (1997). *Technical report writing.* (2nd Ed.). New York: Wiley.

Spyridakis, J.H. & Wenger, M.J. (1992). Writing for human performance: Relating reading research to document design. *Technical Communication, 39,* 202–215.

Suleiman, S.R. & Crosman, I. (Eds.). (1980). *The reader in the text: Essays on audience and interpretation.* Princeton, NJ: Princeton University Press.

Thompson, L.H. & Coney, M.B. (1995). Putting reader roles to the test: An ethnomethodological approach. *IEEE Transactions on Professional Communication, 38,* 100–109.

Tompkins, J.P. (Ed.). (1980). *Reader response criticism: From formalism to post-structuralism.* Baltimore, MD: Johns Hopkins University Press.

Van Pelt, W. (1994, December). Toward a postmodern rhetoric for technical communication. Paper presented at the annual meeting of the Modern Language Association of America. Toronto, Canada.

Whitburn, M.D., et al. (1978). The plain style in scientific and technical writing. *Journal of Technical Writing and Communication, 8,* 349–358.

Williams, J.M. (1994). *Style: Ten lesson in clarity & grace.* (4th Ed.). New York: Harper-Collins.

Winkler, V.M. (1983). The role of models in technical and scientific writing. In P.V. Anderson, R.J. Brockmann & C.R. Miller (Eds.), *New essays in technical and scientific communication: Research, theory, practice* (pp. 111–122). Farmingdale, NY: Baywood.

2

ON TAKING ORGANIZATIONS SERIOUSLY: ORGANIZATIONS AS SOCIAL CONTEXTS FOR TECHNICAL COMMUNICATION

Teresa M. Harrison

Rensselaer Polytechnic Institute

Susan M. Katz

North Carolina State University

INTRODUCTION

It is now almost a cliché to observe that all writing—and certainly that done by technical communicators—is undertaken within social contexts that affect the nature of the text produced. One of the most important developments in composition theory in the 1980s was the articulation of a "social perspective" on writing (Faigley, 1985). The social perspective views writing as more than simply a mode of individual expression or a vehicle for transmitting information. It proposes instead that composing processes and the texts produced reflect complex interrelationships between authors, audiences, and the social contexts in which they are all situated. Although writing obviously takes place in other nonacademic contexts, many would acknowledge that organizations are the most frequent social context in which technical communication takes place. Thus, it is crucial to understand what kind of social context organizations are and what aspects of their character need to be considered in thinking about how to teach and perform as technical communicators. Many composition theorists view social context as best defined by the concept of the "discourse community" (Faigley, 1985), but this concept does not eliminate the need to examine more closely the specialized nature of organizational life. All organizations are discourse communities, but not all discourse communities are organizations. Some features central to organizational contexts, beyond those addressed in the concept of a discourse community, present important implications for technical communication.

In this chapter, we consider certain specialized aspects of organizational life that are critical to teaching technical communication. We begin by describing what an organization is; in so doing we wish to distinguish between conceptions of the organization as a relatively static object in which behaviors occur and stress instead that organizations are dynamic processes comprised of behaviors. We turn then to the concept of "organizational culture" to discuss how organizations create a world characterized by idiosyncratic knowledge and patterns of symbolic expression.

Viewing organizations in this way implies that technical communicators must learn to appreciate what is basic to the nature of organizational contexts as well as the relatively unique character of the organization in which they work and its conventions for communication. Part of this education will take place through organizational socialization processes, but part of it can take place in the classroom as technical communication teachers prepare students to become professionals. Technical communicators will need to learn about the role of diverse modes of communication in an organization, including interpersonal, visual, and electronic communication, as well as writing. Teachers must equip students with an understanding of how relations of authority and power affect the possibilities for collaboration with other organizational members. Finally, we suggest that teachers must complement their focus on the development of skills with a consideration of the ethical consequences of the behavior of technical communicators in organizations.

WHAT IS AN ORGANIZATION?

Most people think of organizations as containers, as more or less static objects in which various activities, such as jobs and other behaviors, are performed. This view is consistent with the idea that organizations are social contexts in which technical communication and other communication activities take place. However, it is important to recognize that, although members of an organization are geographically situated, the organization itself is not a physical entity. Instead, an organization is a social collectivity that is brought into existence when two or more individuals recognize that some of their goals are better accomplished through working together than by independent efforts.

Individuals become organized when they establish interdependence, that is, when each participant recognizes that the accomplishment of an individual goal depends on another participant's performance of certain behavior. When participant A agrees to perform behaviors of type Y in return for participant B's performance of behaviors of type X, we say that behaviors have become "interlocked" and that A and B have formed a collective structure (Weick, 1979). When patterns of interlocked behavior are established and repeated reliably, an organization is created.

It is commonly assumed that organizations begin with groups of people who agree to combine their efforts in the accomplishment of a common goal. But this view begs the question of how such groups come into existence and how they come to agree on common goals. According to Weick, it is more accurate to assume that collective structures are begun by individuals who need each other's respective actions to accomplish their own particular goals. Over time, individuals who have established a successful collective structure begin to develop common goals, if only to continue to preserve the structure that has been successful in enabling all parties to get what they want. Further and more complex sequences of interlocked behavior develop to ensure that the organization as a whole will continue to function. Interlocked behaviors are performed repetitively to decrease uncertainty so that the social collective as well as its members can continue to achieve their respective goals.

Without the joint behavior in which members engage, there is no organization. One important implication of this view is that organizations must be re-created every day. Because re-creation is essential to their nature, organizations are more accurately viewed as processes than as things. This view further implies that an organization is capable of change at any time through changes in the behaviors of its members. Although cycles of behavior become stabilized and repetitive, they can change; thus, the organization can also change. Empirically, however, organizations are slow to change because organizations are also "culture-bearing milieux" (Louis, 1980), characterized by idiosyncratic systems of cognition, meaning, and expression that maintain and render sensible the patterns of behavior of their members.

ORGANIZATIONAL CULTURES

The Weickian model of organization tells us that organizations comprise interlocked behavior cycles, but it says very little about the character of the behaviors that comprise those cycles. What specific actions enter into the behavior cycles that comprise organizations? The concept of organizational culture helps to answer this question. Edgar Schein (1990, p. 111) presents a carefully argued definition of culture:

> Culture can now be defined as (a) a pattern of basic assumptions, (b) invented, discovered, or developed by a given group, (c) as it learns to cope with its problems of external adaptation and internal integration, (d) that has worked well enough to be considered valid and, therefore (e) is to be taught to new members as the (f) correct way to perceive, think, and feel in relation to those problems. The focus of research in organizational culture is to learn what these assumptions are, where they came from, how they influence the behavior of individuals and groups, and how they are maintained and/or changed.

One perspective on organizational culture emphasizes the knowledge that members acquire about organizational life; such knowledge influences members' understandings of what behaviors are required, which are appropriate, which are legitimate, and what behaviors are ultimately possible and impossible in organizational processes (Smircich, 1983). More specifically, cultural knowledge encompasses the technologies of the organization (financial, manufacturing, human resources, etc.) as well as social knowledge, including roles and positions of members and rights accorded thereto and appropriate attitudes, beliefs, and values. Culture provides what members need to know to be able to behave appropriately in specific circumstances.

Another perspective on organizational culture, complementary to the preceding, sees organizational cultures as patterns of symbolic discourse (Smircich, 1983). This perspective focuses on what people say and do in their performance of the culture. Research from this perspective examines how members of a culture express what they know, what they mean, and what they feel through their use of idiosyncratic vocabularies, images, metaphors, slogans, rituals, and stories.

These perspectives on organizational culture are useful for understanding what one needs to know to be a member of an organization and how members of an organization express themselves. All new organizational members must become schooled in organizational culture to perform successfully, including students who, in their future roles as technical communicators, will be speaking and writing as spokespersons for the organization.

EMPHASIZING ORGANIZATION IN TECHNICAL COMMUNICATION

Students must learn certain conceptual and analytic skills to make use of cultural knowledge when they become new organizational members. One strategy that teachers might use is to show students how to incorporate an analysis of organizational discourse into their repertoire of analytical tools (Harrison, 1987). Such analysis can encourage technical communicators to identify commonalities in reasoning, arguments, language, and style that may serve as the basis for making rhetorical choices in communication products. Another way to encourage students' ability to make use of cultural knowledge is to sensitize them in the classroom to some contextual features they are likely to encounter fully only when they become organizational members, such as the socialization processes they will undergo, the role and function of communication media in organizations, and relations of authority and power that affect the creation of communication products.

Socialization Theory and Technical Communication

Two aspects of research on organizational culture have not been emphasized in research on discourse communities but are particularly useful for teachers of technical communication: where basic assumptions about organizational life come from and how these assumptions are maintained. If communicators understand the reasons for a particular convention, see both the assumptions that led to the convention and understand where those assumptions originated, they will more easily incorporate the required features into communication products. This understanding thus helps to maintain the culture, but can also lead to change in situations where a technical communicator can show a more effective means of meeting the needs of the organization—if he or she also understands the mechanisms for change that work in the culture. (See Lutz, 1989, p. 128–133, for a discussion of how writers can effect changes that benefit the organization.)

We have long realized that writing that is appropriate for one audience, situation, or organization is not necessarily appropriate for another. There are differences in genre, style, tone, voice, and format, to name a few of the distinguishing characteristics of written discourse, and much research in writing has focused on describing this rich variety (see Odell and Goswami, 1985; Bazerman and Paradis, 1991; and Spilka, 1993b for descriptions of writing in diverse workplace settings). In recent years, however, interest has been increasing not only in what it is that writers must learn to write appropriately for an organization, but also in how they are enabled by the organization to learn what they need to know. That is, we are interested in how writers are socialized to the discourse conventions of the organization.

Even though the content of socialization varies dramatically depending on situation, scholars who have studied socialization processes have theorized that individuals have similar experiences as they change from newcomers to experienced members of a group. Socialization process literature (for example, Jablin, 1982; Louis, 1990; Schein, 1990; Van Maanen, 1976) focuses on the stages individuals go through (anticipation, entry, assimilation), characteristic reactions to the process (for example, frustration, anxiety), the social and technical aspects of the information to be learned, and the practices engaged in by the organization to effect socialization (for example, formal training or informal mentoring, group orientation or individualized meetings). These discussions include detailed information about newcomer expectations, the resources newcomers use, and the situations in which newcomers can learn about the new environment, all of which is extremely useful in looking at and thinking about writers in organizations.

In fact, we can use these theories to help explain some of the problems described in current research on writing. For example, Meryl Reis Louis's discussion of information-seeking strategies used by newcomers (1990, p. 105–109) informs Chris Anson and Lee Forsberg's (1990) finding that student interns had trouble knowing who to ask for help and how to approach others in their organization. Anson and Forsberg also relate several very different relationships that developed between interns and their supervisors, a finding that is elucidated by Jablin's (1987) discussion of leaders and supervisors as resources for newcomers.

In addition to helping us understand the findings of research on writing in organizations, an awareness of socialization theories may help students as they enter the workplace. The transition from student to professional may become easier if they are prepared with strategies for gathering information and an understanding of what to expect from themselves, their coworkers, and their supervisors.

The Artificiality of Distinctions Between Communication Modes

The concept of a discourse community was created to help composition researchers and teachers understand how writing fits into the ongoing communication activity of social groups. The social perspective in general emphasizes that texts are not "detached objects possessing meaning on their own, but [are] links in communicative chains, with their meaning emerging from their relationships to previous texts and the present context" (Faigley, 1985, p. 237). From this perspective, it seems somewhat artificial to distinguish between speaking, writing, and other modes of communication because all modes of communication contribute to the creation and maintenance of meaning. But the "discourse community" focuses on understanding how written texts function within social life and thus tends to separate writing as a communication activity from other forms of communication in which organization members engage.

In contrast, the concept of organizational culture does not make in principle distinctions between modes of communication. Talking, writing, rituals and ceremonies, graphics and other visual stimuli, electronic communication—all modes of expression help to convey and create meaning in an organization, all serve as the basis for creating, maintaining, and changing organizational culture, and all may contribute to the development of a communication product. Within particular organizational cultures, different modes of communication will serve different organizational purposes. As Schmitz and Fulk (1991) point out, the properties of different communication media, their objective features as well as the uses to which communication media are put, are, at least in part, socially constructed.

Clearly, special pedagogical attention must be paid to developing skills in using different modes of communication and understanding how they work. Technical communication students must learn how to acquire information, how to give public presentations, how to draft computer documentation, how to design graphic and other visual images, and how to create electronic texts.

Students must also consider some of the potential inherent in each type of medium. Toward that end, Kaufer and Carley (1994) have begun to develop a theory of proximate and distant communication that focuses on a comparative assessment of oral, written, and electronic communication. Their theory implies that each mode of communication may be more or less effective for different tasks and that writing (and by extension, electronic communication that is text based) is particularly well suited for communicating over geographic and temporal distance. In fact, they point out that it was the development of writing that has made organizations, which must coordinate members' actions over time and space, possible at all. They suggest that writing classrooms, which are currently organized around interaction with individuals who are proximate in time and space, should be organized to reflect the distance characteristics of written and print communication that students are likely to find relevant in their professional lives.

But just as important as this will be the guidance that instructors can offer technical communicators about learning when to use face-to-face conversations or meetings, when to send electronic mail or speak face-to-face, when to design a graphic or use text, and when to put a document online or on paper. Part of those decisions will be made through sensitivity to the organizational culture, that is, to the socially constructed conventions that organizations follow for using one medium versus another. It should also be recognized, as Spilka (1993a) suggests for orality and written discourse, that modes of communication work together "to enable professionals to fulfill various project goals and to contribute to an organizational culture" (p. 72).

Relations of Authority and Power in Organizations

One thing that all organizational newcomers discover quickly is that relationships between members of an organization are characterized by differential authority and power; however, the formal organizational chart does not always express the clearest view of those relationships. Most organizations structure relationships between members hierarchically; that is, some individuals are granted authority over the work and performance of others as well as differential access to material resources, and nearly everyone is subordinate to someone. Part of becoming a member of an organization requires that one relinquish some degree of control over personal choices in favor of the coordination that is required to achieve organizational as well as personal goals.

Technical communicators occupy positions somewhere on the hierarchy; where they reside can be important in understanding how organizational authority structures their work. Further, the nature of hierarchical relationships in an organization may be critical to understanding whether communication products are created through "collaborative" processes involving cooperation among relevant organizational members or processes that are more traditionally top-down. In top-down hierarchical processes, relevant organizational actors constitute an internal "audience" that must be accommodated in much the same way that communicators accommodate external audiences, but who impose far more explicit demands on the text.

Consider the organization studied by Raven (1992). In this case, a relatively rigid organizational structure required that documentation produced for external use be approved by multiple layers of information providers and management within several different units of the organization (sources of technical information, technical management, document editors, document management, project funders, and others), who all had somewhat different purposes for the text. Technical writers were required to understand the orientations and interests of each type of internal organizational member and were responsible for producing a text that satisfied all these interests simultaneously. These different members also offered suggestions for revisions that were sometimes at odds with each other. Thus, technical writers needed to accommodate widely differing internal demands imposed on the text while representing the needs of external users. In cases where the writer's opinion conflicted with that of other organizational members, the writer was generally overruled. In cases where two hierarchically equal managers conflicted, an individual at the next higher layer of management was required to arbitrate final decisions. In this kind of situation, technical communicators seem to be under the control of organizational actors who are able to impose demands on the text without bearing responsibility for accommodating other interests. Apart from initial information sharing between the writer and other organizational members, there seems to be little that is "collaborative" about such a process.

On the other hand, the organization studied by Debs (1986) structured writers and product developers into teams whose members worked together to produce both the product and the accompanying documentation. Technical and management staff provided information to writers who were responsible for producing text, but review and approval of documents took place at joint meetings where members of the team and other relevant organizational actors were able to confront each other's differing perspectives on the document and negotiate. In such an arrangement, the effect of hierarchy can be minimized by creating a context that allows project members to interact more equally. This is not to say that individuals do not still wield personal power by virtue of factors such as expertise, information, and personal persuasiveness; it is to say that hierarchical authority is not the only or primary basis on which decisions about documents are made. Within such a context, writers are able to exert their own influence as well as to negotiate other members' requirements for communication products, justifying the claim that members collaborate in the creation of organizational documents.

As Kleiman's (1993) research has documented, both collaborative and hierarchical climates may exist within the same organization. This is possible because, although the organization may be hierarchical, idiosyncratic cultures within subunits create informal modes of operation that can undermine or reinforce the formal authority of the hierarchy. Kleiman described how a type of culture can undermine the hierarchy by deemphasizing formal authority in favor of writers' expertise, avoiding sequential text reviews through multiple layers of the organization in favor of consolidated comments from all relevant participants, and valuing face-to-face meetings where consolidated comments could be prioritized and where teams could create joint ownership of documents.

It is up to technical communication instructors to show students how to understand the effects of hierarchy, and of the informal cultural processes that support or transform it, on the creation of communication products. Students need to be aware of distinctions between formal and informal authority and how those distinctions are reflected in communication processes for accomplishing tasks. Students must also appreciate how the nature of authority and power relationships will affect the role that they play as communicators in the organization. Such information may help students in making job choices upon graduation. It may further be useful in providing technical communicators with models they can consult in attempting to alter the nature of organizational conditions in which they work.

Organizations as Ethical Systems

So far, we have argued that taking organizations seriously means helping students develop an appreciation for the kind of social context that organizations represent and using that appreciation to enhance their performance as technical communicators. In making this argument, we have acknowledged that organizations are communities that share conventions for producing, understanding, and evaluating texts. But we have also emphasized that organizations are processes that create a world of their own, with shared knowledge and technologies, shared language, shared norms for using communication media, and relations of authority and power between members. We have pointed out that new members of an organization are socialized into an understanding, if not an acceptance, of this world view. It is important to add that organizations also embody their own ethical systems. As Denhardt (1981, p. 32) has written, "We originally designed and employed organizations to help us in attaining our goals. Yet now organization seems to have assumed an institutional character so strong that it comprises a model of thought and action which we are compelled to follow. The ethic of organization suggests itself as a new model for living."

When we equip students with the capacity for appreciating and using their knowledge of organizational context to enhance their performance as technical communicators, we are contributing to the progress of their socialization. This bodes well for organizational performance, but it also creates conditions under which students becoming professionals can more easily accept the organizational world—the technological, expressive, authoritative, and ethical systems it encompasses—as legitimate and immune to critical reflection.

Within organizational contexts, communication is both a means for creating, maintaining, and changing the organization as well as part or all of the product that an organization sells. Thus, our responsibilities as teachers of technical communication must go beyond simply teaching students the skills of creating a communication product. We must emphasize to students that communication contributes to the ongoing constitution of the organization and the world it embodies; thus all participants must bear responsibility for reflecting on the kind of world that our efforts create.

Students need to recognize that the particular features of organizational life they encounter are neither natural nor necessary, but conventional and, as such, fundamentally arbitrary. The idiosyncrasies of organizational life—the culture in which members are socialized, norms for the use of communication media, and the particular configuration of power and authority—are products of a socially constructed world that members of an organization individually participate in creating. Students, and sometimes their teachers, need to be reminded that life within an organization could be different.

We noted earlier that the organizational world can change with changes in the behaviors of its members. But all too frequently organizational change fails to take place because members passively accept the results of prior constructions. Members forget that when, in an effort to become good organizational citizens, they submit to organizational authority, they do not relinquish responsibility for their actions or the power to change their behavior.

But meaningful change can take place only when organizational members are equipped to reflect critically on the organizational world they wish to inhabit. The possibilities for such reflection will certainly improve if students are aware that a range of alternatives may exist for any given set of organizational norms, conventions, and practices. Teachers can help students understand how various types of organizational contexts create more or less desirable conditions for their own work and for society at large. Moreover, they can encourage students to reflect on the values that underlie their criteria for desirability. In so doing, they will also help students to develop strong preferences for the kind of organizational world that they, as technical communicators and organizational citizens, may wish to create and to understand how their efforts can contribute to or detract from that vision.

CONCLUSION

Taking organizations seriously means recognizing that they are discourse communities, but also quite a bit more. Beyond sharing conventions for discourse and common ways of knowing, believing, and persuading, members of an organization are relatively tightly connected in interdependent relationships, upon which they stake their prospects for short- and long-term goal accomplishment. Thus, members strive to achieve a high degree of predictability and reliability for their organizational system; the particular culture they create makes sense of, justifies, and stabilizes particular patterns of behavior that interconnect members. The net result is the construction of a social context that exerts profound effects on members' behavior.

We have suggested that both the basic nature of organizational contexts as well as aspects of culture idiosyncratic to a particular organization must be understood in order for students to perform effectively in their future roles as technical communicators. By understanding the particular features of an organization's culture, students will gain insight into how they can improve their job performance. But if students' lives as technical communicators are to have any meaning beyond that of simple job performance, then students must also understand how their actions contribute to the construction, maintenance, and potential transformation of the organization and its culture. Ours is a society comprised of organizations; our students will perform their jobs and conduct most of their social lives within organizational communities. Thus, educators have a dual responsibility to help students work effectively in organizations and to help them build the organizations in which they will wish to work.

REFERENCES

Anson, C.M. & Forsberg, L.L. (1990). Moving beyond the academic community: Transitional stages in professional writing. *Written Communication, 7,* 200–231.

Bazerman, C. & Paradis, J. (Eds.). (1991). *Textual dynamics of the professions: Historical and contemporary studies of writing in professional communities.* Madison, WI: University of Wisconsin Press.

Debs, MB. (1986). Collaborative writing: A study of technical writing in the computer industry. Unpublished doctoral dissertation, Rensselaer Polytechnic Institute.

Denhardt, R. B. (1981) *In the shadow of organization.* Lawrence, KS: University Press of Kansas.

Faigley, L. (1985). Nonacademic writing: The social perspective. In L. Odell & D. Goswami (Eds.), *Writing in nonacademic settings.* New York: Guilford.

Harrison, T. (1987). Frameworks for the study of writing in organizational contexts. *Written Communication, 4,* 3–23.

Jablin, F.M. (1982). Organizational communication: An assimilation approach. In M. E. Roloff & C. R. Berger (Eds.), *Social cognition and communication* (pp. 255–286). Beverly Hills: Sage.

Jablin, F.M. (1987). Organizational entry, assimilation, and exit. In F.M. Jablin, L.L. Putnam, K. H. Roberts & L.W. Porter (Eds.), *Handbook of organizational communication* (pp. 679–740). Newbury Park, CA: Sage.

Kaufer, D. & Carley, K. (1994). Some concepts and axioms about communication: Proximate and at a distance. *Written Communication, 11,* 8–42.

Kleiman, S. (1993). The reciprocal relationship of workplace culture and review. In R. Spilka (Ed.), *Writing in the workplace: New research perspectives* (pp. 56–70). Carbondale, IL: Southern Illinois University Press.

Louis, M.R. (1980). Surprise and sense making: What newcomers experience in entering unfamiliar organizational settings. *Administrative Science Quarterly, 25,* 226–251.

Louis, M.R. (1990). Acculturation in the workplace: Newcomers as lay ethnographers. In B. Scneider, (Ed.), *Organizational climate and culture* (pp. 85–129). San Francisco, CA: Jossey-Bass.

Lutz, J.A. (1989). Writers in organizations and how they learn the image: Theory, research, and implications. In C. Matalene (Ed.), *Worlds of writing: Teaching and learning in discourse communities of work* (pp. 113–135). New York: Random.

Odell, L. & Goswami, D. (Eds.). (1985). *Writing in nonacademic settings.* New York: Guilford.

Raven, M.E. (1992). Analyzing and adapting to a multiple audience: A study of two writers in the computer industry. Unpublished doctoral dissertation, Rensselaer Polytechnic Institute.

Schein, E.H. (1990). Organizational culture. *American Psychologist, 45,* 109–119.

Schmitz, J. & Fulk, J. (1991). Organizational colleagues, media richness, and electronic mail: A test of the social influence model of technology use. *Communication Research, 18,* 487–523.

Smircich, L. (1983). Concepts of culture and organizational analysis. *Administrative Science Quarterly, 28,* 339–358.

Spilka, R. (1993a). Moving between oral and written discourse to fulfill rhetorical and social goals. In R. Spilka (Ed.), *Writing in the workplace: New research perspectives* (pp. 71–83). Carbondale, IL: Southern Illinois University Press.

Spilka, R. (Ed.). (1993b). *Writing in the workplace: New research perspectives.* Carbondale, IL: Southern Illinois University Press.

Van Maanen, J. (1976). Breaking in: Socialization to work. In R. Dubin (Ed.), *Handbook of work, organization, and society* (pp. 67–130). Chicago, IL: Rand McNally.

Weick, K. (1979). *The social psychology of organizing.* Reading, MA: Addison-Wesley.

3

TECHNICAL COMMUNICATION AND RHETORIC

Cezar M. Ornatowski

San Diego State University

INTRODUCTION

In his classic *Anatomy of Criticism,* Northrop Frye (1957) suggests that "anything which makes a functional use of words will always be involved in all the technical problems of words, including rhetorical problems." "The only road from grammar to logic," Frye argues, "runs through the intermediate territory of rhetoric" (p. 331).

Although most technical communicators would readily acknowledge that technical communication makes a functional use of words, it is only relatively recently that they have begun to acknowledge that it may also be involved with the rhetorical problems of words. That acknowledgment did not come without resistance; many, especially among practitioners in business and industry, remain cautious as to the viability and usefulness of seeing technical communication in rhetorical terms. A decade ago, Thomas Girill (1985) noted two diametrically opposed schools of thought on the issue: one that saw rhetorical principles as "crucial for understanding what technical writers do," and the other that found "almost nothing" of interest to rhetoricians in the work of technical communicators (p. 44).

Although today the latter position might perhaps appear less tenable, such polarization reveals that the problem of the relationship between technical communication and rhetoric involves deeper issues. At stake is not merely whether and in what way technical communication is bound up with rhetoric. Implicit in any answer are fundamental philosophical, disciplinary, and professional assumptions and values: the scope and role of technical communication in organizations and in society; its relationship to technology and to other forms of human activity; conceptions of professional ethics and social responsibility for technical communicators; and the scope and function of technical communication education.

The goal of this essay is to outline the major rhetorical dimensions of technical communication as they emerge from relevant research in a variety of disciplines. The major question this essay tries to answer is this: In what ways can we think of technical communication as rhetorical, or as involving rhetoric? My aim is to bring some order into this complicated territory, rather than retrace or update earlier reviews of the issue by cataloging current work. I will begin with a brief discussion of the philosophical roots of the problem. Then I will discuss the various conceptions of rhetoric applicable to technical communication, beginning with applications of classical rhetoric.

THE PROBLEM IN PHILOSOPHICAL PERSPECTIVE

The problem of the relationship between technical communication and rhetoric is among the historically more recent manifestations of a debate that reaches back to the foundations of Western intellectual history. Stanley Fish (1989) has traced this debate to the classical conflict between the sophists and the philosophers, a conflict rooted in "a disagreement about the basic constituents of human activity and about the nature of human nature itself" (p. 482). Using Richard Lanham's distinction between "serious man" and "rhetorical man," Fish described this conflict as a clash between two radically divergent worldviews: the "foundational" versus the "rhetorical" (p. 482). "Serious man," wrote Lanham,

> possesses a central self, an irreducible entity. These selves combine into a single, homogeneously real society which constitutes a referent reality for the men living in it. This referent society is in turn contained in a physical nature itself referential, standing 'out there' independent of man. Man has invented language to communicate with his fellow man. He communicates facts and concepts about both nature and society. He can also communicate

> a third category of response, emotions. When he is communicating facts or concepts, success is measured by something we call clarity. When he is communicating feelings, success is measured by something we call sincerity, faithfulness to the self who is doing the feeling.

"Rhetorical man," on the other hand,

> is centered in time and concrete local event. The lowest common denominator of his life is a social situation.... He is thus committed to no single construction of the world; much rather, to prevailing in the game at hand.... Rhetorical man is trained not to discover reality but to manipulate it. Reality is what is accepted as reality, what is useful. (Quoted in Fish, pp. 482–83)

Until recently, the disjunction between "serious man" and "rhetorical man," or—as Richard Rorty (1987) suggestively put it—"objective fact and something softer, squishier, and more dubious"—appeared to mark a boundary between radically different epistemological, disciplinary, and discursive domains (p. 40). On one side were scientists and engineers in laboratories, offices, and test cells engaged in discovering the secrets of nature and translating scientific principles into complex technologies to serve human needs. They employed systematic methods of inquiry to produce specialized, cumulative, and verifiable knowledge, which they used to perfect progressively more refined designs. They communicated their findings and coordinated their work through documents written in conventional formats with objective language and plain, neutral style. On the other side were poets, fiction writers, essayists, columnists, popularizers of science and technology, and politicians. They wrote for diverse audiences, using the rhetorical and stylistic resources of language to delight, amuse, edify, argue, seduce, arouse, and cajole. Fish emphasizes that the perspectives of the "serious man" and "rhetorical man" are ultimately incompatible and perhaps irreconcilable; they constitute enduring poles of our philosophical horizon. "It is," he insists, "the difference that remains" (p. 502).

The complexity of the problem of the relationship between technical communication and rhetoric is largely due to the fact that technical communication is located—as both a theory and a practice, an academic discipline and a profession, as related to the imperatives of technology and business on one hand and to the vagaries of meaning and the dynamics of human interaction on the other hand—at the very boundary of this disjunction.

In the last 20 years or so, however, as part of a general challenge to positivism across a range of disciplines, the very foundations of this disjunction have come under intense questioning. Scholars in rhetoric have argued that technical texts contain a strong element of persuasion and exhibit many affinities with the canons and principles of classical rhetoric. Social constructionism has reconceived all discourse, including technical communication, as a product of disciplinary and professional communities, grounded in collective norms and values and in concrete contexts of action. Studies of writing in professional contexts have revealed the complex embedment of technical documents in social, institutional, and technological processes. Philosophy and sociology of science and technology have revealed that the products of science (scientific facts) and technology (technological artifacts) are products of encounters between people, needs, resources, and exigencies, mediated through discourse, and thus are not immune to problems of communication, including rhetorical problems. All of these perspectives made it possible to begin closing the apparent gap between technical communication and rhetoric and to begin reconceiving their relationship in increasingly complex ways.

TECHNICAL COMMUNICATION AND CLASSICAL RHETORIC

One major way to theorize the relationship between technical communication and rhetoric is look at technical communication through the framework of classical rhetoric. Edward Corbett (1989) has perhaps most clearly articulated the assumptions behind such a perspective:

> [w]hether the writing is scientific, technical, business, professional, or any other kind of specialized writing, the main and persistent problems resolve themselves into a concern for finding something to say and then selecting, organizing, and expressing what has been found. Those concerns are traditionally the concerns of the academic discipline known as rhetoric, a discipline that can most broadly be defined as 'the art of effective communication in the oral and written medium' (p. 65).

The application of the classical framework to technical communication focuses attention on the four canons of rhetoric (invention, arrangement, style, and delivery) as they apply to technical discourse and on the three dimensions of the rhetorical act: ethos (the writer), pathos (audience adaptation), and logos (the message). (For a review of this work, see Broadhead, 1985; Keene & Barnes-Ostrander, 1985; Massee & Benz, 1989; Miller, 1985; Selzer, 1989.) Research from this perspective has examined the "systems of special topoi" characteristic of the "rhetorical environments in which technical discourse is conducted" (Miller, 1985, pp. 122–123), "ordering principles" characteristic of technical documents (Selzer, 1989), figurative devices characteristic of scientific and technical texts (Halloran & Bradford, 1984), and ways to enhance the readability and comprehensibility of the technical text (Broadhead, 1985).

Much of the work influenced by the application of the framework of classical rhetoric to technical communication implies the conception of rhetoric as communicative effectivity. Such a conception leads to a search for better ways to "get the message across"—to what Robert Corey (1978) has termed, somewhat oxymoronically, the "science of technical rhetoric" (p. 6). This search has resulted in a better understanding of how writers work, how readers read and use documents, and what communicative strategies work best—knowledge that has underpinned the document design movement and contributed to a significant improvement in the quality of documentation, especially during the 1980s (see Doheny-Farina, 1988). Such rhetorical "science," however, while congenial to the business/industrial ethos of efficiency and result-orientation, does not, in any fundamental way, challenge the assumptions of "serious men"; on the contrary, it conceives of rhetoric as a kind of "technology" of text and text production, emphasizing its formal aspects.

According to Aristotle, however, rhetoric is an art (and not a science) precisely to the extent that it is concerned with probabilities, not certainties, with the realm of human choice and decisionmaking, and not with the immutabilities of nature—and thus with persuasive effectivity, not informational one. Aristotle's identification of rhetoric with probability, uncertainty, choice, and persuasion implies that to see classical rhetoric as relevant for technical communication one must reconceive technical communication as involved, at least to a significant extent, not only with the imperatives and recalcitrancies of the material and institutional worlds but also with the fallibilities and uncertainties of human reason and judgment and thus with the dynamics of persuasion. Therefore, one way to think of technical communication as involved with rhetoric is to show that it involves persuasion, that it is essentially (and not only occasionally or incidentally) persuasive.

Several conceptions of technical communication as essentially persuasive have been proposed. Marilyn Samuels (1985) has suggested that the technical writer is a "rhetorician who must design in an appropriate context" a "persuasive view of reality" (p. 7). Samuels begins with the assumption that "[a]ll writers are creative" and "everything written is a creation or recreation of reality" (p. 3). Technical writing involves a special kind of creativity in which a manager writing a report, for example, "must integrate several kinds of realities in order to produce an effective communication": the facts, the tacit assumptions and understandings of the industry and of the customer, precedents, and personal judgment (p. 11). In this sense, "technical writing is a recreation of reality for special purposes," but it is also "an act of creation without departing from the truth" (p. 11). In Samuels's conception, technical communication, while grounded on the one side in the recalcitrancy of "facts," is open to the uncertainties of "personal judgment" and is persuasive in essence, since persuasiveness constitutes the very condition of its effectivity (without, however, implying that it cannot thereby also be true).

A different conception of technical communication as persuasion has been suggested by Robert Williams (1983). For Williams, the apparent "effectivity" of technical communication, guaranteed by the traditional constraints of format and style, constitutes the condition of its persuasiveness. Within the constraints of format and style, the technical report writer is "engaged in perceptual play, a running game between writer and reader bound by conventions and unstated rules" (p. 11). In this game,

> the very conventionality of format works in the writer's favor. The message of standard format is that *this* is a sound document. Furthermore, unless the writer disabuses them, readers will associate the report with those read in the past. That is, they anticipate a certain mode of reading, assume a certain set of mind. It is likely that they will read with two deeply embedded assumptions:
>
> - first, the document is rational and objective, and
> - second, words are only vehicles for conveying meaning.
>
> Coupled with the assurance of format, these two assumptions make up the essential elements of play. (p.12)

In this way, the writer "controls the gridwork of perception, and to the extent that the medium is the message, the writer controls the message" (pp. 12–13). Concerning the assumptions of objectivity and factuality, Williams suggests, "[t]he writer would do well to foster that impression irrespective of the facts" (p. 12). And while Williams concedes that "substance . . . is primary and up to a point unyielding," he suggests that "the more unbudgeable the content, the more deeply satisfying the game" (p. 13).

While for Samuels technical documents are inevitably and essentially persuasive because they involve a (re)shaping of reality, for Williams they provide relatively neutral (in themselves) arenas for persuasive action, the only checks on which are the twin recalcitrances of substance and convention. In Samuels's conception, the central issues for technical rhetoric would appear to be those of control and awareness: control of the writer over the creative power of discourse to shape reality, and the awareness, on both the writer's and reader's part, of the choices that have been made and of the realities that have been created by and for them. For Williams, on the other hand, the central issue would be ethical (since the writer controls the arena of the game): the checks and balances on the writer's persuasive intent and skill and the limits of the reader's gullibility.

A conception of technical rhetoric that provides for both control and ethics was proposed by Carolyn Miller (1989), who suggested that technical communication constitutes a "practical rhetoric" that focuses on "arguing in a prudent way toward the good of the community rather than [on] constructing texts" (p. 23). At the heart of such rhetoric lies the doctrine of "phronesis" or prudence. Prudential reasoning mediates between the imperatives of efficiency and effectiveness on the one hand and the diversity of human individual and communal interests on the other, and provides "a locus for questioning, criticism, for distinguishing good practice from bad" (p. 23). For Miller, then, a rhetoric of technical communication would provide a theory of good reasons for deliberations involving simultaneously the recalcitrancies and imperatives of technology and the market on the one hand, and the contingencies of human judgment and action on the other. Such a rhetoric would become the "rhetoric of the world of work" (p. 24). This kind of rhetoric is not primarily concerned with communicative effectiveness, nor even with texts; it is concerned primarily with the deliberative process through which not only texts but decisions (including personal judgments) are made.

Such neoclassical conceptions of technical rhetoric have largely come into being following the well-publicized disasters involving technology and communication, such as Three Mile Island, the space shuttle Challenger, or the Exxon Valdez (Dombrowski, 1992; Farrell and Goodnight, 1981; Herndl, Fennell, & Miller, 1991; Walzer & Gross, 1994; Winsor, 1988, 1990). Arthur Walzer and Alan Gross, for example, have recently suggested that Aristotelian conceptions of technical communication as deliberation directed at the discovery of the best reasons for accepting certain beliefs in view of available knowledge and facts (along the lines proposed by Miller, 1989) offer the best available means of analyzing and understanding failures such as the Challenger disaster, as well as the best hope for preventing like occurrences in the future. Walzer and Gross analyze what they see as prevailing conceptions of technical communication (positivist, postmodern, and Aristotelian) in terms of their ability to account for the complexities of the decision-making process that resulted in the Challenger tragedy. They argue that only such conceptions as Miller's (which they call "Aristotelian") "do full justice to the Challenger engineers and managers as responsible human beings with the capacity to deliberate about an unknown future" (p. 432).

The problem with neoclassical conceptions of technical rhetoric is that they appear to leave the bulk of what the technical communicator does out of the domain of rhetoric. Many technical communicators might object, for instance, that prudential deliberation (while critically important) constitutes only a special case of technical communication, or that it involves technical communication only occasionally (for instance, in the form of supporting analytical reports). It is relatively marginal, however, to the routine tasks, mundane transactions, and standard formats that constitute so much of technical communication on the job. How, they may ask, can one see the writing of a computer or staple-gun manual as an argument for the good of the community? In what sense does an engine performance report constitute a "persuasive version of reality" if all it does is record data and demonstrate compliance with specifications? How can one think rhetorically of a customer spec or a parts list?

Another limitation of neoclassical conceptions of technical communication is that they do not address the fundamental disjunction between "objective fact and something softer, squishier, and more dubious," that is, they have little to say about technical communication as epistemology—a discursive construction of a way of knowing and relating to the material and social world.

To begin to address these two apparent limitations, one must, first, look at technical communication in terms of its context and, second, acknowledge that rhetoric deals not only with the dissemination but also with the generation and organization of knowledge, with strategies of inquiry as well as of persuasion. The first perspective connects technical communication with the dynamics of organizational action as well as technology development and transfer; the second involves it with problems of epistemology and disciplinary inquiry. Both perspectives are implicit in the major assumptions of social constructionism (see also the essay by Subbiah, this collection).

TECHNICAL COMMUNICATION AS RHETORICAL ACTION IN CONTEXT

The advent of social constructionism, the realization that all meaningful practices (including all writing) have a collective origin (thus are "social") and that reality is "constructed" through such practices (Berger & Luckman, 1966), has probably been the most important theoretical development in terms of opening the way for a rethinking of technical communication along rhetorical lines. According to these assumptions, meaning is indeterminate apart from concrete contexts of action in which it is constituted by conditions, interpretations, expectations, constraints, norms, prior knowledge, and other factors (Rafoth & Rubin, 1988). Charles Bazerman (1988) has perhaps articulated the implications of this realization in a way most relevant for technical communicators. "Writing," Bazerman suggested, "is a form of social action; texts help organize social activities and social structure; and reading is a form of social participation" (p. 10). Therefore, one cannot understand what constitutes an appropriate text in any field or situation "without considering the social and intellectual activity which the text [is] part of" and cannot "see what the text [is] doing without looking at the worlds in which [this text] served as significant activity. . . ." (p. 4). Among technical communication scholars, Miller (1978) was one of the first to suggest that because technology is "fundamentally a matter of doing, its rhetorical consequences may be found by looking closely at the activities or actions that we understand as 'technological.'" (p. 228). (See also Zappen, 1983.)

Studies of technical communication in context have revealed that documents serve to coordinate the activities of groups and individuals, promote the progression of organizational tasks, control activities, monitor output, and make "the individual's work advance the organization's established objectives" (Paradis, Dobrin, & Miller, 1985, p. 293). The writing of professionals is shaped by the conventions of the profession or discipline (Miller & Selzer, 1985; Winsor, 1989), by professional publications, meetings, and other "identity-shaping" factors (Lipson, 1988), as well as by organizational structure, relationships of authority and power (Cross, 1990), beliefs and values (Roundy & Mair, 1982), expectations of organizational readers (Barabas, 1970), and by the larger business, professional, and social context of which the organization is a part (Broadhead & Freed, 1986; Mirel, 1988; Odell, Goswami, Herrington, & Quick, 1983; Paradis, Dobrin, & Miller, 1985; Selzer, 1989). The realization of these multiple connections between, on the one hand, documents, writers, and the activity of writing, and, on the other hand, the various contexts, immediate and remote, in which documents and writing function as significant activities, provides the foundation for conceiving more complex connections between technical communication and rhetoric.

In one study of document development in context, Stephen Doheny-Farina (1986) found that the collaborative writing of a business plan in an emerging organization reflected and brought to the surface the simmering conflict over power and authority and the disagreements of members over the mission and goals of the organization. The act of negotiating textual choices among the organization's managers became a "struggle for power in which the stakes [were] the shape, philosophy, and future of the organization" (p. 178). Doheny-Farina's study showed that textual decisions may not only articulate, but actually constitute, organizational decisions. The final draft of the document, far from being simply a report of organizational and financial information (which was its ostensible purpose), became, as it were, a record of the bargains that were struck in order for it to be able to "report" what it did. Rhetorically, therefore, the document was quite complex: it was, at once, a report of financial information (to outside readers), a report on the outcome of a struggle between competing visions (to organizational insiders), a "wish list" (to senior management), and marching orders (to lower management and the rank and file).

In a study of the political efficacy of a computer manual in a college bursar's office, Barbara Mirel (1988) showed that the aspect of the rhetorical situation usually referred to as "users' needs" actually constitutes a complex social context into which a technology is inserted. In this context, even an ostensibly "simple" document such as a computer manual may perform many rhetorical functions. Mirel showed that the computer manual ostensibly intended to teach office workers how to use a new computer system actually fulfilled three social and political functions beyond its "technical" purpose: reactive ("helping to resolve existing problems associated with conflict and uncertainty"), proactive ("avoiding potential difficulties"), and policymaking ("enabling administrators to use its mere existence to represent an organization's commitment to a new system"). These functions were at best only tangentially related to the manual's usefulness as a manual. In fact, as an instructional document the manual turned out to be quite useless because it was conceived for political purposes and nobody really bothered to make it a decent manual. However, Mirel concluded, the manual was successful in terms of achieving its ultimate organizational purpose: helping the organization "tacitly negotiate stability in the midst of technological change" (p. 290). Steven Mailloux (1989) has suggested that rhetoric is the "political effectivity of trope and figure in the culture" (p. xii). In those terms, one could say that the manual was rhetorically successful, even though it was a bad manual.

Studies such as those of Doheny-Farina (1986) and Mirel (1988) suggest that technical documents may have purposes and dimensions quite separate from their ostensible "technical" purpose. Moreover, the document's "rhetorical power" (Mailloux, 1989) may be focused along these purposes and dimensions, in the sense that they constitute the action performed by the document and provide measures of the document's effectivity.

A still different rhetorical dimension of technical text is revealed by James Paradis (1991) in his study of the legal ramifications of a staple-gun manual. Paradis concludes that "[w]ritten discourse is inherently accountable," since

> evidence that a given technology is a reasonable solution to a problem is a matter of demonstration, in which texts—quite frequently the operator's manuals—will inevitably play a powerful testimonial and illustrative role. The document is a testament that the technology can be explained, which is to say made understandable and controllable for the lay user. Language plays a crucial role in this rendering of technology into human terms . . . . Indeed, rendering public technologies into written procedures is a decisive step in the socialization of a technology. The operator's manual not only assumes a

> contractual importance in its capacity as written claim, but also becomes evidence that the expert, who usually has an exclusive hold on the expertise, has sufficiently reasoned out and articulated how it is to be made fit for public use. (p. 269)

One must note that what Paradis calls "inherent accountability" constitutes but another form of "arguing in a prudential way for the good of the community." Technical description and instruction as "testimony" to the viability and fitness of the technology for public use involve a form of deliberation (although perhaps only implicit and internal) in which one reasons from technical data to the uncertainties of actual practice and conceptions of public welfare to arrive at communicative choices that inevitably have ethical implications. In rhetorical terms, at least, it appears that the space shuttle is not that different from a staplegun, nor is a manual from a Congressional debate.

All of the above examples suggest that a distinction may be made between ostensible and implicit rhetoricity: While a document may ostensibly appear to be doing one thing, it may also implicitly be doing something else, somewhere else. Both kinds of rhetoricity, but especially implicit rhetoricity, arise as a function of the embedment of documents in particular social, organizational, and technological processes and contexts. Implicit rhetoricity of a document often escapes the attention of writers and readers because a particular writer or reader may have a limited view of the document's potential circulation and use, or of the sorts of choices that went into its preparation.

One important aspect of implicit rhetoricity is genre. Both Miller (1984) and Bazerman (1988) have offered rhetorical definitions of genre. For Miller, genres represent "typified rhetorical actions based in recurrent situations" (p. 159), while for Bazerman genre is "a socially recognized, repeated strategy for achieving similar goals in situations socially perceived as being similar" (p. 62). In their study of the typical formats of engineering reports, Miller and Selzer (1985) argued that since Aristotle's rhetorical topics derive from "both the political institutions and the generic functions of public discourse," features of professional discourse related to specific discourse communities and specific professional genres (i.e., typical "contents" of scientific and engineering research reports) are also "topical" in the rhetorical sense. For example, the expected presence of such headings as Introduction, Methods, Results, and Conclusions and Recommendations carries implicit messages about the rationality of the research process, the soundness of the argument, the professionalism of the writer, and perhaps even—as in the case of obligatory subheadings in construction reports about accommodations for the handicapped—about the political "correctness" of the approach. Miller and Selzer see the typical forms of technical reports as stylized forms with persuasive power, rather than merely "logical" arrangements of subject matter. (See also Smart, 1993.)

The consideration of genre as implicitly rhetorical carries us closer to the conception of rhetoric as epistemic, as involved with the process of communal creation, and not only dissemination, of knowledge. This conception, deriving largely from the work of Thomas Kuhn, has had profound influence on the reconceptualization of science along rhetorical lines and has recently become increasingly influential in technical communication.

TECHNICAL COMMUNICATION, EPISTEMOLOGY, AND THE RHETORIC OF SCIENCE

Walzer and Gross (1994) have recently suggested that the history of scholarship in rhetoric as applied to technical communication "has been characterized by a movement away from the positivistic assumptions of pioneering textbooks in technical communication and toward the 'social constructionist' assumptions of Kuhnian philosophy of science that mark recent scholarship" (p. 420).

The constructivist assumptions deriving from the philosophy and sociology of science question such givens as "fact" or "method." Rather than assuming that scientific statements represent descriptions of "objectively" existing realities of nature, constructivist research approaches the products of science as resulting from a process of fabrication, focusing attention on the "processes by which outcomes are brought about through the mundane transactions of participants" (Knorr-Cetina & Mulkey, 1983, p. 3). Accordingly, the constructivist approach is primarily concerned with investigating how scientific knowledge (i.e., "facts") is produced, both in the practical actions of scientists in the laboratory as well as in the process of scientific exchange (Knorr, 1977; Knorr-Cetina, 1981, 1983; Knorr-Cetina & Mulkey, 1983; Latour & Woolgar, 1979). Such an approach relocates the problem of facticity from the relationship between scientific statements and external nature to the relationship between the activity of "doing science" and nature. Since both the laboratory activities of scientists and exchanges between scientists appear to be mediated and conducted through language, most of these activities can be seen as directed not toward "reality" but toward operations on statements (Latour, 1980; Latour & Woolgar, 1979). These operations turn out to be largely of a rhetorical kind; they consist of "selections designed to transform the subjective into the objective, the unbelievable into the believed, the fabricated into the finding, and the painstakingly constructed into the objective scientific fact" (Knorr-Cetina, 1983, p. 122).

Based on the assumptions of the constructivist program, scholars (Bazerman, 1988; Gross, 1988, 1990; Prelli, 1989; Weimer, 1977) have constructed a rhetorical conception of science based on three major propositions:

1. Scientific "realities" (including "facts") are not given, and therefore also not *discovered*, but *constructed* by scientists partially in situ (in the laboratory) through various actions, including talk and scriptive activities.
2. The construction of these realities also includes larger contextual ex-situ elements, the more general practices of science as a community of knowledge and discourse, including again talk, both formal and informal, and writing (the norms, conventions, and genres of formal discourse).
3. Because it is always a construction of a world view, scientific discourse is fundamentally (not just occasionally) persuasive.

The assumptions of the constructivist program in the sociology of science and of the rhetoric of science led to suggestions that technical communication may also be seen as constituting a specific manner of seeing and acting in the world, a manner characteristic of technology and the "technical." The most famous early attempt to articulate such a view was Carolyn Miller's essay, "A Humanistic Rationale for Technical Writing." Miller (1979) argued against what she saw as naive, positivistic, unrhetorical assumptions prevalent in technical writing textbooks and called for a conception of technical communication based on a view of scientific knowledge as constructed by disciplinary conventions and intepretive norms and validated by disciplinary communities, rather than discovered in a reality outside of human action and communication. In such a view, Miller argued, "technical writing becomes, rather than the revelation of absolute reality, a persuasive version of experience" (p. 616).

It is important to note that "persuasive" here implies not argument in the classical sense ("arguing in a prudent way towards the good of the community") but a different order of rhetorical effect altogether: the creation of the immanent effect of "factuality" and "technicality" as constitutive conditions of a specific form of discourse (technical discourse). In this sense, technical communication is essentially (and not only occasionally or marginally) rhetorical in that it constitutes a specific way of viewing the world and of being in the world, a way congruent with the imperatives of technology and of the organizational contexts in which it constitutes a mode of action. As a way of viewing and acting in the world, technical communication embodies both the assumptions, values, norms, and conventions of a particular organization as well as those of the industry and the more general practices of technology as a community of knowledge and discourse.

TECHNICAL COMMUNICATION AND TECHNOLOGY

Another aspect of the rhetoricity of technical communication emerges from considering its relationship to technology. To examine this relationship, it is necessary to look at the process of technology marketing, design, and development and to examine the role played by technical communication in this process.

A group of sociologists of technology associated with the "Belgrade" group (Bijker, Hughes, & Pinch, 1987) have examined technologies as products of interaction and communication, rather than of merely mechanical operations based on specialized and esoteric knowledge. They argue that technological artifacts such as airplane engines or bicycles are creations of people working within social collectivities and influenced by a multitude of cultural, political, and ideological factors and interests; as Donald MacKenzie (1987) has pointed out, "a technological enterprise is simultaneously a social, an economic, and a political enterprise" (p. 198).

In examining how technical artifacts are created, sociologists of technology have focused on what Trevor Pinch and Wiebe Bijker (1987) have called the "interpretive flexibility" of the technological artifact, that is, on showing that technical considerations alone do not account for the final shape of emerging technologies, but that technologies result from complex decision-making processes, in which language plays an important part. Using the first bicycles as their example, Pinch and Bijker show that widespread business and public acceptance of a new technological device—and thus its economic and technological viability—is based not on the intrinsic "technical" superiority or performance of the accepted design over other, competing designs, but on the success of the manufacturers and backers in achieving "closure"—a disappearance of controversy and problems surrounding the device. This closure, they show, does not mean that objectionable "technical" problems of design or safety were "solved," but rather that the key constituencies—the relevant social groups that had interlocking interests in the success of the particular design, as well as the public that was to buy it—had to see the problems as solved. Such a "rhetorical" solution to "technical" problems is achieved through manipulating different definitions of the problem, until one is reached such that the problems become "solvable" within parameters satisfactory to all the interested groups, especially those with political and economic interests. In this process of re-presentation, competing interests mobilized resources, including statements by "technical" experts, experiments and tests, and advertising. It is through such a process, rather than through some purely "technical" process of refinement and testing that the shape of bicycle technology was effectively determined. In this process, technical communication plays a persuasive and always interested part, although one of its major effects is to deflect attention from this process of shaping and to lend the human decisions through which technologies are shaped the aura of "technical" necessity.

While the work of the sociologists of technology examines the role of technical communication in shaping emerging technologies, David Dobrin (1983) has suggested a conception of technical communication that sees it as shaping both technology and its users to achieve a particular deployment of material and human resources in relation to the world. Dobrin suggests that technology is more than an array of tools and procedures; it extends also to "the way human beings deploy themselves in the use and production of material goods and services" (p. 243). Technical communication does not simply occur alongside technology; it is itself both a product of technology and a technology: a way of deploying ourselves in our relations to the material and social world. "Technological discourse," Dobrin argues, "converted all things, natural or human, into function, so that it could dominate man and matter simultaneously, using the same discourse to bring man into complicated systems of control and organization as it used to bring matter into complicated systems of manipulation" (p. 245). As "writing that accommodates technology to the user" (p. 242), technical communication represents a kind of "rhetoric of technology" (my phrase) that serves to bridge the gap between technical imperatives and human aspirations and capabilities. Such a formulation opens technical communication to the problematics of technological practice and its social institutionalizations, as well as to the philosophical and ideological aspects of technology.

CONCLUSION

The relationship between technical communication and rhetoric is complex and multifaceted. Any conception of that relationship inevitably involves conceptions of rhetoric, as well as of technical communication. Conceptions of rhetoric associated with technical communication have ranged from communicative effectivity to persuasiveness, prudential reasoning, and ideological force. Conceptions of technical communication range from instructional discourse to the entirety of symbolic operations that accompany organized productive activities and the deployments of technology in our society.

What is perhaps most important to realize about the relationship between technical communication and rhetoric is that this relationship is dialectical, that conceptions of rhetoric and technical communication are mutually interdependent: the scope given to the one constrains or broadens how one can think of the other. That is why this relationship is so vexed; that is why it is so important, especially to teachers of technical communication. How one talks about rhetoric in a technical communication classroom both depends on and determines, to a large extent, how one talks about technical communication, as well as what scope (in terms of personal and social agency) one gives to the technical communicator in professional contexts. The professional, ethical, and ideological implications of that should be obvious.

In the end, it is not possible perhaps to define the relationship between technical communication and rhetoric once and for all, since it depends on so many fundamental assumptions about discourse, subjectivity, and society. Technical communication encompasses a range of communicative activities, some of which may—in any particular instance—appear more rhetorical than others. In this sense, the rhetoricity of a particular act of communication may be determined by what Couture and Rymer (1993) call a writer's "functional relationship to writing": the ensemble of conditions, exigencies, tasks, and purposes in relation to which writers produce texts and which form the larger social context for communicative action (p. 19). However, the research examined in this essay suggests the following broad assumptions for a rhetorical perspective on technical communication:

1. Technical documents are forms of action in the relevant social and institutional contexts. These contexts include not only the internal context of the organization itself but also the larger economic, political, and discursive context of the industry, government, and culture.
2. Within diverse contexts, technical documents serve as arenas for negotiating diverse and often conflicting needs and interests, both public and private.
3. The stylized and formal character of technical documents serves a variety of rhetorical functions, among which are establishing ethos, directing attention, controlling the extent of available interpretations, and providing a legal framework for the negotiation of mutual interests.
4. Technical documents may be ostensibly rhetorical or implicitly rhetorical, fulfilling several functions at once (for example, informational, persuasive, and political).
5. Technical communication represents a specific world view and a specific relationship to the material and social world.

The recent turn towards the problematics of language and interpretation across all disciplines has made us inescapably aware, as John Clifford and George Marcus (1996) have pointed out, of the "systematic and situational verbal structures that determine all representations of reality" (p. 10). As a domain that encompasses a certain class of "systematic and situational verbal structures," technical communication represents a specific deployment of symbols in those areas of culture that involve organized productive activity and the human relationship to technology and its products. To theorize about the relationship of technical communication and rhetoric means to think about the fundamental conditions, principles, and effects of that deployment. In this sense, rhetoric is not a set of strategies, or a special category of effect, or even the principle of communicative effectivity. It is an inherent condition of all discourse, including technical discourse. As Douglas Ehninger has suggested,

> the notion that rhetoric is something added to discourse is gradually giving way to the quite different assumption that rhetoric not only is inherent in all human communication, but that it also informs and conditions every aspect of thought and behavior: that man himself is inevitably and inescapably a rhetorical animal. (p. 10)

To see the relationship between technical communication and rhetoric in such inclusive terms means that claims to "functionality," "objectivity," and "clarity" signal not the absence of rhetoric but the presence of a different class of rhetorical weapons: weapons that are specifically modern, forged over four centuries of Western rationalism and honed in the marketplace, the countinghouse, the factory, on the shop floor, on the launching pad—places where the business of the modern is primarily conducted. In these contexts—all messages—including the most ostensibly "technical"—circulate to direct, coordinate, organize, support, permit, enable, facilitate, and prohibit. They become the means through which people and institutions garner resources, induce action, and realize payoffs. Whether they wield a scholarly treatise, a scientific article, a corporate report, or a stack of engineering drawings, "serious men" participate in transactions characteristic of modern scientific, industrial, and business enterprises and of the larger social institutions of science, business, and technology. Many may choose to ignore the conditions of their participation, and to remain indifferent to its effects. But, as Steven Katz has pointed out in his discussion of technical discourse in the Holocaust, they do so at their, and our, peril.

REFERENCES

Anderson, P.R., Brockmann, R.J. & Miller, C.R. (Eds.). (1983). *New essays in technical and scientific communication: Research, theory, practice.* Farmingdale, NY: Baywood.

Barabas, C. (1990). *Technical writing in a corporate culture: A study of the nature of information.* Norwood, NJ: Ablex.

Bazerman, C. (1988). *Shaping written knowledge: The genre and activity of the experimental article in science.* Madison, WI: University of Wisconsin Press.

Bazerman, C. & Paradis, J. (Eds.). (1991). *Textual dynamics of the professions: Historical and contemporary studies in writing in professional communities.* Madison, WI: University of Wisconsin Press.

Berger, P. & Luckmann, T. (1966). *The social construction of reality.* Garden City, NJ: Doubleday.

Bijker, W.E., Hughes, T.P. & Pinch, T.J. (Eds.). (1987). *The social construction of technological systems: New directions in the sociology and history of technology.* Cambridge, MA: MIT Press.

Broadhead, G.J. (1985). Style in technical and scientific writing. In M.G. Moran & D. Journet (Eds.), *Research in technical communication: A bibliographic sourcebook* (pp. 217–254). Westport, CT: Greenwood.

Broadhead, G.J. & Freed, R.C. (1986). *The variables of composition: Process and product in a business setting.* Carbondale, IL: Southern Illinois University Press.

Clifford, J. & Marcus, G.E. (1986). *Writing culture: The poetics and politics of ethnography.* Berkeley: University of California Press.

Corbett, E.P.J. (1989). What classical rhetoric has to offer the teacher and the student of business and professional writing. In M. Kogen (Ed.), *Writing in the business professions* (pp. 65–72). Urbana, IL: NCTE.

Corey, R. (1978). Rhetoric and technical writing: Black magic or science. *Technical Communication,* 2–6.

Couture, B. & Rymer, J. (1993). Situational exigence: Composing processes on the job by writer's role and task value. In R. Spilka (Ed.), *Writing in the workplace: New research perspectives* (pp. 4–20). Carbondale, IL: Southern Illinois University Press.

Cross, G.A. (1990). A Bakhtinian exploration of factors affecting the collaborative writing of an executive letter of an annual report. *Research in the Teaching of English, 24,*173–202.

Dobrin, D. (1983). What's technical about technical writing? In P.R. Anderson, R.J. Brockmann & C.R. Miller (Eds.), *New essays in technical and scientific communication: Research, theory, practice* (pp. 227–250). Farmingdale, NY: Baywood.

Doheny-Farina, S. (1986). Writing in an emerging organization: An ethnographic study. *Written Communication, 3,* 158–185.

Doheny-Farina, S. (Ed.). (1988). *Effective documentation: What we have learned from research.* Cambridge, MA: MIT Press.

Dombrowski, P.M. (1992). Challenger and the social contingency of meaning: Two lessons for the technical communication classroom. *Technical Communication Quarterly, 1,* 73–86.

Ehninger, D. (Ed.). (1972). *Contemporary rhetoric: A reader's coursebook.* Glenview, IL: Scott.

Farrell, T.B. & Goodnight, G.T. (1981). Accidental rhetoric: The root metaphors of Three Mile Island. *Communication Monographs, 48,* 271–300.

Fish, S. (1989). Rhetoric. *Doing what comes naturally: Change, rhetoric, and the practice of theory in literary and legal studies* (pp. 471–502). Durham, NC: Duke University Press.

Frye, N. (1957). *Anatomy of criticism.* Princeton, NJ: Princeton University Press.

Girill, T.R. (1985). Among the professions: Technical communication and rhetoric. *Technical Communication, 32,* 44.

Gross, A.G. (1988). Discourse on method: The rhetorical analysis of scientific texts. *Pre/Text, 9,* 169–186.

Gross, A.G. (1990). *The rhetoric of science.* Cambridge, MA: Harvard University Press.

Halloran, S.M. & Bradford, A.N. (1984). Figures of speech in the rhetoric of science and technology. In R.J. Connors, L.S. Ede & A.A. Lunsford (Eds.), *Essays on classical rhetoric and modern discourse.* Carbondale, IL: Southern Illinois University Press.

Herndl, C.G., Fennell, B.A. & Miller, C.R. (1991). Understanding failures in organizational discourse: The accident at Three Mile Island and the shuttle Challenger disaster. In C. Bazerman & J. Paradis (Eds.), *Textual dynamics of the professions: Historical and contemporary studies in writing in professional communities* (pp. 279–305). Madison, WI: University of Wisconsin Press.

Katz, S. (1992). The ethic of expediency: Classical rhetoric, technology, and the Holocaust. *College English, 54,* 255–275.

Keene, M. & Barnes-Ostrander, M. (1985). Audience analysis and adaptation. In M.G. Moran & D. Journet (Eds.), *Research in technical communication: A bibliographic sourcebook* (pp. 163–216). Westport, CT: Greenwood.

Knorr, K. (1997). Producing and reproducing knowledge: Descriptive or constructive? Towards a model of research production. *Social Science Information, 16,* 669–696.

Knorr-Cetina, K.D. (1981). *The manufacture of knowledge: An essay on the constructivist and contextual nature of science.* Oxford: Pergamon.

Knorr-Cetina, K.D. (1983). The ethnographic study of scientific work: Towards a constructivist interpretation of science. In K.D. Knorr-Cetina & M. Mulkey (Eds.), *Science observed: Perspectives in the social study of science* (pp. 115–140). Beverly Hills, CA: Sage.

Knorr-Cetina, K.D. & Mulkey, M. (Eds.). (1983). *Science observed: Perspectives in the social study of science.* Beverly Hills, CA: Sage.

Kogen, M. (Ed.). (1989). *Writing in the business professions.* Urbana, IL: NCTE.

Kuhn, T.S. (1970). *The structure of scientific revolutions.* (2nd Ed.). Chicago, IL: University of Chicago Press.

Latour, B. (1980). Is it possible to reconstruct the research process? Sociology of a brain peptide. In K. Knorr, R. Krohn, & R. Whitley

(Eds.), *The social process of scientific investigation. Sociology of the sciences yearbook.* (Vol. 4, pp. 56–76). Boston, MA: Reidel.

Latour, B. & Woolgar, S. (1979). *Laboratory life: The social construction of scientific facts.* Beverly Hills, CA: Sage.

Lipson, C. (1988). A social view of technical writing. *Journal of Business and Technical Communication, 2,* 7–20.

MacKenzie, D. (1987). Missile accuracy: A case study in the social processes of technological change. In W.E. Bijker, T.P. Hughes & T.J. Pinch (Eds.), *The social construction of technological systems: New directions in the sociology and history of technology* (pp. 195–222). Cambridge, MA: MIT Press.

Mailloux, S. (1989). *Rhetorical power.* Ithaca, NY: Cornell University Press.

Masse, R.E. & Benz, M.D. (1989). Technical communication and rhetoric. In C.H. Sides (Ed.), *Technical and business communication: Bibliographic essays for teachers and corporate trainers* (pp. 5–38). Urbana, IL: NCTE.

Miller, C.R. (1978). Technology as a form of consciousness: A study of contemporary ethos. *Central States Speech Journal, 29,* 228–236.

Miller, C.R. (1979). A humanistic rationale for technical writing. *College English, 40,* 610–667.

Miller, C. R. (1984). Genre as social action. *Quarterly Journal of Speech, 70,* 151–167.

Miller, C.R. (1985). Invention in technical and scientific discourse. In M.G. Moran & D. Journet (Eds.), *Research in technical communication: A bibliographic sourcebook* (pp. 117–162). Westport, CT: Greenwood.

Miller, C.R. (1989). What's practical about technical writing? In B. E. Fearing & W. Keats Sparrow (Eds.), *Technical writing: Theory and practice* (pp. 14–24). New York: MLA.

Miller, C. & Selzer, J. (1985). Special topics of argument in engineering reports. In L. Odell & D. Goswami (Eds.), *Writing in nonacademic settings* (pp. 231–249). New York: Guilford.

Mirel, B. (1988). The politics of usability: The organizational functions of an in-house manual. In S. Doheny-Farina (Ed.). *Effective documentation: What we have learned from research* (pp. 277–297). Cambridge, MA: MIT Press.

Odell, L. & Goswami, D. (Eds.). (1985). *Writing in nonacademic settings.* New York: Guilford.

Odell, L., Goswami, D., Herrington, A. & Quick, D. (1983). Studying writing in non-academic settings. In P.R. Anderson, R.J. Brockmann & C.R. Miller (Eds.), *New essays in technical and scientific communication: Research, theory, practice* (pp. 17–40). Farmingdale, NY: Baywood.

Paradis, J. (1991). Text and action: The operator's manual in context and in court. In C. Bazerman & J. Paradis (Eds.), *Textual dynamics of the professions: Historical and contemporary studies in writing in professional communities* (pp. 256–278). Madison: University of Wisconsin Press.

Paradis, J., Dobrin, D. & Miller, R. (1985). Writing at Exxon ITD: Notes on the writing environment of an R&D organization. In L. Odell & D.

Goswami (Eds.), *Writing in nonacademic settings* (pp. 281–308). New York: Guilford.

Pinch, T. & Bijker, W. (1987). The social construction of facts and artifacts: Or how the sociology of science and the sociology of technology might benefit from each other. In W.E. Bijker, T.P. Hughes & T.J. Pinch (Eds.), *The social construction of technological systems: New directions in the sociology and history of technology* (pp. 17–50). Cambridge, MA: MIT Press.

Prelli, L. (1989). *A rhetoric of science: Inventing scientific discourse.* Columbia, SC: University of South Carolina Press.

Rafoth, B.A. & Rubin, D.L. (Eds.). (1988). *The social construction of written communication.* Norwood, NJ: Ablex.

Rorty, R. (1987). Science as solidarity. In J.S. Nelson, A. Megill & D.M. McCloskey (Eds.), *The rhetoric of the human sciences: Language and argument in scholarship and public affairs* (pp. 39–52). Madison, WI: University of Wisconsin Press.

Roundy, N. & Mair, D. (1982). The composing process of technical writers: A preliminary study. *Journal of Advanced Composition, 3,* 89–101.

Samuels, M.S. (1985). Technical writing and the recreation of reality. *Journal of Technical Writing and Communication, 15,* 3–13.

Selzer, J. (1983). The composing process of an engineer. *College Composition and Communication, 34,* 178–187.

Selzer, J. (1989). Arranging business prose. In M. Kogen (Ed.), *Writing in the business professions* (pp. 37–54). Urbana, IL: NCTE.

Smart, G. (1993). Genre as community invention: A central bank's response to its executives' expectations as readers. In R. Spilka (Ed.), *Writing in the workplace: New research perspectives* (pp. 124–140). Carbondale, IL: Southern Illinois University Press.

Walzer, A.E. & Gross, A. (1994). Positivists, postmodernists, Aristotelians, and the Challenger disaster. *College English, 56,* 420–433.

Weimer, W.B. (1977). Science as a rhetorical transaction: Toward a non-justificational conception of rhetoric. *Philosophy and Rhetoric, 10,* 1–29.

Williams, R.I. (1983). Playing with format, style, and reader assumptions. *Technical Communication, 30,* 11–13.

Winsor, D.A. (1988). Communication failures contributing to the Challenger accident: An example for technical communicators. *IEEE Transactions on Technical Communication, 31,* 101–107.

Winsor, D.A. (1989). An engineer's writing and the corporate construction of knowledge. *Written Communication, 6,* 270–285.

Winsor, D.A. (1990). The construction of knowledge in organizations: Asking the right questions about the Challenger. *Journal of Business and Technical Communication, 4,* 7–20.

Zappen, J.P. (1983). A rhetoric for research in sciences and technologies. In P.R. Anderson, R.J. Brockmann & C.R. Miller (Eds.), *New essays in technical and scientific communication: Research, theory, practice* (pp. 123–138). Farmingdale, NY: Baywood.

4

SOCIAL CONSTRUCTION THEORY AND TECHNICAL COMMUNICATION

Mahalingam Subbiah

Weber State University

"No man is an island, entire of itself; . . . Any man's death diminishes me, because I'm involved in mankind; and therefore never send to know for whom the bell tolls; it tolls for thee."

—John Donne, (Meditation XVII)

INTRODUCTION

I am a member of a faculty writing group in my university. The members of the group routinely review each other's writing at various stages: brainstorming, outlining, drafting, revising. The group makes suggestions concerning content, organization, style, mechanics, audience, and potential publication outlets. My colleagues have always noticed that their writing takes shapes that they never initially considered, and they are often pleased (and sometimes even dismayed) at the final draft. Increasingly, scholars appear to explicitly recognize the input of others into their work. Check a recent journal article written by a single individual; often you find the author acknowledging significant contributions by others.

Still, "single" authorship of texts may be more prevalent in the academe than in industry, where texts are produced collaboratively all the time. In nonacademic settings, scientists, engineers, and other professionals often work together in teams to produce written documents. In such contexts, writing seems more a social act than an individual effort.

John Donne's well-known lines eloquently capture the spirit of social constructionist thought, which does not isolate the individual mind from the collective knowledge-making processes of the community. The term "social constructionism" subsumes a number of theories of social knowledge evolving from many disciplines: sociology (Karl Mannheim and others), anthropology (Clifford Geertz), linguistics (Edward Sapir), literary criticism (Michel Foucalt), history of science (Thomas Kuhn), and philosophy (Richard Rorty).

The present essay draws mainly on discussions of social constructionist thought in composition and related disciplines.

The first section of this essay summarizes the major tenets of social constructionism, while the second focuses on the implications of social constructionist thought for technical communication practitioners and teachers.

SOCIAL CONSTRUCTIONIST THEORY

What is knowledge? Where does it originate? What is reality? Truth? Fact? How does one come to know them?

Different intellectual traditions and perspectives have offered different answers to such questions. One broad perspective, which Kenneth Gergen (1985) calls the exogenic and which includes the postulates of such philosophers as John Locke, David Hume, and John Stuart Mill, sees the source of human knowledge in the external and objective world, which knowledge merely mirrors. Another perspective, which Gergen calls the endogenic and which is represented by such thinkers as Spinoza, Kant, and Nietzsche, sees human beings as the source of knowledge. According to this perspective, knowledge is fashioned by the human capabilities for thinking, categorizing, and processing information (Gergen, 1985, pp. 269–270).

Both the exogenic and endogenic perspectives emphasize the objectivity of external reality and see such entities as "reality," "thought," "knowledge," "fact," and "text" as existing outside the human mind. Both traditions also empower the human mind with two faculties: One, like a mirror, perceives external, objective reality; the other, like an inner eye, contemplates reality, internalizes it, and formulates it into concepts, ideas, or theories. The mind then adds these perceptions to an already existing body of knowledge, which in turn is retrieved in the act of learning. This is the traditional cognitive theory of knowledge that social constructionism opposes.

Major Tenets of Social Constructionism

Of the various interpretations of social constructionism, Kenneth Bruffee's (1986) has perhaps been the most influential (and certainly seminal) among students of language and communication. Other, alternative interpretations challenging major assumptions of Bruffee's view have been offered by, among others, Timothy Weiss (1991) and Thomas Kent (1993). This section summarizes Bruffee's interpretation of social constructionism and discusses how the other interpretations challenge it and differ from it. The discussion lays the groundwork for the rest of the essay, which discusses the implications of the different interpretations of social constructionism for technical communication teaching and scholarship.

According to Bruffee (1986), while social constructionism affirms the existence of physical reality, it denies the objectivity of the mental constructs generated by encounters with it. Instead, social constructionism considers the knowledge thus generated to constitute only a perceived reality, which has no existence outside the mind. Furthermore, this knowledge has a collective origin, grounded in the conventions, norms, discourse, and culture of the appropriate community. As Bruffee summarizes it, "[a] social constructionist position in any discipline assumes that entities we normally call reality, knowledge, thought, facts, and texts, selves and so on are constructs generated by communities of like-minded peers" (p. 774).

Thus, while cognitive theory focuses on the individual and examines primarily individual acts of cognition (however, see the essay by Redish, this collection), social constructionism focuses on the community and on the moment of mutuality and dialogue among its members, shifting the locus of knowledge from the individual mind to communal processes. From this perspective, individual thought becomes part of collective consciousness. Furthermore, cognitive theory focuses on knowledge as the product of the relationship between the individual and the world. As a consequence, Bruffee suggests, it assumes that not all potential knowledge is accessible; gaps may exist between the learner and what can be learned. Social constructionism, on the other hand, sees the locus of knowledge in relationships between and among individuals; knowledge emerges as the product of these relationships. Gaps in knowledge are therefore a matter external to the individual and are traceable to communal processes of knowledge making. From a cognitive perspective, an individual's knowledge is a measure of intellectual growth, and individuals can claim knowledge as their own. For social constructionism, individual thought is an internalized version of a conversation carried out in the community. Such thought cannot be a measure of individual intellectual growth, and thus both knowledge and authorship are artifacts of the community.

Finally, the cognitive perspective separates knowledge from language, which serves merely as a conduit for communicating knowledge. Thus, language is peripheral to knowledge. Social constructionism, by contrast, sees language as integral to knowledge; the two are inseparable because language is at the center of knowledgemaking, and knowledge is identified with the language in which it is formulated. Language is always community-specific (consider, for instance, the technical languages of computer scientists, physicists, or mathematicians) and marked by the conventions of the community that uses it. Therefore, language binds members into a knowledge community.

Challenges to Bruffee's Interpretation of Social Constructionism

Several scholars have challenged Bruffee's (1986) interpretation of social constructionism in terms of its implications for technical and scientific communication. The most important among these challenges have been advanced by Timothy Weiss (1991) and Thomas Kent (1993).

Weiss finds two of Bruffee's assumptions especially problematic. First, he points out that Bruffee's interpretation favors consensus and accord, ignoring disagreement and conflict, which inevitably occur when any professional group engages in a common pursuit. Bruffee equates knowledge with consensus and belief, making no distinction between knowledge, on one hand, and opinion and belief, on the other. As a result, knowledge asserted by the consensus of one community appears as valid as the knowledge asserted by the consensus of another. In contrast, Weiss argues that knowledge and belief are different entities and points to the persecutions in medieval Europe, Nazi Germany, and apartheid South Africa as examples of "socially justified belief" that one would hesitate to equate with knowledge (pp. 37–38). Weiss refers to the work of Imre Lakatos, who, in his *The Methodology of Scientific Research Programs* (1978), has argued the dangers of accepting such socially justified beliefs as truth. Both Weiss and Lakatos insist that knowledge cannot be determined solely by communal consensus and belief.

Second, Weiss criticizes what he sees as Bruffee's orientation toward the humanities, as opposed to science, an orientation that creates problems for technical and professional communicators. Bruffee suggests, following Thomas Kuhn (1970), that changes in knowledge occur when a community's collective consciousness shifts from one knowledge base to another. Weiss, on the other hand, argues that such an approach cannot account for progress made in such disciplines as medicine (p. 38).

Another challenge to Bruffee's view of social construction comes from Thomas Kent's (1993) "paralogic hermeneutic" approach (p. 83). Kent, like many other social theorists, believes that knowledge is made through mediation. Like Bruffee, he sees knowledge as constructed through interpretive acts—hence as hermeneutic. However, he differs from Bruffee in his interpretation of the exact relationship between language and knowledge. For Bruffee, communities are defined and bound by shared language, practices, and values; therefore, community membership is contingent on an understanding of these community-specific elements. This implies that community members first learn the community's language, practices, and values, before understanding community-constructed knowledge. This view places language outside of the domain of knowledge proper. Kent, however, emphasizes the uncodifiable—hence paralogic—nature of interpretation (pp. 88–90). Both knowledge and language grow together through interactive, dialogic practices of community members.

Other scholars have also challenged aspects of Bruffee's interpretation of social constructionism. They point out that Bruffee and his followers consider knowledge making a "benign and apolitical process," ignoring issues of power and control that inevitably emerge in any research community (Blyler & Thralls, 1993, p. 15). Research in academic and professional writing that has followed Bruffee's tenets has tended to treat communal values and practices as given, natural, and normal. In any group, however, those in power wield political influence, in large measure establishing values and practices. Scholars such as Greg Myers, James Berlin, John Trimbur, Patricia Bizzell, and Carolyn Miller have pointed out the existence of power structures within communities and shown how these structures influence the practices and values to which members adhere. The awareness of how these structures operate in relation to communal knowledge construction is an important element in fostering a critical stance toward received knowledge and in helping community members, especially professional communicators, take an active role in shaping communal discourse, rather than allowing it to be shaped by existing power elites and by unexamined agendas and interests.

In general, therefore, social constructionism assumes that knowledge is constructed in communities by members who share beliefs, language, practices, and values. Community members construct knowledge among themselves by consultation, negotiation, and consensus, as well as through struggle and contention. The knowledge thus constructed in turn influences members of the community. In this view, "culture," including organizational culture, appears as a site of negotiation of diverse and competing interests, with language and communicative practices playing a major role in this negotiation and struggle. These assumptions have major implications for technical communication scholarship and teaching.

THE IMPLICATION OF SOCIAL CONSTRUCTIONISM FOR TECHNICAL COMMUNICATION

Social constructionist research in such disciplines as science, philosophy, sociology, psychology, political science, composition, and literary criticism has implications for three concepts central to any theory of communication: the self, language, and thinking and writing.

The Concept of Self

Social constructionism calls for a change in our perception of the self, a change that can be troublesome to those deeply entrenched in the humanistic tradition that views self and society as diametrically opposed. As Charles Bazerman (cited in Blyler & Thralls, 1993, p. vii) points out, humanists tend to see the self as imaginative, creative, and free, while society is oppressive, restrictive, and suffocating. They thus assert the independence of the self and celebrate its struggles against society. Social constructionists provide an alternative vision of the self (Coulter, 1979; Gergen, 1982; Harre, 1984). According to this vision, the following traits apply:

- The self does not exist in a vacuum or alone.
- The self is embedded in a matrix of other selves.
- The self is defined in terms of the society in which it lives.
- The self is judged by the standards of the community to which it belongs.

Such a vision of the self as a social construct has two immediate implications for technical communication. First, it enables technical communicators to see themselves as part of a larger community that they influence through their communicative practices and that, in turn, influences these practices. Second, communication and communicative activities appear as critical constituents of community culture.

Variously referred to as "atmosphere," "company spirit," and "ethos," organizational culture is defined by Terrence Deal and Allen Kennedy (1982) as the internalized values, attitudes, and beliefs shared by members of an organization. Identifying the culture of an organization may take an employee many years, and the learning process is subtle, even subconscious (Paradis, Dobrin, & Miller, 1985, p. 302). Nevertheless, the awareness of the self in a community and the awareness of the community's culture enable technical communication professionals to become responsible contributors to the communal meaning-making process. Such awareness empowers technical communication professionals in open, receptive, and collaborative organizations; in autocratic, top-down organizations, this perspective becomes, as Bruffee (1986) points out, "potentially a democratic corrective" (p. 787). The major implication of this realization for technical communication teachers is that to become successful in organizations, their students need more than strong writing skills; students must also be able to adapt, socially and intellectually, to organizational communities (Anson & Forsberg, 1990, p. 225). Such adaptation requires that students develop the concept of self in society. Teachers must help students understand what it means to be an employee in an organization. They must emphasize that students need to identify themselves with the organizational cultures they will be joining after graduation. (See also the essay by Harrison and Katz, this collection.)

Many theorists suggest that understanding the culture of an organization can take place only after an employee joins a company and that culture cannot be taught in schools (Lutz, 1986). However, teachers can sensitize students to the socialization process and its implications for students as future employees by incorporating these issues in the technical communication curriculum. Teachers' efforts to highlight these concepts can prepare students to interact more successfully with organizational communities and can motivate students to learn about prospective organizations before joining them.

However, teachers must also recognize that the social constructionist perspective on self-in-society inevitably raises ethical issues. Who is a good employee? What happens to the students' selves, to their beliefs and values, when they join an organizational community? Will joining an organization call for some compromise of their beliefs and values? Does good communication mean compromising for the good of the organization, or should teachers teach students to defend their beliefs and values at any cost? Such questions have been raised and debated especially in the literature concerning the space shuttle Challenger disaster (Boisjoly, 1987; Brown, 1990; Herndl, Fennell & Miller, 1991; Walzer & Gross, 1994; Winsor, 1988, 1990).

The Concept of Language

Social constructionist thought also radically redefines the relationship of technical communicators to both knowledge and language. Social constructionism posits the following:

- Language is inseparable from knowledge.
- Language is knowledge.
- Language binds a community.
- Language is bound by conventions specific to the community.

Mikhail Bakhtin (1986) has suggested that language by itself has no stable meaning; meaning arises in use as people use language to interact in social contexts (p. 86). Thus, as Greg Myers (1985) has suggested, changes in knowledge are brought about by changes in language following negotiations with members of the community. Therefore, technical communicators actively participate in the formation of communal knowledge, just as they shape communal language through processes of negotiation, struggle, and consensus (Hagge & Kostlenick, 1989; Walzer, 1985).

Technical communication teachers must therefore remind students that academic preparation in any given field provides students with only the necessary entry permit to an organization. Beyond the entry point, however, students must be able to converse in the value-laden language of their peers, and they won't necessarily learn this specific, convention-bound language in academe. In addition, students must be made aware that their communicative practices help shape those values and the emerging knowledge, as much as they are shaped by them. Teachers of technical communication should sensitize students to this reciprocal dynamic.

The Concept of Thinking and Writing

Thinking and writing are social acts. Even though thinking and writing may be performed by an apparently isolated individual, these acts are carried out in response to, or to meet the obligations of, the organizational community to which an individual belongs. Therefore thinking becomes an act of internalizing and writing an act of externalizing, the conversation of the community. An understanding of this tenet of social constructionism helps professional communicators connect their thinking and writing activities to the broader organizational context in which they are functioning. This understanding helps them to see their community as the locale where knowledge is constructed by members who share similar beliefs, values, and practices. It also helps them to operate and govern themselves with some shared norms or standard behaviors. Professional communicators construct knowledge among themselves by consultation, negotiation, consensus, or struggle and contention. Knowing this helps them synchronize their communication efforts effectively with organizational goals and objectives. As Paradis, Dobrin, and Miller (1985) point out, many writers working in industries are unable to understand their supervisors' criticism of their writing; they consider the suggestions for revision mere managerial whims, failing to recognize the managerial priorities and experience that prompted the suggestions (p. 300).

However, the interconnectedness between organizational values, conventions, and goals, on the one hand, and communicative practices (including technical communication), on the other hand, raises serious ethical questions: How far should professional communicators go in lending their rhetorical expertise to simply further organizational purposes? When should their communicative practices actively question established communal knowledge? Tragedies such as the Challenger disaster illustrate the practical consequences of not considering such issues. (See also the essay by Sanders, this collection.)

Recent studies of nonacademic writing (Cooper, 1986; Doheny-Farina, 1986; Odell, 1985) have firmly established that, as Richard Freed (1993) has put it, "professional communication is eminently and complexly social" (p. 198). (For more discussion of social constructionism, as well as of the social involvements of technical communication in government, industry, and business organizations, see Barabas, 1990; Blyler & Thralls, 1993; Forman, 1992; Kogen, 1989; Lay & Karis, 1991; Matalene, 1989; Odell & Goswami, 1985; Rafoth & Rubin, 1988; Spilka, 1993). These studies highlight the significant skills that professional communicators must have to function successfully as writers in organizations: interaction (Winsor, 1988), listening (Lewis & Reinsh, 1988), negotiation (Rogers & Horton, 1992), conflict resolution (Spilka, 1990; Winsor, 1989), and consensus building (Rogers and Horton, 1992; Spilka, 1990; Winsor, 1990).

The technical communication teacher's major goal is to prepare the students to function successfully as professionals in the organizational discourse community. Social constructionism demonstrates that as part of that goal teachers must strive to make students critical and responsible community members, not merely teaching discourse practices or discourse genres, but also preparing students to participate fully in the communal meaning- and knowledge-making process (Rymer, 1993). Anson and Forsberg (1990) discuss the kinds of problems students may experience in moving from academe to industry. Students, they say, need to adapt to the social setting of the organization, which is characterized by "not only the idiosyncratic textual features of a discourse community but a shifting array of political, managerial, and social influences as well" (p. 225). This means that discourse, discourse communities, and communal knowledge-making processes must become an important focus in technical writing education.

This shift requires that teachers help students understand that texts in the workplace are usually collaborative in the social constructionist sense, resulting from a "community of peers," even if their authors appear to be individuals. Such understanding is a necessary part of the acculturation of students into their professions, including the profession of technical communication (Rogers & Horton, 1992). One of the best ways to foster such understanding is to engage students in collaborative learning projects that would make students participate in communities of peers constructing knowledge. As Janis Forman (1992) points out, certain core issues emerge in collaboration: power, conflict, decision making, influences of organizational structures and norms, politics, culture, and socio-economic structures. An awareness and discussion of these issues need to be incorporated into the technical communication curriculum; specific ways of doing so are suggested by studies on collaborative practices in professional settings (see, for example, Lay & Karis, 1991). (See also the essay by Burnett, White, & Duin, this collection.)

CONCLUSION

The social constructionist view alters our perceptions of classrooms, teachers and students, and educational goals:

- Classrooms become communities of discourse.
- Teachers and students become members of discourse communities.
- The focus of attention shifts from the individual writer and communicative principles and conventions toward discourse communities and the processes of communal knowledge construction.

As a result, technical communication students should be able to do the following:

- Identify with the culture of an organization.
- Be alert to the ethical implications of such identification.
- Be open to diverse points of view.
- Learn to accept, accommodate, and negotiate, as well as, when necessary, question, argue, and defend their own points of view and principles.
- See knowledge and texts as constructed through such processes of accommodation, negotiation, and argument.

It is a vision that makes professional communicators, as William Blake put it, "behold the world in a grain of sand."

REFERENCES

Anson, C.M. & Forsberg, L.L. (1990). Moving beyond the academic community: Transitional stages in professional writing. *Written Communication, 7,* 200–231.

Bakhtin, M. (V.N. Voloshinov). (1986). *Marxism and the philosophy of language.* (Ladislav Matejka & I.R. Titunik, Trans.). Cambridge: Harvard University Press.

Barabas, C. (1990). *Technical writing in a corporate culture: A study of the nature of information.* Norwood, NJ: Ablex.

Blyler, N.R. & Thralls, T. (Eds.). (1993). *Professional communication: The social perspective.* Newbury Park, CA: Sage.

Boisjoly, R.M. (1987). Ethical decisions: Morton Thiokol and the space shuttle Challenger disaster. Paper presented at the American Society of Mechanical Engineers Annual Meeting, Boston, MA.

Brown, M.H. (1990). Past and present images of Challenger in NASA's organizational culture. In B. D. Sypher (Ed.), *Case studies in organizational communication* (pp. 111–123). New York: Guilford.

Bruffee, K.A. (1986). Social construction, language, and the authority of knowledge: A bibliographical essay. *College English, 48,* 773–790.

Cooper, M. (1986). The ecology of writing. *College English, 48,* 364–375.

Coulter, J. (1979). *The social construction of mind: Studies in ethnomethodology and linguistic philosophy.* Totowa, NJ: Rowman.

Deal, T.E. & Kennedy, A. (1982). *Corporate cultures: The rites and rituals of corporate life.* Reading, MA: Addison-Wesley.

Doheny-Farina, S. (1986). Writing in an emerging organization. *Written Communication, 3,* 158–185.

Forman, J. (Ed.). (1992). *New visions of collaborative writing.* Portsmouth, NH: Boynton.

Freed, R.C. (1993). Postmodern practice: perspectives and prospects. In N.R. Blyler & T. Thralls (Eds.), *Professional communication: The social perspective* (pp. 196–214). Newbury Park, CA: Sage.

Gergen, K.J. (1982). *Toward transformation in social knowledge.* New York: Springer-Verlag.

Gergen, K.J. (1985). The social constructionist movement in modern psychology. *American Psychologist, 40,* 266–275.

Hagge, J. & Kostelnick, C. (1989). Linguistic politeness in professional prose: A discourse analysis of auditors' suggestion letters, with implications for business communication pedagogy. *Written Communication, 6,* 312–339.

Harre, R. (1984). *Personal being: A theory for individual psychology.* Cambridge: Harvard University Press.

Herndl, C.G., Fennell, B.A. & Miller, C.R. (1991). Understanding failures in organizational discourse: The accident at Three Mile Island and the shuttle Challenger disaster. In C. Bazerman & J. Paradis (Eds.), *Textual dynamics of the professions: Historical and contemporary studies in writing in professional communities* (pp. 271–299). Madison, WI: University of Wisconsin Press.

Kent, T. (1993). Formalism, social construction, and the problem of interpretive authority. In N.R. Blyler & T. Thralls (Eds.), *Professional communication: The social perspective* (pp. 79–91). Newbury Park, CA: Sage.

Kogen, M. (Ed.). (1989). *Writing in the business professions.* Urbana, IL: National Council of Teachers of English.

Kuhn, T.S. (1970). *The structure of scientific revolutions.* (2nd Ed.). Chicago, IL: University of Chicago Press.

Lakatos, I. (1978). *The methodology of scientific research programs.* (Vol. 1). Cambridge, UK: Cambridge University Press.

Lay, M.M. & Karis, W.M. (Eds.). (1991). *Collaborative writing in industry: Investigations in theory and practice.* Amityville, NY: Baywood.

Lewis, M.H. & Reinsh, N.L., Jr. (1988). Listening in organizational environments. *Journal of Business Communication, 25* (3), 49–67.

Lipson, C. (1988). A social view of technical writing. *Journal of Business and Technical Communication, 2,* 7–20.

Lunsford, A. & Ede, L. (1990). *Singular texts/plural authors: Perspectives on collaborative writing.* Carbondale, IL: Southern Illinois University Press.

Lutz, J. (1986). The influence of organizations on writers' texts and training. *Technical Writing Teacher, 12,* 187–190.

Matalene, C.B. (1989). *Worlds of writing: Teaching and learning in discourse communities of work.* New York: Random House.

Myers, G. (1985). The social construction of two biologists' proposals. *Written Communication, 2,* 219–245.

Odell, L. (1985). Beyond the text: Relations between writing and social context. In L. Odell & D. Goswami (Eds.), *Writing in nonacademic settings* (pp. 249–280). New York: Guilford.

Odell, L. & Goswami, D. (Eds.). (1985). *Writing in nonacademic settings.* New York: Guilford.

Paradis, J., Dobrin, D. & Miller, R. (1985). Writing at Exxon ITD: Notes on the writing environment of an R&D organization. In L. Odell & D. Goswami (Eds.), *Writing in nonacademic settings* (pp. 281–307). New York: Guilford.

Rafoth, B.A. & Rubin, D.L. (Eds.). (1988). *The social construction of written communication.* Norwood, NJ: Ablex.

Rogers, P.S. & Horton, M. (1992). Face-to-face collaborative writing. In J. Forman (Ed.), *New_visions of collaborative writing* (pp. 120–146). Portsmouth, NH: Boynton.

Rymer, J. (1993). Collaboration and conversation in learning communities: The discipline and the classroom. In N.R. Blyler & T. Thralls

(Eds.), *Professional communication: The social perspective* (pp. 179–195). Newbury Park, CA: Sage.

Spilka, R. (1990). Orality and literacy in the workplace: Process and text based strategies for multiple-audience adaptation. *Journal of Business and Technical Communication, 4,* 44–67.

Spilka, R. (Ed.). (1993). *Writing in the workplace: New research perspectives.* Carbondale, IL: Southern Illinois University Press.

Walzer, A.E. (1985). Articles from the "California Divorce Project": A case study of the concept of audience. *College Composition and Communication, 36,* 150–159.

Walzer, A.E. & Gross, A. (1994). Positivists, postmodernists, Aristotelians, and the Challenger disaster. *College English, 56,* 420–433.

Weiss, T. (1991). Bruffee, the Bakhtin Circle, and the concept of collaboration. In M.M. Lay & W.M. Karis (Eds.), *Collaborative writing in industry: Investigations in theory and practice* (pp. 31–48). Amityville, NY: Baywood.

Winsor, D.A. (1988). Communication failures contributing to the Challenger accident: An example for technical communicators. *IEEE Transactions in Professional Communication, 31,* 101–107.

Winsor, D.A. (1989). An engineer's writing and the corporate construction of knowledge. *Written Communication, 6,* 270–285.

Winsor, D.A. (1990). The construction of knowledge in organizations: Asking the right questions about the Challenger. *Journal of Business and Technical Communication, 4,* 7–19.

5

UNDERSTANDING PEOPLE: THE RELEVANCE OF COGNITIVE PSYCHOLOGY TO TECHNICAL COMMUNICATION

Janice C. Redish

Redish & Associates, Inc.

INTRODUCTION

This essay has three parts. The first briefly introduces some of the major themes in cognitive psychology research. The second relates cognitive psychology to some of the other theories in this section of the book. The third explores some of the ways in which cognitive psychology applies to technical communicators and teachers of technical communication as they try to understand readers, writers, and students.

INTRODUCING COGNITIVE PSYCHOLOGY

Cognitive psychology is concerned with how people perceive and remember information. Let us first briefly consider perception and memory. Then let us consider two critical aspects of how people organize information in memory so that they can get to, retrieve, and use that information.

Considering Perception and Memory

Perception

Perception is more than just what we physically see or hear. It is also deciding (subconsciously) what to attend to. We may believe that we see something even when it *is not* actually there. Conversely, we may feel absolutely certain that we did not see something when it *is* actually there.

A case that illustrates both of these points is the difficulty we all have in proofreading our own work when we have already read a draft several times. Technical communicators know that all writers need someone else to proofread their work. If a writer knows what a sentence should say, his or her mind may fill in a missing word, leave out an extra word, or correct a mistyped word to fit what the mind expects. We simply don't "see" the mistakes in our own work after we've read it a few times.

Readers working with documents, attendees at an oral presentation, and students in the classroom are constantly deciding what of all they are seeing and hearing should be perceived and brought into memory.

Short-term memory

Psychologists now believe that the information we perceive goes first into short-term memory, and then some of what we've taken into short-term memory is taken into long-term memory and connected to other information that we've stored away. As George Miller (1956) explains in his well-known paper, "The Magical Number Seven, Plus or Minus Two," people, in general, can hold only five to nine pieces of information in short-term memory at one time.

One of the principles that technical communicators learn is "chunking"—dividing text into meaningful and manageable units. Chunking helps people deal with the limitations of short-term memory.

Long-term memory

The issues of greatest interest to most cognitive psychologists are how people organize information in their minds and how they get to and retrieve that information. Various terms have been proposed for these forms of mental organization: scripts (Schank & Abelson, 1977), frames (Minsky, 1977), schemas (Bartlett, 1932; Rumelhart & Norman, 1985), mental models (Norman, 1983), "MOPs" or memory organization packets (Schank, 1985), and patterns (Margolis, 1987).

Probably the most common term used today is "schemas." David Rumelhart and Donald Norman (1985) describe them this way: "Roughly, schemas are like models of the outside world. To process information with the use of a schema is to determine which model best fits the incoming information" (p. 36).

Considering Two Critical Aspects of Schemas and Mental Models

Current theory in cognitive psychology points to two aspects of schemas and mental models that are particularly important for technical communicators and teachers of technical communication:

- Each individual constructs his or her own schemas and mental models.
- Schemas and mental models may be highly unstructured, more like clouds and webs than like buildings.

Each individual constructs his or her own schemas and mental models

One of the central tenets of cognitive psychology is "constructivism": that we each individually construct our own models of the many worlds we live in. As Roger Schank (1985) writes, "Memory is highly idiosyncratic. One person's organization is not another's" (p. 233).

One of the clearest examples of constructivism is children learning their native language. Every parent knows that children say things which they cannot have heard and which are incorrect in the grammar of the adults' language. The theory that best explains why English-speaking children go through a stage of saying "see two mans" and "I comed" is that they are overgeneralizing the rules for plural and for past tense that they are busy constructing. No one explicitly taught them the rules. They make their own rules for themselves from the information they are taking in.

Constructivism, in turn, has two very important implications for technical communicators and teachers of technical communication. First, each reader, writer, and student has his or her own schemas and mental models that affect how he or she perceives and remembers what happens in a document or writing assignment. Second, because people really know something only when they have assimilated it into their own schemas, they must be actively involved in working on a project: reading, writing, or learning.

As I will discuss again in the last part of this essay, listening to lectures is seldom as useful a learning experience as actually doing relevant work.

Schemas and mental models may be highly unstructured, more like clouds and webs than like buildings

Schemas may be loose associations that are formed and reformed as new information arrives. Schemas have subschemas. Schemas represent knowledge at all levels of abstraction. Schemas are not only pieces of information; they are also processes for linking information. Schemas incorporate all media: pictures, words, and sounds. The information that is perceived and brought into schemas may come from all modes: seeing, hearing, smelling, and touching.

Some schemas may be more structured than others. For example, one of the earliest types of schemas to be described were *scripts* (Schank & Abelson, 1977). In Western culture, most of us have a script for "going to a restaurant." In fact, most of us now have at least two, if not three, restaurant scripts. We expect events to happen in a different order in a restaurant with table service than we do in a fast food restaurant or in a cafeteria. Suppose I say, "We went to a restaurant last night. The hostess showed us to a table. Then the waitress came and gave us the bill." You might say, "Wait a minute! You didn't order and get the food yet." How did you know to say that? You knew because my story triggered associations in your mind. The words "hostess" and "waitress" made you call up your script (or schema) for a restaurant with table service where the food comes before the bill.

Roger Schank, who first described scripts, now believes that even scripts do not exist as permanent memory structures (1985, p. 232). Rather "script-like" structures are recreated as needed. Furthermore, instead of "scripts," Schank now writes of "memory organization packets" (1985, p. 238). Schank may be using the words "memory organization packets" now because many people associate the word "script" with something that is highly structured and he wants to deemphasize the idea that people have scripts as permanent structures in memory.

The words "mental model," like the word "script," may also make many people think of highly structured entities—and different perceptions of the word "model" may be causing confusion and miscommunication between cognitive psychologists and product developers. Technical communicators, human factors specialists, and interface designers speak of readers or users having "mental models," but it is not clear how structured these models are. They are certainly not models in the same sense in which a hardware or software developer builds a mock-up or prototype of a system. They are not models of the sort that young children build of their favorite ships or planes.

As John Wilson and Andrew Rutherford (1989) point out, cognitive psychologists and developers may have difficulty communicating about mental models because they have different associations for the words. Cognitive psychologists exhort hardware and software developers to take the users' mental model into account, but they cannot draw a picture of or describe in the detail needed by the developer what that model is. "Mental model" as a psychology term refers to a vague, amorphous, individual, and changeable collection of associations in people's minds. To the developer, who most likely comes from an engineering background, "model" may mean something much more concrete.

Does "mental model" then have any practical use as a concept for technical communicators and interface designers? The answer must be "yes" for at least three reasons:

- People do make associations.
- We can find out what some of the relevant associations are for a given situation.
- Taking these associations into account helps in developing useful technical communications and computer interfaces.

For example, using a picture of a trash can as the icon for discarding materials, as the Macintosh developers did, was a good example of connecting to most users' mental models. Making the same trash can later the means for ejecting a floppy disk from the computer, however, was *not* a consistent and logical extension of that mental model for most users.

RELATING COGNITIVE PSYCHOLOGY TO OTHER THEORIES

Each of the essays in this section of the book focuses attention on different areas of theory relevant to technical communication. These areas, however, are not mutually exclusive. None by itself leads to total understanding of either people or processes. In what follows, I briefly explore how society and organizations—and emotion and motivation—interact with cognitive psychology.

Society and Organizations Influence Cognition

I do not want to be seen as taking a cognitive perspective in opposition to a contextual (social, cultural, organizational) perspective. It is true that American research on cognition has generally focused on the individual rather than on the social, cultural, or organizational context. However, each individual lives in all these contexts. Each act of reading is done within contexts. Each act of writing is done within contexts.

In 1982, Melissa Holland and I published a model of the interaction between readers and documents that incorporated both cognitive and contextual features, including the person's social environment, expectations, motivations, and experiences with documents. The model also included the social and physical context in which the document would be used and the purposes the document serves within an organizational system as factors that influence how the reader deals with and interprets the document (Holland & Redish, 1982; also Redish, 1993). All of the elements in that model are part of the communication process.

Cognitive psychologists have also come to recognize the importance of social context in the ways that people build and use schemas. Donald Norman (1985) says that "the human is a social animal, interacting with others, with the environment, and with itself," although he admits that "the core disciplines of cognitive science have tended to ignore these [contextual] aspects of behavior" (p. 310).

Although each person creates his or her own scripts or schemas, most readers will understand the problems in my restaurant story because they have common experiences that make their scripts similar. Each child must construct his or her native language, and each person's language is different. But the differences cannot be too great. The experiences from which the language is constructed are not identical, but they are similar. The need to use the outcome of the construction to communicate constrains what can be constructed. As Schank says, "experiences are constantly being organized and reorganized on the basis of similar experiences *and cultural norms*" (1985, p. 237, emphasis added).

Emotion and Motivation Also Influence Cognition

Cognitive psychology emphasizes intellectual rather than affective aspects of an experience, although both are clearly important. As Alice Brand (1987) suggests, "a realistic and complete psychology of writing must include affective as well as cognitive phenomena" (p. 436). Emotion and motivation affect how and what people perceive and remember.

Emotions that have nothing intellectually to do with a particular experience may affect how a person interprets a new experience. Readers who have struggled with a particular type of document in the past may be less willing to attempt to deal with a similar document in the future.

Motivation also influences how people deal with experiences. On the one hand, readers who are highly motivated about a particular topic can sometimes manage text that would otherwise be considered too difficult for them. Sylvia Ashton-Warner (1963) found that Maori children in New Zealand could learn to read and spell words that were well beyond their grade level by "readability" standards if the words related to important elements in their life. On the other hand, readers who are not highly motivated will not make the effort to deal with text that they could manage, but don't want to. In using a computer, most users are motivated to get a job done. The computer program is only a tool for doing the job. The manual is only a tool for using the tool for doing the job. Most computer users, therefore, are not highly motivated to read computer manuals, and technical communicators must take that low motivation into account in preparing manuals that busy users can easily get into, grab information from, and get out of.

Until recently, cognitive psychologists tended not to focus on affect. Referring to the early work of Linda Flower and John Richard Hayes (1981), Brand (1987) argues that "the cognitive model...fail[ed] to capture the rich, psychological dynamics of humans in the very act of cognizing" (p. 440). Schriver calls for studies that explore the "mutual embeddedness of cognition, context, motivation, and affect" (1992, p. 193). More recent work by scholars who look at cognition and writing has indeed begun to take the affective context into account, too. (See, for example, Flower et al., 1990 and Flower, 1994.)

APPLYING COGNITIVE PSYCHOLOGY

Cognitive psychology has much to offer technical communicators and teachers of technical communication in understanding readers, writers, and students.

Understanding Readers

Teresa Harrison and Susan Katz (this collection) argue that technical communicators must view organizations not as "relatively static object[s] in which behaviors occur" but as "dynamic processes comprised of behaviors." In the same way, readers must be viewed as dynamic processors of information. As I have written elsewhere: "Meaning does not reside in the text of a document; it exists only in the minds of communicators who produce documents and readers who use documents" (Redish, 1993, p. 22).

Each individual reader brings his or her own experiences and interpretations to any communication. Technical communicators can never be sure just how anything that they write (or draw or say) will be interpreted. All is not hopeless, however, because of these four factors:

- Many readers share experiences and, therefore, have similar schemas.
- The text (or product) influences and constrains readers' interpretations.

- Guidelines derived from empirical research can help technical communicators meet their readers' needs.
- Techniques exist for getting feedback from audiences on draft materials.

Many readers share experiences and, therefore, have similar schemas

Many members of an audience are likely to have shared experiences because they come from similar social and cultural backgrounds. Technical communicators can find out what those shared experiences are by analyzing their audiences, and, in particular, by getting out of their own offices or classrooms and observing and interviewing representative readers (or computer users) in the readers' (users') own environment.

Technical communicators whose documents are going to readers in cultures that are different from their own must be aware of their own schemas and go out to learn enough about the culture of their readers to adapt their communications as needed. (That's a fancy way of saying that a successful technical communicator will use the readers' words, avoid jargon that readers won't understand, know the readers' expectations, and use examples that come from the readers' lives.)

Those other cultures may be in different parts of the world, but they need not be. Lawyers writing for laypeople, software developers creating applications for financial analysts, or technical communication professors writing for practitioners in business—all may be in cross-cultural situations.

The text (or product) influences and constrains readers' interpretations

Readers (users) interpret in light of both knowledge in their heads (their schemas) and knowledge in the world (what they are looking at). As Thomas Huckin says, "texts exist. . . . Although texts are usually open to multiple interpretations, the number of plausible interpretations is constrained by various linguistic conventions that are manifested in the text." Furthermore, Huckin continues, "texts are the product of an attempt by a writer to communicate meaning to one or more readers." The writer invests time and effort into making his or her meaning clear. "If writers are competent, many if not most of their intended readers will be able to glean their intended meaning" (1992, p. 86).

Writers can improve the chances that readers will interpret the text as they meant it to be interpreted by analyzing their audiences, understanding their audiences' schemas, applying guidelines that make it cognitively easy for those audiences to deal with the text, and having representative readers try out drafts.

Guidelines derived from empirical research can help technical communicators meet their readers' needs

Several decades of cognitive psychology research have given us guidelines on how to make documents (and now computer interfaces) easier for readers to understand and use.

Technical communicators and teachers of technical communication must, of course, realize that the guidelines derived from research in cognitive psychology (or rhetoric or any other discipline) are just that—guidelines, not standards. Every sentence does not have to be in the active voice. Introducing a new element into the page layout may be just what is needed to make a specific point. Furthermore, the very basic point of cognitive psychology is that any guideline must be applied within the broader cognitive principle of knowing what the audiences expect, knowing what their schemas are, and knowing what the right vocabulary for them is.

In this essay, I can cite only a few examples of guidelines for technical communicators that come from cognitive research. I have chosen four: invoking an appropriate schema, following the "given-new" principle, writing in the active voice, and creating consistent patterns. (For more information on specific principles and guidelines based on cognitive theory, see Redish, 1989, 1993; Kent, 1987; Redish, Battison, & Gold, 1985; Huckin, 1983; and Felker, Pickering, Charrow, Holland, & Redish, 1981. For cognitively based principles and guidelines in designing computer interfaces, see Dumas, 1988; and Mayhew, 1992. For reviews of this cognitive research as it applies to technical communication, see Felker, et al., 1980; Spyridakis & Wenger, 1992.)

Invoking an appropriate schema Bransford and Johnson (1972) showed that readers recall more from a text if the title or an appropriate illustration helps them make associations to an appropriate schema. Technical communicators follow this principle when they organize computer manuals by users' tasks or when they organize information brochures as questions and answers.

Following the "given-new" principle Clark and Haviland (1975) showed that people involved in a conversation expect information that is new to them to be linked to information that they already know or that the other person has just given them. The "given-new" principle that comes from Clark and Haviland's work (and from later research studies) is as applicable in technical communication as it is in conversation. Technical communicators follow this principle when they make sure that pronouns have obvious antecedents. They also follow this principle when they construct tables in which the left-hand column is the contextual information that readers already have and the right-hand column is the new information that readers are seeking.

Writing in scenarios On the sentence level, many studies have shown that, in general, active voice is easier for readers to understand than passive voice. When Linda Flower and her colleagues (Flower, Hayes, & Swarts, 1983) listened to readers trying to understand a government regulation, they found that the readers spent time and energy translating the typical bureaucratic prose into "scenarios"—sentences with actors and with action verbs in the active voice. Technical communicators make use of these findings when they address the reader directly rather than talking about an entity or system.

Creating consistent patterns Once readers have found a pattern in the text, they can grasp new information most easily if it fits into that same pattern. Changes in wording, in syntax, or in page layout that violate the patterns they have come to expect require more time for readers to process. Writers help readers by being consistent in their choice of words, by using parallel sentence structure for headings, by making all the items in a list structurally similar, and by creating a useful page layout and then following it consistently.

Techniques exist for getting feedback from audiences on draft materials

The best way for technical communicators to know how well they are succeeding as they prepare materials is to get feedback from representative members of the audience before developing the final version. Techniques like protocol analysis (Schriver, 1991) and usability testing (Dumas & Redish, 1993) allow writers and developers to watch and listen to people as they try to read, understand, and use materials that are being developed.

Understanding Writers

Just as each individual reader brings his or her own experiences and interpretations to any communication, so does each individual writer. Early cognitive research on writers focused primarily on the processes of individual writers as they dealt with specific writing assignments. This early research (Flower & Hayes, 1981; Hayes & Flower, 1980) identified writers' processes, such as planning, including the sub-processes of generating ideas, setting goals, and organizing; translating (that is writing); and reviewing, with the sub-processes of evaluating and revising. Protocol analysis (having writers think aloud as they work) gave researchers insights into how writers went about these processes, how they monitored their progress, how they drew on long-term memory.

A major focus of this work was to compare the cognitive processes of expert and novice writers. The research showed, for example, that expert writers construct more elaborate plans, monitor their progress more, reflect critically on their plans, resolve conflicting plans, and give more attention to audience than do novice writers.

This early research focused primarily on individual writers, not on writers in their social or organizational contexts. It focused on the interaction between the writer and the emerging text, not on the influences or schemas writers drew on in forming that text. As Donald Norman (1985) said of other cognitive research endeavors, context was not of primary concern.

More recently, researchers who study cognition and writing have come to realize how important contexts are. Flower has written that, "we need . . . a far more integrated theoretical vision which can explain how context cues cognition, which in its turn mediates and interprets the particular world that context provides" (1989a, p. 282). Flower's recent model of the writing process (Flower, 1990, p. 13) shows that the writer is influenced by his or her own social context, purpose and goals, activated knowledge, language, and discourse conventions. All of these influence the writer as he or she forms mental representations that are then interpreted into text. (Flower's model is also reprinted in Redish, 1993.)

Future work on cognitive aspects of writing is likely to focus on this interplay between social, organizational, and cultural contexts and the choices that individual writers make. As Karen Schriver suggests,

> [i]t is too simple to assume that either individual cognition weighs most heavily in the choices people make during composing or that context is the more potent force. Individual agency is likely to be more possible in some contexts than in others. The relative balance between cognition and context is a complex empirical issue that warrants sustained attention from the research and teaching community. (1992, p. 199)

Another point to consider is that cognitively-based studies of writers have been done almost exclusively with university students, not with writers in the workplace. Studies of writers in the workplace have focused more on the choices that these writers make for social and organizational reasons (Odell, 1985) or on how writers interact with other writers and reviewers (Paradis, Dobrin, & Miller, 1985). Future work might blend cognitive and contextual considerations in studies of both university students and workplace writers.

Understanding Students

Cognitive psychology also has much to say to teachers of technical communication. Just as readers bring their experiences and expectations to any act of communication, students bring their experiences and expectations to technical communication courses. Students (like readers and writers) may not be able to directly articulate the schemas they are using, but those schemas are implicit in the answers they give and the work they do. The schemas are there, and teachers (and technical communicators and interface designers) are faced with what John M. Carroll and Mary Beth Rosson (1987) call *the assimilation paradox.*

The paradox is this: On one hand, people interpret new information in light of what they know. If you make no links to users' (students', readers') experiences and schemas, they may have no clue as to what you are talking about (or how to use the document you've written or the interface you've designed). They may not even "hear" you.

On the other hand, those earlier experiences and schemas may lead people astray. They may lead to false expectations or incorrect interpretations. They may keep people from seeing new possibilities.

In resolving apparent contradictions between old schemas and new information, students (readers, users) may develop contextually based schemas that tell them to interpret the same information differently in different contexts. Contextualizing information may sometimes be appropriate. You may have three different restaurant schemas: one is called up when you think "cafeteria," another when you think "fast food outlet," and the third when you think "table service." You may have one set of associations for "window" when you are thinking about your house and another when you are thinking about your computer.

Contextualizing information may sometimes be inappropriate. Students may develop schemas that tell them there is one truth in the classroom and another in the real world. For example, many students taking physics classes can repeat Newton's first law, "An object in motion continues in motion unless acted upon by an outside force," yet they still drive too closely behind another car on the highway as if Newton's law did not apply to real cars. In English classes, students may think that they must write perfect five-paragraph essays even though they are reading examples of good essays that regularly violate that structure.

Just as technical communicators must understand their readers' mental models to write text that will reach their readers, teachers must understand their students' mental models to develop curricula that will reach their students. Teachers must also be aware of the schemas that are implicit in what they teach and how they teach.

Students have schemas both about school and about specific subject matter that may differ from the ones that teachers want them to have.

Mismatches in schemas about school

Students and teachers may be operating under very different expectations for what is and should be happening in their courses. Jennie Nelson (1990) interviewed college freshmen and had them keep diaries of their experiences in writing for their courses. She found that, contrary to teachers' expectations, students often saw writing assignments as busy work, not as an opportunity to learn and practice. Many physics students think that learning physics is just memorizing formulas, while physics teachers want students to understand the concepts behind the formulas.

Mismatches in schemas about subject matter

There is also extensive literature on the preconceptions (misconceptions) that students bring with them about specific subject matter in the sciences and mathematics. For example, many college students believe that just placing a flashlight bulb on top of a battery will cause it to light. They do not realize that a circuit must be closed to permit current to flow. They do not realize that real flashlights have a metal strip that closes the circuit back from the bulb to the battery.

Students bring the schemas that they have developed from their earlier experiences to all their classes. Some of those schemas come from their lives outside of school. Some come from earlier school experiences.

Let me cite an example from composition research: Kathleen McCormick (1990) found that the college students in her study were unwilling to express their own opinions in their essays. She suggests that these students have been told throughout their schooling not to say "I" in papers. She further suggests that they therefore think that they must always be "objective" and that "objective" means not putting themselves into their essays. Even though their teachers are now saying, "Interpret the works you've read and give your own insight and opinion," the students cannot get over their deeply held schema that teachers do not want them to put themselves into what they write. As McCormick says, "This gap between what the teacher is supposedly teaching and what the student is supposedly learning should not be dismissed lightly as a simple misunderstanding" (p. 197).

Deeply held schemas are hard to overcome. Furthermore, teachers, and the institutions they are part of, may well still be sending mixed messages to students. Teachers may voice one position and reward another.

Getting students to change their schemas

How can teachers reach students and get them to change their schemas about school or subject matter? Three important strategies are identifying and addressing specific preconceptions, getting students actively engaged in the work, and helping students to understand and monitor their own learning.

Identifying and addressing incorrect or incomplete preconceptions In other fields, researchers are using interviews with students to understand the schemas that they bring with them about specific subject matter. They then develop curricula that help students articulate those schemas, see how new information does not fit into the old schemas, and change their schemas appropriately. Curriculum changes based on cognitive theory in other fields are showing significant improvement in students' grasp of critical concepts. (See, for example, the work of Lillian McDermott and her group in the Physics Department at the University of Washington [McDermott, 1991].)

Engaging students actively in their own learning In the first part of this essay, I pointed out the importance of "constructivism" as one of the key themes of cognitive psychology. A corollary of constructivism is that students truly learn only when they are actively engaged in constructing knowledge for themselves. Lecturing at students seldom results in real learning. But activity by itself is also not enough. The activity has to be situated in realistic contexts, in what John Seely Brown, Allan Collins, and Paul Duguid (1989) call *cognitive apprenticeships*. Fortunately, because technical communication is about writing, most technical communication courses involve students in creating communications. The major issue that constructivism and cognitive psychology pose for teachers of technical communication is to consider the realism of the situations in which their students write. Are the students getting mixed messages? Are they being told that they should write for a "real audience" when they know that their product will be read only by an instructor who is not part of the real audience?

Monitoring their own learning Schemas are usually implicit, not explicitly articulated. However, schemas can be "teased out," as McCormick (1990) says (p. 198), in interviews and group discussions. Getting students to understand that they have schemas, what those schemas are, and how new information fits into or conflicts with those schemas is necessary to true learning.

Linda Flower puts this point in perspective for technical communication teachers when she writes, "Writers, I would suggest, need to operate with at least four levels of knowing. I choose the word 'knowing' to suggest that a writer's knowledge goes beyond having statable 'knowledge about' something. It includes procedural knowledge—knowing 'how to' manage one's own thinking process" (1989b, pp. 13–14). Flower's four levels of knowing are topic knowledge, discourse knowledge, rhetorical problem solving, and metaknowledge—knowing what you know.

Flower's point is relevant to teachers as well as to students of technical communication. Teachers also have schemas both about what should be happening in classrooms and about specific subject matter. Teachers must also have metaknowledge—understanding and monitoring their own thinking processes. Getting teachers to stop lecturing and to engage students in meaningful activity may require significant changes in *their* schemas, and changing teachers' schemas is every bit as difficult as changing students' schemas.

REFERENCES

Aitkenhead, A.M. & Slack, J.M. (Eds.). (1985). *Issues in cognitive modeling.* Hillsdale, NJ: Erlbaum.

Anderson, P.R., Brockmann, R.J. & Miller, C.R. (Eds.). (1983). *New essays in technical and scientific communication: Research, theory, practice.* Farmingdale, NY: Baywood.

Ashton-Warner, S. (1963). *Teacher.* New York: Simon & Schuster.

Bartlett, F.C. (1932). *Remembering.* Cambridge, UK: Cambridge University Press.

Brand, A.G. (1987). The why of cognition: Emotion and the writing process. *College Composition and Communication, 38,* 436–443.

Bransford, J.D. & Johnson, M.K. (1972). Contextual prerequisites for understanding: Some investigations of comprehension and recall. *Journal of Verbal Learning and Verbal Behavior, 11,* 717–726.

Brown, J.S., Collins, A. & Duguid, P. (1989). Situated cognition and the culture of learning. *Educational Researcher, 18,* 32–43.

Carroll, J.M. & Rosson, M.B. (1987). The paradox of the active user. In J. M. Carroll (Ed.), *Interfacing thought: Cognitive aspects of human-computer interaction* (pp. 80–111). Cambridge, MA: MIT Press.

Clark, H. & Haviland, S. (1975). Comprehension and the given-new contract. In R. Freedle (Ed.), *Discourse production and comprehension* (pp. 1–40). Hillsdale, NJ: Erlbaum.

Dumas, J.S. (1988). *Designing user interfaces for software.* Englewood Cliffs, NJ: Prentice–Hall.

Dumas, J.S. & Redish, J.C. (1993). *A practical guide to usability testing.* Norwood, NJ: Ablex.

Felker, D., Pickering, F., Atlans, M., Charrow, V.R., Holland, V.M., Olkes, C., Redish, J.C. & A.M. (1980). *Document design: A review of the relevant research.* Washington, DC: American Institutes for Research.

Felker, D., Pickering, F., Charrow, V.R., Holland, V.M. & Redish, J.C. (1981). *Guidelines for document designers.* Washington, DC: American Institutes for Research.

Flower, L. (1989a). Cognition, context, and theory building. *College Composition and Communication, 40,* 282–311.

Flower, L. (1989b). Rhetorical problem solving: Cognition and professional writing. In M. Kogen (Ed.), *Writing in the business professions* (pp. 3–36). Urbana, IL: NCTE.

Flower, L. (1990). Introduction: Studying cognition in context. In L. Flower, V. Stein, J. Ackerman, M.J. Kantz, K. McCormick & W.C. Peck (Eds.), *Reading-to-write: Exploring a cognitive and social process* (pp. 3–32). New York: Oxford University Press.

Flower, L. (1994). *The construction of negotiated meaning. A social cognitive theory of writing.* Carbondale, IL: Southern Illinois University Press.

Flower, L. & Hayes, J.R. (1981). A cognitive process theory of writing. *College Composition and Communication, 32,* 365–387.

Flower, L., Stein, V., Ackerman, J., Kantz, M.J., McCormick, K. & Peck, W.C. (Eds.). (1990). *Reading-to-write: Exploring a cognitive and social process.* New York: Oxford University Press.

Flower, L., Hayes, J.R. & Swarts, H. (1983). Revising functional documents: The scenario principle. In P.R. Anderson, R.J. Brockmann & C.R. Miller (Eds.), *New essays in technical and scientific communication: Research, theory, practice* (pp. 41–58). Farmingdale, NY: Baywood.

Hayes, J.R. & Flower, L. (1980). Identifying the organization of writing processes. In W. Lee Gregg & E.R. Steinberg (Eds.), *Cognitive processes in writing: An interdisciplinary approach* (pp. 3–30). Hillsdale, NJ: Erlbaum.

Holland, V.M. & Redish, J.C. (1982). Strategies for reading forms and other documents. In D. Tannen (Ed.), *Proceedings of the Georgetown roundtable on language and linguistics: Text and talk* (pp. 205–218). Washington, DC: Georgetown University Press.

Huckin, T.N. (1983). A cognitive approach to readability. In P.R. Anderson, R.J. Brockmann & C.R. Miller (Eds.), *New essays in technical and scientific communication: Research, theory, practice* (pp. 90–108). Farmingdale, NY: Baywood.

Huckin, T.N. (1992). Context-sensitive text analysis. In G. Kirsch & P.A. Sullivan (Eds.), *Methods and methodology in composition research* (pp. 84–104). Carbondale, IL: Southern Illinois University Press.

Johnson-Laird, P.N. & Wason, P.C. (Eds.). (1977). *Thinking: Readings in cognitive science.* Cambridge, UK: Cambridge University Press.

Kent, T. (1987). Schema theory and technical communication. *Journal of Technical Writing and Communication, 12,* 243–252.

Kirsch, G. & Sullivan, P.A. (Eds.). (1992). *Methods and methodology in composition research.* Carbondale, IL: Southern Illinois University Press.

Kogen, M. (Ed.). (1989). *Writing in the business professions.* Urbana, IL: NCTE.

Margolis, H. (1987). *Patterns, thinking, and cognition: A theory of judgment.* Chicago, IL: University of Chicago Press.

Mayhew, D.J. (1992). *Principles and guidelines in software user interface design.* Englewood Cliffs, NJ: Prentice Hall.

McCormick, K. (1990). The cultural imperatives underlying cognitive acts. In L. Flower, V. Stein, J. Ackerman, M.J. Kantz, K. McCormick & W.C. Peck (Eds.), *Reading-to-write: Exploring a cognitive and social process* (pp. 194–218). New York: Oxford University Press.

McDermott, L. (1991). Millikan lecture 1990: What we teach and what is learned - closing the gap. *American Journal of Physics, 59,* 301–315.

Miller, G.A. (1956). The magical number seven, plus or minus two: Some limits on our capacity for processing information. *Psychological Review, 63,* 81–97.

Minsky, M. (1977). Frame-system theory. In P.N. Johnson-Laird. & P.C. Wason (Eds.), *Thinking: readings in cognitive science* (pp.355–376). Cambridge, UK: Cambridge University Press.

Nelson, J. (1990). This was an easy assignment: Examining how students interpret academic writing tasks. *Research in the Teaching of English, 24,* 362–396.

Norman, D. (1983). Some observations on mental models. In D. Gentner & A.L. Stevens, *Mental models* (pp. 7–14). Hillsdale, NJ: Erlbaum.

Norman, D. (1985). Twelve issues for cognitive science. In A.M. Aitkenhead & J.M. Slack (Eds.), *Issues in cognitive modeling* (pp. 309–336). Hillsdale, NJ: Erlbaum, 1985.

Odell, L. (1985). Beyond the Text: Relations between Writing and Social Context. In L. Odell & D. Goswami (Eds.), *Writing in nonacademic settings* (pp. 249–280). New York: Guilford.

Odell, L. & Goswami, D. (Eds.). (1985). *Writing in nonacademic settings.* New York: Guilford.

Paradis, J., Dobrin, D. & Miller, R. (1985). Writing at Exxon ITD: Notes on the writing environment of an R&D organization. In L. Odell & D. Goswami (Eds.), *Writing in nonacademic settings* (pp. 281–307). New York: Guilford.

Redish, J.C. (1989). Writing in organizations. In M. Kogen (Ed.), *Writing in the business professions* (pp. 97–124). Urbana, IL: NCTE.

Redish, J.C. (1993) Understanding readers. In C. Barnum & S. Carliner (Eds.), *Techniques for technical communicators* (pp. 14–41). New York: Macmillan.

Redish, J.C., Battison, R.M. & Gold, E.S. (1985). Making information accessible to readers. In L. Odell & D. Goswami (Eds.), *Writing in nonacademic settings* (pp. 129–153). New York: Guilford.

Rumelhart, D.E.& Norman, D.A. (1985). Representation of knowledge. In A.M. Aitkenhead & J.M. Slack (Eds.), *Issues in cognitive modeling* (pp. 15–62). Hillsdale, NJ: Erlbaum.

Schank, R.C. (1985). Reminding and memory organization. In A.M. Aitkenhead & J.M. Slack (Eds.), *Issues in cognitive modeling* (pp. 229–249). Hillsdale, NJ: Erlbaum.

Schank, R.C. & Abelson, R.P. (1977). Scripts, plans, and knowledge. In P.N. Johnson-Laird & P.C. Wason (Eds.), *Thinking: readings in cognitive science* (pp.421–432). Cambridge, UK: Cambridge University Press.

Schriver, K. (1991). Plain language through protocol-aided revision. In E.R. Steinberg (Ed.), *Plain language: Principles and practice* (pp. 148–172). Detroit, MI: Wayne State University Press.

Schriver, K. (1992). Connecting cognition and context in composition. In G. Kirsch & P.A. Sullivan (Eds.), *Methods and methodology in composition research* (pp. 190–216). Carbondale, IL: Southern Illinois University Press.

Spyridakis, J.H. & Wenger, M.J. (1992). Writing for human performance: Relating reading research to document design. *Technical Communication, 39,* 202–215.

Wilson, J.R. & Rutherford, A. (1989). Mental models: Theory and application in human factors. *Human Factors, 31,* 617–634.

PRACTICAL FOUNDATIONS

6

WORKPLACE REALITIES AND THE TECHNICAL COMMUNICATION CURRICULUM: A CALL FOR CHANGE

Paul R. Meyer

Texas Higher Education Coordinating Board

Stephen A. Bernhardt

New Mexico State University

INTRODUCTION

Programs in technical communication strive to be well informed by prevailing practices in the workplace. In fact, a whole genre of essays and research builds on the relationship between what is taught in the academy and what is expected in the workplace, often with a strong element of self-critical appraisal. More than most university programs, and certainly more than other areas of emphasis within English departments, technical communication programs pursue a good understanding of and a close articulation with business and industry.

Our goal in this paper is to call attention to a useful area of discussion with which some technical communicators may not be familiar: **workplace literacy**. The workplace literacy movement and what it implies about the needs of the workplace have led us to rethink the curricula and goals of our technical communication program. We hope you will find this information equally provocative.

Beyond simply the ability to read and write at a basic level, definitions of workplace literacy attempt to nail down exactly what skills are essential for successful entry into the workplace. These defined skills are undergoing rapid reconceptualization as the nature of work and the workplace changes. It is very common now to hear talk of "upskilling" the workforce—of giving all workers the skills to produce quality goods and services and to play responsible, decision-making roles in their organizations. ISO 9000, a European-based workplace quality and standards initiative that is spreading to the United States, provides a good example of the practical consequences of this upskilling. To be certified as an ISO 9000 manufacturer, a company must prove through detailed documentation that every worker who uses or even cleans a machine is able to explain the machine's purpose, how the machine works, what manufacturing processes the machine is used for, and what should be done in the event of a breakdown or emergency.

Workplace literacy has emerged within the past few years as a shared concern of government, business, and industry. There is a remarkable consensus among various groups regarding the nature of the central competencies or basic skills that collectively constitute workplace literacy. For example, the U. S. Department of Labor's SCANS report identifies workplace know-how with five competencies that rest on a three-part foundation of skills and personal qualities (see Figure 6.1).

Anthony Carnevale, Leila Gainer, and Ann Meltzer (1990) offer a slightly different configuration of the same basic competencies. (See Figure 6.2, which is meant to be read from the bottom up.)

As Figures 6.1 and 6.2 show, workplace literacy includes not only the traditionally defined literacies of reading, writing, and math, but also computer skills, oral communication, teamwork, problem-solving, and effective interpersonal communication. The workplace needs people who can apply these skills creatively and in combination to get things done.

As technical communication teachers develop courses and programs, they must consider the increasingly strident call for graduates with better

COMPETENCIES—effective workers can productively use:

- **Resources**—allocating time, money, materials, space, and staff.
- **Interpersonal Skills**—working on teams, teaching others, serving customers, leading, negotiating, and working well with people from culturally diverse backgrounds.
- **Information**—acquiring and evaluating data, organizing and maintaining files, interpreting and communicating, and using computers to process information.
- **Systems**—understanding social, organizational, and technological systems, monitoring and correcting performance, and designing or improving systems.
- **Technology**—selecting equipment and tools, applying technology to specific tasks, and maintaining and troubleshooting technologies.

THE FOUNDATION—competence requires:

- **Basic Skills**—reading, writing, arithmetic and mathematics, speaking, and listening.
- **Thinking Skills**—thinking creatively, making decisions, solving problems, seeing things in the mind's eye, knowing how to learn, and reasoning.
- **Personal Qualities**—individual responsibility, self-esteem, sociability, self-management, and integrity.

Figure 6.1 Workplace know-how as defined by the U. S. Department of Labor's SCANS report.

skills. It is in their interest to be aware of what's going on in workplace literacy, who is leading the initiatives, what the prevailing philosophies are, and how schools might respond. To a large extent, workplace literacy initiatives are dominated by two federal departments: Labor and Education. Both have issued reports, funded demonstration projects, and convened blue ribbon panels to construct programs for workplace development. Additional initiatives are sponsored by the American Society for Training and Development (ASTD), where many of the materials and methods of instruction in basic workplace skills are being developed. Labor,

The Seven Skill Groups

Organizational Effectiveness/Leadership

Interpersonal/Negotiation/Teamwork

Self-Esteem/Goal Setting–Motivation/Employability-Career Development

Creative Thinking/Problem Solving

Communication: Listening and Oral Communication

3 R's (Reading, Writing, and Computation)

Learning to Learn

Figure 6.2 Carnevale, Gainer, and Meltzer (1990) identify these seven skill groups as the foundational skills upon which effective workers build more complex personal and interpersonal skills.

Education, and ASTD's interests are cross-fertilized—the same experts turn up on different committees and panels.

The thinking of these groups about workplace skills has resulted in some very concrete ideas about how education should change both in schools and in the workplace. Figure 6.3 lists some of the goals identified by the U. S. Department of Education in *America 2000: An Education Strategy* (1991).

Teachers of technical communication, the subject area most focused on preparing students for the workplace, should consider the extent to which technical communication programs support these goals. Do courses in technical communication teach students how to think critically and solve complex problems? Do students become good writers? Do enough of them develop the knowledge and skills that will enable them to become scientists and engineers?

Technical communication educators need to look toward the workplace to assess its demands as well as look back toward the public schools to assess their performance. As they do so, they should take into account that students in technical communication classes actually comprise two groups: those students who complete their undergraduate degrees within a reasonable time frame (four to six years) and the large proportion of students

Selected Objectives from America 2000

- By the year 2000, every adult American will be literate and will possess the knowledge and skills necessary to compete in a global economy and exercise the rights and responsibilities of citizenship.
- The percentage of students who demonstrate the ability to reason, solve problems, apply knowledge, and write and communicate effectively will increase substantially.
- The number of United States undergraduate and graduate students, especially women and minorities, who complete degrees in mathematics, science, and engineering, will increase substantially.
- Every major American business will be involved in strengthening the connection between education and work.
- All workers will have the opportunity to acquire the knowledge and skills, from basic to highly technical, needed to adapt to emerging new technologies, work methods, and markets through public and private educational, vocational, technical, workplace, or other programs.
- The proportion of those qualified students, especially minorities, who enter college, who complete at least two years, and who complete their degree programs will increase substantially.
- The proportion of college graduates who demonstrate an advanced ability to think critically, communicate effectively, and solve problems will increase substantially.

Figure 6.3 Selected Objectives from U.S. Department of Education, *America 2000.*

who drop out of college sometime during their first or second year (about half at many universities) and who may or may not return intermittently for further education or training. Educators should also consider the government's projection that by the year 2000, more than 70% of the jobs in America will *not* require a college education (National Center on Education and the Economy, 1990, p. 3). Some forms of post-secondary training and education will be much in demand, but colleges and universities already appear close to meeting the workplace's need for people with traditional college degrees.

The situation is really much more complex than college educators typically imagine it to be. College programs are preparing students both to complete college and to drop out (or take an educational sabbatical). And colleges are offering degrees to many people who will take jobs that do not require college degrees. It is not that these jobs will be non-technical or undemanding. It's just that they will not call for the sorts of learning typically provided by colleges and universities. Consider the kinds of skills the workplace is calling for and the ways technical communication programs might adapt to meet them.

BEHAVIORAL AND SOCIAL SKILLS: A GOOD WORK ETHIC

The calls for improved workplace literacy often redefine what is meant by basic skills. Featured prominently are skills that are largely behavioral or social, behaviors that when taken together constitute a strong work ethic (Natriello, 1989). *America's Choice: High Skills or Low Wages* reports:

> Our research did reveal a wide range of concerns covered under the blanket term of "skills." While businesses everywhere complained about the quality of their applicants, few talked about the kinds of skills acquired in school. The primary concern of more than 80 percent of employers was finding workers with a good work ethic and appropriate social behavior: 'reliable,' 'a good attitude,' 'a pleasant appearance,' 'a good personality.' (National Center on Education and the Economy, 1990, p. 3)

When asked, business says it needs people who have good attitudes, who can work independently, who can function as team members, who are responsible and dependable, and who show other behaviors that generally characterize a good work ethic.

In many ways, technical communication courses offer a good opportunity to develop these sorts of skills. Favored here would be assignments that pose real problems, that require students to work within time and resource constraints, and that require students to work with classmates and people outside the course. To be truly beneficial, such projects would need to include ways for participating students to receive feedback on their attitudes, appearance, and personal interaction.

Some within the technical communication profession may suggest that we are recommending the production of "good little worker bees" for business and industry. We think that this issue should be consciously addressed within technical communication programs. To what extent should programs contribute to developing an effective workforce—with all that this implies? The nature of the workplace literacy movement suggests that public education does not currently produce diligent workers in the numbers desired by business and industry. Critics could suggest that responding to this need constitutes capitulation to the worst, capitalistic demands for docile and cooperative workers.

Businesses recognize that they can give on-the-job training in necessary technical skills. A willing, cooperative worker will generally learn what it takes to do the job. When a business fires a worker, it is not usually because of a lack of skill, but because of personal/interpersonal habits. In the same way, schools have never tossed aside students who have trouble learning; they toss aside the trouble makers, those without the willingness or sufficient self-discipline to behave in ways the system will tolerate. In this negative sense, schools have always shaped behavior. The question is whether schools ought to take a proactive stance in identifying and helping students consciously develop the behavioral and social skills that comprise a good work ethic.

How universally accepted are such qualities as observing deadlines, being cooperative, being dependable, and so on? As teachers of professional communication, both of us watch students, undergraduate and graduate, repeatedly having trouble meeting deadlines, coordinating group activities, and acting in ways that we would characterize as dependable. We could ignore these problems, perhaps by passing them off as caused by the challenging university environment. Instead, our inclination is to push students to demonstrate frequently those behaviors that collectively constitute what would be called a good work ethic and to hold students responsible for their successes and failures. In doing so, we recognize that we open ourselves up to the criticisms outlined above. In the final analysis, we come down on the side of the work ethic. Our students expect us to prepare them for the workplace, and our main responsibility is to them.

PERSONAL DEVELOPMENT SKILLS

Increasingly, one of the themes of workplace literacy is the need for workers with well-defined senses of self—people with high self-esteem, high motivation, and the ability to set high goals. Additionally, organizations need people with leadership skills and the ability to work effectively. Such people will recognize how they fit into organizations and how they can promote both individual and organizational goals.

Alongside this demand is a parallel demand for people who know how to learn. The ruling assumption is that most knowledge has a very short half-life. What people learn in school might carry them a short distance, but new jobs, new technologies, and new patterns of work organization quickly make obsolete what people learn in school. So the emerging model is one of constant learning in the workplace: constant training and constant adaptation to change.

The question for universities and for technical communication programs is clear: to what extent do these programs develop in students both self-motivation and the ability to learn in self-directed ways? Conversely, to what extent do the courses and the programs establish requirements that students must fulfill, but which also encourage them to be passive consumers?

INTERPERSONAL SKILLS: ORAL COMMUNICATION, NEGOTIATION, AND TEAMWORK

In addition to general behaviors and social skills, the calls for workplace literacy tend to stress strong oral communication skills. The workplace needs people who can listen well, respond to both content and feeling in other people's words, negotiate and compromise, and participate in efficient and supportive ways in group discussion. At least some businesses call for people with aggressive interpersonal skills—strong negotiation or persuasive skills, the ability to direct others, and the willingness to defend positions and offer criticism. The need for heightened oral communication skills is increased by the general movement toward a service economy within an information-based society. One prediction holds that about 90% of new jobs through 1995 will be in services, compared with about 8% in manufacturing (U.S. Department of Labor and U.S. Department of Education, 1988, p. 3). The drive toward restructured industries based, in part, on participatory management through increased front-line authority and reduced middle management also increases the pressure on industry to look for workers with highly developed oral communication skills.

Many businesses recognize the need for employees who can communicate well face-to-face or via the telephone. The training industry is largely geared toward giving existing workers these skills. Seminars in client relations, conflict resolution, sales presentations, telephone etiquette, management communication, and dealing with the press are among the more popular topics for training seminars. Traditionally, organizations have sought such training for management and professional staff alone. Now, they are increasingly seeing the value of training in oral communication for workers at other levels.

Teachers of professional communication need to reconsider the place of oral and interpersonal communication in their programs. It is all too common for oral communication, if incorporated into programs at all, to consist of a unit on short speeches or project presentations. There are better ways to develop communicative competence among students. Role playing is one avenue—having students act out scenarios where communication is likely to be difficult or strained. Again, assignments that partner students with human resources in the university or the community encourage the development of interaction skills. Here, too, is where legitimate issues of power in discourse can be raised: Who does the speaking? When? And under what rules?

A wealth of scholarship exists on gender roles in communication (see the essay by LaDuc, this collection), on cross-cultural communication (see the essay by Thrush, this collection), and on the ways that status and power are reflected in and created through shared discourse (see the essays by Subbiah and by Burnett, White, and Duin, this collection). Just as technical communication students are asked to develop metacognitive awareness of their own writing processes, they should be given the tools and be encouraged to be analytical about their own processes and patterns of interpersonal interaction.

Technical communication faculty can also carve out roles for themselves as on-campus advocates of active participation by students in their own learning. Education that expects students to be passive absorbers of information cannot turn out workers who take the kind of active, participatory roles in work settings that business and industry currently demand. Educational reform has been a constant issue in elementary and secondary education for ten years; it is now also reaching post-secondary education. It is up to those who understand workplace realities to influence reform efforts on campuses in ways that encourage students to develop strong skills in oral communication, teamwork, and active, participatory learning.

Technical communication journals, programs of study, and conventions tend to reflect the fact that teachers of technical communication see themselves as involved in a larger enterprise than simply *technical writing*. They favor terms such as *technical communication* or *professional communication* to remind themselves and to indicate to the world that their provenance is larger than written reports. Yet the bulk of the profession's discussion, research, and course work focuses on written communication. The field of technical communication needs to achieve more balance between oral and written communication in both pedagogy and research. Students of technical communication need to learn to integrate the full range of oral and written competencies in their work.

ADAPTIVE READING AND WRITING SKILLS: HANDLING THE INFORMATION LOAD

In thinking about the place of reading and writing within the curriculum, teachers of technical communication should consider the paperwork demands of typical office and production environments. Doing so calls attention to the need for adaptive reading and writing strategies. Workers need strategies for sifting through large quantities of information to find what is useful. They have to be able to quickly find information in complex documents in order to take appropriate actions. They have to be able to *use* documents, not so much to *read* them.

Typically, the reading strategies that are reflected in academic classes presuppose behaviors that are more characteristic of students than of workers. In technical communication classes, students should be encouraged to develop reading strategies that rely on navigating, searching, skimming, and filtering large pools of information. Instead, too often, they are offered short textbook chapters to read, followed by discussions of this limited amount of text. Classrooms must find ways to introduce students to the complexities of naturally occurring texts: the thick manuals and long shelves of manuals typical of large information systems, the complex sets of regulations or specifications governing technical processes, or the volumes of bureaucratic prose, forms, and procedures that surround funded projects.

Similarly, educators need to examine their presuppositions about writing—including conventions of authorship, ownership, and use of information. Many businesses now build or assemble documents, rather than creating them from scratch. Authorship is important in different ways than it is in the academy, and so are the rules governing the use and attribution of information. Students need to know how to boilerplate documents, what the fair use rules are for graphics or written materials, and what the conventions are (if there are any consistent ones) for documenting sources.

Few people in the workplace write research papers with long bibliographies. Much more important for the vast majority of workers is the ability to write effective memos, short reports, and briefing papers of one or a few pages. Workplace writers need to be able to write quick overviews for their superiors, clear instructions for their subordinates, and careful notes for themselves. It is more important that they are able to reshape information than to produce it from scratch. What we need to move toward is defining reading and writing not as ends in themselves, but as information skills. The abilities to move around in and make use of large pools of information are critical survival skills as technical communication students move into the information age.

COMPUTER SKILLS

Computer skills are rapidly entering into the standard definitions of basic skills. The U.S. Department of Education, in particular, has been receiving a steady stream of suggestions to include computer skills as a basic sort of literacy, not a specialized technical skill. The SCANS report (U.S. Department of Labor, 1991) targets computer/information skills under several of its competencies:

- **Information**—acquiring and evaluating data, organizing and maintaining files, interpreting and communicating, and using computers to process information.
- **Systems**—understanding social, organizational, and technological systems, monitoring and correcting performance, and designing or improving systems.
- **Technology**—selecting equipment and tools, applying technology to specific tasks, and maintaining and troubleshooting technologies.

The commission suggests that all public school graduates should have these skills to be productive in the workforce. Reread that list and ask yourself whether all high school graduates have such skills. Then, ask yourself whether all college graduates have them.

Defining skills or learning in these ways is a very recent development. It is interesting to note how the SCANS report integrates skills from across several traditional school domains: math, science, computer science, engineering, and communication. Seeing computers as information tools tends to blur the distinction between reading and using computers: It is all about working with information. It is also interesting to note how these skills are tightly embedded in task domains: doing things with people, machines, or data, and not just knowing facts or manipulating printed sources. Thinking about necessary worker skills in such broad, inclusive terms forces educators to reconceptualize the cross-disciplinary thrusts of professional communication courses and programs of study within universities. It forces those who design programs to consider the extent to which the programs focus on content versus performance, with the clear edge in the new workplace going to those who can perform.

WHO NEEDS WORKPLACE LITERACY?

Up to this point, we have only hinted at the relationship between the college students in technical communication programs and the workers "out there" who need to improve their basic skills. In the best of all possible worlds, there would be little overlap in the two groups. Students would come to college with good basic skills, and all college graduates would find the niche into which they and their skills could nestle.

The truth requires a reconsideration of both the college and the workplace. It would be nice if all students had good literacy skills when they entered college and if all of them became managers, scientists, and engineers or went on to graduate school. In fact, many students come to college without adequate skills. Many manage to graduate from college without college-level skills. Some drop out; others complete limited technical training.

To serve students well, those who build college programs must recognize the across-the-board need for better literacy skills. Programs need to encourage students to develop a strong work ethic. Courses should give them practical skill in solving problems, understanding systems, working with resources, and using technology. Students need help in becoming better readers, writers, and communicators in complex information environments.

The workplace is beginning to recognize both that it has workers who need better skills and that these workers are not all at the lowest level of the workplace hierarchy. Supervisors with great interpersonal communication skills run into a brick wall when the job setting changes and their inability to read and write is revealed. College graduates, some with advanced degrees, lose their jobs because of poor interpersonal skills. Hard-working minority workers turn down promotions because of a lack of experience with computers or poor writing skills.

For individuals in the workplace, poor literacy skills are an insurmountable barrier to advancement. For businesses, poor worker skills hinder the implementation of total quality management and prevent the best use of good workers. Workplaces are beginning to turn to career-long workplace training and to workplace literacy programs as a partial solution to these problems. Those at colleges and universities who are building technical communication programs should also consider what can be done to prepare a workforce for the next century.

CONCLUSION

An interesting cultural shift is reflected in the calls for improved workforce literacy. In particular, these calls represent what many would construe as a somewhat conservative agenda; if there is a consensus, it is among those with vested interests—the business/industrial complex. When business or industry makes demands on the schools, many teachers become uncomfortable. They object that schools and universities are not trade or vocational schools, that they have larger missions related to the whole lives of their students, not just to preparation for work.

And yet the current goals and the ways of talking about these goals could easily be construed as reflecting an earlier liberal/pragmatic agenda. The emphases on doing, on problem solving, on teamwork, and on project-based learning all sound a lot like an earlier Deweyan agenda for the schools. That earlier agenda was, like the current one, a response to arid, formalist instruction that was seen to be inadequate to the needs of a literate citizenry. The current agenda, as described above, aligns itself easily with "outcomes-based" approaches to education, with their emphasis on performance and on an education that leads to the ability to "do things" as opposed to simply "knowing things." The outcomes-based approach looks sufficiently liberal to arch-conservative Phyllis Schlafly (1993) to serve as a prime target for a scathing attack. She objects to the schools' attempts to help students develop values and attitudes, to rely on performance as opposed to paper-and-pencil standardized tests, and to government agendas for education in general.

It is ironic that what appeared liberal in the 1930s now looks conservative in the 1990s to liberal cultural critics but appears liberal to conservative thinkers. We are not sure whether what we have described above is an appropriation of liberal educational theory by vested conservative interests, or a continuing and maturing Deweyan pragmatism.

Lest anyone assume that we think the path toward enhanced workplace literacy is clear, we would end on a note of caution. Suppose, for example, that a technical communication teacher did attempt to give greater attention to oral communication skills in the workplace. The question still remains: "What oral communication skills? On what model?" No one can assume that there is agreement on what constitutes good communication. Gender studies, in particular, point up the essential underlying fact of variation in styles (see the essay by LaDuc, this collection). Should students be taught verbal dueling in an aggressive, "masculine" style? Should they be taught compromise and concession, or hardball negotiation? Should classes encourage students to be open and nondefensive, to show concern and caring, or should they teach people to be crafty and calculating, with an eye on their rear flanks?

And what should technical communication teachers think about the issue of work ethic, the issue that business repeatedly stresses as so important? Is there anything close to agreement on what a good work ethic is? What happens as the discussion moves across the boundaries of social class and ethnicity? It would be a mistake to assume that there is a single, unifying work ethic that students need to develop. Many of the models that business is so enamored of derive directly from a foreign culture—from Japan—and it is important to maintain a healthy skepticism about expecting or even wanting the same levels of fierce corporate loyalty or commitment to work among workers in this country. The trade-offs inherent in the Japanese model are just becoming apparent: the gender inequities, the psychological malaise, and the distorted value systems that follow unquestioning loyalty and devotion.

We don't pretend to have the answers to these troubling questions. Yet, we feel that programs in technical communication will surely be better informed if they take into account the calls for enhancing workforce literacy. Technical communication teachers need to participate in the dialogues that are today defining what a good worker is, what education is appropriate for that worker, and how full literacy in a participatory democracy might be defined.

REFERENCES

Carnevale, A., Gainer, L.J. & Meltzer, A.S. (1990). *Workplace basics: The essential skills employers want.* San Francisco, CA: Jossey-Bass.

Johnson, WB. & Packer, A. (1987). *Workforce 2000: Work and workers for the 21st century.* Indianapolis, IN: Hudson Institute. (Available from U. S. Government Printing Office, Washington, DC 20402).

National Center on Education and the Economy. (1990, June). *America's choice: High skills or low wages. The Report of the Commission on the Skills of the American Workforce.* (Available from the National Center on Education and the Economy, 39 State Street, Suite 500, Rochester, NY 14614).

Natriello, G. (1989). *What do employers want in entry-Level workers?* ERIC Clearinghouse on Urban Education: ED 308 279.

Schlafly, P. (1993, May). What's wrong with outcome-based education? *The Phyllis Schlafly Report, 26* (10), n.p.

United States. Department of Education. (1991). *America 2000: An Education Strategy.* Washington, DC: U.S. Department of Education. (Available from 1-800-USA-LEARN).

United States. Department of Labor. (1991, June). *What work requires of schools: A SCANS Report for America 2000.* Washington, D.C.: U.S. Department of Labor, Secretary's Commission on Achieving Necessary Skills. (Available from the U.S. Department of Labor, 200 Constitution Avenue, NW, Washington, DC).

United States. Department of Labor and Department of Education. (1988). *The Bottom line: Basic skills in the workplace.* Washington, DC: U.S. Government Printing Office.

7

TECHNICAL COMMUNICATION AND ETHICS

Scott P. Sanders

University of New Mexico

INTRODUCTION

Over the past several years and across the entire field of technical communication—in workplaces large and small, in college writing classrooms, and in the pages of academic and professional journals—ethics has become the topic of increasing debate. In each of these venues, the fundamental notion of what it means to be an ethical technical communicator appears to be changing. As is often the case when an age-old intellectual concern (the study of ethics in the Western tradition traces its lineage back nearly 2,500 years to the Sophists, Plato, and Aristotle) is challenged by changing methods of analysis and understanding, the discussion is vigorous, sometimes contentious.

The increased interest in ethics and technical communication stems largely from a shift in the focus of analytical concern: away from the product of ethical deliberation—the action itself and its potential outcomes—and toward an increasingly complex analysis of the cluster of processes that influence the decision to act. Arthur E. Walzer, writing in the Society for Technical Communication's (STC) 1989 anthology on ethics, concludes his essay by calling for a redirection of attention:

> . . . with few exceptions, . . . [ethical] debate has so far tended to move too cavalierly from exhortation on the importance of ethics to a consideration of particular examples, without due consideration of the mediating questions concerning the motives, purposes, goals, and efficacy of ethics and of ethics codes. (1989b, p. 105)

Many recent discussions of ethics in technical communication have followed Walzer's implicit advice: They analyze "motives, purposes, goals, and efficacy." In short, they pursue rhetorical analyses of ethics, primarily by investigating the concept of ethos, which they develop by posing what we might call "mediating questions" that probe the myriad relationships that obtain in the interaction of the writer (or writers), the document, and the reader (or readers) who read the document.

In this essay I survey and organize into topical categories much of the literature on ethics and technical communication. Along the way, I hope first to distinguish the several approaches to ethics that commentators have taken and then to compare those approaches, drawing the reader's attention to their relative strengths and weaknesses.

LOCATING THE DOMAINS OF ETHICS IN TECHNICAL COMMUNICATION

The first bibliographical anthology (Moran & Journet, 1985) devoted to research in technical communication did not offer a chapter devoted entirely to ethics. In their "Preface," Moran and Journet describe the "tradition of research" in technical communication as coming "from a variety of fields," and they suggest that "because of its heterogenous nature, research in technical communication is often difficult to assess in a coherent and unified manner" (p. ix). The subject index of this book of 515 pages cites four pages specifically on "ethics," all of them in Philip M. Rubens' (1985) essay, of which a two-page discussion under the subheading "Science, Technology, and Ethics" is the principal offering. Rubens reviews several books on ethics and values in science and concludes by remarking that "not much work has been done in ethics in technical and scientific communication" (p. 10).

A secondary subject index listing for "ethics and audience" directs the reader to six pages in Carolyn R. Miller's essay, "Invention in Technical and Scientific Discourse" (1985). In this short section of her much longer essay, Miller considers the rhetoric of persuasion in scientific and technical writing. She notes that persuasion "involves the need to understand one's audience and to seek more or less deliberately for proofs that the audience will accept as good reasons for assenting" (p. 137), and she explicitly points out that "the relationship between rhetor and audience is the concern of ethics" (p. 138). Miller moves on to discuss "the *ethos* of science," not the ethics of technical communication, but her explicit linking of ethics, audience analysis, and ethos succinctly describes how many subsequent arguments locate rhetoric, and specifically ethos and audience analysis, as the dominant domain of ethics in technical communication.

Four years later, Stephen Doheny-Farina's bibliographical essay, "Ethics and Technical Communication" (1989), surveys the relevant literature on the topic published to that point. Doheny-Farina's essay is especially useful for its historical account of the STC's efforts to write and agree to pronounce an official "Code of Ethics." This story is described at length in a section headed "Technical Communication Ethics in Practice" (pp. 53-63). The next section, "Technical Communication in Theory," is equally valuable for its discussion of articles that consider the relationships between ethics, ethos, and persona in technical communication (63-65). In this discussion, Doheny-Farina cites more than 20 articles, and he quotes tellingly from several of them on the "infusion of authorial identity and responsibility in technical communication" (p. 65). The essay continues by looking briefly at mass media ethics (pp. 66–67) and approaches to teaching ethics in technical communication courses (pp. 67–69). Also in 1989, an STC anthology edited by R. John Brockmann and Fern Rook reprinted several articles on ethics that had originally appeared in the society's journal, *Technical Communication.* Doheny-Farina mentions some of these articles in his bibliographical essay.

Doheny-Farina demonstrates that a fair body of work on ethics and technical communication did exist by 1989 and that it could be presented in a coherent, unified manner. In the discussions that follow, I extend the categorical distinctions that Doheny-Farina makes; with very few exceptions, I limit my comments to literature published since 1989 to avoid duplicating Doheny-Farina's work, which ably presents the state of the topic at the time of its publication.

PRACTICAL ETHICS

By "practical ethics," I mean the domain of much of the literature on business ethics, which, as Walzer complained, often moves directly "from exhortation on the importance of ethics to a consideration of particular examples" (1989b, p. 105). Between the exhortation and the examples, guidelines for ethical conduct are usually given.

A representative example applied specifically to technical communication is Herbert Michaelson's "How an Author Can Avoid the Pitfalls of Practical Ethics" (1990). Michaelson locates the source of most ethical problems for technical communicators in "the rather subtle conflict between an author's self-interest and the obligation to provide adequate information for readers" (p. 58), and he admonishes writers that "violations of practical ethics can defeat your purposes. . . . Attempts to bolster your professional reputation will fall flat . . . [T]hey disturb the integrity of your manuscript and will eventually expose you to criticism" (p. 58). The body of the article offers examples of specific ethical pitfalls, from the 10 "Sins of Omission" (pp. 58–59) to "Unfair Bias" (pp. 59–60), "Ambiguity and Speculation" (p. 60), "Plagiarism" (pp. 60–61), and "Indiscriminate Publication" (p. 61). The examples given are clear and to the point: "the omission of outlier points from a graph because they wouldn't look good" and "neglecting to mention significant failures that occurred during the course of the design effort" simply "isn't cricket" (p. 59). The advice that derives from most of Michaelson's examples is disarmingly simple, direct, and eminently practical: Just don't do it.

The simplicity of such ethical advice does not necessarily make it simplistic. As Lauren Mund and Gary Perez (1992) note in their newsletter article, "Developing Usable Ethics," many professionals find ethics "an abstract subject"; "it is difficult," they suggest, "to see how [ethical considerations] directly apply to our work as technical communicators" (p. 6). Mund and Perez offer "ethical guidelines that support craft values" that are all plain statements of such common sense advice as "Avoid lying, exaggeration, unverified value judgment, and editorializing" (p. 6). The simplicity of these statements helps diffuse practitioners' fears about the complexity of the ethical contexts in which this advice must be applied. The focus on common sense reflects the practical nature of this approach to ethics: It encourages the busy professional first to recognize ethical considerations and then, perhaps, to act upon them.

Most professional codes of ethics are similarly practical and straightforward. A typical code of ethics will cite "such obvious items as prohibitions against receiving or giving bribes, restrictions on outside business activities and employment, and conflicts of interest in the size or value of a gift that employees can receive from suppliers" (Cox, 1993, p.16). Writing in the introduction to an anthology of 54 reprinted articles on business ethics, John E. Richardson (1989) asserts that "corporate America struggles to find its ethical identity in a business environment that grows increasingly complex. . . . Does a company have any obligation to help solve social problems. . . ? What ethical responsibilities should a multinational corporation assume in foreign countries?" The practical ethics approach to sorting out these knotty questions is to discover a rule-based guideline and then apply the guideline to the question: "as individuals and managers, we formulate our ethics (i.e., the standards of 'right' and 'wrong' behavior that we set for ourselves) based upon family, peer, and religious influences, our past experiences, and our own unique value systems" (Richardson, 1989, p. 4).

Still, one must choose which guideline to follow, so how does one devise a practical method for evaluating the guidelines? David L. Sturges (1992) asserts that "most of the rhetoric about business ethics in textbooks results more often in confusion" and fails "to provide students or practitioners with solid guidance" (p. 44). Sturges develops an "Ethical Dilemma Decision Model that practitioners can use as a disciplined guide"; it is, in effect, a practical guide to the guidelines that helps a student or practitioner "evaluate [ethical] decisions" (p. 44). Sturges offers an overview of the literature on ethics and business communication, and he distinguishes between "two basic approaches": the teleological (or consequentialist) approach, which is based on "concern for the consequences for given behavior," and the deontological (or nonconsequentialist) approach, which is based on "the duty of the individual as a member of a social collective" (p. 44). Sturges cites an article from a special issue of the *Journal of Business Communication* (27:3, 1990) that "confirms that the majority of approaches to ethics are grounded in philosophical and theological foundations" (p. 44).

PHILOSOPHICAL ETHICS

The advice offered by commentators on practical ethics is rule-based, and the rules are derived from the long tradition of philosophical and theological study of ethics. Sturges notes that one source finds "more than 34 theories [of business communication ethics] associated with" the deontological approach alone (p. 44). However, when one looks specifically at technical communication, analyses derived from philosophical ethical theory are not so numerous.

Mark R. Wicclair and David K. Farkas, writing in a 1984 article cited and discussed by Doheny-Farina (1989) in his bibliographical essay, offer a brief overview of philosophical approaches intended to "clarify the nature of ethical problems" and "distinguish between the ethical perspective and several other perspectives" (p. 15). Wicclair and Farkas describe "three types of ethical principles [Goal-Based, Duty-Based, and Rights-Based Principles]" that together "make up a conceptual framework that will help illuminate almost any ethical problem" (p. 16). They then demonstrate how these principles may be used to analyze three hypothetical cases. The third case is presented without discussion. Readers are invited to "resolve it for themselves using the conceptual framework" (p. 19). The authors pose four questions to guide readers' responses to this final case: "Is there an ethical problem here? If so, what is it, what ethical principles are involved, and what kinds of responses are called for?" (p. 19). The method is first to identify the three philosophical principles of ethical analysis, apply them to the specifics of the particular case, and then judge the ethicality of potential actions by weighing how their probable outcomes will affect all parties involved. For example, the first case they present considers whether a fictional technical communicator should write a report that intentionally misconstrues some data. The analysis concludes that all three ethical perspectives agree: the fictional communicator "should not write the report" (p. 18). But this determination leads the writer to another problem, "whether to act ethically or to protect his self-interest" (p. 18). Readers are left with that choice. The essay does not pursue the philosophical arguments that justify the ethical perspectives presented beyond four paragraphs; readers interested in the philosophy are referred to four books on ethics (see note 2, p. 19 in Wicclair and Farkas).

Writing nearly 10 years later, Mike Markel (1993) observes that articles on ethics and technical communication "risk oversimplification of the theories" when "discussions of natural law, utilitarianism, and Kant's categorical imperative all fit on one page" (p. 81). After an extensive review of the literature, Markel suggests that "in our desire to make ethics as palatable as we can, we leave out the philosophical justification . . . which is really the essence of the argument" and focus too quickly and too squarely on practical guidelines; the result is that students are quite right to be "unimpressed by such advice as 'Don't lie'" (p. 81). Markel carefully sets out a deontological ethic that critiques the consequentialist values of utilitarian approaches to ethics. He offers "a powerful ethical foundation for technical communicators" derived from "Kant's second formulation of the categorical imperative—to treat ourselves and others not merely as means but also as ends" and from the "concept of the ideal society" described in the work of the contemporary American philosopher John Rawls (p. 81).

RHETORICAL ETHICS

When Markel (1993) appeals to the need for "a powerful foundation" for analyzing ethical questions, he defines an essential difference that separates the practical and philosophical approaches to ethics from many of the more recent rhetorical approaches to ethical analysis. These approaches are antifoundational; that is, they "view ethics not so much as a set of fundamental and abstract principles to be applied to situations but as a process of inquiry necessarily tied to the act of composing" (Porter, 1993a, p. 208). This shift mirrors the movement in the past thirty years of composition studies away from analyzing writing by evaluating the product (the finished document) according to how well it reflects accepted principles of style to analyzing the composing processes that lead to the finished product.

This approach to the rhetorical study of ethics, the postmodern rhetorical approach, probes an "enlarged understanding of *ethos*," which is analyzed as "the complex representation of a communal character created by the co-inherence of the writer and the audience as they are figured in the text" (Martin and Sanders, 1994, p. 149). Audience analysis, long a defining feature of technical communication studies, takes on renewed importance as the part of the composing process through which ethos, the embodiment of the ethical character, forms:

> through ethos . . . the writer creates and becomes one with the audience that has been created [and] . . . the reader re-creates this process in the act of reading, if the ethical appeal has created presence enough. (Enos, 1990, 106)

Audience analysis of this sort, when it is employed in the composing process, "leads to the production of texts that evince an ethical rhetoric, a rhetoric that is as willing to change the self as it is to influence the reader" (Martin and Sanders, 1994, p. 148). When this happens, James Porter suggests that

> . . . the audience-writer binary breaks down: Collaboration occurs between writer and audience, the audience becomes the writer, the writer becomes one with the audience. The ethical implication here then is not just that it is to the advantage of the writer to "analyze" audience, but that it is the writer's ethical obligation to "identify" with audience, negotiate meaning with the audience, and work to blur those roles that traditional rhetoric has staunchly maintained. (1993b, p. 134)

Although in the passage above Porter distinguishes the rhetoric of his approach to ethics from "traditional rhetoric," he maintains elsewhere that

> The ethical axis pertains in crucial ways to questions about the writer's relationship with various audiences and about the loci of authority for rhetorical acts and also provides rhetoric with a means of discussing motives—the reasons people communicate in the first place, the driving force of rhetorical activity. (1993a, p. 208)

Porter's claim that the "postmodern" approach to ethics and professional writing "provides rhetoric a means of discussing motives" would seem, at first, to answer Arthur E. Walzer's earlier call for "consideration of the mediating questions concerning the motives, purposes, goals, and efficacy of ethics" (1989b, p. 105). But the postmodern rhetoric of ethics that Porter and others explore is not traditional rhetoric, largely because of its need "to blur" (in Porter's words) the distinctions that traditional rhetoric draws between the writer, the text, and the reader.

Traditional rhetoric draws its inspiration directly from the work of classical rhetoricians. The basic texts include the writings of Aristotle, Plato, and Quintilian. Readers interested in the primary works of rhetoric will find excerpts from classical to contemporary commentators presented with useful introductions in *The Rhetorical Tradition*, an anthology edited by Patricia Bizzell and Bruce Herzberg (1990). See also essays by George E. Yoos (1979) and by Nan Johnson (1984), which discuss ethics and ethos in the context of contemporary writing theory. Yoos's later essay, "Rational Appeal and the Ethics of Advocacy" (1984), is also interesting for its rhetorical analysis of ethos and ethics and persuasion.

Arthur E. Walzer writes specifically about ethics and technical communication in "The Ethics of False *Implicature* in Technical and Professional Writing Courses" (1989a). Walzer demonstrates how an instructor might use traditional "rhetorical theory, with its emphasis on discovering and meeting the needs and expectations of an audience" (p. 149) to create "an assignment that requires students to judge the morality of particular suspect rhetorical practices" (p. 150). Walzer considers how technical and professional writers might be tempted into "intentionally fostering false inference . . . to avoid writing what is demonstrably literally untrue but . . . in order to achieve their ends . . . imply what they know to be false" (p. 150). The analysis uses H. Paul Grice's "famous lecture on 'implicature'" (p. 152) to develop analytical principles for discovering "what the readers can be presumed to know, whether the reader has access to information, and what expectations are fostered by external factors and by the immediate context in which the implicature appears" (p. 154). The purpose of the rhetorical analysis is to arrive at a "judgment of the readers' susceptibility and responsibility and of the writer's culpability" (p. 155) for the inferences that might be drawn from a text. The method is then worked out in a case that involves reporting the results of tests of a hypothetical "rail car" (pp. 155–157).

Also addressing the issues of ethics in technical writing, I cite the work of classical and contemporary rhetoricians ranging from Plato and Aristotle to Booth and Perelman to argue that "persuasive rhetoric is appropriate in technical writing" (1988, p. 63) and suggest that rhetoric derived from the work of the American psychologist Carl Rogers may be used to effect "persuasion deriving from mediation [that] uses audience analysis to promote understanding, both intellectual and affectual, and then persuades through the mediation that occurs in the act of understanding" (p. 61). I argue that the use of such persuasive rhetoric in technical communication is "effective and ethical" (p. 64).

Both the traditional and the postmodern rhetorical approaches to ethics in technical communication direct attention away from analyzing the features of finished documents to analyzing the processes that inform the community that gives rise to the need for the communication. Carolyn R. Miller urges this view of technical communication when she argues that

> . . . understanding . . . practical rhetoric [for example, technical communication] as a matter of conduct rather than of production, as a matter of arguing in a prudent way toward the good of the community rather than of constructing texts . . . provides . . . a locus for questioning, for criticism, for distinguishing good practice from bad." (1989, p. 23)

Miller calls for an ethic of technical communication that is closely bound up in ethos, in analysis of the complicated and various ways in which writers and readers engage documents and in that engagement express the ethos of individuals and of communities.

Both the traditional and postmodern rhetorical methods of analysis respond to this call. But how different the two approaches are. In the traditional rhetorical approaches to ethics and technical communication, the roles played by the writer, the text, and the reader are clearly drawn. Walzer judges the "culpability" of writers and readers; I urge writers to "demonstrate understanding of the reader's point of view" in part by using "active voice, second- or third-person verb constructions" (Sanders, 1988, p. 67). In the postmodern rhetoric of ethics described by Porter (1993a), Martin and Sanders (1994), and Enos (1990), responsibility and influence cannot be attributed and judged so clearly when, as Porter puts it, "the audience-writer binary breaks down . . . the audience becomes the writer, the writer becomes one with the audience" and the text becomes, not the printed page, but an indeterminate space. Readers seeking practical advice on how to act when faced with an ethical issue might well scratch their heads.

CONTRAST, CONFLICT, AND CONVERGENCE

To illustrate how different the postmodern rhetorical approach to ethics is from the traditional approaches—whether practical, philosophical, or rhetorical—consider the contrasting treatment of ethics in two recent technical communication textbooks. Diana C. Reep's *Technical Communication, Principles, Strategies, and Readings* offers a two-page, sub-chapter discussion, "Writing Ethically," that appears in Chapter One, "Technical Writing on the Job." Ethics is defined as "a broad term that applies to a set of moral principles" that many companies apply to "a written corporate code of ethics" that "includes rules of ethical behavior" (p. 22). Working with ethics following this approach focuses on the potential actions an individual may take and tests the probable consequences of those actions against "rules of ethical behavior" specifically and "set(s) of moral principles" more generally to consider how "communication choices affect readers, the company, and other writers" (p. 23).

Reep cites the Ford Motor Company's "40-page publication called *Integrity*, which sets forth the company's ethical code: 'Integrity is never compromised'" (p. 22). She includes several readings to help students recognize the "moral principles" involved in ethical analysis and offers a checklist of 12 questions pertaining to potential ethical problems, for example, "Have you warned readers of all possible hazards in specific terms?" (p. 23). One of the readings is the Wicclair and Farkas (1984) essay discussed above, which insistently focuses on the product of "ethical reasoning," arguing that "typically, when faced with an ethical problem, we ask, 'What should I do?'" (in Reep, 1991, p. 605). Ethical analysis, as Reep presents it, focuses on the action itself, on "What should I do?" This is the approach of traditional, practical ethics.

In contrast, in the 1995 textbook *Technical Communication*, written by eight authors (Lay et al.), the word "ethics" does not appear in the index. Instead, "ethos" is listed, with references to 26 pages, 14 of which make up a subdiscussion of Chapter 5: "The Persuasive Nature of Technical Communication," titled "*Ethos*: Creating a Reliable, Trustworthy Persona" (p. 120). Here ethics becomes a part of the writing (and reading) process, most specifically part of the complex, shifting relationships that evolve in the matrix that brings together writer(s), text(s), and reader(s): "every document . . . is delivered by a created character, a persona, who may or may not have much in common with the real author of the piece" (p. 121). Two documents may "contain the same information, but their *ethos*—their ethical appeal—is very different" (121). And those "two documents" with "the same information" may also be read very differently (with very different ethical appeals understood) by any number of different readers. The treatment of ethics in *Technical Communication* is strongly rhetorical, with more than a hint of postmodern influence: Ethical analysis is part of the complicated mix of audience analysis and self-analysis that goes into creating "*the kind of persona that will be most persuasive in a given case*" (p. 123, original emphasis).

The conflict between traditional and postmodern rhetorical approaches to ethics is the principal topic of an article in which Arthur E. Walzer and Alan Gross (1994) analyze more than half a dozen articles that discuss the Challenger disaster. Walzer and Gross suggest that "the different explanations for the failure in deliberation [among the engineers who approved the launch] enact, in microcosm, the recent history of scholarship in rhetoric as applied to technical communication" (p. 420). Walzer and Gross "champion . . . Aristotle's *Rhetoric*, which . . . can explain what happened better than can the explanations that rely on either positivistic or postmodernist assumptions" (p. 420). Their analysis of the Challenger engineers' and managers' deliberations finds that "two types of knowledge were sought . . . technical knowledge and normative or ethical knowledge" (p. 427). The authors offer an Aristotelian critique of the positivist notion that the facts speak for themselves (a critique in which postmodern rhetoric joins) and the postmodern notion that "no 'facts' . . . speak for themselves; meaning comes only with interpretation" (p. 422). Walzer and Gross conclude that "both are in essence anti-rhetorical, finding either rhetoric unnecessary or persuasion impossible" (p. 426). To be "anti-rhetorical" is also to risk being anti-ethical, for Aristotelian rhetoric "helps find the best reasons for assent or dissent and the best reasons for decision and action," and "the discovery of this normative knowledge is rhetoric's traditional epistemic role" (p. 427). In this light, "the managers . . . who overruled their engineers stand condemned . . . for their failure to respect the deliberative process in reaching their managerial decision" (p. 430). Actions that work "to minimize deliberation" work also to "circumvent ethics" (p. 420). When postmodern analysis of the same deliberations finds that "the managers' and engineers' different roles resulted in different 'argumentation styles' that lead them initially to interpret the evidence differently" and concludes "that these differences made it *impossible* for the managers to appreciate the engineers' arguments" (p. 425), Walzer and Gross assert that it denies rhetoric's traditional, and true, role in developing normative, ethical knowledge.

Another historical example of the development of rhetorical ethics as applied to technical communication offers a good sampling of contrast and conflict among the different points of view. A "reprint issue" of *The Journal of Computer Documentation* (18:3, 1994) features an essay by Gregory Clark that appeared in the special issue on ethics Stephen Doheny-Farina edited for the *IEEE Transactions on Professional Communication* (30:3, 1987). In his original essay, Clark argued for a "rhetorical perspective on ethics" that would foster "ethical technical communication . . . as a cooperative exchange between the people who can provide information and the people who need to use it" (1987, p. 195). In the reprint issue, Clark's essay is the occasion for four rejoinders, with a fifth being an essay on Clark by Clark himself. All of the respondents' essays are interesting. The response of Michael Davis offers specific criticism from the perspective of practical, professional ethics.

Davis offers a pointedly definitional argument: "Clark's article is mistitled. Its subject is not ethics but how to define the competence of technical communicators" (p. 18). Davis criticizes Clark's definition of ethics as "over-broad . . . it does not limit ethics to morally permissible agreements (allowing for such travesties as torturer's ethics)" (p. 18). In addition, Clark's definition "makes every contract a code of ethics" (p. 18). Davis attacks the social constructionist basis of Clark's article, specifically Clark's definition of ethics, which Davis quotes as "'[any] agreement about what people are together attempting to accomplish (p. 190)'" (p. 18). For Davis, debate about ethics considers "the question of defining the *ethical* standards that should govern exercise of [professional] competence" (p. 17, original emphasis). This appeal to ethical standards signals Davis's definitional grounding in what we have called practical ethics. Davis's critique of the inclusiveness of Clark's definition of ethics points to a key problem with postmodern rhetorical ethics: the suggestion that all manner of contractual or consensual agreements—even the hazily implied and vaguely understood agreements whereby readers interpret texts and writers hope to reach readers through texts—should be understood as fundamentally ethical, or, in James Porter's words, the assertion that "ethics [may be understood] as a process of inquiry necessarily tied to the act of composing" (1993a, p. 208).

Clark, writing in response to his earlier essay, acknowledges that several of his positions have changed over the seven years since the reprinted essay was published, especially his earlier emphasis on "cooperative exchange" leading to consensus as the defining feature of ethical technical communication:

> people cooperate voluntarily but . . . what prompts the choice to cooperate is not so much their agreements about principles and purposes as their agreements about the necessity of working across present differences. (1994a, pp. 32–33)

All four of Clark's respondents point out that the cause of rhetoric and ethics is furthered more by debate, by differences, than by cooperation. Davis notes that "an organization is more likely to make the right decision when its decision-makers disagree" (p. 16). Arthur E. Walzer, another of Clark's respondents, writes that "rhetoric more often spurs contention than cooperation" (1994, p. 25), and, recalling his own Challenger essay, suggests that

> if the . . . deliberation [of the engineers and the managers] had involved more contentious debate and less cooperative silence, rhetoric would have had rein to play its traditional role of generating ideas. . . . The result in the Challenger case might have been a better decision than the one the managers made. (p. 31)

In another essay published in a different journal at about the same time on this same topic, Clark describes an "ethics that directs people to value their differences because that is what enables their cooperation as equals" (1994b, p. 62). Competing viewpoints must be recognized and attended to, but "how this concept might be put into practice in the work of technical communication," writes Clark, "I cannot claim the expertise to say" (1994a, p. 38).

Among the academic theorists there does not appear to be much convergence of opinion. But in the workplace, a process-oriented and rhetorically informed approach to work, and to the ethics of work, is emerging that holds some promise for bringing together the disparate perspectives examined above. The new notion of quality, as being inherent in a process rather than as a judgment rendered on a finished product, has led to understanding ethics as a function of the character, or ethos, that an individual brings to the collective enterprise. For example, in *Reengineering the Corporation*, Michael Hammer and James Champy (1993) propose radical changes for businesses that want to enter "the postindustrial business age" in which "corporations will be founded and built around the idea of reunifying . . . tasks into coherent business *processes*" (p. 2, original emphasis). To do this, corporations must "look across and beyond functional departments to processes" (p. 3). This shift results in a "radical change in the shape and character" of the organization (p. 4). One result of these changes is that formerly linear chains of command are now more webs or nets of interconnection (in many organizations made electronically imminent via e-mail), that have enormously complicated (or enriched) the rhetorical dynamics of corporate decisionmaking and action. In the words of Richard C. Freed (1993), the "new organization, a mosaic of structures, voices and texts, constantly changes not only internally but in its relationship to the decentered space of flows that characterizes the larger system of organized knowledge" (p. 211).

In this fluid redefinition of the corporate arena, ethics is tied to ethos—to character, beginning with the character of the individual. Hammer and Champy warn that "companies that reengineer must consider additional criteria in their hiring. It is no longer enough merely to look at prospective employees' education, training, and skills; their *character* becomes an issue as well" (p. 71, original emphasis). Writing specifically on technical communication, Charles P. Campbell (1995) suggests that if the problem of character reappears as a concern in the corporate quality movement, then technical communicators should consider what the rhetorical tradition has to say, not only about how to cater to an audience, but also about how to develop and project aspects of the author's character, or the character of the organization that the author represents. Campbell explores Aristotle's concept of ethos to discover more than a set of techniques for manipulating personae, "a richer concept, involving the individual in a deliberative community and thus having, as the Greek root implies, an ethical dimension as well as a transactional one" (in press). The emerging redefinition of quality in the workplace—as a process that evolves from the consciously ethical actions of individuals—may offer a structure for understanding the complex rhetoric of ethics in technical communication, in which individuals are called upon to act based on their personal ethical convictions, but those actions are also seen as the necessary catalysts for constructing the larger social organization that is the modern corporation. And if ethics are inherent in the quality of this corporate construction, so the theory goes, quality will be inherent in the corporate products.

CONCLUSION

The newer analyses of ethics and ethos, with their postmodern emphasis on social communities and the carefully articulated rhetoric that constructs them, should not be read as new, improved models of ethical analysis and behavior meant to replace old or outdated ethics based on established philosophical or moral principles. There are problems with the postmodern rhetorical approach. Carolyn R. Miller notes that

> . . . without idealist or realist foundations to justify belief and verify knowledge, discourse must draw exclusively upon the knowledge and beliefs that circulate within a human community . . . . A good reason is a reason that will be accepted as a good reason. It is this flattery, this vicious circularity . . . that has made of rhetoric so many enemies. . . . Such circularity troubles many . . . who believe it leads to self-righteousness, intolerance, and mass delusion (Auschwitz, for example, or Jonestown). (1993, p. 86)

When read out of context, the statement about persona and persuasion from the Lay et al. textbook's discussion of ethos, that the problem facing the professional writer is to create "*the kind of persona that will be most persuasive in a given case*" (123, original emphasis), risks the "vicious circularity" Miller warns against.

And there are other murmurs in the heartland. Stephen Katz considers ethics and ethos in technical writing in the context of the Holocaust in his analysis of a Nazi technical writer's memo on "the modification of vehicles not only to improve efficiency, but also to exterminate people" (p. 257). Katz (1992) reveals what he terms an "ethic of expediency . . . . [that is] symptomatic of a highly scientific, technological age" (p. 266). Dale L. Sullivan (1990) warns teachers of technical communication that by teaching "thought forms and discourse forms demanded by the workplace" (p. 375) they risk "defining technical communication . . . as the rhetoric appropriate for slaves—those barred from making decisions about ends, those whose decision-making authority is restricted to determining the most efficient means of obtaining predetermined ends" (p. 380). The ethic of expediency in the context Katz describes is clearly evil, as is the wretched state of existence of Sullivan's slaves. Katz suggests that by beginning to recognize "the essentially ethical character of all rhetoric, including our writing theory, pedagogy, and practice, and the role that expediency plays in rhetoric" (1992, p. 272), teachers of technical communication might resist the evil of the ethic of expediency. But it is hard to feel confident that these foundational evils are effectively countered without appealing to foundational ethical tenets. Markel's urging of Kant's second formulation of the categorical imperative "to treat ourselves and others not merely as means but also as ends" (1993, p. 81) seems very appropriate and very reasonable in these contexts.

Perhaps, finally, the ethics question is not central, it is centripetal, and therein lies much of the confusion of perspectives described in the pages above. Richard A. Lanham (1988) suggests this when he considers "The 'Q' Question," meaning Quintilian's query: "Is the Perfect Orator . . . a good *man* as well as a good orator?" (p. 653, original emphasis). That is, what are we to make of rhetoric, of language itself, when it is employed for evil purposes, when the art of writing well, in Lanham's words, turns "language, man's best friend, into a potential enemy" (653)? That, in short, is the ethical dilemma of the technical communicator, indeed, of any communicator.

Lanham considers different answers to the "Q" question, but he focuses in particular on Peter Ramus, the 16th century rhetorician, who answered the "Q" question by severing rhetoric from philosophy, whereby

> . . . rhetoric and grammar thus become cosmetic arts, and speech—and of course writing—along with them. Reason breaks free of speech and takes on a Platonic self-standing freedom . . . breaking rhetoric down the middle, . . . [reversing] the centripetal flow the rhetorical paideia had built into its heart. . . . From now on, ethics would have a special "department," religion first and then philosophy, where it could be studied in and for itself. (pp. 656–657)

One result of the Ramist redefinition of rhetoric is to "render problematic the relation of thought to action" (p. 657).

The heterologue of voices we hear when we read what is being written today on ethics and technical communication illustrates the centripetal nature of rhetorical deliberation and the possibility that all those concerned with technical communication are learning to revalue what Lanham describes as the "mixture of play, game, and purpose [that] was the characteristic product, if not always the avowed purpose, of the rhetorical" (p. 691). But in the ethical arena, the problem of action remains. Rhetorical play with the "mediating questions" that Walzer called attention to in 1989 has perhaps become oddly Ramist in its self-fascination. Academic theorists may have developed so many intriguing ways to analyze what may prompt a technical communicator to act in a situation that has strong ethical consequences, that, like Hamlet (himself caught in Ramus's trap), they risk leading those who seek to act ethically into being caught up in the intrigue; they may neglect to act at all, or, finally, act rashly when unforeseen circumstances force an outcome. Perhaps the new quality movement in industry, with its emphasis on continuous improvement through continuous dialogue, debate, and action, may offer a venue for bringing together the very different analytical approaches to ethics described in this essay in a way that will promote vigorous ethical deliberation and decisive ethical action.

ACKNOWLEDGMENTS

Thanks to my colleague at UNM, Charles Paine, for bringing Richard A. Lanham's article, "The 'Q' Question" to my attention. Thanks also to Professor Barbara Mirel of DePaul University for leading me to *The Journal of Computer Documentation* reprint issue on ethics. Thanks also to M. Jimmie Killingsworth of Texas A & M University for his permission to use, in revised form, some of the text from our coauthored introduction to the special issue on ethics of *IEEE Transactions on Professional Communication* (September 1995).

REFERENCES

Beene, L. & White, P. (Eds.). (1988). *Solving problems in technical writing.* New York: Oxford University Press.

Bizzell, P. & Herzberg, B. (1990). *The rhetorical tradition: Readings from classical time to the present.* New York: St. Martins

Blyler, N. R. & Thralls, C. (1993). *Professional writing: The Social Perspective.* Newbury Park, CA: Sage.

Brockmann, R. J. & Rook, F. (Eds.). (1989). *Technical communication and ethics.* Washington, DC: Society for Technical Communication.

Campbell, C. P. (1995). *Ethos: character, persona, purpose, and ethics in technical writing.* IEEE Transactions on Professional Communication, 38.

Clark, G. (1987). *Ethics in technical communication: A rhetorical perspective.* IEEE Transactions on Professional Communication, *30,* 190–195.

Clark, G. (1994a). Rescuing the discourse of community. *College English, 45,* 61–74.

Clark, G. (1994b). Professional ethics from an academic perspective. *Journal of Computer Documentation, 18,* 32–38.

Connors, R.J., Ede, L.S. & Lunsford, A.A. (Eds.). (1984). *Essays on classical rhetoric and modern discourse.* Carbondale, IL: Southern Illinois University Press.

Cox, B. (1993, April). Good ethics: Companies emphasize standards in hard times with sidebar story, provisions of a typical ethics policy. *Albuquerque Journal, Business Outlook* [insert] *12,* 16–17.

Doheny-Farina, S. (1987). Legal and ethical aspects of technical communication: A special issue. *IEEE Transactions on Professional Communication, 30,* 119–120.

Doheny-Farina, S. (1989). Ethics and technical communication. In C.H. Sides (Ed.), *Technical and business communication: Bibliographic essays for teachers and corporate trainers* (pp. 53–73). Urbana, IL: NCTE.

Enos, T. (1990). "An eternal golden braid": Rhetor as audience, audience as rhetor. In G. Kirsch & D. H. Roen (Eds.), *A sense of audience in written communication* (pp. 99–114). Newbury Park, CA: Sage.

Enos, T. & Brown, S.C. (Eds.). (1993). *Defining the new rhetorics.* Newbury Park, CA: Sage.

Fearing, B. & Sparrow, W. K. (Eds.). (1989). *Technical writing: Theory and practice.* New York: Modern Language Association.

Freed, R. C. (1993). Postmodern practice: Perspectives and prospects. N.R. Blyler & C. Thralls *Professional writing: The Social Perspective* (pp. 196–214). Newbury Park, CA: Sage.

Hammer, M. & Champy, J. (1993). *Reengineering the corporation: A manifesto for business revolution.* New York: Harper.

Johnson, N. (1984). Ethos and the aims of rhetoric. In R.J. Connors, L.S. Ede & A.A. Lunsford (Eds.). *Essays on classical rhetoric and modern discourse* (pp. 98–114). Carbondale, IL: Southern Illinois University Press.

Katz, S. B. (1992). The ethic of expediency: Classical rhetoric, technology, and the Holocaust. *College English, 54,* 255–275.

Kirsch, G. & Roen, D. H. (Eds.). (1990). *A sense of audience in written communication.* Newbury Park, CA: Sage.

Lanham, R. A. (1988). The "Q" question. *South Atlantic Quarterly, 87,* 653–700.

Markel, M. H. (1993). An ethical imperative for technical communicators. *IEEE Transactions on Professional Communication, 36,* 81–86.

Martin, W. & Sanders, S.P. (1994). Ethics, audience, and the writing process: Bringing public policy issues into the classroom. *Technical Communication Quarterly, 3,* 147–163.

Michaelson, H. (1990). How an author can avoid the pitfalls of practical ethics. *IEEE Transactions on Professional Communication, 33,* 58–61.

Miller, C. R. (1985). Invention in technical and scientific discourse. In M.G. Moran & D. Journet (Eds.), *Research in technical communication: A bibliographic sourcebook* (pp. 117–162). Westport, CT: Greenwood.

Miller, C.R. (1989). What's practical about technical writing? In B. Fearing, B. & W.K. Sparrow (Eds.), *Technical writing: Theory and practice* (pp. 14–24). New York: Modern Language Association.

Miller, C.R. (1993). Rhetoric and community: The problem of the one and the many. In T. Enos & S.C. Brown (Eds.), *Defining the new rhetorics* (pp. 79–94). Newbury Park, CA: Sage.

Moran, M. G. & Journet, D. (Eds.). (1985). *Research in technical communication: A bibliographic sourcebook.* Westport, CT: Greenwood.

Mund, L. & Perez, G.(1992). Developing usable ethics. *Intercom, 38,* 6–7.

Porter, J. E. (1993a). Developing a postmodern ethics of rhetoric and composition. In T. Enos & S.C. Brown (Eds.), *Defining the new rhetorics* (pp. 207–226). Newbury Park, CA: Sage.

Porter, J.E. (1993b). The role of law, policy, and ethics in corporate composing: toward a practical ethics for professional writing. In N.R. Blyler. & C. Thralls (Eds.), *Professional writing: The Social Perspective* (pp. 128–143). Newbury Park, CA: Sage.

Richardson, J.E. (Ed.). (1989). To the reader. *Annual Editions: Business Ethics 89/90.* Guilford, CT: Dushkin.

Richardson, J.E. (1989). Ethics in business. *Annual Editions, 4.*

Rubens, P. M. (1985). Technical and scientific writing and the humanities. In M.G. Moran & D. Journet (Eds.), *Research in technical communication: A bibliographic sourcebook* (pp. 3–23). Westport, CT: Greenwood.

Sanders, S.P. (1988). How can technical writing be persuasive? In L. Beene & P. White (Eds.), *Solving problems in technical writing* (pp. 55–78). New York: Oxford University Press.

Sides, C. H. (Ed.). (1989). *Technical and business communication: Bibliographic essays for teachers and corporate trainers.* Urbana, IL: NCTE.

Sturges, D. L. (1992). Overcoming the ethical dilemma: Communication decisions in the ethic ecosystem. *IEEE Transactions on Professional Communication, 35,* 44–50.

Sullivan, D.L. (1990). Political-ethical implications of defining technical communication as a practice. *Journal of Advanced Composition, 10,* 375–386.

Walzer, A.E. (1989a). The ethics of false implicature in technical and professional writing courses. *Journal of Technical Writing and Communication,* 149–160.

Walzer, A.E. (1989b). Professional ethics, codes of conduct, and the society for technical communication. In R.J. Brockmann & F. Rook (Eds.), *Technical communication and ethics* (pp. 101–105). Washington, DC: Society for Technical Communication.

Walzer, A.E. (1994). Ethical norms for technical communication: Plato, Aristotle, and Clark's "rhetorical perspective." *Journal of Computer Documentation, 18,* 25–31.

Walzer, A. E. & Gross, A. (1994). Positivists, postmodernists, Aristotelians, and the Challenger disaster. *College English, 56,* 420–433.

Wicclair, M. R. & Farkas, D.K. (1984). Ethical reasoning in technical communication: A practical framework. Technical Communication, 31, 15–19. Reprinted in D.C. Reep, *Technical writing: Principles, strategies, and readings.* (2nd Ed.). Boston, MA: Allyn & Bacon.

Yoos, G.E. (1979). A revision of the concept of ethical appeal. *Philosophy and Rhetoric, 12,* 41–58.

Yoos, G. E. (1984). Rational appeal and the ethics of advocacy. In R.J. Connors, L.S. Ede & A.A. Lunsford (Eds.), *Essays on classical rhetoric and modern discourse* (pp. 82–97). Carbondale, IL: Southern Illinois University Press.

8

FROM SCHROEDINGER'S CAT TO FLAMING ON THE INTERNET: EXPLORING GENDER'S RELEVANCE FOR TECHNICAL/PROFESSIONAL COMMUNICATION

Linda M. LaDuc

University of Massachusetts, Amherst

INTRODUCTION

Like the traditional "jack-in-the-box," gender usually remains hidden; you know it's in there, but when it pops out it's always a bit of a surprise. Erwin Schroedinger's famous 1935 thought puzzle in quantum physics, an academic jack-in-the-box in the form of an experiment, illustrates how critical elements such as gender can remain hidden in fields of expertise.

In Schroedinger's classic conundrum, a live cat is placed in a box from which it cannot escape and into which no one can see. A device will trigger either poison or food into the box with a 50/50 probability. The trigger goes off after a random period of time, and the cat either dies (or not) or eats (or not). It's impossible for physicists to know what happened until someone opens the box, measures and observes the cat's state, and informs others of the results. Schroedinger constructed this problem to demonstrate to the physics community how human observation is inextricably tied to our understanding of scientific phenomena. Upon analyzing the problem, we are apt to conclude that observation "determines" outcomes, yet we cannot "know" objectively (Wheatley, 1994). Often overlooked in considerations of this puzzle, however, are the related effects of power and expertise in bringing about experimental results—and the very real consequences of the physicists' practices for the cat.

In the ensuing decades since Schroedinger articulated his puzzle, physicists and philosophers of science (e.g., Kuhn, 1970) have come to understand how scientific knowledge is a result of socially created methods and frameworks. In tandem with this development, in the field of professional communication we now largely eschew the likelihood that there is scientific "truth" to be conveyed without human intervention. Having also redefined our field as concerned with social action, at least since Carolyn Miller (1979) criticized the "windowpane" theory of language on which Western positivist science has long relied, we have further admitted the potentially wide variability of interpretation and the necessity for considering multiple viewpoints. Despite this philosophical maturity, we have only just begun to understand gender complexities as they are implicated in our practices. Thus, this essay calls for more attention to gender, and from a perspective that holds gender to have such significance that it would be as unwise to relegate it to a minor variable as it would be to ignore its role.

In this essay I will offer definitions of gender, briefly survey relevant scholarship, review knowledge to be gained by attending to gender, caution about negative consequences of ignoring or suppressing gender, and pinpoint trends in gender scholarship that are increasingly relevant to technical communication.

WHAT IS GENDER? WHY IS IT A CONCERN FOR TECHNICAL COMMUNICATORS?

The Origins of Gender as a Concept

Never uni-dimensional or tidy (it is cross-cut by other concerns that may assume more or less significance depending on the situation), gender is nevertheless highly salient for human beings: In its reproductive role it is as central to our lives as are movement, growth, and nourishment. In addition, however, because gender features as part of a constructed "social system of power relations," to focus on gender is also to analyze the social consequences of differences that, while originating in sexual reproductive physiology, are massively transformed by culture into a wide variety of roles, functions, and forms (Langellier, Carter, and Hantzis, 1993, p. 95).

The concept of gender was originally conceived as a rhetorical strategy to circumvent the tendency to treat relations between "the sexes" as part of a "natural," physiologically determined order (and thus as normal or unproblematic). Thus, an early and strong tendency to look for "sex differences" in research was offset by a more or less socio-political decision to focus on "gender differences" and to define sexual identity to be the result of social and cultural construction (Oakley, 1979). We are now at a point where scholars have established a wider range of gender-related issues, some unthinkable even a decade ago, issues that have greatly complicated our understanding of gender.

We know that gender variation occurs along a socially constructed continuum, the anchors of which are prototypical categories of female and male, feminine and masculine, although we know little about what drives people to categorize and to maintain, often rigidly, gendered distinctions when they have no immediately apparent relevance (Rosch and Lloyd, 1978). We know that social practices extend, distort, and even change sexual behavior as humans develop norms and patterns of interacting in culture; that cultures demand and constrain sex and gender practices; and that culture surrounds, permeates, shapes, and is shaped by our work practices. Despite all this knowledge, however, and our awareness of the lacunae, we have hesitated to fully investigate how sex and gender are intertwined with professional communication.

When not reflected upon, gender relations can cloud over other communication-related variables, obscuring them by acting as what Kenneth Burke (1961) called "terministic screens"—filters through which we interpret our worlds and our places in these worlds. Thus, as gendered beings, we see through the lens of gender; as experts, we ought to acknowledge this fact, and thus analyze and understand gender both as obstacle and as interpretive scheme. Framed in this manner, the concept of gender can help us to uncover differences and pinpoint problem areas, direct us to investigate why such differences arise, and encourage us to formulate accounts of the dynamics of gender relationships as they emerge in our practice. For just these reasons, technical communicators have begun to pay attention to gender, as several articles and three recent special issues of journals attest (See *JBTC* 5 [1991]; *IEEETPC* 35 [1992]; *TCQ* 3 [1994]).

The Emergence of Gender as a Concern in Technical Communication

Gender has emerged as a prominent concern across most disciplines and fields of expertise, largely as a result of feminist politics. In some fields where considerable resistance to change developed (e.g., philosophy), gender scholarship has been ignored or contested. For the most part, however, such negative reactions have not characterized gender's entrance into the field of technical communication because in our field gender has come to our attention as one of many practical variables such as race, class, and ethnicity with which we need to be concerned as communicators. We are, at our roots, rhetoricians; we know we work with the probable, the social, the relational, and we know that gender is somehow implicated in all of this and that we must respond to it as a new challenge. *How* we respond, however, matters significantly.

Several streams of scholarship have been incorporated into knowledge about gender in technical communication. Some early articles issued directly from research in technical communication and were both practical and well focused. Examples include J. M. Stalnaker's 1941 study of sex differences in the ability to write. Stalnaker reported that girls showed a superior ability in writing English, an early positive finding in marked contrast to reports from most research during that time. (For example, Bernard Bass reports significant bias in much early management research, the result of which has been to reinforce men's superiority [1981]). In fact, even before some ground-breaking studies of women and language (e.g., Robin Lakoff, 1975), Janet Emig (1971) had discussed gender differences in writing modes in her study *The Composing Processes of 12th Graders.* As in Emig's case, reported gender-related observations in technical communication research were usually but one feature of studies whose focus and intent were to assess the effectiveness of discourse generally. Beginning in the 1980s and 1990s, however, writers started to address issues of sexist language, in response to feminist political efforts across all disciplines, but couched in field-pragmatic terms. For example, Duane Roen and Donna Johnson (1992) discussed features of complimenting in association with male/female language use in relation to the effectiveness of written discourse, and Sherry Dell (1990) issued a practitioner-based call for technical communicators to promote equality through technical writing by avoiding sexist language, as a natural concomitant of the requirement for precise language.

Also appearing at about this time were articles addressing gender issues in the context of other concerns, such as collaboration or nonverbal communication. Increasingly, such articles reflected business communication problems and issues in addition to more traditional issues and emphases in composition and in technical and scientific writing. Deborah Bosley and Meg Morgan (1991), for example, introduced gender as a concern in designing effective technical communication teams. Gerald Graham, Jeanne Unruh, and Paul Jennings (1991) discussed perceptions of women as better decoders and encoders of nonverbal cues in the context of organizations. Margaret Ann Baker (1991) offered a model for reducing gender bias in managerial communication, and Marlene Fine (1991) suggested considering gender in terms of multiculturalism in the workplace. Some studies, such as Claire Anderson and Giovanna Impeira's (1992) photo analysis of male and female portrayals in corporate annual reports, have begun to reflect an even more explicit focus on gender.

Reflecting the increasing range of issues in which gender figures for technical/professional communicators, scholars in technical communication have also mined a second stream of gender scholarship for technical communication: research consisting of studies that explicitly focus on gender but that have issued largely from other fields, primarily interpersonal and nonverbal communication, sociology, and social and cognitive psychology, but also reader response research by feminist literary scholars, small group and organizational communication studies, and linguistics. Mary Lay (1994) offers a definitive survey of such studies, articulating their value for professional communication. In "The Value of Gender Studies to Professional Communication Research," Lay links gender and writing, speaking, language choice, visual communication, collaboration, reading, management, and a host of other concerns in a tour de force that leaves no ground for not including gender as a variable in professional communication. Having surveyed two decades of gender-related scholarship, she goes further by asking how we can make accessible to both women and men a wide range of communication strategies to meet the demands of the next century—once again exemplifying the kind of balanced gender-related thinking that has prevailed in technical communication.

Additional examples of useful gender scholarship also appeared in the December special issue of *IEEETPC* 1992. In the editor's introduction to that issue, Beverly Sauer (1992b) focuses on the idea of women and gender difference in the science and technology workplace, pointing to potential connections between gender and user interface design, documentation, visual formatting, hypertext development, task analysis, and encoding and retrieval of information, to name just a few topics. From Maria de Armas Ladd and Marion Tangum's (1992) exploration of culture and gender to Sauer's analysis of gender bias in the concept of rationality as it guides specific engineering practices (1992a), these heuristic articles reflected a growing awareness that not attending to gender can lead to certain, sometimes harmful, consequences.

A third stream of gender-related research that contributes to professional communication is explicitly feminist scholarship. This stream of contributions can be characterized as more politically committed than discourse studies tangentially addressing gender, or gender-focused research efforts in which gender is treated as a (sometimes minor) variable. Despite its more overtly political aims, however, as contrasted with feminist research and writing in other fields such as literary studies, feminist scholarship concerned with science and technology has not taken as polemical a tone and stance; further, it has not confined itself to any predominant perspective within feminist thought (such as liberal or radical feminism). Instead, it has demonstrated greater awareness of the needs of the various technical audiences it addresses as well as of the complexity of the issues involved.

To this stream belong works by feminist critics of science and technology (Donna Haraway, 1991; Sandra Harding, 1987; Evelyn Keller, 1983), feminist scholarship aimed at teaching technology in gender-affirming ways (Joan Rothschild, 1988; Judy Wajcman, 1991), and scholarship that seeks to affirm feminist theory and praxis as useful to technical communication (Mary Lay, 1991; Jo Allen, 1991). Recent research in this stream is exemplified by two special issues of key journals devoted to bringing in feminist theory and practice to technical communication (*Journal of Business and Technical Communication* and *Technical Communication Quarterly*). The aim of these research efforts has been to explore the direct contributions of women to the field, define feminist approaches to research and how these relate to professional communication, and analyze relations between gender and social and communication practices in order both to illuminate implicit relations of power and to resist and change harmful practices that are arguably the result of gendered power relations (LaDuc & Goldrick-Jones, 1994).

Mary Lay has been at the forefront of much of this scholarship, demonstrating that feminist theory is largely congruent with the aims of technical communicators in its concern for audience, its emphasis on cooperation and collaboration as processes intrinsic to practice, and its attention to situation and context (1991). Other feminist scholars have contributed by attempting to rewrite the history of technology to include women and women's technologies (Helen Deiss Irvin, 1982), or by studying ways that technology affects women and organizations (Jan Zimmerman, 1983). Still others have analysized the relationship of human beings and technology, especially gender problems in new "cyberspace" forums (Susan Herring, in press).

WHAT WE HAVE LEARNED—
AND WHAT WE NEED TO CONSIDER...

As is clear from this small number of studies, technical communication has made progress in acknowledging and analyzing gender's significance, but much remains to be done. We have learned from the sex-difference and gender-difference research of the 1970s and 1980s that differences do abound—in language, learning styles, writing characteristics, reader responses, visual perception habits, and so on. From research in the 1990s we have learned that gender issues are embedded in situations in ways that are hard to decipher. We will probably never know whether gender differences originate in physiology or in culture, but we have largely come to agree that regardless of origins, gender shapes and is shaped by culture and by our cultural practices. In particular, we have come to understand that as a basic and enduring constituent of human identity and of human action (Wood, 1993), gender affects all we do and say communicatively; this understanding is especially relevant to professional communicators.

However, despite the pragmatic tendency to consider gender as part of audience analysis and as the province of rhetoric and communication, and despite the prevalence of women in technical communication (Dragga, 1993) (and the attendant concern about women's advancement and thus about gender), technical communicators have not yet fully explored how gender is intertwined in professional practices, organizations, interactions with students, processes of communicating information, and the products designed and constructed for readers and clients. Some of the consequences of these gaps in knowledge are just now emerging.

Consequences of Not Attending to Gender

Gender is almost the first information we try to gather about a person when we meet face to face, and it has been demonstrated to be a deep concern and problem for people in most everyday social interactions (Tannen, 1990). Not to know someone's gender can be a "disequilibriating" experience because gender structures provide a kind of certainty for interaction, even if we have to grandly generalize, categorize, and even stereotype to arrive at such certainties.

The centrality of gender to both our communication and our psychological well-being is one reason feminist (and sympathetic) literary and linguistic scholars have fought to rid professional language of the generic "he" and of derogatory or sexist language. That generations of women had to read literature, history, and politics "as men" occurred at a significant psychic cost for women individually; for women to read themselves as negated and derogated was destructive to women's identities as human beings; for men to read themselves as absolutely powerful in language was corrupting to men's identities as well. We recognize these gendered consequences now, but we have not yet explored a multitude of other gendered practices that daily affect us. Just as clothes are constructed to project gender difference, cars are designed to project gendered images, and organizations are organized according to historical gendered preferences, so too we use gender, often unconsciously, as a conceptual scheme to assign meaning and value to our lives and our work.

Many problems emerge precisely because we use gender to make sense of large domains of experience, as Beverly Sauer (1994) demonstrated in her critique of sexually loaded metaphors in James Paradis' analysis of the problem of expert knowledge in technical operators' manuals for the stud-gun, a tool commonly used in the construction industry. Sauer observes that while also a subject of humor, sexually loaded metaphors and assumptions in the discourse of science and technology can lead to less effective documentation and to users' taking unnecessary risks. Alternatively, Susan Ross (1994) points to how technical communicators working on environmental projects who do not understand how gender may be implicated in alternative world views of groups involved in remedial action plans risk producing less effective communication for their clients. Explorations such as these are now increasing in number and quality, but more are needed. In addition, there is a need for studies that focus on specific technical communication problems, such as gender differences in learning approaches, in navigating hypertext, or in decoding icons (as Deborah Bosley [1994] did, for example, in her research into verbal and visual representation).

Because gendered schemes and distinctions reflect power relations, in ways that either dominate or enable, gender and "engendered structures" are constantly in the process of being created, maintained, and challenged by individuals, collectivities, and communities (Wolffensperger, 1991). Sometimes what seem to be harmless manifestations of gender, however, can have far-reaching negative effects. A recent and prominent example of one such potentially negative manifestation is the phenomenon of "flaming," which has emerged as a prominent feature of computer communication on the Internet.

Flaming and Its Consequences

"Flaming" has been defined as attack-like exchanges in which participants assault each other verbally. Such exchanges have increasingly proliferated in certain Internet forums (e.g., Usenet) and on occasion have come to dominate conversational interactions in those forums. Some researchers have become concerned about flaming and have speculated that "flame wars" are a masculine-gendered communication phenomenon. Susan Herring (in press), for example, concluded that young men who are the most frequent "flamers" are demonstrating a different politeness convention than the majority of women who communicate on the Internet.

Despite the fact that computer-mediated communication would appear to be theoretically accessible by all who know how to use the technology, gender politics or styles of communication emerge here as patterns of display and reaction. It may be, in fact, because the medium is gender-neutral that such displays occur: As in face-to-face communication, some of us want that critical gender information, or are unable or unwilling to submerge it when it is part of an individual style. Regardless of its cause, feminist scholars assert that flaming is a cogent example of how problems of gender, power, and authority are embedded in social action in cyberculture as elsewhere (see Balsamo, 1993).

Whether one takes a feminist position or not, however, flaming has consequences, just as physicists' practices have certain consequences for Shroedinger's cat. Episodes of flaming caused some bulletin board facilitators to moderate usage, to set rules, to drop users; some users objected, dropped their subscriptions, or claimed to be intimidated. What is of critical concern to technical/professional communicators is that some interactants are displaying gender and dominating discourse—and this communication display is an exigency for communicative action. Technical communicators use electronic media in expert practice; they produce documents for such uses; they are concerned about audiences' responses in this media set, as in others. Reflective practice calls for an investigation of the potential for gendered effects even when such effects cannot be seen clearly.

TRENDS AND FUTURE DEVELOPMENTS

Other gender-related matters of consequence for technical communication practice arise daily, as we reflect on the processes in which we participate and the products we produce. One trend in technical communication has been to investigate workplace processes such as collaboration to try to understand the role of gender in forming and maintaining writing groups or in managing communication teams. Another trend has been to investigate specific communication phenomenoma, such as flaming or virtual reality products. Still another, and one I especially think we need to engage in more often, is to investigate how gender plays a part in users' and readers' responses to communication products. For example, in terms of usability one may ask such questions as the following:

- Do women and men respond similarly to on-line help systems, or are there differences that might variably affect performance?

- Are there visual cues, colors, shapes, or processing patterns that vary according to gender—in processing information as well as in displaying information?
- Do people demonstrate gender differences in the way they navigate hypertext-based applications, and does this matter?
- How and where is gender implicated in legal writing? In medical writing? In other kinds of writing?

It seems obvious to state that men and women differ in certain physiological characteristics, but some of these differences may have relevance (as do color-blindness and visual phoria in computer-user screen interaction), and to some extent such factors must be accounted for in document and screen design. If we do not "interrogate" users to find out about such possible differences, we may assume all is well, when instead there are hidden obstacles to communication—or to learning.

Thus, in addition to usability concerns, there are instructional concerns:

- To what extent do we need to take gender differences in learning style into account as we design user interfaces and on-line instructional programs?
- How do we address gender concerns in teaching technical communication—at what points should we bring in relevant research and how can we shape problems that students can use to develop their thinking about gender issues?
- In international contexts, how is gender apt to vary as a factor by which to analyze audience, purpose, the appropriateness of content?

These are but a few of the many questions to be asked in the next decade of technical communication research.

CONCLUSION

Technical communication is a profession that, because of its relationship to technology, can greatly affect the social construction of work-related assumptions, organizational structures and plans for action, the implementation of specific technologies, and even gender roles and functions. One needs only to think about the effect that linotype technology has had on women: Many young women were first brought into business as linotype operators and then as typists. A century later, women dominate technical writing. Gendered actions, gendered consequences.

Gender as a topic of major interest has emerged alongside the developing understanding of technical communication; it has also emerged along with more encompassing concerns about the increasingly critical role of technical communicators in the creation of effective communication processes and products in the context of international relations and of intercultural communication (see the essay by Thrush, this collection). In a global context, it is even clearer that technical communication is a social practice, as David Dobrin (1983), Lester Faigley (1985), and James Zappen (1989) have all suggested.

Dale Sullivan (1990), in particular, has argued for the need to admit and explore political and ethical concerns and objections connected to technical reading and writing practices. Because gender relations are seldom symmetrical (some concerns may regularly prevail over others, whether due to rules, resources, or variable access to resources), and since such asymmetries are at the heart of differences in power relations, ethical questions that include gender concerns must be considered to be questions of power as well. Furthermore, because technical communicators work in a domain of rhetoric, they need not only to be sensitive to concerns about gender in connection to issues of audience, but to actively explore such concerns.

Scholarship and teaching have become more sophisticated both conceptually and methodologically, progressing from uncovering how gender politics limit and oppress women to investigating how gender, as a complex of social, cultural, and psychological phenomena attached to sex, affects us all. Technical communication scholars, feminist theorists, and gender researchers have attempted to uncover hidden gender assumptions in work practices, silent power structures that limit practice, and models of reasoning that sustain outdated theoretical frameworks. As professional communication becomes ever more important to a world in need of translation of knowledge from scientific domains into practical applications that affect people's lives, questions of gender must be addressed at the very least to avoid disadvantaging women in the profession, in the classroom, and in the workplace. At the most, questions of gender may lead to a rethinking of professional communication practices that disadvantage the general public.

In this matter, we are all like Schroedinger's cats.

REFERENCES

Allen, J. (1991). Gender issues in technical communication studies: An overview of the implications for the profession, research, and pedagogy. *Journal of Business and Technical Communication, 5*, 371–392.

Anderson, C.J. & Impeira, G. (1992). The corporate annual report: A photo analysis of male and female portrayals. *Journal of Business Communication, 29,* 113–118.

Baker, M.A. (1991). Reciprocal accommodation: A model for reducing gender bias in managerial communication. *Journal of Business Communication, 28,* 113–130.

Balsamo, A. (1993). Feminism for the incurably informed. In M. Dery (Ed.), *Flame wars: The discourse of cyberculture. South Atlantic Quarterly, 92,* 681–712.

Bass, B.M. (1981). *Stogdill's handbook of leadership.* New York: Macmillan.

Bosley, D.S. (1994). Feminist theory, audience analysis, and verbal and visual representation in a technical communication writing task. *Technical Communication Quarterly, 3,* 293–308.

Bosley, D.S. & Morgan, M. (1991). Designing effective technical communication teams. *Technical Communication, 38,* 504–512.

Burke, K. (1961). *A Rhetoric of Motives.* Berkeley, CA: University of California Press.

Dell, S. (1990). Promoting equality of the sexes through technical writing. *Technical Communication, 37,* 90–91.

Dobrin, D. (1983). What's technical about technical writing? In P.R. Anderson, R.J. Brockmann & C.R. Miller (Eds.), *New essays in technical and scientific communication: Research, theory, practice* (pp. 227–250). Farmingdale, NY: Baywood.

Dragga, S. (1993). Women and the profession of technical writing. *Journal of Business and Technical Commmunication, 7,* 312–321.

Emig, J. (1971). *The composing processes of 12th graders.* Urbana, IL: NCTE.

Faigley, L. (1985). Nonacademic writing: The social perspective. In L. Odell & D. Goswami (Eds.), *Writing in nonacademic settings* (pp. 231–248). New York: Guilford.

Fine, M.G. (1991). New voices in the workplace: Research directions in multi-cultural communication. *Journal of Business Communication, 28,* 259–276.

Graham, G.H., Unruh, J. & Jennings, P. (1991). The impact of non-verbal communication in organizations: A survey of perceptions. *Journal of Business Communication, 28,* 45–62.

Haraway, D.J. (1991). *Simians, cyborgs, and women: the reinvention of nature.* New York: Routledge.

Harding, S. (1987). Introduction: Is there a feminist method? In S. Harding (Ed.), *Feminism and methodology* (pp. 1–14). Bloomington, IN: Indiana University Press.

Herring, S. (in press). Politeness in computer culture: Why women thank and men flame. In Bucholtz, M. & Sutton, L. (Eds.), *Communication across cultures: proceedings of the third Berkeley women and language conference.* Berkeley, CA: Berkeley Women and Language Group.

Irvin, H.D. (1982).The machine in utopia: Shaker women and technology. In J. Rothschild (Ed.), *Women, technology and innovation.* New York: Pergamon.

Keller, E.F. (1983). *A feeling for the organism: The life and work of Barbara McClintock.* San Francisco, CA: Freeman.

Kuhn, T. (1970). *The structure of scientific revolutions.* Chicago, IL: University of Chicago Press.

Ladd, M. & Tangum, M. (1992). What difference does inherited difference make? Exploring culture and gender in scientific and technical professions. *IEEETPC, 35,* 183–190.

LaDuc, L. & Goldrick-Jones, A. (1994). The critical eye, the gendered lens, and "situated insights": Feminist contributions to professional communication. *Technical Communication Quarterly, 3,* 245–256.

Lakoff, R. (1975). *Language and woman's place.* New York: Harper & Row.

Langellier, K.M., Carter, K. & Hantzis, D. (1993). Performing differences: feminism and performance studies. In S.P. Bowen & N. Wyatt (Eds.), *Transforming visions: Feminist critiques in communication studies* (pp. 87–124). Cresskill, NJ: Hampton.

Lay, M.M. (1991). Feminist theory and the redefinition of technical communication. *Journal of Business and Technical Communication, 5,* 348–370.

Lay, M.M. (1994). The value of gender studies to professional communication research. *Journal of Business and Technical Communication, 8,* 58–90.

Miller, C.R. (1979). A humanistic rationale for technical writing. *College English, 40,* 610–617.

Oakley, A. (1979). *Sex, gender and society.* New York: Harper and Row.

Roen, D.H. & Johnson, D.M. (1992). Perceiving effectiveness of written discourse through gender lenses: The contribution of complimenting. *Written Communication, 9,* 435–464.

Rosch, E. & Lloyd, B.B. (Eds.). (1978). *Cognition and categorization.* Hillsdale, NJ: Erlbaum.

Ross, S.M. (1994). A feminist perspective on technical communicative action: Exploring how alternative worldviews affect environmental remediation efforts. *Technical Communication Quarterly, 3,* 325–342.

Rothschild, J. (1988). *Teaching technology from a feminist perspective.* New York: Pergamon.

Sauer, B.A. (1992a). The engineer as rational man: The problem of imminent danger in a non-rational environment. *IEEE Transactions in Professional Communication, 35,* 242–249.

Sauer, B.A. (1992b). Introduction: Gender and technical communication. *IEEE Transactions in Professional Communication, 35,* 193–195.

Sauer, B.A. (1994). Sexual dynamics of the profession: Articulating the ecriture masculine of science and technology. *Technical Communication Quarterly, 3,* 309–324.

Stalnaker, J.M. (1941). Sex differences in the ability to write. *School and Society, 54,* 532–535.

Sullivan, D. (1990). Political-ethical implications of defining technical communication as a practice. *Journal of Advanced Composition, 10,* 375–386.

Tannen, D. (1990). *You don't know what I mean: Women and men in conversation.* New York: Morrow.

Wajcman, J. (1991). *Feminism confronts technology.* University Park, PA: Penn State University Press.

Wheatley, M.J. (1994). *Leadership and the new science.* San Francisco, CA: Berrett-Koehler.

Wolffensperger, J. (1991). Engendered structure: Giddens and the conceptualization of gender. In K. Davis, M. Leijenaar & J. Oldersma (Eds.), *The gender of power* (pp. 87–110). London: Sage.

Wood, J. (1993). Enlarging conceptual boundaries: A critique of research in interpersonal communication. In S.P. Bowen & N. Wyatt (Eds.), *Transforming visions: Feminist critiques in communication studies* (pp. 19–50). Cresskill, NJ: Hampton.

Zappen, J.P. (1989). The discourse community in scientific and technical communication: Institutional and social views. *Journal of Technical Writing and Communication, 19,* 1–11.

Zimmerman, J. (Ed.). (1983). *The technological woman: Interfacing with tomorrow.* New York: Praeger.

9

LOCATING COLLABORATION: REFLECTIONS, FEATURES, AND INFLUENCES

Rebecca E. Burnett

Iowa State University

Christianna I. White

Iowa State University

Ann Hill Duin

University of Minnesota

Ames, IA, Riverside Drive...The teapot is still half full of orange ginger mint tea. Pieces of chocolate cake have been reduced to a few crumbs. Christianna and Rebecca sit side by side in front of the computer and create a coherent sequence of definitions.

Northwest Airlines...somewhere over Indiana. The engines of the 727 drone. Ann and Rebecca use a PowerBook® to record the ideas they're brainstorming about team characteristics.

Ames, IA...Department of English. Christianna writes about vantage theory and wonders if she needs to check with anyone about what she's going to write.

St. Paul, MN...Department of Rhetoric. When Ann retrieves her email from Rebecca and Christianna, she accesses the draft they've attached with Binhex so she can refine the section of the essay dealing with technology.

Ames, IA, Department of English...Rebecca decides on key questions to focus the discussion about authority.

Cyberspace...in the silent ether, not really in Ames or St. Paul. Ann, Christianna, and Rebecca work through problematic places in the essay.

INTRODUCTION

In this essay, we discuss face-to-face and computer-mediated collaboration as they are complicated by issues of culture, authority, conflict, and gender. In part, simply raising such issues is important by acknowledging that they influence our work as collaborators and as researchers about collaboration. But these issues also signal an evolution in the theory, research, and practice of collaboration as attention moves beyond establishing that collaboration exists and focuses instead on contextual factors that influence (and sometimes interfere with) collaborative interaction. These issues are pursued in theoretical speculations, in both quantitative and qualitative research (though those boundaries are becoming increasingly blurred), and in guidelines for practitioners. As we've developed this chapter, we've refined what we mean by collaboration; examined sites of collaborative interaction, both traditional face-to-face interactions and computer-mediated communication; and, investigated what makes the issues of culture, authority, conflict, and gender worthwhile for ongoing inquiry.

WHAT IS COLLABORATION?

We define collaboration so that the term is not used as a label for every type of human interaction. However, working definitions of collaboration vary dramatically, incorporating or ignoring factors such as the context of the collaboration, the complexity of the task, the nature of the interaction, the structure of the group, the division of work, and so on. In sorting through the ways to define collaboration, we begin with a broad, historical perspective and then explore the complexities of developing a more focused definition.

Joseph McGrath (1984) explains that collaboration occurs in a group—that is, a "relatively small and relatively structured or organized" social aggregate that involves "mutual awareness and potential mutual interaction" (p. 7). McGrath goes on to explain that

> [s]uch mutual awareness and potential interaction provide at least a minimum degree of interdependence; that is, members' choices and behaviors take one another into account. Interdependence, in turn, implies some degree of continuity over time: these relationships have, or quickly acquire, some history, and some anticipated future. A time based, mutual interdependence can reasonably be termed "dynamic." In other words a group is an aggregation of two or more people who are to some degree in dynamic interrelation with one another. (p. 8)

But as Barbara Couture and Jone Rymer (1991) point out, we need to differentiate between simply *interacting* with a group and *writing* with a group because both the frequency and nature of the interaction change as the purpose of the collaboration changes. For example, Couture and Rymer's respondents interacted with others far more (76%-81%) than they planned or wrote with others (24%-37%).

Even when we concentrate on collaborative writing, we see a range of definitions. Nancy Allen, Dianne Atkinson, Meg Morgan, Teresa Moore, and Craig Snow (1987) focus specifically on interaction and product when they define shared document production, which includes substantive interaction among group members and shared decision-making and responsibility. Lisa Ede and Andrea Lunsford (1990) focus more broadly on interaction and product when they suggest that collaborative writing is "any writing done in collaboration with one or more persons" (p. 15).

Although these definitions focus primarily on interaction and product, recent theorists locate collaboration within a social web in which all writing occurs. Charlotte Thralls (1992), for example, argues convincingly that "collaboration is a complex and comprehensive activity that extends well beyond joint authorship. . . [and that] all writing is inherently collaborative" (pp. 63-64). Similarly, Rachel Spilka (1993) situates collaboration as cross-cultural "communication across project groups, departments, divisions, and other social configurations" based on a definition of collaboration "in a broad sense as interacting, working together, and negotiating before and during the production of a document" (p. 128).

The task of culling just one definition from existing collaboration literature presents a challenge. If collaboration is defined too narrowly (e.g., individuals working in a face-to-face group with a common commitment to achieve a common goal), then many kinds of collaborative interaction are neglected (e.g., computer-mediated collaboration or teams with members committing unequal time/contributions to the project). If collaboration is defined too broadly (e.g., interaction among individuals), then it comes to mean nothing because any kind of verbal or nonverbal communication might be construed as collaborative. The challenge then is to develop a definition that acknowledges that collaboration involves the following contextual complications:

- The participants may have unequal commitments and devote unequal time and energy to the task.
- The group may be structured in numerous ways—e.g., hierarchical or nonhierarchical, single or shared leadership, individual responsibilities or shared responsibilities, and so on.
- The interaction may be face to face and/or computer mediated.

As the investigation of collaboration evolves, theorists, researchers, and practitioners alike acknowledge the importance of contextual factors that influence collaborative interaction. Factors such as culture, authority, conflict, and gender represent a productive way to examine the nature of collaboration.[1] Before discussing each of these factors, though, we briefly explore collaboration in the classroom and the workplace and consider how technology shapes computer-mediated collaboration.

WHAT EXPLAINS COLLABORATION?

One way to explain collaboration is to consider the syllogistic argument that some people create: All communication is interactive; all interaction is collaborative; therefore, all communication is collaborative. And, in fact, if one communicates, one engages in the interactive process of making meaning. For example, Thomas Kent (1993) suggests that "without collaboration. . . no communicative interaction is possible. . . . If we are communicating, we are collaborating" (pp. 160-161). Extending his argument about communicating as collaborating, Kent says that

---

1. Other factors such as duration of team life (Forman) and self-direction (Bosley) continue to be extraordinarily important in the productivity of a team.

> the act of collaborating with others. . . cannot be reduced to a strict pedagogical methodology. Consequently, teachers cannot provide students with a methodological framework that will tell them how to collaborate. . . . [nor can teachers] provide students with a framework that explains the process of collaborative interaction. (p. 165)

If we accept this reasoning, then we are called to fully explore and understand the contextual complications and factors that influence collaboration. However, we believe that there is a fundamental flaw in the oversimplification that all communication is collaborative. Directly put, interaction is a necessary but not sufficient element for collaboration; rather, two additional elements, intentionality and purpose, are required in order for interaction to be collaborative. While intentionality and purpose are intricately bound, collaboration must include the idea that people plan or intend to act together in a purposeful manner, with an understanding that their activity has a common goal. In addition, we argue that culture, authority, conflict, and gender are among the factors that teachers can introduce to help students better understand face-to-face and computer-mediated interactions in the classroom and in the workplace. While Kent agrees that "teachers can offer helpful advice" (p. 165), we go further by suggesting that learning about the issues of culture, authority, conflict, and gender goes beyond learning about being "polite, cooperative, and politically astute in . . . interactions with others" (p. 165).

One way to approach a more complete understanding is to consider explanations such as those addressed by Anne Ruggles Gere (1987) when she identifies three broad and sometimes overlapping categories of collaboration: a response to socio-economic factors, a way to bring writers and readers closer, or a result of knowledge as community property. In explaining these positions, Gere reminds readers that 19th century sociologist Emile Durkheim saw collaboration as a way to stimulate and release creative energy and power in individuals who were "freed from the alienation of isolation" (p. 64). She also notes that "collaboration ameliorates alienation by reorienting writers toward their readers" (p. 68). And finally, she recognizes the influence of the social-constructivist perspective brought by theorists such as Thomas Kuhn whose *Structure of Scientific Revolutions* demonstrated, as Gere explains, that "objectivity is a social construct [and that] scientific knowledge is community property and science should be seen as a social activity. . . shaped by observers' preconceptions and circumstances" (pp. 71-72).

The perspectives discussed by Kent and those reviewed by Gere often result in classroom and workplace collaborations with different purposes and different forms. Typically, classroom collaboration seems to focus on process as well as on the product. In addition to completing tasks more accurately and easily, student collaborators gain insight into their own thinking and problem solving. In contrast, workplace collaboration typically focuses more on the product. Workplace process is usually a concern only insofar as it promotes the more efficient or effective means to the end product. Distinctions aside, however, collaboration is a critical kind of interaction in both the classroom and the workplace.

Collaboration in the Classroom

The importance of peer interaction is highlighted by a range of theorists and practitioners who agree that collaboration belongs in the classroom. Specifically, traditions emerging from Jean Piaget, Lev Vygotsky, and Harry Stack Sullivan all support the view that peer interaction contributes to students' intellectual and social development. All three theoretical perspectives provide a foundation for collaboration, arguing that such interaction enhances motivation and provides a forum for creative thinking in which participants generate ideas and solutions, receive and respond to criticism, and develop social and cognitive processes.

What Classroom Collaboration Does

Educational theory and practice have typically viewed collaboration as a problem-solving activity that increases students' engagement in their learning and works as scaffolding because they can accomplish more collaboratively than they can individually (Johnson and Johnson, 1979, 1987; Sharan, 1980, 1990; Sharan et al., 1984; Slavin, 1980, 1990). This scaffolding aspect of collaboration has been capitalized on by writing-across-the-curriculum (WAC) programs, which generally treat collaboration as a problem-solving tool within the content area. For example, Duin, Simmons, and Lampaers (1994) studied the development and use of decision case studies as a WAC component in science courses. Students worked in groups and individually to analyze current state, national, and international environmental problems; they read copies of documents developed by different constituencies to argue their positions; and students had to develop options for the decision makers. All this involved extensive amounts of collaborative talk and collaborative writing and required at least some awareness of the issues of cultural and gender difference, negotiated authority, and possible conflicts within and among the people affected by the students' projects.

In other writing classrooms, however, collaboration has often been treated less as problem solving and more as an activity to give students feedback about their writing (e.g., DiPardo & Freedman, 1988). And frequently, collaboration in classroom writing has emphasized the benefits that come from sharing and agreeing on ideas (e.g., Bruffee, 1985;

Clifford, 1981) or on the emotional support, dialectical opportunities, and mutual commitment (Gebhardt, 1980).

What Classroom Collaboration Doesn't Do

In many classrooms, working toward a social consensus too often involves collaboration without "intellectual negotiation" (Trimbur in Wiener, 1986, p. 54) and ignores or suppresses conflict. In a shift from his early writings that seemed to privilege consensus as the desired end-product of collaborative interaction, Bruffee now specifically includes dissent in his definition of consensus and suggests that dissent is essential for the nonfoundational social construction of knowledge (1993, p. 221). The shift away from an emphasis on consensus arose, in part, from problems in writing classes that stripped collaboration of one of its most valuable features, the emphasis on substantive conflict—that is, conflict focusing on the content and other rhetorical elements of the discussion (Burnett, 1993).[2]

Students are not usually encouraged to see collaboration as a way to explore other points of view or develop alternative approaches. If students are encouraged to work toward a common goal of consensus, they may be deprived of the experience of negotiating the rhetoric of dissensus as described by John Trimbur (1989, p. 610). In short, collaboration doesn't automatically ensure optimal process or products if consensus is privileged over dissensus. This perspective is reinforced in an article by Patricia Kelvin and Scott Leonard (in press) who identify five fields of dissonance—logistical, personal, cognitive, epistemic, and social—that operate together to contribute to conflict that results in "collaborative breakdown." While we hesitate to draw direct parallels with the five fields of dissonance identified by Kelvin and Leonard and the issues we discuss in more detail later in this essay, we find that Kelvin and Leonard reveal the possibilities for exploring issues that influence classroom collaboration.

Classroom collaboration also doesn't solve the problem of entirely equal engagement—some students prefer to work individually; others prefer not to work at all. While we know that effective collaborative groups increase comprehension and retention of content and develop social skills (Sharan, 1990; Sharan et al., 1984), students need training to take advantage of these benefits—training that is too often missing from classrooms, regardless of grade level, subject matter, or student ability. These student experiences, too, are influenced, either consciously or unconsciously, by the issues of technology, culture, gender, conflict, and authority.

---

2. Work in social psychology as early as Thorndike in the 1930s reports that group discussion creates a pressure, generated by the nature of the group discussion, to move toward unanimity (Kelley & Thibaut, 1969). Some people argue that urging conflict is counter-intuitive and runs contrary to their own experiences in collaboration. Generating cooperative, constructive conflict—even though it can result in better decisions and higher-quality products—takes a conscious effort on the part of the collaborators.

COLLABORATION IS IMPORTANT IN THE WORKPLACE

Team building and quality circles are examples of workplace commitment to collaboration. For example, teams are a large part of the reason that Solectron Corporation, a leading independent provider of customized integrated manufacturing services to original equipment manufacturers in the electronics industry, received a coveted Malcolm Baldrige National Quality Award.[3] "[E]ach Solectron customer is supported by two teams that work to ensure quality performance and on-time delivery.

- A project planning team works with customers in planning, scheduling, and defining material requirements and lead time.
- A total quality control team meets weekly for monitoring and evaluating production with the aim of preventing potential problems and identifying ways to improve process yields." ("Three Companies," 1991, p. 6).

Despite a multilingual workforce composed of workers from more than 20 cultures, Solectron uses a highly participatory management style (*rather than traditional, authoritarian leadership structures*), providing coaching and mentoring while allowing autonomy. Because customers are seen as part of a Solectron team, they are given weekly service reports for analysis and encouraged to provide direct and frequent feedback in several ways, including a weekly survey, which forms the basis of a customer satisfaction index ("Three Electronic Firms," 1991).

Solectron's teams, with their successful structure and function, are often used as benchmarks by companies that would like to improve their internal management and their interaction with customers. Successful teams are often credited with major breakthroughs and important initiatives; in fact, the team concept is central to the success of many companies.

What Workplace Collaboration Does

While there is some disagreement about how prevalent collaboration is in the workplace and exactly what falls within the boundaries of what is considered collaboration, no one argues about its importance. Workplace teams typically resolve problems, generate new ideas, or manage complex operations. In *TeamWork: What Must Go Right/What Can Go Wrong*, Larson and LaFasto (1989) identify team characteristics, examples, and operations, as shown in Figure 9.1.

What Workplace Collaboration Doesn't Do

The emphasis on workplace teams is typically on the task, not on individuals making up a team. As a result, workplace teams usually don't build

---

3. The Malcolm Baldrige National Quality Award was established by legislation in 1987, named for the late Secretary of Commerce Malcolm Baldrige, "to raise awareness about quality management and to recognize U.S. companies that have a world-class system for managing their operations and people and for satisfying ther customers" ("Three Companies," 2).

Team Characteristics and Examples	*Operations*
Problem-resolution Teams • Focus on issues that need to be resolved. • Depend on each member trusting the other members to be truthful and demonstrate integrity. • Example: A *problem-solving team* might be asked to develop a docking and transfer system to eliminate the ongoing problem of accidental spills during loading and offloading of oil tankers.	• Select tasks that require careful investigation. • Do not start with predetermined assumptions or conclusions. • Take advantage of team members' expertise. • Collect information from those closest to the problem.
Creative Teams • Focus on exploring possibilities and alternatives. • Depend on team being autonomous from organization's systems and procedures. • Example: A *creative team* might venture into new territory to develop a financially feasible, environmentally safe additive that would prevent spilled fuel oil from contaminating a water supply and causing unrecoverable environmental damage.	• Abandon "normative thinking." • Don't reject any ideas prematurely. • Impose few constraints on the team. • Ignore organizational conventions.
Tactical Teams • Focus on well-defined operations. • Depend on team having an unambiguous definition of the task and each member's role in completing the task. • Example: A *tactical team* might be called in an emergency to prevent a large fuel oil spill from contaminating a city's water supply, spoiling the beach front property, and damaging a nearby wildlife preserve.	• Define each role on the team. • Establish clear performance standards for each role. • Assign each team member to a specific role, with well-defined responsibilities. • Direct the implementation of tasks.

Figure 9.1 Team Characteristics and Operations (modified from Larson and LaFasto, 1989)

stars (though star teams may emerge). Attention and energy are given to the problem and its solution.

Unfortunately, though, using a team to address a problem or accomplish a complex task doesn't guarantee success. The presence of certain situations can virtually assure that a project will have problems and maybe even fail. One of the most widely analyzed failures (Moore, 1992; Pace, 1988; United States Congress, 1986; United States Presidential Commission, 1986; Windsor, 1990) is the Challenger disaster. This disaster exhibited at least three complicating situations that may occur in other complex collaborations.

- If vested interests prevail over common good, the project is likely to fail.
- If the organizational culture privileges decisions based on a person's position rather than a person's knowledge, the project is likely to fail.
- If the communities from which various team members are drawn don't understand or aren't willing to translate each other's conventions (e.g., when "you should consider the risk of..." really means "DANGER"), the project is likely to fail.

TECHNOLOGY ENABLING COMPUTER-MEDIATED COMMUNICATION

Whether in the classroom or the workplace, technology provides both public and private forums for collaboration, both real-time and delayed-time options for collaborators to meet and exchange information. Technology can no longer be considered a tangential influence on collaboration; instead, it should be recognized as a critical medium that is affected—just as face-to-face collaboration is affected—by the issues of culture, authority, conflict, and gender. In fact, we would venture to say that many collaborative writers meet electronically far more than they meet face to face. Cyberspace locations for collaborative writing—virtual classrooms (Selfe and Hilligoss, 1994), virtual corporations (Cronin, 1994; Duin & Archee, in press; Ellsworth and Ellsworth, 1995), and virtual communities (Gurak, in press; Star, 1995; Rheingold, 1993)—alter our definition of collaboration for those in academia and for those in the workplace.

Technological advances offer collaborators the opportunity to transform their collaboration from a one-directional transfer of information to a dynamic dialectic in which they see and hear each other, sharing and comparing ideas and text (Duin & Hansen, 1996; Duin, Mason, & Jorn, 1994). Collaborators can now monitor changes across drafts; individuals who complain that they work harder than other members can verify this complaint through programs such as David Kaufer and Chris Neuwirth's PrepEditor (1995).

Technologies used widely by collaborators are systems that support the following kinds of tasks and interactions:

- real-time discussion of projects (e.g., IRCs [Internet Relay Chats], MOOs [multi-user object-oriented environments], World Wide Web chat systems, and desktop videoconferencing systems)
- delayed-time exchange of messages (e.g., electronic mail, computer conferencing, and listservs)
- real- and delayed-time development of drafts (e.g., groupware such as Lotus Notes, Microsoft Access, and PrepEditor)
- retrieval of information from the Internet (e.g., Gopher and WWW)

More specifically, nearly all classroom and workplace collaborators use electronic mail to discuss their projects and share and edit drafts. Increasing numbers of faculty and students are using IRCs and MOOs to locate communities of scholars interested in collaborative projects and to discuss in real-time the projects underway (Bruckman & Resnick, 1993; Mehlenbacher, in press; Mehlenbacher et al., 1994). According to Mehlenbacher, MOOs now facilitate collaborative discussions of issues like postmodern culture (PMC-MOO), new media and technology (MediaMOO), hypertexts and fiction (Brown Hypertext Hotel), bioinformatics (BioMOO), and the anthropological and social evolution of MOOs themselves (Point MOOt). Workplace collaborators also are using MOOs to gain valuable information from users about their products and the accompanying documentation.

The collaborative outlet currently expanding at the fastest rate is the World Wide Web (WWW). As of the writing of this chapter, more than six million WWW pages may be searched and accessed. As an attempt to produce some sort of convergence out of the tumultuous collection of files on the Internet, the WWW now seamlessly incorporates electronic services collaborators use widely. From a given WWW page, collaborators can access chat boxes for synchronous discussion, they can retrieve and share information with other members, and they can use desktop videoconferencing during their meetings.

Collaborators with a direct TCP/IP connection such as SLIP or PPP can now set themselves up as a WWW server and publish their collaborative work globally. In Ann Hill Duin's recent experience collaborating with Ray Archee, (in press) who was located on another continent, they used the NetSearch capabilities on the Netscape Navigator and then immediately saved their searches as home pages on their home servers. They placed the papers they had developed for upcoming conferences on WWW sites, and they regularly logged the sources they discovered onto these same sites so that their students might access this information.

As access to broadband services increases, desktop videoconferencing will expand exponentially as a tool for collaborators. Market researchers say the desktop videoconferencing market will reach $5 billion by the time this essay is published. Assuming that the essential technology is in place, the cost for a one-hour, coast-to-coast desktop videoconferencing call is now less than $15 an hour. According to one desktop videoconferencing developer—PictureTel—desktop videoconferencing is filling a need in the global marketplace for meetings at a distance. Industry analysts estimate that videoconferencing will become as widely accepted as the fax machine is today. Research laboratories including Bellcore, Olivetti, and Hewlett-Packard have multimillion dollar projects devoted to establishing videoconferencing connections between their collaborators.

Just as universities are slow to recognize collaborative efforts as having merit when considering promotion and tenure issues, some institutions are slow to extend support and approval to employees who use these services to facilitate collaboration and who then publish their work electronically. However, the rapid expansion of WWW sites (some estimates state that a new WWW site appears every two seconds) suggests that electronic publishing of collaborative work will soon surpass traditional outlets.

Virtual Reality Markup Language (VRML) will further expand opportunities for collaboration as collaborators use VRML to create the environments within which they work. We will likely study how student and workplace collaborators meet in cyberspace where computers will locally render realistic images of fellow collaborators opting to meet in a cafe, in a lounge, or atop a mountain. Via the high-bandwidth cabled computer, collaborators will have immediate access to any reference in the world and will collaborate within these sites (Duin & Archee, in press).

All of the above forms for electronic interaction force us to consider the role of culture, authority, conflict, and gender—because all of these change when the interaction is electronic rather than face to face. For example, as Linda LaDuc notes in her essay in this collection, numerous researchers have observed that gender seems to influence adherence or violation of politeness conventions in electronic communication, with young men being the most likely flamers. Thus, if a team of high school or college students is interacting primarily electronically, there is an increased possibility that unproductive conflicts may emerge—conflicts that can be traced to gender.

There is also a tendency to view technological advances as simply more efficient methods or tools for confronting or improving collaborative writing in workplace and classroom settings. But technologies that link collaborators create communities as well as boundaries to those communities. Technologies create new matrices of social relations—and concerns about access, support systems, the reduction of face-to-face interaction, and anonymity (see Figure 9.2). Technologies inextricably link us to notions of power and to attention on issues of culture, authority, conflict, and gender.

Furthermore, as Steven Jones (1995) notes in *CyberSociety*, these technologies ensnarl already difficult legal matters concerning privacy, copyright, and ethics. Although copyright and ethics in electronic work are being discussed

Technology issues and instances	*Questions about technology's influence on collaboration*
Access to Technology Think of two companies that have sophisticated computer networks but cannot easily communicate with each other because their systems aren't compatible.	Is access dictated by cost? Is access related to quality? How can technology improve a team's effectiveness and efficiency?
Support Systems Think of the increase in the personnel budget necessary to support a systems operator.	How much do workplace professionals on teams need access to human support—e.g., technicians to answer questions? How do they use helplines? Helpscreens? Other support systems? How do they use information available on listservs, email, or other electronic options?
Reduction of Face-to-face Interaction Think of chemists in France and Indiana who collaboratively conduct research and jointly publish a scholarly article yet who have not met face-to-face for several years.	What percentage of time should group members spend in face-to-face interaction? Can the entire work of a productive team be electronic, with no face-to-face interaction? How will the increase in telecommuting affect the productivity of teams?
Anonymity Think of the problems in a company where employees could send email anonymously. Before management stopped their email system, there was a rash of sexually suggestive and obscene email sent to female employees, insulting email messages sent to unpopular managers, and widely distributed messages sent to clients and competitors about serious problems with several of the company's key projects (Schrage, 1994).	Do workplace professionals generate different messages if they know the information can be posted anonymously? Do readers react differently to signed messages and to anonymous messages? How should workplace professionals respond to anonymous messages? In what situations might anonymous messages be acceptable or appropriate?

Figure 9.2 Technology issues affecting collaboration

(Helyar & Doudnikoff, 1994), few collaborators protect their work by means of encryption programs. One author has experienced network-level censorship and activity monitoring on a range of systems on two continents. The fact that all systems administration staff members usually have global privileges to any file on that system should caution against misplaced trust in the security of any file on the Internet. Encryption programs such as Pretty Good Privacy will become a necessity to ensure the integrity of a collaborator's work and to authenticate its authorship.

WHERE IS COLLABORATIVE RESEARCH MOVING?

Although collaboration has long been a subject of study, the past decade has produced a number of important and widely cited works focusing specifically on collaboration in technical and professional communication.[4] Classroom and workplace collaboration continue to be rich sites for extending the broad disciplinary conversation.

Multiplicity of Culture

Practitioners and researchers are interested in exploring the ways in which culture—in its broadest sense—affects collaboration. The workplace looks increasingly like the global village Marshall McLuhan (1964) forecast in the 1960s. Interesting segments of this global village are reported in *Hoover's Handbook of World Business*, (Hoover, et al., 1991). For example, "America's high-end stereo makers ship 60 percent of their product to Japan. GE TVs and RCA camcorders are made by a French company. . . . Jaguar and Lotus are part of Ford and GM" (Hoover et al., 1991, p. 8). More specifically, Japanese Sony—with manufacturing and distribution facilities in the United States (having purchased, among other companies, CBS Records and Columbia Pictures)—is well-known for its effective collaborative relationships with other companies such as the Dutch electronics giant, Philips, with whom Sony developed the standard for interactive CDs (Hoover et al., 1991).

The multicultural nature of some teams can make team interaction complex, even difficult. Multicultural collaboration would be difficult enough if "multicultural" simply referred to people from various countries (Victor 1992). However, "multicultural" refers additionally to cultural differences that may be the result of geography, ethnicity, education, sociopolitical views, and so on. Figure 9.3 suggests some of the cultural issues that potentially influence interactions on workplace or classroom teams. A critical concern is whether people even think about any of these cultures when they're working on teams.

---

4. Among these works are books and collections: Ede and Lunsford (1990), Lay and Karis (1991), Forman (1992), Cross (1994), Burnett and Duin (in press); and special issues of journals: Couture and Rymer (1990), Morgan and Bosley (1991), Duin and Burnett (1993).

Cultural issues and instances	*Questions about culture's influence on collaboration*
site of collaborative interaction Think of classrooms and boardrooms.	How do students and workplace professionals differ in their views of academic assignments and workplace tasks? How do they differ in their relations with team leaders? With pressures of time? With criteria for success?
workplace cultures Think of Ben & Jerry's and Citicorp.	How do people from different corporate cultures approach management? How do they approach problem-solving? What do they consider appropriate rewards? How do they relate to the corporate hierarchy?
cultures based on intellectual traditions Think of human resource professionals and computer engineers.	How do professionals from different intellectual traditions approach problems? How do they share information? What kind of on-the-job training is typical?
national cultures Think of the United States and Saudi Arabia.	Do people from different national cultures have different perceptions of time? Do they have different expectations of interpersonal interaction? Do they have different ways of determining priorities?
racial and ethnic cultures Think of African-Americans and Japanese Americans.	How do people from different racial and/or ethnic backgrounds interpret history or current events in ways that might influence on-the-job attitudes or actions? Do they have different educational and employment opportunities?
religious cultures Think of Episcopalians and Seventh Day Adventists.	What links do people from different religions see between their religious beliefs and their workplace decisions and actions?
political cultures Think of labor unions and management, Republicans and Democrats.	How do people with different political views feel about centralized authority? How do they feel about the power of a collective voice? How do they feel about individual initiative? How do people act out their political beliefs?
gender cultures Think of women and men.	How do men and women listen? How do they interact on teams? How do they express disagreement?

Figure 9.3 Cultural issues affecting collaboration

Collaborators can usually anticipate generalities about cultural characteristics, but they can't predict specific individual behaviors because each person brings specialized interests to team interaction. For example, an engineer on a team to survey and select new battery vendors for his division's battery-operated fork-lift vehicles could anticipate that the financial analyst on the team would complete a cost-benefit analysis of each option and check each vendor's financial position. However, he might not anticipate that the financial analyst, who works with an environmental conservation group in his spare time, would have strong opinions about each vendor's recycling efforts or R&D work in developing nontoxic batteries.

Multicultural teams are potentially poly-vocal; however, team members may have to go out of their way to privilege minority voices—making room in conversation for alternative views and uncomfortable perspectives, re-seeing options from a different perspective. One new research tool uses vantage theory (MacLaury, 1995; Preston, 1994) to identify interactions where participants shift between *specialized language* (which emphasizes distinctions such as jargon or technical terms with very specific meanings) and *generalist language* (which emphasizes similarities, such as analogies or vernacular terms with meanings that link ideas). Awareness of differences in and shifts between specialist and generalist language can allow team members to understand how their colleagues view the interaction and possibly allow insight into culturally influenced values that influence interactions among team members (White, 1995).

For example, many people use the term hypertext to refer to nearly all of what we find on the World Wide Web, including QuickTime movies and audio clips—the whole environment is hypertextual. However, for the community of scholars and practitioners who specialize in hypertext, the term has a specific meaning and is distinct from related terms like *hypermedia* or even context-sensitive *on-line help.* If members of these two groups of people work collaboratively, they would need to negotiate the meanings of the words they use. Within the context of this sort of negotiation, the specialists are likely to be viewed as authoritative because of their reliance on specialized terminology or jargon that their less knowledgeable colleagues might find slightly off-putting. Vantage analysis offers a way for people to understand and talk about their different uses of terms and also enables researchers and practitioners to see how authority is assumed and operates in collaborative interactions.

Authority

Authority, which deals with control, affects collaborative interaction in at least three ways: gatekeeping, dissemination or hoarding of knowledge, and leadership.

Authority based on gatekeeping—"Who's in charge?"—focuses on concerns ranging from team membership and structure to topics of inquiry, from resource sharing to conflict resolution. Gatekeeping is a way of enforcing authority by controlling the availability of information, determining access to resources, and limiting those involved with substantive decision making. The control exerted by gatekeeping can come from an individual on a team or from the team itself. While authority may be imposed by some external agent outside the team, benefits of self-governing teams are widely recognized (Bosley, 1991) because they're likely to be more committed to their task.

Authority based on knowledge—"Who's the expert?"—privileges selected team members so that their information is either emphasized or marginalized. Knowledge and expertise don't necessarily correspond with organizational rank or position. For example, a problem-solving team charged with eliminating the resolution problems in satellite telescopes may have a team manager with the authority to approve or reject the purchase of a $30,000 piece of test equipment. But the technical knowledge to determine the need for the test equipment and to select the appropriate features of the equipment may lie with an aerospace engineer who can offer a recommendation but has no decision-making authority. Or on a software development team, the documentation specialist may have to demonstrate that her knowledge is as valuable to the team's goals as the knowledge of the computer engineers or programmers (Doheny-Farina, 1992). Sharing or disseminating knowledge, hoarding knowledge, and restricting the release of knowledge are all controlling behaviors that affect authority.

Authority based on leadership—"Who's the boss?"—determines who directs and facilitates the actions of a team. Just as authority can be shared or restricted by gatekeeping and dissemination of knowledge, so too can authority be shared or restricted by leadership. For example, more than one person can assume a leadership role, depending on available time, knowledge, and interest. Effective leaders generally provide two important kinds of support for a team: task leadership and interpersonal leadership. Nearly 50 years ago (1948), Benne and Sheats developed what are now classical lists that describe these roles as illustrated in Figures 9.4 and 9.5.

In addition to these functions of leadership, both personal style and cultural expectations influence collaborations, too. For example, a groupmember might remain quiet during most of a meeting and then express one idea that changes the course of the project. Similarly, no matter what strategy we might think we are teaching or employing, there may be one person who has ultimate authority over the group.

Task leadership	*Roles to provide task support*
Leaders can provide *task support* by focusing on the work to be done—helping to define the problem, coordinate activities, and provide evaluation.	*Initiator contributors* recommend novel ideas about the problem at hand, new ways to approach the problem, or possible solutions not yet considered. *Information seekers* emphasize getting the facts by calling for background information from others. *Opinion seekers* ask for more qualitative types of data, such as attitudes, values, and feelings. *Information givers* provide data for forming decisions, including facts that derive from expertise. *Opinion givers* provide opinions, values, and feelings. *Elaborators* give additional information—examples, rephrasings, implications—about points made by others. *Coordinators* show the relevance of each idea and its relationship to the overall problem. *Orienters* refocus discussion of the topic whenever necessary. *Evaluator-critics* appraise the quality of the group's efforts in terms of logic, practicality, or method. *Energizers* stimulate the group to continue working when discussion flags. *Procedural technicians* care for operational details such as the materials, machinery, and so on. *Recorders* provide a secretarial function.

Figure 9.4 Task functions of leadership (modified from Beene and Sheats, 1948)

Interpersonal leadership	***Roles to provide interpersonal support***
Leaders can provide *interpersonal support* by focusing on affective and interpersonal concerns—making sure that team members work in a positive atmosphere and feel part of the group.	*Encouragers* reward others through agreement, warmth, and praise. *Harmonizers* mediate conflicts among groups members. *Compromisers* shift their own positions on issues in order to reduce conflict in the group. *Gatekeepers and expediters* smooth communication by setting up procedures and ensuring equal participation from members. *Standard setters* express calls for discussion of and standards for evaluating the quality of the group process. *Group observers* informally point out the positive and negative aspects of the group's dynamics and call for change if necessary. *Followers* accept the ideas offered by others and serve as an audience for the group.

Figure 9.5 Interpersonal functions of leadership (modified from Beene and Sheats appearing in Donelson, 1993)

Conflict

Collaborators increase the likelihood of being more productive if they anticipate and thus avoid destructive conflicts—those that interfere with interpersonal interaction, exploration of the issues, or decision-making. Borrowing from the language of social psychologists (Putnam, 1986) and previous work about conflict in professional communication (Burnett, 1991), we identify conflicts as affective, procedural, or substantive. A conflict among collaborators is usually affective if it deals with interpersonal and emotional reactions. It's usually procedural if it deals with how things should be done. And a conflict is usually substantive if it deals with content, context, and concepts. Typically, affective and procedural conflicts—if left unresolved—are destructive and can interfere with all aspects of collaboration. And, typically, substantive conflict is usually productive, giving collaborators the opportunity to explore alternative perspectives.

In disciplines such as small group behavior, cooperative learning, and social psychology and more recently in rhetoric, composition, and technical communication, theorists and researchers have argued that substantive conflict enhances collaborative decision making (e.g., Burnett, 1993b; Clark and Ede, 1990; Karis, 1989; Trimbur, 1989). Substantive conflict during collaboration not only is normal, but also can be productive, in large part because it gives collaborators more time to generate and critically examine alternatives and to voice disagreements on their way to making a decision. In fact, ignoring cooperative, substantive conflict can reduce the effectiveness of a group and lower the quality of the decisions. On the other hand, engaging in substantive conflict can increase the effectiveness of a group, improve the quality of the decisions, and increase members' commitment to the decisions they do reach (Gouran, 1986; Putnam, 1986). Experienced collaborators often defer, and in some cases even resist, consensus in order to explore alternatives, and they value explicit disagreement to help them focus on potential problems.

Virtually every conflict, however—even those that stem from content, context, and concepts—has the potential to become unproductive or even destructive. For example, substantive disagreements between collaborators about the nature of evidence used to illustrate points in a paper may become affective, involving issues of politics and power if one of the collaborators simply deletes another team member's examples and substitutes his own. Rather than considering that the substitution may, in fact, be more appropriate support given the purpose or the audience, other collaborators may feel threatened or marginalized.

Most of the work about the importance of substantive conflict is either theoretical or has been done with student groups. Theorists and researchers who argue the importance of conflict in productive collaboration need to extend their work to detailed investigations of short-term and long-term workplace teams.

Gender

The confirmation of physiological differences in the brains of women and men will fuel ongoing interest in gender as a factor in collaborative interaction. Much of the scholarship where gender and collaboration converge suggests that the structure of the team, leadership styles and functions, team roles, and cultural biases can all be influenced by gender issues (Allen, 1991; Lay, 1989; Tebeaux, 1990). Some of these issues and influences are summarized in Figure 9.6.

Gender issues and instances	*Questions about gender's influence on collaboration*
team structure Think of a team that is highly imbalanced by gender—for example, one woman and five men or five women and one man.	What is the most productive gender balance on a team? Is an androgynous approach desirable? Is it possible?
leadership Think of the "alpha male" approach to leadership—the person with the most physical and political power.	What qualifies someone to be a team leader? What are the ramifications of selecting various people as team leader?
team roles Think of a woman always being asked to be the recorder or secretary.	Who is most qualified for each role on a team? What are the implications of having men or women in various roles?
cultural biases Think of a cross-cultural team with men and women from various professions (e.g., engineering, technical communication, marketing) and with various national heritages (e.g., Korean, Lebanese, United States).	How are women treated in traditionally male professions such as mechanical engineering or agricultural engineering? How will people from cultures in which men are dominate treat women on a team?

Figure 9.6 Gender issues affecting collaboration

The questions in Figure 9.6 suggest ways of looking at collaboration by appropriating gender research and theory and experience grounded in feminist interpretations. Although their essay is not topically focused specifically on collaboration, Gesa Kirsch and Joy Ritchie (1995) situate their examples within collaborative interactions in order to articulate their argument about the politics of location. Through their examples, Kirsch and Ritchie develop issues of cultural biases, roles in collaborative interactions, leadership and power issues, and the way interactions are structured.

> It is not enough, then, to begin locating ourselves and our experiences. In doing so naively, we risk ignoring the hierarchies . . . . we risk defining gender biologically rather than recognizing it as a varied set of social relationships. . . . researchers need to resist the drive to generalize about men and women, that we can learn much from studying the multiple ways in which both men and women can express themselves, and that composition teachers need to develop pedagogical practices that encourage students to write in a wide variety of discourse forms. (p. 11)

We extend this argument into the workplace as well. Collaboration, especially among team members conversant with the gender issues influencing collaborative interaction, is one way to foster understanding while at the same time enhance interactions and maximize team productivity.

CONCLUSION

In the beginning of this essay, we raised the issues of culture, authority, conflict, and gender as central to both face-to-face and computer-mediated collaboration. The importance of these issues signals the development of collaboration as classroom strategy, workplace practice, and research agenda. No longer is the focus exclusively on what collaboration is, where it is done, or how frequently it occurs. Instead, attention has moved to issues that influence the interaction. These issues are neither new nor mutually exclusive; rather, they are deeply interrelated, which complicates any inquiries. However, such inquiries may help teachers, researchers, and practitioners heighten their understanding of collaboration, smooth group interactions, reflect on their experiences, analyze their interactions, and consider these nested and interrelated issues that influence collaboration.

We suggest the following conclusions both as reflections of current research and practice and as springboards for future research:

- The *cultural issues* that influence collaboration extend beyond traditional nationalistic understandings of culture to encompass cultural issues related to sites of collaborative interaction; workplace cultures; cultures of intellectual tradition; racial, ethnic, and religious cultures; political cultures; and gender cultures.
- *Authority issues,* whether control based on gatekeeping, knowledge, or leadership, exert powerful influences on collaborative interactions.

Awareness of these issues is an increasingly important skill to teach and to examine in future research, particularly in light of the relationships among authority, culture, conflict, and gender.

- Understanding and productively managing *conflict* are essential skills that must be taught to students as well as workplace collaborators. Research into the effects of conflict on short- and long-term workplace collaborations should be undertaken in order to confirm or disconfirm findings based on academic collaborations.
- *Gender* influences general factors such as cultural biases and more specific factors such as team structure, leadership, and team roles. Appropriating and utilizing gender research can help enhance and facilitate collaborations in which all participants contribute cooperatively and productively.

Rapid shifts in technology pervade our classrooms and workplaces and create new tensions as well as new opportunities for collaborators. Just as the sites of collaboration have changed as the result of technological innovations, ways of collaborating have changed and will, indeed, continue to change.

REFERENCES

Allen, J. (1991). Gender issues in technical communication studies. *Journal of Business and Technical Communication, 5*, 371–92.

Allen, N., Atkinson, D., Morgan, M., Moore, T. & Snow, C. (1987). What experienced collaborators say about collaborative writing. *Journal of Business and Technical Communication, 1*, 70–90.

Beene, K.D. & Sheats, P. (1948). Functional roles of group members. *Journal of Social Issues, 4* (2), 41–49. Reprinted in R. Donelson & R. Forsyth (Eds.). (1993). *Group dynamics* (2nd Ed.). (p. 113). Brooks/Cole: Pacific Grove, CA

Bosley, D.S. (1991). Designing effective technical teams. *Technical Communication, 38*, 504–512.

Bruckman, A. & Resnick, M. (1993). Virtual professional community: Results from the MediaMOO Project. *Third International Conference on Cyberspace.* Austin, TX: (Available via anonymous ftp from media.mit.edu in pub/MediaMOO/papers/MediaMOO-3cyberconf, 1993).

Bruffee, K.A. (1985). *A short course in writing.* (3rd ed.). Boston, MA: Little.

Bruffee, K.A. (1993). *Collaborative learning: Higher education, interdependence, and the authority of knowledge.* Baltimore, MD: Johns Hopkins University Press.

Burnett, R.E. (1991) Cooperative, substantive conflict in collaboration: A way to improve the planning of workplace documents. *Technical Communication 8* (2), 532–539.

Burnett, R.E. (1993a). Conflict in collaborative decision-making. In N. Blyler & C. Thralls (Eds.), *Social perspectives in professional communication* (pp. 144–162). Newbury Park, CA: Sage.

Burnett, R.E. (1993b). Decision-making during the collaborative planning of coauthors. In A. Penrose & B. Sitko (Eds.), *Hearing ourselves think: Cognitive research in the college writing classroom* (pp. 125–146). New York: Oxford University Press.

Burnett, R.E. & Duin, A.H. (Eds.). (in press). *Collaboration in technical and professional communication: A research perspective.* Hillsdale, NJ: Erlbaum.

Clark, S. & Ede, L. (1990). Collaboration, resistance, and the teaching of writing. In A. Lunsford, H. Moglen, & J. Slevin (Eds.), *The Right to literacy* (pp. 276–285). New York: MLA.

Clifford, J. (1981). Composing in stages: The effects of a collaborative pedagogy. *Research in the Teaching of English, 15,* 37–53.

Couture, B. & Rymer, J. (Eds.). (1990). [Special issue on collaboration]. *Bulletin of the Association for Business Communication, 53* (2).

Couture, B. & Rymer, J. (1991). Discourse interaction between writer and supervisor: A primary collaboration in workplace writing. In M.M. Lay and W.M. Karis (Eds.), *Collaborative writing in industry: Investigations in theory and practice* (pp. 87–108). Amityville, NY: Baywood.

Cronin, M.J. (1994). *Doing business on the Internet: How the electronic highway is transforming American companies.* New York: Van Nostrand Reinhold.

Cross, G. A. (1994). *Collaboration and conflict: A contextual exploration of group writing and positive emphasis.* Cresskill, NJ: Hampton Press.

DiPardo, A. & Freedman, S.W. (1988). Peer response groups in the writing classroom: Theoretical foundations and new directions. *Review of Educational Research, 58,* 119–149.

Doheny-Farina, S. (1992). *Rhetoric, innovation, and technology: Case studies of technical communication in technology transfers.* Cambridge, MA: MIT Press.

Duin, A.H., & Archee, R. (in press). Distance learning via the World Wide Web: Information, engagement, community. In S. Selber (Ed.), *Computers and technical communication.* Norwood, NJ: Ablex.

Duin, A.H. & Burnett, R.E. (Eds.). (1993, Winter). [Special issue on collaboration]. *Technical Communication Quarterly, 2* (1).

Duin, A.H. & Hansen, C.J. (1996). Setting a sociotechnological agenda in nonacademic writing. In A.H.Duin & C.J. Hansen (Eds.), *Nonacademic writing: Social theory and technology.* Hillsdale, NJ: Erlbaum.

Duin, A.H., Mason, L.D. & Jorn, L.A. (1994). Structuring distance-meeting environments. *Journal of Technical Communication, 41,* 695–708.

Duin, A.H., Simmons, S. & Lammers, E. (1994). *Decision cases for writing across the curriculum: A report for the center for interdisciplinary studies of writing.* Minneapolis, MN: University of Minnesota.

Ede, L. & Lunsford, A. (1990). *Singular texts/plural authors: Perspectives on collaborative writing.* Carbondale, IL: Southern Illinois University Press.

Ellsworth, J.H. & Ellsworth, M.V. (1995). *Marketing on the Internet: Multimedia strategies for the World Wide Web.* New York: Wiley.

Forman, J. (Ed.). (1992). *New visions of collaborative writing.* Portsmouth, NH: Boynton/Cook.

Forman, J. (1993). Task groups and their writing: Relationships between group characteristics and group reports. *Technical Communication Quarterly, 2* (1), 75–88.

Gebhardt, R. (1980). Teamwork and feedback: Broadening the base of collaborative writing. *College English, 42,* 69–74.

Gere, A.R. (1987). *Writing groups: History, theory, and implications.* Carbondale, IL: Southern Illinois University Press.

Gouran, D.S. (1986). Inferential errors, interaction, and group decision-making. In R. Y. Hirokawa & M. S. Poole (Eds.), *Communication and group decision-making* (pp. 93–111). Beverly Hills, CA: Sage.

Gurak, L.J. (1996). *Cyberspace, rhetoric, and community: Privacy and persuasion on the virtual forums of the Internet.* New Haven, CT: Yale University Press.

Helyar, P.S. & Doudnikoff, G.M. (1994). Walking the labyrinth of multimedia law. *Technical Communication, 41,* 662–671.

Hoover, G., Campbell, A., Chai, A. & Spain, P.J. (1991). *Hoover's handbook of world business 1992.* Emeryville, CA: Publishers Group West.

Johnson, D.W. & Johnson, R.T. (1979). Conflict in the classroom: Controversy and learning. *Review of Educational Research, 49,* 51–70.

Johnson, D.W. & Johnson, R.T. (1987). *Learning together and alone: Cooperative, competitive, and individualistic learning.* (2nd ed.). Englewood Cliffs, NJ: Prentice-Hall.

Jones, S. (Ed.). (1995). *Cybersociety: Computer-mediated communication and community.* Thousand Oaks, CA: Sage.

Karis, B. (1989). Conflict in collaboration: A Burkean perspective. *Rhetoric Review, 8,* 113–126.

Kaufer, D. & Neuwirth, C. (1995). Supporting online team editing: Using technology to shape performance and to monitor individual and group action. *Computers and Composition, 12,* 113–124.

Kelley, H.H. & Thibaut, J.W. (1969). Group problem solving. In G. Lindzey & E. Aronson. *The handbook of social psychology.* (Vol. 4). (2nd Ed.) Reading, MA: Addison-Wesley.

Kelvin, P.R. & Leonard, S.A. (in press). Fields of dissonance in the collaborative writing classroom. In R.E. Burnett & A.H. Duin (Eds.), *Collaboration in technical and professional communication: A research perspective.*Hillsdale, NJ: Erlbaum.

Kent, T. (1993). Paralogy and the teaching of rhetoric. *Paralogic rhetoric: A theory of communicative interaction* Lewisburg, PA : Bucknell University Press.

Kirsch, G.E. & Ritchie, J.S. (1995). Beyond the personal: Theorizing a politics of location in composition research. *College Composition and Communication, 46* (1), 7–29.

Larson, C.E. & LaFasto, F.M.J. (1989). *Teamwork: What must go right/what can go wrong.* Newbury Park, CA: Sage.

Lay, M.M. (1989). Interpersonal conflict in collaborative writing: What we can learn from gender studies. *Journal of Business and Technical Communication, 3,* 5–28.

Lay, M.M. & Karis, W. (Eds.). (1991). *Collaborative writing in industry: Investigations in theory and practice.* Amityville, NY: Baywood.

MacLaury, R.E. (1995). Vantage theory. In J.R.Taylor & R.E. MacLaury (Eds.), *Language and the cognitive construal of the world* (pp. 231–276). New York: Mouton de Gruyter.

McGrath, J. (1984). *Groups: Interaction and performance.* Englewood Cliffs, NJ: Prentice.

McLuhan, M. (1964). *Understanding media: The extensions of man.* New York: McGraw-Hill.

Mehlenbacher, B. (in press). Listservs, MOOs, and Mosaic: Playing professionals and technical communication pedagogy. In S. Selber (Ed.), *Computers and technical communication.* Norwood, NJ: Ablex.

Mehlenbacher, B., Hardin, B., Barrett, C. & Clagett, J. (1994). Multi-user domains and virtual campuses: Implications for computer-mediated collaboration and technical communication. In *SIGDOC'94: The 12th annual international conference proceedings.* [Special Interest Group on Documentation] (pp. 213–219). New York: The Association for Computing Machinery (ACM).

Moore, P. (1992). When politeness is fatal: Technical communication and the Challenger accident. *Journal of Business and Technical Communication, 6* (3), 269–292.

Morgan, M. & Bosley, D. (Eds.). (1991, November). [Special issue on collaboration]. *Technical Communication, 8* (2).

O'Hara-Devereaux, M. & Johansen, R. (1994). A multicultural perspective: Transcending the barriers of behavior and language. *Globalwork.* San Francisco, CA: Jossey-Bass.

Pace, R.C. (1988). Technical communication, group differentiation, and the decision to launch the space shuttle Challenger. *Journal of Technical Writing and Communication, 18* (3), 207–20.

Preston, D.R. (1994). Content-oriented discourse analysis and folk linguistics. Unpublished manuscript.

Putnam, L.L. (1986). Conflict in group decision-making. In R. Y. Hirokawa & M. S. Poole (Eds.), *Communication and group decision-making* (pp. 175–196). Beverly Hills, CA: Sage.

Rheingold, H. (1993) *The virtual community: Homesteading on the electronic frontier.* Reading, MA: Addison.

Selfe, C.L. & Hilligoss, S. (Eds.). (1994). *Literacy and computers: The complications of teaching and learning with technology.* New York: MLA.

Sharan, S. (1980). Cooperative learning in small groups: Recent methods and effects on achievement, attitudes, and ethnic relations. *Review of Educational Research, 50,* 241–271.

Sharan, S. (Ed.). (1990). *Cooperative learning: Theory and research.* New York: Praeger.

Sharan, S., Kussell, P., Hertz-Lazarowitz, R., Bejarano, Y., Raviv, S., Sharan, Y., Brosh, T. & Peleg, R. (1984). *Cooperative learning in the classroom: Research in desegregated schools.* Hillsdale, NJ: Erlbaum.

Slavin, R.E. (1980). Cooperative learning. *Review of Educational Research, 50,* 315–342.

Slavin, R.E. (1990). *Cooperative learning: Theory, research, and practice.* Englewood Cliffs, NJ: Prentice.

Spilka, R. (1993). Collaboration across multiple organizations cultures. *Technical Communication Quarterly, 2* (2), 125–145.

Star, S.L. (Ed.). (1995). *The cultures of computing.* Cambridge, UK: Blackwell.

Tebeaux, E. (1990). Toward an understanding of gender differences in written business communication: A suggested perspective for future research. *Journal of Business and Technical Communication, 4* (1) 23–43.

Thralls, C. (1992). Bakhtin, collaborative partners, and published discourse: A collaborative view of composing. In J. Forman (Ed.), *New visions of collaborative writing.* Portsmouth, NH: Boynton/Cook.

Three companies win 1991 Baldrige Quality Award. (1991, October 21). *Business America, 112,* 2–9.

Three electronic firms win 1991 Baldrige Award. (1991, November 1991). *Quality Progress, 24* (11), 39–41.

Trimbur, J. (1989). Consensus and difference in collaborative learning. *College English, 51* (6), 602–616.

United States. Congress. (1986). House of Representatives Committee on Science and Technology Hearings. 99th Congress. (2nd Session). (2 vols.). Washington: GPO.

United States. Presidential Commission on the Space Shuttle Challenger Accident. (1986). *Report of the Presidential commission on the space shuttle Challenger accident.* (Vol. 1). Washington: The Commission.

Victor, D.A. (1992). *International business communication.* New York: HarperCollins.

White, C.I. (1995). Common knowledge and specialized discourse: Situating vantage theory in professional communication. Unpublished manuscript.

Wiener, H.S. (1986). Collaborative learning in the classroom: A guide to evaluation. *College English, 48,* 52–61.

Windsor, D.A. (1990). The construction of knowledge in organizations: Asking the right questions about the Challenger. *Journal of Business and Technical Communication, 4* (2), 7–20.

ACKNOWLEDGMENT

We would like to thank Susan Booker and Mark Zachry for their insightful comments.

10

MULTICULTURAL ISSUES IN TECHNICAL COMMUNICATION

Emily A. Thrush

The University of Memphis

INTRODUCTION

Does anyone still doubt the need of today's technical communicator to be aware of cultural differences in reading and writing? Most practitioners have probably encountered cultural differences directly on their jobs—in writing computer documentation for products to be sold worldwide, in designing maintenance manuals to be used by technicians of varying cultural backgrounds, or in working with the managers of their foreign-owned companies.

The numbers have often been recited: more than 35,000 Americans are working for foreign-owned companies overseas (Lathan, 1982, p. 16), 300,000 are working for Japanese-owned companies in the United States

(Haight, 1991, p. 1), and more than 30,000 American companies are involved in exporting goods (Lathan p. 16), often equaling 25–50% of their total sales (Sprung, 1990, p. 71). According to a 1992 *Newsweek* article (Samuelson, 1992), between 1989 and 1991, United States exports to Mexico increased 62% to a total of $33.3 billion a year (p. 48)—and that was before the passage of NAFTA.

The implications for the technical communicator are clear, especially if one looks more closely at the software industry, a major employer of technical writers. In the countries making up the new European Union, for example, 19 of the 30 best selling software packages are American, and American software products account for 60% of total sales. Britain's *Economist* magazine ("Europe's Software Debacle," 1994) has recently reported that because of the various advantages (in expertise and financing) enjoyed by high-tech firms in the United States, many of Europe's largest software companies are opening management offices in the United States and transferring much of their operations here, where American and European designers, programmers, and managers will work side by side (pp. 77–78). Design and documentation for all these products, whether American or European produced, will need to take into account audiences on both sides of the Atlantic. The *Economist* reports that when Microsoft, purchaser of the Intuit line of software, wanted to market the very successful personal financial management package *Quicken* in France, the interface had to be redesigned to use an image other than that of a check, familiar to United States users, but much less widely used in France (p. 77).

There's no escaping the increasing internationalization of business. Even in my area, Memphis, Tennessee—not known as a center for international business nor as a destination for immigrants to the United States —we feel the effects of the changing world. One local writer, Steve Gillespie, has recently moved from rewriting installation manuals for Korean-made escalators at Dover Elevator Company, to working with Japanese managers and writing user instructions for Brother typewriters. Federal Express, a major employer in the area with its home office here, has gone international in a big way (even changing its name to FedEx, partly because it's more pronounceable for non-English speakers) and regularly trains employees for transfer overseas. We even have an International MBA program, one of many springing up around the country, in which American students take intensive language instruction and do internships abroad while international students study English and intern locally.

The signing of NAFTA, the APEC agreement with Asian countries, and the GATT treaty with Europe mean that new opportunities, and challenges, will open up for many industries all across the country. With increasing exports comes increasing need for documentation, manuals, and instructional materials of all kinds, from the simplest to the most complex. (Remember the story of Kellogg's Corn Flakes in England? Nobody bought any until the company put instructions on the box for adding sugar and milk.) Those who sell their skills in communicating for a living need to be prepared to meet the new challenges and take advantage of the opportunities.

Members of the technical and professional writing community generally agree that there is a need to:

- Raise awareness of the differences in communication styles and strategies across national and cultural boundaries.
- Demonstrate sensitivity to those cultures and avoid implications that we are measuring other cultures by our own or that we are trying to manipulate members of the other cultures.
- Avoid the cultural imperialism implicit even in such statements as "people are really all alike underneath," because this statement often means "people are just like me, want the same things I want, and will eventually learn to get them the same way I do, therefore I can just continue to do things the way I always have."

The question, of course, is how to do that? The danger is falling back on "tips" on international communication ("this is how the Japanese write a business letter" or "here's what a French computer manual looks like"), when those may not be the best models and certainly may reflect only the choices made by one writer in one particular context. What is needed is a framework for looking at cultures, a framework that will help technical communicators make reasonable hypotheses about how members of the culture will communicate and how they will receive and interpret attempts at communication.

In the rest of this chapter, I will review briefly what is known about technical and business writing in other cultures, then attempt to set up a preliminary framework—based on concepts from anthropology, sociology, history, political science, and economics—through which communicators can better analyze culturally diverse audiences to make informed communication choices.

CONCEPTS FROM LINGUISTICS

Contrastive Rhetoric

Much of what we know about international and intercultural communications comes from an area of linguistic study called contrastive rhetoric. People engaged in contrastive rhetoric research look at how members of various cultures accomplish certain communication tasks. They look at such features of a text as its pattern of organization, length, phrasing, and format. They are also interested in how members of different cultures accomplish specific speech acts such as persuasion or requests.

One problem with contrastive rhetoric is that it deals with individual documents, thereby making generalization difficult and risky. Also, to analyze a text and make reasonable assumptions about what is going on in it, the researcher must have not only a great facility with the language, but also a depth of understanding of the culture that is rare even in linguists. Many of the contrastive rhetoric studies in the literature were done using texts written by nonnative speakers of English in their English classes. While these texts reveal differences from the way native speakers of English would write, it's tricky to separate what features remain from the native language and what is the result of previous learning about English. It's also difficult to make statements about how other members of the culture would handle a similar communication task even in English because individual styles within a culture may vary depending on whether the writer was educated in another country (often Britain, the United States or France) or whether the country was recently a colony, in which case the writing style typical of the colonizing culture may be found side by side with the native style (Eggington, 1987).

Here's a sampling of what contrastive rhetoric teaches about documents in different cultures:

- In France, business documents such as proposals and reports tend to include more detailed information, statistics, and technical specifications in the body of the text than do American documents. On the other hand, business correspondence may include few details. Business transactions are often based on trust developed through long-term relationships between companies, so correspondence can use the kind of "shorthand" commonly found in communications between individuals who know each other well (Hall & Hall, 1990, p. 23).
- German documents tend to include considerable elaboration on the history of the organizations and their business relations (Hall & Hall, 1990, p. 35).
- Some cultures, including the Japanese, often prefer a narrative organization in business documents, which can place the main point of the text near the end rather than at the beginning, as is preferred in United States business documents (Haneda & Shima, 1982).
- Japanese writing tends to be writer-oriented (that is, designed to express the thoughts and feelings of the writer) while United States writing is reader-oriented (that is, with emphasis placed on the needs and wants of the reader). Chinese writing may be changing from

writer-oriented to reader-oriented (Hinds, 1987). Traditional Chinese texts of all kinds use extensive imagery and discourage the intrusion of the individual (Shen, 1989).

- Many cultures, including the French (Hall & Hall, 1990, pp. 103–104) and some African cultures (Boiarsky, 1995), value sophisticated, complex linguistic structures as reflective of a high level of education and competence in their fields. The short, simple sentences often favored by Americans may be viewed in these cultures as the product of carelessness or ignorance.
- Writing in Middle Eastern cultures traditionally does not focus on cause and effect relationships as much as writing in Western cultures (Leibman-Kleine, 1986).
- What counts as evidence to prove a point or to persuade varies from culture to culture: repetition and citation of authority in the Middle East (Leibman-Kleine, 1986), appeals to the emotion in Latin countries (Hall & Hall, 1990).
- Preference for graphics varies; some research indicates that certain types of graphics (three-tone drawings, line drawings, color photographs, etc.) may be processed better by members of some cultures than others (Sukaviriya & Moran, 1990), colors may carry different connotations (red versus green for warnings, for example) or evoke different feelings (del Galdo, 1990, p. 7), and ambiguity in images may be better tolerated by some cultures than is typical of Americans (Heba, 1994).

For more information on these findings from contrastive rhetoric, the reader should consult the work of researchers such as Ulla Connor, Robert Kaplan, and Ilona Leki. I have also discussed the issues mentioned above at greater length elsewhere (Thrush, 1993). The point I want to make here is that technical communicators can't and shouldn't wait for contrastive rhetoric researchers to examine documents from even the major cultures before the material on communicating across cultures is incorporated into professional writing classes. The texts subjected to contrastive rhetoric research represent a particular communicator in a particular organization at a particular point in time. There are obviously individual differences within cultures as well due, for instance, to the influence of "corporate cultures." Also, communication styles change with time; many English language programs in Asia are beginning to use American business writing texts, and a recent British text, *International Business English* by Leo Jones and Richard Alexander (1989), espouses principles strikingly closer to current American style than to traditional British business writing.

Masculinity versus Femininity

From linguistics, technical communication also got the concepts of masculinity and femininity in communication styles. According to the ways men and women communicate in mainstream United States culture, masculine style is defined as confrontational and assertive while feminine style is consensus-seeking, more intuitive, and emotional. Cross-cultural research shows that in some countries the "feminine" style of communication is widespread and characteristic of business and political negotiations, while in others the "masculine" style is prevalent (Dorfman, 1994). The Netherlands and France, for example, rank on the feminine side of the scale, while the United States and, perhaps surprisingly, Japan fall on the masculine side (Hofstede, 1993). Surprisingly, because the Japanese are known for seeking consensus, but their communication style is certainly not emotional or intuitive. The implications of this for designers and writers of technical and business communications are clear. The direct, unelaborated style of American business writing with its emphasis on facts and statistics is directly related to the dominance of the masculine style in our business environment.

CONCEPTS FROM ANTHROPOLOGY

High versus Low Context

Anthropologists classify cultures on a continuum from high context to low context. In a high-context culture, the members share a great deal of information because of a common education, religion, ethnic background, and so on. In a high-context culture, writers and speakers do not need to give extensive details or to give much support for their opinions because they can assume that the audience shares their values and attitudes. A low-context culture, on the other hand, is one in which the members have differing religious, ethnic, and educational backgrounds, so the writer must work hard to make sure that analogies are clear, details are inclusive, and sufficient support is included to persuade someone who comes to the text with entirely different assumptions about the world and how it works. The United States is an excellent example of a low-context culture, which explains why good business writing contains all relevant details and is explicit in expressing what the writer wants the reader to do. Take, for example, this letter from an insurance company to an insured individual who has just bought a new car:

> Enclosed is the application on your new Nissan Altima. Please sign this at the bottom where indicated in yellow, and return the form to our office with a check for $60.17. A stamped return envelope is enclosed for your convenience.

Not a word is wasted, and the reader is left with no doubt about what to do next.

Most contrastive rhetoric texts that contrast documents from a high-context culture to documents from a low context culture point out that members of high-context cultures are irritated by instructions such as those in the example above. They feel that their intelligence is in question and that the writer is being condescending. Because most of the researchers are American and their purpose is often to show Americans how to communicate better with other cultures, less has been written about the reverse effects. One exception is a case study in Andrews and Andrews' *Business Communication* (1992) that describes an interaction between an American and a Japanese company. After a face-to-face meeting where they set a schedule for a number of shipments, the representatives of the two firms returned to their countries. As the time for the first shipment approached, the Americans became concerned because they hadn't heard anything from the Japanese. Eventually they sent a fax that said, in essence, "Do you still plan to ship on time? *Please respond.*" The Japanese were puzzled—why should there be any question about whether they were keeping to the schedule? The problem was that the Japanese assumed there was no need for further communication as long as everything proceeded as planned, while the Americans expected to receive updates and confirmations. The lack of a continual flow of communication caused considerable anxiety among the low context Americans.

I saw the same principle at work recently when I acted as United States contact for a Summer Institute in languages and the Teaching of English as a Foreign Language to be held in the Czech Republic. I sent out information on the program, but people had to write or fax the administrators of the program directly. Most received an initial confirmation that they were registered for the program. Some received an information packet with a housing request form; other didn't because of the vagaries of international mail. When the applicants called me, I was usually able to confirm that the administrators knew they were coming because I was in e-mail contact with a colleague who was there on a Fulbright fellowship. For many, this was enough. Others, however, became extremely frustrated with the lack of communication and called or wrote me constantly, looking for reassurance. One even mailed a check to the Czech Republic as a deposit, even though the initial information specifically said that they were unable to deal with American checks and preferred people to pay with travelers' checks on arrival. (The check disappeared somewhere—either in the mail or in the hands of a Czech who didn't know what to do with it.)

The degree of frustration and even anger expressed by the (low-context) Americans was surprising and illuminating. These were people who teach students from all over the world—if they were unprepared and unwilling to cope with differences in amount and type of communications, how could others be expected to? I also learned that explaining the basis for the differences satisfied some on the surface, but never really removed the underlying discomfort. My colleague had also tried to explain to the Czechs that the Americans needed more information, but with limited success. The moral of this story seemed to be that advocating change of deep-seated, culturally determined communication patterns is risky and often unproductive, while encouraging understanding may yield only limited results.

Concepts of Time and Space

Two other concepts from anthropology that may be relevant to our study of written documents have to do with time and space. Anthropologists talk about monochronic versus polychronic cultures. In a monochronic culture, such as the mainstream United States, the members are most comfortable doing one task at a time. All of their time and attention are devoted, at least for a short period of time, to that one task. In a polychronic culture, on the other hand, members typically give attention to several activities at once. The classic example of the clash that can result from the meeting of monochronic and polychronic cultures is the business meeting during which the monochronic participants are annoyed and irritated as the polychronic participants take phone calls, talk to visitors, and generally split their attention several different ways.

In written communication, this focus on completion of one task at a time translates into a particular rhetorical style, which influences even academic writing in United States school systems. Composition classes teach that paragraphs, and essays, have one main idea, with supporting details directly related to only that idea. In other words, each essay works to accomplish one, and only one, task. The greater degree of tolerance for discussion of peripherally related ideas in the expository essays of other cultures corresponds to the degree to which members of the culture are willing to divide their time and attention among topics.

Similarly, the advice on writing business letters in American textbooks is to "get to the point quickly" (that is, state the one main idea), then give only information that is directly relevant to what you want to accomplish (do one task at a time). In other cultures, a business letter may be expected to perform social as well as business functions and thus may be more discursive.

Also, when each period of time is devoted to only one task, it becomes important to complete the task quickly to move on to the next item of business. Consequently, conciseness of expression is highly valued in monochronic cultures. A problem encountered by companies selling computer equipment and software internationally is that manuals written in the United States contain very little redundancy of information. Because strategic repetition of important points is often expected in educational materials in other cultures, including most Latin cultures (Mikelonis, 1994), this brevity works against the effectiveness of the documentation when translated.

In addition, cultures treat space differently. It is fairly widely known that members of the mainstream American culture require greater personal space than members of many other cultures. This is expressed in the distances maintained between speakers during conversations, the size of houses and apartments, and the preference for open and uncluttered work spaces. This probably also explains the American preference for large amounts of white space in business and technical documents.

CONCEPTS FROM SOCIOLOGY

Group-orientation versus Individualism

Sociology looks at the behavior of people in groups. The behavior patterns revealed in this research are reflected in, and influence, communication patterns. For example, one continuum on which sociologists place cultures is that of group versus individual orientation. In group-oriented societies, everyone is a part of a group, whether that group be the family or some larger unit. The individual receives rewards from the group and is expected to contribute to the good of the group in return. This translates into loyalty to the employer, emphasis on group decisions, and rewards for conformity. In individualistic societies, individuals may still be members of family and business groups, but they are expected to achieve and survive on their own. This is manifested in "job-hopping" to advance the career, a desire for autonomy, and greater expectation for individual performance (Dorfman, 1994). The United States is placed by most sociologists at the individualistic end of this spectrum. But several of the subcultures within the United States are more group-oriented, which has often resulted in miscommunication between management and workers.

One of the ways in which this difference in orientation manifests itself in business communication is the use of the signature to assign responsibility. In American correspondence, contracts, and other documents, the signature indicates the individual who takes ultimate responsibility for the contents of the document. If an executive, for example, signs a contract containing terms that are unacceptable to the company the executive represents, that executive's job may be at risk. In Japan, on the other hand, contracts are often sealed with the company stamp rather than the signature of an individual, reflecting the fact that the terms of the contract are the result of a group decision-making process. Even though this may seem a minor point, the emphasis on individual responsibility and achievement versus the group affects all phases of business negotiations and conduct.

Competition versus Consensus

Related to the differences in orientation toward the group or the individual is the difference in focus on competition versus consensus. When people strive for individual success, they are likely to be in competition with each other. This increases the emphasis on closing the deal and making the sale. The result is the kind of assertive, self-confident style of expression advocated in American business writing texts. In consensus-seeking, group-oriented cultures, the individual is unlikely to pose as having greater abilities or intellect than others, but will strive to appear humble and self-effacing. This is evident in the samples of Japanese business letters examined by Haneda and Shima (1982) and Chinese correspondence analyzed by Halpern (1983).

It has sometimes been stated, erroneously, that Japanese has no word for "no." What is true is that the Japanese, among other consensus-seeking cultures, are reluctant to say "no" in business negotiations, both for fear of destroying the possibility of reaching consensus and from reluctance to cause another to "lose face." Much anecdotal evidence exists for the problems this causes when correspondence goes unanswered because the answer is "no" or negotiators think an agreement has been reached because no one said "no" during the discussions. However, there is a remedy for this communication problem. English teachers working with students from consensus-seeking cultures have learned not to ask questions that might force the listener into an answer that would embarrass either party. "Do you understand?" is not likely to elicit accurate information, but "Would you like me to repeat?" permits a "yes" answer that insults neither the learner nor the teacher. Even better is "Which part of the lesson would you like to go over?" Similarly, in a business negotiation, training session, or needs analysis, questions that avoid the necessity of "no" responses will be more effective and less awkward.

HISTORY, POLITICAL SCIENCE, AND ECONOMICS

The political and economic history of a culture has a distinct impact on communication strategies. Think about how American business works: rewards, in the form of promotions and raises, are based on individual performance. If you get the deal signed, you get rewarded. If you don't, eventually you will probably find yourself out of a job. In recent history, this has been particularly true for management personnel as companies "downsized." In the 1980s, an estimated 3 million managers lost their jobs. It is easy to see how the strong incentives to get the deal signed, partnered with the fear of being unemployed, led to the aggressiveness of the American business style. If time is money, and money is the way success is measured by the society, then time is too precious to waste on developing relationships with business contacts or indeed on any activity that does not directly lead to increased profits.

In many other countries, including Japan and most of Western and Eastern Europe, instability of employment has not been the case. Employees were seldom fired, and promotions came with seniority, not performance. Also, the net of social services in these countries made the specter of unemployment considerably less frightening. Successful business dealings were still a goal, but there was less pressure to conduct business quickly. According to Robert Samuelson (1992, p. 48), a *Newsweek* analyst, "[G]enerous welfare benefits make it easier for people to survive without work. . . . In 1991, about 6 percent of unemployed Americans had been without a job for more than a year; in Europe, the comparable figure was 46 percent."

There are indications that this is changing. Articles in the European press in the past few years have discussed the need for greater flexibility in hiring, firing, and reassigning employees. Still, most attempts to reform employment practices are met with resistance and, at times, demonstrations and strikes.

The Central and Eastern European countries are in the process of change from a heavily socialized system, in which there were few rewards for individual achievement, but also few penalties for inefficiency or incompetence, to a market economy. Most of these nations have not yet reached a final determination on how much social support will be offered. Already, however, employers and managers have had to learn to give more specific information on business transactions and employment conditions than was true in the days when all these items were determined centrally, by the government, and everyone understood what prices could be charged and how much labor was worth (Hall & Thrush, 1992).

The effect of this difference on communication styles is understandable. If your job is not on the line every morning when you report to work, you are more likely to devote time and energy to long-term goals rather than to turning an immediate profit. Considerable anecdotal evidence exists of American companies losing major contracts because they rushed the negotiations or presented a written proposal, with its emphasis on bottom-line costs and profits, without establishing an interpersonal relationship of trust beforehand and without taking into consideration the values and goals of the foreign organization. On the other hand, where international business arrangements have been successfully completed, as in the opening of McDonald's in the Soviet Union (Puffer & Vikhansky, 1994) or Toys 'R Us in Japan and Europe ("The World," 1992), they have usually resulted from years of negotiation and study of local conditions.

Another effect of the political system seems to be the institutionalization of hierarchy. When political systems and business organizations are highly stratified, that structure is reflected in the communication style, especially in the maintenance of distance between reader and writer. It has often been noted that the Japanese language contains a system of particles that, added to words, indicates precise degrees of status between the reader and writer. Although few other languages have such a finely tuned way of reflecting hierarchy as this, distance is often maintained by formality and impersonality of tone. Or, as an Argentinian commented, "The more closely you approach a dictatorship, the more formal the language becomes." (Boiarsky, 1995). In contrast, the more open, democratic style of American business is reflected in the friendly tone and "you" perspective prevalent in documents, from memos to proposals to operation manuals.

THE MULTICULTURAL WORKFORCE

As little as we know about technical communication in other countries, it is startling how little research has been done on subcultures within the United States, especially in light of the fact that they are expected to make up 21–25% of the workforce by the year 2000. This includes African-Americans, Hispanic-Americans, and Asian-Americans as the largest groups of American-born minorities. The fact that little research has been done on the rhetorical styles of these groups (aside from some discussion of the language of sermons in African-American churches) is probably partly political. Discussion of whether a distinctive Black English vernacular exists has been highly controversial, with objections that the proponents supporting the existence of such a dialect were primarily white (Wolfram, 1990).

However, the problems raised by culturally patterned variances in communication style are widely recognized. The July 1994 issue of the *Journal of Business and Technical Communication* was devoted to articles on workplace diversity, most of them documenting difficulties experienced by companies with increasingly diverse workforces or implementing human resource policies fostering diversity.

Nasreen Rahim (1994) of the Institute for Business and Community Development in the San Jose/Evergreen Community College District teaches courses in workplace English and communication skills for companies in her area. In addition to vocabulary and basic grammar, she has discovered that her students need to learn how to be "politely assertive." That is, they need to be able to communicate with supervisors, particularly about equipment needs and safety concerns, and to learn how to persist until their concerns are heard. She concentrates on the use of expressions such as "could you" and "would you." These expressions moderate questions in English to make them more polite, and they are used much more extensively in English than their equivalents in other languages.

There are programs like Ms. Rahim's all over the United States, but they address almost exclusively the needs of immigrants in low-skill jobs. At the more highly skilled and management levels, many companies provide courses in writing or in making presentations; however, these are seldom focused on the problems caused by cultural differences. Seminars in diversity training address issues of culturally determined behavior and informal, oral communication differences, based on work done by researchers in the field of organizational behavior. But few researchers have looked specifically at differences in writing strategies or the processing of texts in subcultures of the United States. In fact, it is hard to find in the literature any acknowledgment that we need to understand these processes to produce effective technical documents and training materials for workplaces that include members of these subcultures. The need for research in this area is urgent; overcoming the political problems of getting funding and access will not be easy.

CONCLUSION

At the 1st Annual Conference on International Communications, held in Ames, Iowa, in the summer of 1994, two questions were raised that may be unanswerable at this point. Do certain principles of communication, whether from traditional rhetorical theory or from reading research, cut across cultural, national, and organizational differences? Should they be taught universally? One problem with the principles we normally teach in our classrooms is that they are all based on Western culture, whether we are teaching rhetorical principles from Aristotle to Bruffee, or relating research on how readers process texts. All that research was performed on American readers. Are the writing strategies that were successful with those readers successful because they corresponded with the expectations of Western readers or because all brains process text the same way? For example, cognitive linguists claim that readers of English expect to find some kind of statement of the main idea of a text at the end of the first paragraph in a short text, or by the end of the second or third paragraph in a longer text. Is that because American readers are accustomed to seeing main ideas in those locations? Until research can tell us whether members of other cultures process texts in the same way, we cannot be sure even that what we know about the advantages of headings, white space, and active verbs holds true for all audiences in all environments.

Some evidence has been found for similar argumentative structures across some European and American writing, including problem to solution organization, similar means of asserting and justifying claims, and awareness of audience (Connor & Kaplan, 1987). But this study did not examine more disparate cultures to see if those structures also existed in non-Western texts. Then how do we know what to teach to prepare students for the multicultural and international workplace they will be entering? As Nancy Allen (1994) pointed out recently in *Technical Communication Quarterly*, we need to do more than give students formulaic rules for making decisions in their writing. We can do this by referring to research that "illustrates the interactive nature of reading by describing ways in which readers draw on their own backgrounds, values, and communities to create meaning as they respond to verbal, visual, and cultural cues in the text before them" (p. 351). While most of the currently available workplace-based research does not deal with multicultural and international issues, we can enrich our examination of this research with the framework I've suggested in this essay for identifying the values and communities of a wide variety of possible audiences.

REFERENCES

Allen, N. (1994). Review of four technical writing textbooks. *Technical Communication Quarterly, 3*, 351–356.

Andrews, D.C. & Andrews, W.D. (1992). *Business communication.* (2nd Ed.). New York: Macmillan.

Boiarsky, C. (1995). The relationship between cultural and rhetorical conventions: Engaging in international communication. *Technical Communication Quarterly*, 4, 245–259.

Connor, U. & Kaplan, R.B. (Eds.). (1987). *Writing across languages: Analysis of the L2 text.* Reading, MA: Addison-Wesley.

del Galdo, E. (1990). Internationalization and translation: Some guidelines for the design of human-computer interfaces.In J. Nielson (Ed.), *Designing user interfaces for international use* (pp. 1–10). New York: Elsevier.

Dorfman, P. (1988). *Advances in international comparative management.* (Vol. 3). JAI Press. (Reprinted in D. Marcic & S.M. Puffer [Eds.]. [1994], *Management international: Cases, exercises, and readings* [pp. 151–157]. St.Paul, MN: West Publishing).

Eggington, W.G. (1987). Written academic discourse in Korean: Implications for effective communication. In U. Connor & R.B. Kaplan (Eds.), *Writing across languages: Analysis of the L2 text* (pp. 153–168). Reading, MA: Addison-Wesley.

Elashmawi, F. (1993). *Multicultural management: New skills for global success.* Houston: Gulf Publishing.

Europe's software debacle. (1994, November 12–18). *The Economist,* 77–78.

Ferraro, G.P. (1994). *The cultural dimension of international business.* (2nd Ed.). Englewood Cliffs, NJ: Prentice Hall.

Fine, M.G. (1991). New voices in the workplace: Research directions in multicultural communication. *Journal of Business Communication, 28,* 259–575.

Haight, Robert. (1991). *Infusing a global perspective into business communications courses: From rhetorical strategies to cultural awareness.* Unpublished Manuscript.

Hall, C. & Thrush, E.A. (1992, May 10). Technical communications in eastern Europe. 39th Annual Conference of the Society for Technical Communication. Atlanta, GA.

Hall, E.T. & Hall, M.R. (1990). *Understanding cultural differences.* Yarmouth, MA: Intercultural Press.

Halpern, J.W. (1983). Business communication in China: A second perspective. *Journal of Business Communication, 20,* 43–54.

Haneda, S. & Shima, H. (1982). Japanese communication behavior as reflected in letter writing. *Journal of Business Communication 19,* 19–32.

Heba, G. (1994, July 30). After words: A rhetoric of international multimedia communication. InterComm '94, Ames, IA.

Hinds, J. (1987). Reader vs. writer responsibility: A new typology. In U. Connor & R.B. Kaplan (Eds.), *Writing across languages: Analysis of the L2 text* (pp. 141–152). Reading, MA: Addison-Wesley.

Hofstede, G.H. (1991). *Cultures and organizations: Software of the mind.* London: McGraw-Hill.

Hofstede, G.H. (1993). Cultural constraints in management theories. *The Executive, 7,* 81–94.

Johnston, J. (1984). Business communication in Japan. *Journal of Business Communication, 17,* 65–69.

Jones, L. & Alexander, R. (1989). *International business English.* Cambridge, UK: Cambridge University Press.

Kalbfleisch, P.J. & Davies, A.B. (1991). Minorities and mentoring: Managing the multicultural institution. *Communication Education, 40,* 266.

Kaplan, R.B. (1966). Cultural thought patterns in intercultural education. *Language Learning 16,* 1–20.

Kilpatrick, R.H. (1984). International business communication practices. *Journal of Business Communication, 21,* 33–44.

Kozminski, A.K. & Cushman, D.P. (Eds.). (1993). *Organizational communication and management: A global perspective.* Albany, NY: State University of New York Press.

Lathan, M.G. (1982). Internationalizing business communication. *Mid-South Business Journal, 2,* 16–18.

Leki, I. (1991). Twenty-five years of contrastive rhetoric: Text analysis and writing pedagogies. *TESOL Quarterly, 25* (1), 123–143.

Liebman-Kleine, J. (1986). Towards a contrastive new rhetoric — A rhetoric of process. Teachers of English to Speakers of Other Languages. 20th Annual Meeting, Atlanta, GA.

Limaye, M.R. (1994). Facilitating research in multicultural business communication. *Bulletin of the Association for Business Communication, 57,* 37–45.

Limaye, M.R. & Victor, D.A. (1991). Cross-cultural communication research: State of the art and hypotheses for the 1990s. *Journal of Business Communication, 28,* 277–299.

Marcic, D. & Puffer, S.M. (1994). *Management international: Cases, exercises, and readings.* St.Paul, MN: West Publishing.

Matalene, C. (1985). Contrastive rhetoric: An American writing teacher in China. *College English, 47,* 789–808.

Mikelonis, V. (1994, July 30). Rhetoric of transition in central and eastern Europe. InterCom '94, Ames, IA.

Nielsen, J. (1990). *Designing user interfaces for international use.* New York: Elsevier.

Puffer, S.M. & Vikhansky, O.S. (1993). Management education and employee training at Moscow McDonald's. *European Management Journal, 11,* 102–107. (Reprinted in D. Marcic & S.M. Puffer [Eds.]. [1994], *Management international: Cases, exercises, and readings* [pp. 151–157]. St.Paul, MN: West Publishing).

Purves, A.C. (Ed.). (1988). *Writing across languages and cultures: Issues in contrastive rhetoric.* Newbury Park: Sage.

Rahim, N. (1994, July 30). Linguistic and cultural diversity on practical, on-the-job problems and changing roles in teaching and training communication skills. 1st Annual Conference on International Communications, Ames, IA.

Ruch, W.V. (1988). *International handbook of corporate communication.* Jefferson, NC: McFarland.

Samuelson, R.J. (1992, March 23). The gloom behind the boom. *Newsweek,* 48.

Shen, F. (1989). The classroom and the wider culture: Identity as a key to learning English composition. *College Composition and Communication, 40,* 459–466.

Sprung, R.C. (1990). Two faces of America: Polyglot and tongue-tied. In J. Nielson (Ed.), *Designing interfaces for international use* (pp. 71–101). New York: Elsevier.

Sukaviriya, P. & Moran, L. (1990). User interface in Asia. In J. Nielson (Ed.), *Designing interfaces for international use* (pp. 189–218). New York: Elsevier.

Thrush, E. (1993). Bridging the gaps: Technical communication in an international and multicultural society. *Technical Communication Quarterly, 2,* 271–285.

Varner, I. (1988). A comparison of American and French business correspondence. *Journal of Business Communication, 25,* 55–65.

Victor, D.A. (1994). Advancing research in international business communication. *Bulletin of the Association for Business Communication, 57,* 37–43.

Weiss, T. (1992). "Ourselves among others": A new metaphor for business and technical writing. *Technical Communication Quarterly, 1,* 23–36.

Wolfram, W. (1990). *Dialects and American English.* Englewood Cliffs, NJ: Prentice Hall.

The World "S" Ours. (1992, March 23). *Newsweek,* 46–47.

11

THE IMPACT OF NEW TECHNOLOGIES ON TECHNICAL COMMUNICATION

Henrietta Nickels Shirk

University of North Texas

INTRODUCTION: LEADING EDGE VERSUS LAGGING EDGE

For many technical communication professionals, the task of remaining on the "leading edge" of computer technology is often viewed with enough apprehension to make them believe they are rather on technology's "lagging edge." There is simply too much to learn, and once new computer technologies are learned, these technologies change too rapidly for most technical communicators to remain consistently well informed about their current status and potential developments. How, then, are technical communication teachers, students, and practitioners to cope with the masses of evolving information that surround technology?

This essay offers several tools to assist those in the field of technical communication with the task of making sense of and remaining current with new computer technologies (both hardware and software) that impact technical communication. It also examines how existing technologies have influenced and changed the professional work that technical communicators accomplish, the specific challenges for technical communicators inherent within each group of technologies, and some of the relevant perspectives on the future of these technologies. It concludes with a consideration of the curricular implications of these technologies for both the teaching and the ongoing study of technical communication.

The approach in this essay is eclectic and categorical. Suggested tools to assist with understanding and tracking technologies are several metaphors that provide "mental maps" that may be superimposed on the chaos and plethora of information that surround computer technologies. As a foundation for this discussion, it is first useful to consider critically some of the assumptions about "computer literacy" that have become associated with technical communicators in general.

THE "COMPUTER-LITERATE" TECHNICAL COMMUNICATOR

The job title of technical communicator has always been somewhat misleading for those not knowledgeable about this profession. The common assumption has been that, because technical communicators communicate about technical subject matters, they necessarily learn about and are well informed concerning the many technologies that can be used to support the creation of their technical communication products. The view is that technical communicators must, by definition, be "technically literate," and, by implication, that they are therefore especially endowed with "computer literacy" because they use computer "tools of the trade" in their profession.

There are, in fact, many different kinds of "literacy" associated with computer literacy for technical communicators. In addition to assumed verbal literacy (as expressed through word processing and desktop publishing), various literacies are associated with visualization. Visual literacy includes the competencies of both evaluating and creating visual images— or, at least, the ability to direct others in the effective creation of such materials. It also encompasses knowledge of color, perspective, typography, page and screen layouts, and other "document packaging" techniques.

The problem of comprehending the multitude of computer technologies can be initially addressed by using a classification system (taxonomy) that helps to clarify the roles that computer technologies are capable of fulfilling within the job responsibilities and processes exercised by technical communicators. At a general level, computer technologies may be categorized in terms of either hardware or software. The computer-literate technical communicator understands the uses that can be made of both hardware and software.

Figure 11.1 presents the various kinds of storage, image manipulation, and communication devices that computer technologies can contribute to accomplishing the tasks required of technical communicators. Figure 11.2 presents the various functions that computer technologies can contribute to the process of creating technical communication products, including planning, writing, editing, and publication. Both figures present minimal topics for computer literacy, and both identify the various roles that computer technologies can fulfill as assistants to technical communicators in their professional work. In various combinations, hardware and software have created a series of metaphors for thinking about technology. These metaphors categorize the functions of computer technologies and provide a method for tracking and monitoring their current and future development. In short, they help to make order of what could be technological

#1 — Remembering *Storage:* Disks CD-ROMs WORMs ***Computer's Role:*** *Extended Memory*	**#2 — Visualizing** *Graphics:* Scanners Printers Light Pens ***Computer's Role:*** *Design Assistant*
#4 — Recording *Capture/Playback Mechanisms:* Audio Video Animation ***Computer's Role:*** *Media Manipulator*	**#3 — Communicating** *Networks:* Modems Fax Machines Satellites ***Computer's Role:*** *Information Facilitator*

Figure 11.1 Hardware to Support Technical Communications

#1 — Pre-writing	**#2 — Writing**
Creativity Heuristics: Audience Analyzers Idea Generators Outline Processors Project Scheduling Programs ***Computer's Role:*** *Planning Assistant*	*Writing Support Tools:* Word Processing Graphic Packages Bibliography Generators Electronic Thesauruses ***Computer's Role:*** *Tool Provider*
#4 — Publishing	**#3 — Editing**
Publishing Implementation: Desktop Publishing Tools: (Layouts, Font Styles and Sizes) Presentation Programs Hypertext and Hypermedia ***Computer's Role:*** *Professional Publisher*	*Editing Assistance:* Spelling Checkers Grammar Checkers Writing Style Analyzers Editing Response Programs (ERPs) ***Computer's Role:*** *Change/Revision Agents*

Figure 11.2 Software to Support Technical Communication

chaos. This essay examines four of these electronic metaphors—the pen, the link, the web, and the mind.

ELECTRONIC PENS TO ASSIST CREATIVITY

During the past decade, the work of technical communicators has been most greatly influenced by the widespread use of computers in the document creation, design, and publication processes. As "electronic pens," computers enable technical communicators to write, edit, and create graphics and page layouts more quickly, and to publish documents with professional appearance from the convenience of their own desktops. In addition to the cost benefits of greater efficiency and improved packaging techniques, these technologies engage their users in the creative space of a computer environment. And this environment, in turn, affects the creativity inherent in technical communication.

Changing Previous Mindsets

The mindset about technical communication that is evolving because of this group of electronic pen technologies is different from the one that technical communicators had in their old paper-based environment. Although computers may indeed be only "dumb machines," they are used and managed by the "smart machines" of human minds. Many technical communicators have made the mistake of assuming that computer technologies will do their professional work for them, or, minimally, do their work better than they are able to do it. They have failed to recognize that technologies are just tools; as tools they do not automatically confer talent, although they can be used with talent. In short, technical communicators have not been serious enough in addressing the challenges and consequent changes that these technologies command.

Such challenges and changes involve responding appropriately to the overabundance of electronic options for the creation of communication products. The wide variety of fonts, styles, type sizes, and page layout formats makes graphical expertise a necessity for technical communicators. Prospective employers now assume that technical communicators know about more than writing. This demand requires learning about skills such as visual design and page layout. Even if technical communicators do not know how to draw, they must learn something about effective visual communication and, at least, how to recognize it. For those who are verbally rather than visually oriented, this may be a daunting task, requiring creativity on many levels.

VIEWING COMPUTERS AS PARTNERS

A more comprehensive view of the pen metaphor as a category for computer technologies relates to the creative environment in which technical communicators participate when they use these technologies to assist in the communication process. To produce communication products with an electronic pen means not only to engage in the greater efficiency of revisions, but also to enter fully into an environment in which the computer becomes a partner as well as a tool. This partnership can enhance creativity, if technical communicators are willing to take risks with these technologies and not only undergo the effort in learning them but also have the desire to experiment with them. Many technical communicators have gotten caught in word processing software and never explored any of the other software options available to assist them in communicating more effectively. Some of those software options are listed in Figure 11.2.

A significant electronic pen that many technical communicators are now wielding is that of the creation of on-line communications—information intended to be presented solely via the computer rather than on paper. Those who are creating on-line publications know that there are no easy rules for doing so. Research in this area of communication has been limited, and technical communicators have tended simply to repeat what they already know about paper-based communication. Because computer screens are not the same as pieces of paper, new ways of presenting information must be explored. Technical communicators have to learn about software design and software psychology, and then take from these fields whatever will help them communicate effectively in the on-line medium. The challenges are great, and, in a sense, everyone is a beginner in relation to on-line communication, especially that which enables linkages.

ELECTRONIC LINKS TO FACILITATE CONNECTIONS

The terms hypertext, hypermedia, multimedia, and interactive video have become a familiar, although sometimes intimidating, new vocabulary for technical communicators. The ability to link texts, graphics, animation, sound, and video electronically has vastly changed the communication methods and products available to technical communicators, as well as placed some new requirements on their ongoing development of effective communication skills.

Understanding New Communication Methods

Now that some of the initial excitement about "hyper" communication has passed, technical communicators must determine how they are going to best use this group of technologies to communicate with their various audiences. In fact, they must decide whether the electronic linking of information is always the most effective choice for communicating. It has been generally assumed that hyper communication is most often the technology of choice for large databases of information—situations where audiences require immediate access to vast bodies of complex information (equipment service and repair manuals, for example). From this somewhat limited perspective, electronic links are simply information access techniques that are faster, and therefore more efficient, than those available on paper. From another perspective, linkages are important when technical communicators need to provide their audiences with information in more than one medium. Hyper communication then becomes the "glue" that holds the whole communication product together, and the size of the communication becomes irrelevant.

Redefining Perceptions of Audiences

While both of these criteria (large size and multiple media) for determining when to use electronic links have practical relevance in further determining when these technologies are appropriate, a third consideration relating to audience needs is even more important for technical communicators. Electronic links make it possible to address multiple levels of audience. This fact places some new demands on technical communicators. Unfortunately, the pedagogy of technical communication has addressed audience on a rather superficial level, mainly because paper publication places economic and practical restrictions on publication length. Almost all technical communication textbooks, as well as the experiences of practicing professionals, have espoused addressing one primary audience (ideally) and perhaps a single secondary audience (if necessary). The unlimited availability and reasonable cost (compared to paper) of electronic storage and the ability to link information in unlimited ways casts a whole new perspective on the notion of audience. Technical communicators have not yet become comfortable or proficient in addressing the notion of multiple levels of audience and the variety of learning styles and needs they might represent. The areas of learning theory and educational psychology must become part of the training programs for technical communicators. Simplistic thinking about addressing the needs of only two levels of audiences is rapidly becoming a practice of the past.

However, another consideration in selecting electronic links is even more basic: the availability of the various hardware and software technologies that make hyper communication possible. For example, if readers of a manual do not have the requisite presentation software and hardware components, such as HyperCard or ToolBook, and a CD-ROM or videodisk player, the best designed electronically linked communication is useless. One major concern in this area is transportability. Linked texts developed to run on one computer platform are usually not easily transported to other platforms. Those who must produce single products that communicate in several computer environments, for instance, know that even translation programs are neither completely effective nor efficient in converting a Macintosh hypertext to one that will run in a DOS environment. It appears that these challenges in electronic link technologies are going to continue to confront technical communicators for some time to come. The solution, of course, is the standardization that so much of computer technology calls for but which has been difficult, if not impossible, to achieve.

Revisioning the Interactivity of Communication

The power of electronic links has resulted in new technical communication products such as interactive on-line documents. One of the most significant groups of these products are those that fall under the heading of computer-based training (CBT) or computer-based instruction (CBI). Because all products of technical communication teach in some way, computer-based methods of linking information from which audiences can learn through interactions with the computer itself should be of interest to technical communicators. Pedagogical branching, which gives learners immediate feedback on their responses and then allows them to proceed to whatever best meets their learning styles and needs, is an important technique for technical communicators. In such learning environments, the computer itself becomes a persona through the dialogue made possible by its software. As creators of one side of such dialogues, technical communicators must pay close attention to style, tone, and voice. In addition, such qualities are not confined to words alone, but are also expressed graphically.

Electronic links not only provide new perspectives on the nature and structure of texts but also redefine the creative process itself. The ability to link text, graphics, animation, sound, and video has changed the one-dimensional realm of paper-based textuality to the multidimensional realm of electronic-based textuality. However, not publishing communication products on paper can be both liberating and restrictive. While it is exciting and challenging to think of multiple audiences and multiple connections of information, it is not always easy to structure this new communication environment in ways that prevent audiences from becoming hopelessly lost and frustrated. Technical communicators must learn to be architects and designers of computer-based information structures and of pathways within these structures in ways still being discovered and tested. In a sense, all technical communicators who create electronically linked communications are exploring and helping to define new creative environments.

From a more sobering perspective, technical communicators must confront the current realities of electronic link technologies. Even with today's "easy" menu-driven hyper authoring systems, the creation of electronically linked communication is time-consuming and labor-intensive. Technical communicators must learn specialized computer languages to accomplish the truly innovative. Finally, technical communicators must develop a whole new range of skills that have traditionally not been a part of their profession. The design and production of professional graphics, animation, and video require new skills and cross-disciplinary efforts. At the minimum, these new directions require teams of experts who can work together productively.

ELECTRONIC WEBS TO SUPPORT COLLABORATION

Although teamwork and collaboration are highly praised in most technical communication environments today, the reasons for their successes and failures are still not fully understood. Even so, both software and hardware to support collaboration are being rapidly developed. These "electronic webs" have most recently been manifested through the growth of the "Information Superhighway," represented by the collection of on-line services available through the Internet, and through groupware products. Both of these manifestations of electronic webs provide evolving perspectives on collaboration, and both are providing technical communicators with changes as well as challenges.

The major changes that have resulted from these electronic web technologies have occurred because of the interconnectivity that they create. Technical communicators no longer have to function in job settings outside of their homes. Instead, through network technology they can connect to other teammates with whom they work and then use software products that assist the whole team in the collaborative process.

Navigating the "Information Superhighway"

The "Information Superhighway" created by on-line network services has revolutionized the dissemination of information and the ability of technical communicators to send and receive information over great distances. There is now no reason, for example, why technical communicators today have to live in the same country as their employers. Technical communication products can be researched, written, reviewed, and even published over the vast web of networks that now connect all major industrial areas on the earth. But what really happens on networks, and can they actually enhance the collaborative communication process?

Anyone who has ever accessed a network bulletin board has probably been overwhelmed by the deluge of available information, as well as exhilarated by its infinite possibilities for connecting with others. Technical communicators can now access information not readily available to them previously. Carried to its extreme, the presence of networks contributes to the image of technical communicators as surveyors (and perhaps also purveyors) of information, ideally located at the center of a web of data flowing in and data flowing out of their circles of creativity. The reality of this image is still evolving.

In truth, all technical communicators who use networks in accomplishing their work must deal not only with the difficulty of oversaturation of information on the crowded "Information Superhighway," but also with learning to function in an electronic web environment. Some humor has been focused on the problems of network etiquette, sometimes called "(n)etiquette." Two extremes of network behavior are "flamers" and "lurkers." The former use the networks to vociferously and usually inappropriately communicate their own biases and prejudices (often anonymously), while the latter quietly read what is going on in network conversations but never say a word or have the courage to enter into such conversations themselves—they simply "lurk" in the background. Both of these types of network users demonstrate a major concern of many technical communicators about using networks—that is, the lack of human contact fostered by and resulting from the use of electronic webs.

Collaborating Through Groupware

Although technical communicators can now participate in and facilitate group work and discussions in collaborative ways not possible before electronic webs, a major concern for many using these technologies is that they do not have direct contact with their collaborators. Although video transmissions are now technologically possible to accompany audio exchange of information, such technology is generally beyond the economic means of most organizations, except on a limited basis. More research is needed on the nature of collaboration, especially on the effects of electronic accessibility on group creativity and productivity. Until such information is available, criticisms of electronic webs to support collaboration may be matters of personal preference rather than the results of verifiable research on the effectiveness of group processes and products.

Technical communicators now have network access to software that enhances collaborative work. "Groupware" products are really combinations of existing technologies, including telephones, computers, electronic mail, videos, image projection, and others. What makes groupware products unique as a software category is that they are all designed to support collaborative efforts. Groupware products help workgroups perform such job responsibilities as exchanging project information (for example, product development and scheduling data), conducting group discussions and group reviews, and filtering content for specially designated audiences. The development of such collaborative technologies is still in its rudimentary stages. To many workgroups, much of the existing groupware appears limited and overly controlling. For now, it seems that groupware designed to meet the general needs of collaborative workgroups fails to meet the needs of specific ones.

Groupware also requires the commitment of all members of a collaborative team. If even one team member refuses to use the groupware or uses it sporadically, the team's collaborative efforts will probably fail or the team will have to revert to noncomputerized collaboration. However, technical communicators can use existing groupware to make the document review process more efficient and manageable. Many products now track changes to documents and allow multiple and simultaneous inputs of changes to them. Technical communicators need to monitor and learn more about this area of developing computer technologies.

Sharing knowledge and information in the collaborative process via the electronic webs of networks and groupware can potentially transform the logistics of the work environment of technical communicators. At the moment, this group of technologies has not reached its full potential. Electronic webs should become easier to use, more adaptable to individual needs, and less expensive. From the perspective of technical communicators, electronic webs require rethinking the nature and value of collaboration itself. Such self-examination will undoubtedly be a healthy exercise for the profession because it will lead to new definitions of creativity and perhaps even of authorship.

ELECTRONIC MINDS TO SIMULATE REALITY

As technical communicators contemplate their creative communication processes, they cannot help but be drawn to a final group of computer technologies that may be identified as "electronic minds." This is the category of technologies that began with artificial intelligence and has most recently taken the form of expert systems, virtual reality, neural networks, and simulations. While it is not the goal here to explain how these technologies work, it is helpful for technical communicators to understand how their participation on design teams for such technologies will require specially developed skills. It is also helpful to consider how these electronic mind technologies might support the education of technical communicators.

Developing New Skills

Artificial intelligence, expert systems, and neural networks have essentially captured processes and products that are as close as possible to the way the human mind works. Although many maintain that the term "artificial intelligence" is an oxymoron, it has long been the challenge of computer software designers to reproduce the workings of the human mind. Although the results of these efforts have, to date, been unsuccessful in electronically creating truly human minds, tremendous strides have been made in developing software that assists humans in solving problems, making decisions, and completing tasks.

Technical communicators can be valuable contributors to design teams for electronic mind software. The electronic mind technologies rely on capturing large amounts of information and on creating a "knowledge engine" or software to access it and rapidly sort through it to answer questions. The large-scale storage and rapid access possible with computers does indeed rival most human minds. Creating software that represents the best ways of thinking by experts in any field requires an understanding of how these experts address and solve problems. This is where technical communicators can lend their interviewing and observational skills to the software design process. Getting information, experiences, and thought processes out of the minds of experts requires communication skills rather than technical skills. And interviewing skills are among those in which technical communicators typically excel. Therefore, as interviewers, technical communicators must refine their skills to include knowledge about cognitive psychology, linguistics, and related fields. In short, they must be able to gain not only content information, but also an understanding of expert problem solving.

Using the New Technologies

Electronic mind technologies can also contribute to the development of technical communicators through simulations (using the computer to present situations simulating real life), although currently very little work done in this area relates to technical communication. The use of simulations in the education and training of technical communicators should be explored by technical communication educators. Technical communicators often do not use the technologies they help to create and document in their own professional development.

CONCLUSION: PIONEERS ON THE INFORMATION HIGHWAY

The metaphors described here are ways of conceptualizing what computer technologies are all about. Two main themes emerge from a consideration of the impact of computer technologies on technical communication. First, because computer technologies are always developing, one can never be completely current on the state of the art. Technology is progressing much more rapidly than technical communicators are able to take advantage of it. Second, technical communicators are users of technologies in creating their products. They must keep up with technological developments, even though it is difficult to do so, because they need to use them in their own profession. Both of these themes suggest the need to rethink the effects of technology on technical communicators and its implications for the teaching of technical communication.

Although the technological tools used by technical communicators have become more sophisticated and more efficient, the basic skills of verbal and visual literacy still have to be taught and learned. Those who teach must decide which technologies can best help technical communicators in their work and what theoretical and practical material from many related disciplines will best help them participate in technological development. To accomplish this task, educators and trainers must reconceptualize the vision of computer technologies that was prevalent in the mid-1980s. They must monitor the progress of technology and try to estimate its present and potential impact on the profession.

What, then, would a technology-driven restructuring of technical communication be like? The new technologies may obviously realign the way technical communicators do their work. Offices in office buildings may not be necessary. Developing technologies are going to continue affecting technical communication publishing, teaching, the way technical communicators do research—in short, everything that they do. The prototypes for the work environment to come are already in the marketplace. This future world will most likely be one of widespread handheld computers, readily available communications devices, and extremely user-friendly software. Voice commands to computers will probably take the place of the current textual and visual directives.

In the meantime, as this "brave new" technological environment looms on the horizon, technical communicators remain pioneers on the "Information Superhighway." Some are the advance scouts, willing to use and develop new technologies. Some are the pioneers who move steadily forward, eager to adapt whatever beneficial innovations technology has to offer, in spite of difficulties. Some turn back to a more comfortable world where technology (like the hardship of the trail) does not threaten their comfortable complacency. The last group does not worry about being left behind; they want to be left behind. Unfortunately, these technical communicators may eventually find themselves professionally unable to compete for jobs in today's—and tomorrow's—marketplace.

Technical communicators need to learn more about new technologies. The metaphors of the electronic pens, links, webs, and minds suggested here provide a framework for doing so. Additional books that might be useful in this ongoing process of understanding and assimilation are listed in the "Reading List" that follows this essay. They provide a starting point for technical communicators who wish to become participants rather than observers of technological change.

New technologies are not without the challenges inherent in change. The education and training of technical communicators must emphasize the fact that technologies are only tools, although powerful ones. These tools do not make better technical communicators, but they do make the jobs of technical communicators easier. In short, they help technical communicators communicate more effectively.

REFERENCES

Bolter, J.D. (1991). *Writing space: The computer, hypertext, and the history of writing.* Hillsdale, NJ: Erlbaum.

Campbell, J. (1989). *The improbable machine: What the upheavals in artificial intelligence tell us about how the mind really works.* New York: Simon & Schuster.

Greenberg, S. (Ed.). (1991). *Computer-supported cooperative work and groupware.* New York:Harcourt Brace Jovanovich.

Hardison, O.B., Jr. (1989). *Disappearing through the skylight: Culture and technology in the twentieth century.* New York: Viking Penguin.

Harmon, P. & King, D. (1985). *Expert systems: Artificial intelligence in business.* New York: Wiley.

Haugeland, J. (Ed.). (1981). *Mind design: Philosophy, psychology, artificial intelligence.* Cambridge, MA: MIT Press.

Haugeland, J. (1985). *Artificial intelligence: The very idea.* Cambridge, MA: MIT Press.

Johansen, R. (1988). *Groupware: Computer support for business teams.* New York: Free Press.

Landow, G.P. (1992). *Hypertext: The convergence of contemporary critical theory and technology.* Baltimore, MD: Johns Hopkins University Press.

Morelli, R. et al. (Eds.). (1992). *Minds, brains and computers: Perspectives in cognitive science and artificial intelligence.* Norwood, NJ: Ablex, 1992.

Olson, M.H. (Ed.). (1989). *Technological support for work group collaboration.* Hillsdale, NJ: Erlbaum.

Penrose, R. (1989). *The emperor's new mind: Concerning computers, minds, and the laws of physics.* New York: Oxford University Press.

Schrage, M. (1990). *Shared minds: The new technologies of collaboration.* New York: Random House.

12

THE POLITICS AND PRACTICE OF MEDIA DESIGN

Stuart A. Selber

Texas Tech University

INTRODUCTION

I recently conducted a one-day course on designing on-line documentation for a manuals and forms group at a popular Northwest branch bank. The manager, an experienced technical communicator and employee of 15 years, requested this course because her writers commonly lose such projects to subject matter experts within the corporation. Moreover, her boss estimates that the corporation can save more than $200,000 per fiscal year by converting 20 paper-based manuals to on-line manuals, so this group's success (or failure) clearly rests on their ability to compete for on-line documentation projects. They have experienced little success, thus far, because writers in this corporation are viewed narrowly as production or support specialists, an unfortunate and all too common perspective on technical communicators in workplace settings. By soliciting this course and through participating in other professional development activities, this manager is attempting to reverse common attitudes that locate the practice of on-line media design solely within the realm of programming and product development.

While preparing this course, I was reminded that designing media is complicated work because this activity is informed by interdisciplinary perspectives. Although there is much discussion about designing on-line information, many technical communicators are still primarily experienced in writing paper-based documentation. But the physical and rhetorical differences between pages and screens, for instance, pose significant challenges for writers and often force them to rethink how they organize and structure information, both on macro and micro levels (Bernhardt, 1993; Selfe, 1989). These differences also pose substantial problems for readers, who often read more slowly and less accurately, and struggle to "[get] a sense of text" in on-line information space (Haas, 1989). In addition to the challenges of writing and reading, few standards exist for designing human-computer interfaces in general and hypertext documentation systems in particular (Boyle & Ratliff, 1992), a worrisome condition given the expanded rate at which such systems are being developed. Combine these challenges and concerns with the constraints any one technology places on design tasks (such as how you can and cannot link information), as well as the design decisions encouraged or discouraged by any one technology (through default structures and templates provided by software manufacturers), and it becomes clear that there is much to know about designing media projects, both practically and theoretically.

This essay addresses issues technical communicators face when designing on-line media projects. It begins broadly, defining media design and the interdisciplinary realms that inform such work. It then offers a note of caution about the ideological nature of software applications that support projects. Next, this essay looks more narrowly at issues and principles for designing on-line media, paying particular attention to those for organizing information and structuring the human-computer interface. With an eye toward helping both professionals and teachers, it briefly outlines three challenges for productively educating technical communicators as the next generation of media designers.

DEFINING MEDIA AND MEDIA DESIGN

The domain of media design potentially includes all print and electronic technologies that mediate technical communication. This essay, however, considers computers in general and the design of multimedia and hypertext in particular. The expanded roles of technical communicators in workplace settings increasingly require them to use these environments for authoring on-line applications and for promoting productivity, information sharing, and collaborative work (see edited collections by Barrett, 1992; Doheny-Farina, 1988; Greenberg, 1991), Therefore, a discussion about foundations for teaching technical communication that ignored the design of multimedia and hypertext would be, at best, incomplete. Before discussing design issues, however, we need definitions for multimedia and hypertext which are often confused and/or conflated; we also need definitions for the activity of media design, which moves beyond the traditional tasks that technical communicators often engage in in workplace settings.

The Differences Between Multimedia and Hypertext

Although technical communication has articulated many of the physical and rhetorical differences between printed and on-line information (Cohen, 1991; Nord & Tanner, 1993), we have tended to treat the various types of on-line information more uniformly (because they require, in all cases, a computer for access), as opposed to recognizing the potential differences that might exist between them. Perhaps obstructing our vision of the ways in which multimedia and hypertext diverge are definitions that center exclusively on technological features, as opposed to pedagogical purposes or rhetorical approaches. For example, both environments commonly provide media designers with the ability to link information across screens, although hypertext, in certain forms, also provides users with this same capability. Depending on our perspectives, we may or may not find such user-centered design attractive. But understanding the potential differences between and applications of various media types requires us to consider how their technological features may or may not support the goals of communication activities.

Multimedia is commonly used to present information dynamically through some combination of text, graphics, animation, audio, and video. Numerous examples exist in technical communication, particularly for product demonstrations, tutorials, and guided tours. In many cases, users of multimedia systems have some control over the sequence and pace of information and almost no control over its content and structure. Designers often use interactivity to simulate processes or support metaphors that structure human-computer interfaces, and they look for ways of presenting information effectively and efficiently to a wide range of audiences for many different purposes: to inform, persuade, and educate (see the edited collection by Ambron and Hooper [1990] and *IEEE*

Multimedia, a new journal associated with the Institute of Electrical and Electronics Engineers, Computer Society). Although multimedia systems can be quite dynamic and robust, users tend to assume passive roles in their operation.

In contrast, hypertexts (or hypermedia) are networked structured chunks of information that users engage by following paths through multiply connected texts. Like multimedia, these chunks of information can include some combination of text, graphics, animation, audio, and video. In its most powerful sense, however, hypertext attempts to elevate the status of users by allowing them to co-author texts they encounter in the act of reading to engage the structure of information. As Gygi (1990) explains, "The so-called dynamism in hypermedia results from the user's ability to alter the medium, not from a dynamic presentation" (p. 281). Although this vision seems valuable, technical communication has adopted rather conservative approaches to hypertext, primarily considering its potential to automate rather than transform tasks (Johnson-Eilola & Selber, 1996). We commonly use hypertext as a delivery medium, for example, but rarely explore its generative uses in collaborative writing or product development. While some envision hypertext primarily as a new medium requiring a new rhetoric (Moulthrop, 1991; Shirk, 1991; Slatin, 1990), others view it more cautiously, retaining certain principles from the technology of print (Farkas, 1992; Horton, 1990). Regardless of any particular position, however, because it commonly includes graphics, audio clips, and video clips, the realm of hypertext will often include those issues important to the design of multimedia.

The Activity of Media Design

In many ways, designing multimedia and hypertext requires technical communicators to blend the tasks of architects, cartographers, and rhetoricians, particularly if we view on-line environments as spaces we build, navigate, and inhabit. As architects, media designers are involved in many stages of product development, from blueprinting specifications and deciding on tools and systems to coordinating and directing the work of others. And they are responsible for recursively testing the design to ensure its integrity. As cartographers, media designers make decisions about the scale or proportion of design elements, represent and describe their spatial relationships, and highlight or subordinate information depending on its relevance at particular junctures during user tasks. Like architects, they consider the graphical elements that both represent and structure information, although they pay particular attention to navigation issues and navigation aids, and play a more central role in production. Finally, as rhetoricians, media designers create user profiles and understand how to represent user tasks, construct arguments and effectively communicate in on-line information space, and implement pedagogical principles that are consistent with the communication goals of projects. Moreover, they bring critical perspectives that locate media design within human contexts, understanding that the environments they build, navigate, and inhabit are value-laden (see the essay by Ornatowski, this collection).

Contributing Disciplines and Interdisciplinary Education

Any educational model representing the knowledge domains that might inform media design should be interdisciplinary. This claim is hardly novel; in fact, it was implicit in the original mission of the Massachusetts Institute of Technology's Media Lab. According to Stewart Brand (1987), Nicholas Negroponte convinced individuals to support its creation in the late 1970s and early 1980s by forecasting the convergence of the print and publishing industry, the computer industry, and the broadcast and motion picture industry (p. 10). By 1987, the Lab housed 11 interdisciplinary workgroups with many alliances among them: Electronic Publishing; Speech; The Advanced Television Research Program; Movies of the Future; The Visible Language Workshop; Spatial Imaging; Computers and Entertainment; Animation and Computer Graphics; Computer Music; The School of the Future; and Human-Machine Interface (Brand, 1987, pp. 12–13). Negroponte and former MIT President Jerome Weisner assumed that "Graduates [of the Media Lab] will be required to pursue studies in epistemology, experimental psychology, filmmaking, holography, and signal processing, as well as in computer science" (Brand, 1987, p. 11).

Although no one technical communication program has the faculty or budget to support such intensively focused work, which might include larger proportions of influence from English studies and the humanities, we can broadly consider additional intersections and combinations of disciplines that inform projects in these three industries. Historically, the work of technical communication is aligned most closely with the print and publishing industry, and technical communication programs already offer courses in rhetoric, writing, editing, graphic design, and publications management. These kinds of courses constitute the core curriculum of many technical communication programs, in addition to more limited offerings in electronic documentation, human-computer interaction, and usability testing (Selber, 1995). From the computer industry, students need broad exposure to human factors/ergonomics, a conceptual understanding of how hardware and software operate, machine skills, and perhaps some programming skills (although object orientation has simplified the environments in which computer-based media are commonly designed). And, from the broadcast and motion picture industry, they should understand how to design visual effects and animation, and how a particular design "affect[s] the mind and feelings of the viewer" (Nelson, 1990, p. 238). According to Nelson, designing media is akin to making movies because "special talents are required that have nothing to do with the technicalities. The greatest of these is the ability to conceive and realize a unifying vision" (p. 238).

The convergence of these three industries, however, reveals gaps in potential areas of interdisciplinary education for media designers. We might include the creative aspects of theater, architecture, industrial design, and information display (Mountford, 1990), and, as in software documentation, emphasize the fields of linguistics, cognitive science, learning psychology, and reading studies (Barker, 1991). Perhaps most neglected in the education of media designers are discussions about critical theory and technology criticism, two overlapping fields that broadly consider the social and political influences on meaning making in cultural contexts. From these two fields, we learn that humans and human activities both shape and are shaped by computer technologies and that we should, therefore, pay attention to the ethical dimensions of media design. Regardless of where technical communication programs are housed, whether in English, engineering, humanities, or other departments, we face significant challenges in providing students with comprehensive interdisciplinary educations.

ACKNOWLEDGING IDEOLOGIES IN DESIGN TOOLS

Computer technologies that both support and result from media design projects are value-laden. Too often, however, such technologies are talked about uncritically, which discounts the very real influence they exert in a culture. As Winner (1986) explains, "In our accustomed way of thinking technologies are seen as neutral tools that can be used well or poorly, for good, evil, or something in between. But we usually do not stop to inquire whether a given device might have been designed and built in such a way that it produces a set of consequences logically and temporally *prior to any of its professed uses*" (p. 25). Consequences for media design can be traced partially to decisions made by developers of authoring tools and hypertext applications, the computer programs that technical communicators use to create on-line information. The default template in release 1.0 of HyperCard, for example, encouraged designers to approach their tasks with notions of textuality derived from print-based texts and index cards.

In broader ways, metaphors such as this influence how we think about the nature and potential of on-line information, structure relationships between ideas in on-line information space, and envision the activities of writing and reading in on-line environments. (Selber, 1995. See also the essay by Shirk, this collection.)

In addition, many of the decisions made by developers of such environments privilege problem-solving models of cognition, neglecting in their theories of knowledge making that "thinking is to some extent socially, culturally, and historically constructed and that thinkers, as a result, may differ in how they form ideas" (Smith, 1991, p. 225). The intellectual orientations and habits of certain media designers, therefore, may be discouraged or unsupported by various commercially available design environments. Moreover, the interface designs of such environments are often articulated along axes of capitalism, rationalism, and class, discursive, and logocentric privilege, systematically excluding large segments of our culture (Selfe & Selfe, 1994). Technical communication should provide critical perspectives on the dominant ideologies influencing the development of design environments, perspectives that are unlikely to come from outside the humanities.

MAPPING DESIGN ISSUES AND PRINCIPLES

There are many issues and principles to consider when designing multimedia and hypertext, a large proportion of which relate to organizing information and structuring the human-computer interface. Although some of these issues and principles will be familiar to technical communicators primarily experienced in writing paper-based documentation, many will challenge their traditional ways of thinking. As Bolter (1991) notes, "it is hard to think of a marginal technology in the history of writing that the computer cannot imitate, just as it is hard to think of a dominant technology (the papyrus roll, the codex, the printed book) whose elements the computer does not borrow and reinterpret" (p. 40). Moreover, in addition to combining electronic media such as text, audio, and video, on-line information space in general and hypertext in particular provide forums in which the activities of writing and reading are potentially different, and thus our corollary assumptions about textuality, intertextuality, and literacy are complicated (see edited collections by Hawisher & LeBlanc, 1992; Selfe & Hilligoss, 1994). Hypertext environments that provide readers with full authoring privileges, for example, highlight the instability of electronic text and the need, on some level, for alternative visions of collaboration and rhetoric. Technical communicators need a broad understanding of these alternative visions, particularly as they relate to the design of on-line media.

Organizing Information

Many print-based documents, particularly those containing descriptive and procedural information, are organized deductively. Such frameworks for organizing information use propositional logic to create syllogisms and enthymemes that depend on a reader's ability or willingness to work through major and minor premises toward conclusions. In the case of enthymemes, readers must even supply an implied major premise. This approach presupposes a somewhat linear and logocentric reading of texts, as authors establish hierarchies of information that help readers move from page to page and from general to more specific information. Obvious exceptions are modularly constructed reference materials such as encyclopedias and dictionaries, which continue to exercise influence over certain instantiations of on-line media. In all cases, however, the technology of print fixes the content and organization of texts, privileges and makes stable an author's intended message, and subordinates the role of readers. Such effects have profound cultural consequences, particularly for our notions of literacy, pedagogy, and communication (Tuman, 1992; Johnson-Eilola, 1994).

For organizing on-line information, however, deductive frameworks are only one of many possible schemes available to media designers. Moreover, these frameworks may prove less useful under many conditions, such as the design of full-featured hypertexts, which "permit the individual reader to choose his or her own center of investigation and experience" (Landow & Delany, 1991, p. 19) as well as co-author texts. In general, media designers need an expanded set of strategies for organizing on-line information, strategies that complement and support a wide range of pedagogical and rhetorical goals. At the same time, they must contend with increasingly large numbers of computer novices who initially may be uncomfortable with unfamiliar organizing schemes. According to Duffy, Palmer, and Mehlenbacher (1992), rapid growth in information technologies, at least in the foreseeable future, will continue to produce both fewer experts and more first-time computer users (p. 2–4).

Bernstein (1991) and others have adopted a web metaphor to describe the ways in which information is commonly organized in multimedia and hypertext. This metaphor highlights the intertextual connections that exist between and within nodes of information and provides a scheme for representing both the degree of linking and shape of navigational patterns encouraged or discouraged by various organizational structures. It also encourages us to reconceive mechanistic notions of on-line information: As Carlson (1992) notes, "Once we start thinking of electronic text as a web of knowledge, rather than a collection of bits and bytes, all kinds of symbiotic relationships between words and reader(s) are possible" (p. 64). Web-like structures can range from simple to complex, depending on the purpose of an on-line environment and a designer's philosophy of user control. According to Bernstein (1991), the most conservative and rigid webs are monotonous, modeling the hierarchy and linearity encouraged by the technology of print and providing users with few opportunities to explore by association. These webs attempt to constrain the possibility of disorientation, a canonical issue in the literature on hypertext design.

Tangled webs support substantial navigation and provide mechanisms that allow users to read and write in personal ways, build recoverable paths through information, and co-author documents on some level, either by modifying existing text or by adding entirely new text. Perspectives that inform the design of tangled webs are often antithetical to those that inform the design of monotonous ones. For example, in discussing the issue of disorientation, Bernstein (1991) claims that "If readers cannot possibly become lost, they feel little sense of achievement in exploring complex relationships. If readers never stray far, they will not feel that the road they have traveled was either long or significant" (p. 43). Moreover, he maintains that concerns about disorientation are often fundamentally misguided:

> Hypertext disorientation is indistinguishable from bad writing. No convincing evidence exists that interlinked information necessarily disorients the reader, or that linear presentation actually keeps people from getting lost; indeed, anyone who reads difficult essays or listens to challenging lectures is likely to lose the thread of the argument from time to time. (p. 42)

Although monotonous and tangled webs represent radically different visions of hypertext design and of issues such as disorientation, in practice we commonly find spacious, open, and accommodating webs, each supporting varying degrees of author and user control. In the case of accommodating webs, designers provide organizational structures that are dynamic or "intelligent," structures that the computer adapts to decisions made by users in the act of reading.

When organizing information in multimedia and hypertext, therefore, media designers must make decisions about the degree of complexity supported by their web-like structures, and these decisions should be informed in central ways by broad rhetorical concerns, not solely by the available technological features of any one program (Selber, Johnson-Eilola, & Mehlenbacher, in press). Media designers should also recognize that even full-featured hypertexts impose constraints and boundaries on users, and that the claims of freedom and liberation associated with this technology are often overstated (Meyrowitz, 1991; Rosenberg, 1992). In addition, media designers should be concerned with at least two related tasks: (1) providing users with graphical browsers or maps that depict the organizational structures of on-line environment; and (2) chunking information for inclusion in nodes. The former task is encouraged throughout the literature on multimedia and hypertext design because even users of highly rigid applications find both comfort and value in viewing their past and present locations. The latter task attempts to render each node or screen of information semantically meaningful to users, much like structured writing techniques for paper-based documentation. The often undiscussed difficulty of this task lies in assuming that media designers alone can decide what constitutes a meaningful chunk of information for diverse users. But, as Redish (1993) explains, "Meaning does not reside in the text of a document; it exists only in the minds of communicators who produce documents and readers who use documents. Because each reader is an individual with his or her own knowledge, interests, and skills, a text can have as many meanings as it has readers" (p. 22).

Structuring the Human-Computer Interface

In addition to organizing information, media designers face significant challenges in structuring the human-computer interface, the various points at which users engage software and hardware to accomplish work in on-line space. These challenges transcend the design of functional screen elements into psychological, emotional, and cognitive considerations; they also include social and political dimensions. As Heim (1993) explains,

> Interface denotes a contact point where software links the human user to computer processors. This is the mysterious, nonmaterial point where electronic signals become information. It is our interaction with software that creates an interface. Interface means the human being is wired up. Conversely, technology incorporates humans. (p. 78)

It is the nature of this symbiotic relationship—and how we can best build on-line environments that are useful to humans—that should interest media designers. Although user-centered approaches have received much attention lately, historically media designers have concerned themselves primarily with accommodating machines: "much of the research in human factors, from its beginnings over a century ago to the present day, places the needs of technology over the human, thus treating the 'human factor' as an unfortunate impediment in the process of developing emerging technologies" (Johnson,

1994, p. 196). Moreover, media designers have not always thought critically about how technology incorporates humans. For example, stock advice about designing transparent and seamless interfaces discourages both designers and users from considering unproductive and political aspects of computer use, as well as from considering how certain kinds of literacies are privileged in on-line information space. It also assumes that users learn, solve problems, and make meaning in the same ways. But, as Duffy, Palmer, and Mehlenbacher (1992) note, "even if interfaces are simple and clear, which is always a goal, we may expect users with different knowledge bases to interpret the capabilities and perhaps even the procedures differently" (p. 7).

Beyond political and social concerns, Schlusselberg and Harward (1992) provide categories in which to locate many important interface design issues: conceptual, interactive, and visual (pp. 99–100). Not a prescription or strict methodology for structuring human-computer interfaces, these interdependent categories provide a useful scheme for representing and organizing issues individuals should consider when creating multimedia and hypertext. Conceptual design includes two phases: (1) identifying an application's goals, contents, and metaphors; and (2) dividing or chunking the contents in ways that are consistent with those goals and metaphors (p. 101). Technical communicators should find aspects of both phases analogous to planning and organizing paper-based documentation; in fact, needs assessments and document specifications may assume added importance in initial on-line media projects. Metaphors are commonly employed to impose schemata that help users learn and predict the functions of computer programs. They are considered invaluable when users experience such success; conversely, they can do irreparable damage when users struggle to anticipate the operations of programs. Although Schlusselberg and Harward find interface metaphors integral to effective media design, others consider them ultimately limiting for many reasons; for instance, "Once the metaphor is instituted, *every related function has to become part of it*" (Nelson, 1990, p. 237). Media designers should at least recognize the ways in which metaphors filter and delimit the experiences of users, both productively and unproductively. As Blattner (1994) explains, "Metaphors lack the precision required for careful software engineering, but they will continue to provide an intuitive way to design large and complex collections of interface objects, particularly those based on human behavior" (p. 25).

Interactive design examines the relationship between conceptual decisions and constraints imposed by technology (as well as users) by considering the degree to which prevailing interface metaphors support, or should support, the realities they suggest. According to Schlusselberg and Harward (1992), "The art lies in the adaptation" (p. 103). At this stage, media designers construct the ways in which users interact with software, how they navigate within and between various parts of the application, and how multiple audiences might be accommodated. If not sooner, they should make decisions about the degree of complexity supported by their organizing structures.

Visual design considers the composition of screens, which "should reinforce and, therefore, deriv[e] from the application model specified by the conceptual and interactive design" (Schlusselberg & Harward, 1992, p. 103). Among other things, this category includes the appropriate use of emphasis markers (such as color, text attributes, and negative space); the consistent and logical placement of buttons (hot spots that actuate links); and the development of user cues (signposts that help individuals understand on-line conventions). Collectively, the categories of conceptual, interactive, and visual design include important considerations for structuring human-computer interfaces.

EDUCATING THE NEXT GENERATION OF MEDIA DESIGNERS

This essay provides a broad overview of media design, including the differences between various media types, the interdisciplinary nature of media design, and issues and principles central to organizing on-line information and designing human-computer interfaces. In addition to providing technical communicators with robust and comprehensive interdisciplinary learning experiences, teachers face at least three additional challenges when educating and preparing to educate the next generation of media designers.

1. **Acquiring Technology**—Many technical communication programs may find it prohibitive to purchase even one midrange workstation for multimedia and hypertext development, as well as the peripheral devices and supporting software that media designers need to produce even modest projects.[1] Moreover, new developments in hardware and

---

1 The Department of Humanities at Michigan Technological University purchased equipment in January of 1994 to support courses in multimedia and hypertext design. The basic package included a mid-range multimedia workstation (with CD player, 16 MB RAM, and 500 MB hard disk), video editing equipment, memory upgrades, development software, and software upgrades. First-time buyers would spend significantly more on initial software purchases. Including educational discounts, they spent approximately $9,000.00 on the following equipment:

Macintosh Quadra 840 A/V 16/500 w/CD
Apple 14-inch A/V Display
Apple Extended Keyboard II
Audiovision 14 w/adapter kit
Panasonic SVHS VCR
4MB 60ns RAM (upgrade)
Macromedia Director 3.13
Quicktime Starter kit
Midi Translator II (upgrade)
Musicshop (upgrade)
Audioshop (upgrade)

software occur regularly, and these developments are often significant. For example, three generations of multimedia systems were developed between 1989 and 1995, with a new generation available approximately every 2 years (Furht, 1994, p. 57). To acquire and update equipment that allows students to explore current media design issues, faculty may need to form alliances with other academic departments or seek corporate sponsors. In addition, they may need to pursue equipment grants through various funding sources.

2. **Reforming Curricula**—The current curricula of many technical communication programs may not support the theory and practice of media design, let alone offer entire courses in multimedia and hypertext. Many computer-related courses are often skills-based, discouraging students from locating computer use within larger theoretical, cultural, and social contexts (Selber, 1995). Technical communication programs should examine the formal and the informal ways students can pursue media design studies, reforming curricula that offer students few or no opportunities to do so. Because media design is a relatively new area of study for technical communicators, it may not have been included in curricular and programmatic decisions made in the 1980s and even the early 1990s.
3. **Preparing Teachers**—Perhaps the greatest challenge is in preparing teachers to teach media design courses. Many individuals are just beginning to consider how they might approach the design of multimedia and hypertext pedagogically, as well as how design issues relate to other offerings, requirements, and interests in their departments. Moreover, students will increasingly possess sophisticated machine skills, although they will need help, as will teachers, in examining the theoretical and social dimensions of this work (Selber, Johnson-Eilola, & Selfe, 1995). Teachers need forums in which to explore the teaching of media design, such as Internet discussion groups that include the perspectives of other educators and practicing professionals in the field. In addition, the dynamic nature of emerging technologies requires teachers to adopt life-long learning strategies: to prepare for inevitable changes in hardware and software; to develop pedagogical approaches for teaching about and with computers; and to promote an evolving body of research and theory that both informs and is informed by workplace practice.

In the future, as we move from digital to virtual reality, Heim (1993) claims that we will experience an ontological shift, "a change in the world under our feet, in the whole context in which our knowledge and awareness are rooted" (p. xiii). What we learned about structuring human-computer interfaces, for example, will be less valuable because there will be no interface to design (Bricken, 1992). But even if such technological changes are more subtle, teachers need to continually examine traditional notions of rhetoric and how they illuminate and fail to illuminate the design of multimedia and hypertext as discursive spaces.

REFERENCES

Ambron, S. & Hooper, K. (Eds.). (1990). *Learning with interactive multimedia: Developing and using multimedia tools in education.* Redmond, WA: Microsoft Press.

Barker, T.T. (Ed.). (1991). *Perspectives on software documentation: Inquiries and innovations.* Amityville, NY: Baywood.

Barrett, E. (Ed.). (1992). *Sociomedia: Multimedia, hypermedia, and the social construction of knowledge.* Cambridge, MA: MIT Press.

Bernhardt, S.A. (1993). The shape of text to come: The texture of print on screens. *College Composition and Communication, 44,* 151–175.

Bernstein, M. (1991). Deeply intertwingled hypertext: The navigation problem reconsidered. *Technical Communication, 38,* 41–47.

Blattner, M.M. (1994). In our image: Interface design in the 1990s. *IEEE Multimedia, 1,* 25–36.

Bolter, J.D. (1991). *Writing space: The computer, hypertext, and the history of writing.* Hillsdale, NJ: Erlbaum.

Boyle, C. & Ratliff, K. (1992). A survey and classification of hypertext documentation systems. *IEEE Transactions on Professional Communication, 35,* 98–111.

Brande, S. (1987). *The media lab: Inventing the future at MIT.* New York: Viking Penguin.

Bricken, M. (1992). Virtual worlds: No interface to design. In M. Benedikt (Ed.), *Cyberspace: First steps* (pp. 362–382). Cambridge, MA: MIT Press.

Carlson, P.A. (1992). Varieties of virtual: Expanded metaphors for computer-mediated learning. In E. Barrett (Ed.), *Sociomedia: Multimedia, hypermedia, and the social construction of knowledge* (pp. 53–77). Cambridge, MA: MIT Press.

Cohen, N.E. (1991). Problems of form in software documentation. In T.T. Barker (Ed.), *Perspectives on software documentation: Inquiries and innovations* (pp. 123–136). Amityville: Baywood.

Doheny-Farina, S. (Ed.). (1988). *Effective documentation: What we have learned from research.* Cambridge: MIT Press.

Duffy, T., Palmer, J.E. & Mehlenbacher, B. (1992). *Online help: Design and evaluation.* Norwood, NJ: Ablex.

Farkas, D.K. (1992). Applying hypertext to print concepts. *1992 International Professional Communication Conference Proceedings.* Santa Fe, CA: IEEE.

Furht, B. (1994). Multimedia systems: An overview. *IEEE Multimedia, 1,* 47–59.

Greenberg, S. (Ed.). (1991). *Computer-supported cooperative work and groupware.* New York: Harcourt Brace Jovanovich.

Gygi, K. (1990). Recognizing the symptoms of hypertext...and what to do about it. In B. Laurel (Ed.), *The art of human-computer interface design* (pp. 279–287). Reading, MA: Addison-Wesley.

Haas, C. (1989). "Seeing it on the screen isn't really seeing it": Computer writers' reading problems. In G.E. Hawisher & C.L. Selfe (Eds.), *Critical perspectives on computers and composition instruction* (pp. 16–29). New York: Teachers College Press.

Hawisher, G.E. & LeBlanc, P. (Eds.). (1992). Re-imagining computers and composition: *Teaching and research in the virtual age.* Portsmouth, NH: Boynton/Cook.

Heim, M. (1993). *The metaphysics of virtual reality.* New York: Oxford University Press.

Horton, W.K. (1990). *Designing and writing online documentation: Help files to hypertext.* New York: Wiley.

Johnson, R.R. (1994). The unfortunate human factor: A selective history of human factors for technical communicators. *Technical Communication Quarterly, 3,* 195–212.

Johnson-Eilola, J. (1994). Reading and writing in hypertext: Vertigo and euphoria. In C. L. Selfe & S. Hilligoss (Eds.), *Computers and literacy: The complications of teaching and learning with technology* (pp. 195–219). New York: Modern Language Association.

Johnson-Eilola, J. & Selber, S.A. (in press). After automation: Hypertext and corporate structures. In P. Sullivan & J. Dautermann (Eds.), *Electronic literacies in the workplace: Technologies of writing.* Urbana, IL: National Council of Teachers of English.

Landow, G.P. & Delany, P. (1991). Hypertext, hypermedia, and literary studies: The state of the art. In G.P. Landow & P. Delany (Eds.), *Hypermedia and literary studies* (pp. 3–50). Cambridge, MA: MIT Press.

Meyrowitz, N. (1991). Hypertext: Does it reduce cholesterol, too? In J. M. Nyce & P. Kahn (Eds.), *From Memex to hypertext: Vannevar Bush and the mind's machine* (pp. 287–318). New York: Academic Press.

Moulthrop, S. (1991). Beyond the electronic book: A critique of hypertext rhetoric. *Third ACM Conference on Hypertext Proceedings* (pp. 291–298). New York: Association for Computing Machinery.

Mountford, S.J. (1990). Tools and techniques for creative design. In B. Laurel (Ed.), *The art of human-computer interface design* (pp. 17–30). Reading, MA: Addison-Wesley.

Nelson, T.H. (1990). The right way to think about software design. In B. Laurel (Ed.), *The art of human-computer interface design* (pp. 235–243). Reading, WA: Addison-Wesley.

Nord, M.A. & Tanner, B. (1993). Design that delivers: Formatting information for print and online documents. In C.M. Barnum & S. Carliner (Eds.), *Techniques for technical communicators* (pp. 219–252). New York: Macmillan.

Redish, J.C. (1993). Understanding readers. In C.M. Barnum & S. Carliner (Eds.), *Techniques for technical communicators* (pp. 14–41). New York: Macmillan.

Rosenberg, M. (1992). Contingency, liberation, and the seduction of geometry: Hypertext as an avant-garde medium. *Perforations*, 1–12.

Schlusselberg, E. & Harward, V.J. (1992). Multimedia: Informational alchemy or conceptual typography? In E. Barrett (Ed.), *Sociomedia: Multimedia, hypermedia, and the social construction of knowledge* (pp. 95–106). Cambridge, MA: MIT Press.

Selber, S.A. (1995). Metaphorical perspectives on hypertext. *IEEE Transactions on Professional Communications, 2*, 59–67.

Selber, S.A. (in press). Beyond skill building: Challenges facing technical communication teachers in the computer age. *Technical Communication Quarterly.*

Selber, S.A., Johnson-Eilola, J. & Mehlenbacher, B. (in press). Online support systems: tutorials, documentation, and help. In A.B. Tucker (Ed.), *CRC handbook for computer science and engineering.* Boca Raton, FL: CRC Press.

Selber, S.A., Johnson-Eilola, J. & C.L. Selfe. (1995). Contexts for faculty professional development in the age of electronic writing and communication. *Technical communication, 4*, 581–584.

Selfe, C.L. (1989). Redefining literacy: The multilayered grammars of computers. In G.E. Hawisher & C.L. Selfe (Eds.), *Critical perspectives on computers and composition studies* (pp. 3–15). New York: Teachers College Press.

Selfe, C.L. & Hilligoss, S. (Eds.). (1994). *Literacy and computers: The complications of teaching and learning with technology.* New York: Modern Language Association.

Selfe, C.L. & Selfe, R.J. (in press). The politics of the interface: Power and its exercise in electronic contact zones. *College Composition and Communication.*

Shirk, H.N. (1991). "Hyper" rhetoric: Reflections on teaching hypertext. *Technical Writing Teacher, 18*, 189–200.

Slatin, J.M. (1990). Reading hypertext: Order and coherence in a new medium. *College English, 52*, 870–883.

Smith, C.F. (1991). Reconceiving hypertext. In G.E. Hawisher & C.L. Selfe (Eds), *Evolving perspectives on computers and composition studies: Questions for the 1990s* (pp. 43–64). Houghton, MI & Urbana, IL: Computers and Composition Press & National Council of Teachers of English.

Tuman, M.C. (1992). *Word Perfect: Literacy in the computer age.* Pittsburgh, PA: University of Pittsburgh Press.

Winner, L. (1986). *The whale and the reactor: A search for limits in an age of high technology.* Chicago, IL: University of Chicago Press.

PROFESSIONAL ROLES FOR TECHNICAL COMMUNICATORS

13

PROFESSIONAL ROLES: TECHNICAL WRITER

Roger A. Grice

Roger Grice Associates, Inc.

INTRODUCTION

I never knew a person who failed as a technical writer because of comma splices. I do know, however, people who have failed as technical writers for a wide variety of other reasons, often having little to do with their writing ability. Why is this? Two possibilities come to mind:

- Those who teach technical communication are doing a good job of teaching how to write correctly and clearly. Thus, basic writing concerns are not a problem for most technical writers.
- The actual task of writing may not be the most critical part of a technical writer's job. And certainly a good editor can always fix surface blemishes.

Why, then, might someone fail as a technical writer? I offer and examine three possibilities to explain what successful technical writers do that makes them assets to their organizations and that enables them to provide a "value add" to the products on which they work. Technical communicators may fail because they:

1. Lack understanding of the products or processes for which they are to provide information or of the audiences for whom they write and how those audiences will use the product or process and the associated documentation to do their own work
2. Use ineffective collaboration strategies for working with their technical contacts; with other writers, editors, graphic designers, and production specialists; and with the full range of product-team members needed to gain all needed information and perspective
3. View their work as a "solo act" rather than as a part of a team effort to produce a product that will do well in the marketplace

To provide background for this discussion of the technical writer's role, I will briefly review the skills needed to do the job; a typical process that technical writers follow, including their activities, strategies, and critical choices; and the importance of collaborative relationships. I will then discuss some implications for the content and structure of technical communication courses.

SKILLS NEEDED TO DO THE JOB

The list of skills that technical writers need continues to grow as advances in media technology and diversification of audiences proliferate.

Consider the technical writers of the '60s, who provided information on how to use computers. (This was the start of my career in technical communication.) For all intents and purposes, the information was delivered as manuals made up by system programmers who, for the most part, were very knowledgeable and sophisticated; they often knew more about the subject matter than the writers who produced the manuals. This made the task of writing if not easy, at least very clearly defined.

Now consider the technical writer of the '90s, who provides information on how to use computers. Information could be delivered as manuals—manuals with a wide range of sizes and shapes, printed in color, packaged in attractive and functional ways, and designed to be used easily. However, the information could also be delivered in a variety of other ways: on-line help or tutorials displayed on a computer's display screen, videotapes, demo programs, or hypermedia presentations that combine all of the previously named elements into one seamless presentation of information. And who is the audience for the information? It could be anyone, from the most sophisticated computer programmer to someone who knows very little about computers and doesn't care to, but who has to use them to get work done. Will one treatment of information work for this wide range of readers? Most likely not. But the skillful technical writer must develop ways of presenting information so that the needs of all readers are met. This means that technical writers require a more comprehensive and sophisticated education than ever before (Carliner, 1992).

The passage from the 1960s to the 1990s has seen a fundamental shift in the way technical writing is done and the way technical writers work and are perceived by others in their organizations. During this period, technical writing has evolved from writing descriptions of products after the products were already developed to working with product developers during development to produce descriptions of how to use products. The emphasis shifted from completeness of product-oriented information to ease of use of task-oriented information. The information products evolved from isolated manuals to integrated libraries of information supporting the full range of user tasks and information needs.

How did this transition change the skills necessary for a competent or successful technical writer? It caused enormous growth in the range of skills technical writers need. During the '60s, technical writers needed only writing and editing skills to produce documentation. Later, the skill set grew to include audience analysis, text management, graphic design, testing for accuracy and usability, planning, financial accounting, media choice, and information packaging and design. Today, the skill set includes sophisticated knowledge of hypermedia, video and film, training, electronic distribution, database design and management, and research. Technical writers today routinely use skills that were not even imagined by most of their counterparts a few decades ago.

USE OF SOURCE MATERIAL

For source material for documents, writers may draw on written product specifications, discussions and interviews with technical experts, or expertise developed from using the product being documented. Sometimes they may not have a choice. However, usually several varieties of source material may be available, and the success or failure of the documentation may depend on making a wise choice of source materials.

A writer who relies solely on written product specifications, for example, may wind up with a document that is little more than a cleaned up version of the specification—product-oriented, not user-oriented, and probably out of date. On the other hand, a writer who depends solely on discussions and interviews with technical experts may be limited by the availability of those experts and their willingness to help produce and review documentation. A writer may get information from an expert whose knowledge of the product is incomplete or that reflects a strong personal bias. Knowledge derived from working with the product is certainly user-oriented because the writer would need to work though the procedures being described. But there is also the danger that the product might change after the writer has used it to generate information. Perhaps the best choice is to use a combination of sources to gain a well-rounded view of the product and its use and to ensure that different sources are in agreement.

A PROCESS FOR DEVELOPING TECHNICAL INFORMATION

Whether specified as a formal process or done informally as a commonsense approach to developing information, technical writers generally need to do the following:

1. Analyze the product or process to be documented and the documentation requirements. Understand the intended audience and the media available for use.
2. Set objectives—goals to be met—for the documentation.
3. In light of the objectives, define specifications for the documents, as a response to the objectives, describing the documentation and how it will meet the objectives.
4. Write the documentation.
5. Verify the accuracy and suitability of the documentation through review and inspections, editing, and testing. As a result of the verification, the documentation is usually revised—reorganized and rewritten.
6. Publish the information in the chosen media and distribute it or make it available for distribution.
7. Analyze the documentation effort's success and failures and determine how to be more successful on the next project.

TECHNICAL WRITERS' ACTIVITIES AND TASKS

As they move through the process, technical writers must perform a wide variety of tasks, calling on different skills and knowledge. The process is, indeed, a rich one, one that demands the broad viewpoint of a generalist and the work and dedication of a specialist.

During the *analysis* phase, technical writers are called upon to understand the intricacies of the product for which they provide documentation. They must negotiate for the resources (time, equipment, access to people and products) that they will need to do their job. They must gather and understand the requirements that have been set for the product and develop an understanding of how those product requirements will shape the product's information requirements. They must gather, read, and understand product descriptions that have been generated by those who are designing and developing the product, and they need to analyze these documents to help ensure that the product will be usable. They must start, at this very early stage, to do the audience, task, and media analysis that will form the basis for their later documentation work. They need to understand the interface between the product and its users and work to ensure that the interface is usable rather than hope they can make a complex interface simple through documentation. As Paul Heckel tells us, "If you can't communicate it, don't do it" (1984).

During the *objectives* phase, technical writers need to set two different types of objectives: those that relate to quality and those that relate to project management. Quality objectives specify goals to be met for such information characteristics as content, usability, appearance, and readability. Project management objectives address such items as schedules, resource requirements, review procedures, and potential exposures.

During the *specifications* phase, technical writers develop specifications as a response to the information objectives. The specifications define how the goals set in the objectives will be reached. It is in the specifications that technical writers do their design work, producing outlines and prototypes (or "dummies"), and even model sections of the finished documents. Well-thought-out, detailed specifications identify the documents that will be produced, the audiences for each document, required resources, media choices, purposes, and user tasks that will be supported.

During the *development*, or writing phase, technical writers turn the source material they have gathered into drafts according to the specifications that they have defined or that have been defined for them. They must also arrange for such verification as technical reviews, editing, and testing that will be done to ensure that the documents they produce are suitable for their intended audience. The process of producing a draft and verifying its content and presentation may need to be done more than once.

During the *verification* phase, technical writers distribute drafts of the documents they have produced to technical experts, editors, and testing groups for their comments and then incorporate the comments as part of the work to produce the next level of draft. Writers may also try to get members of the intended audience—customers—involved in verifying the drafts to help ensure that the finished documents will, in fact, meet the needs of the audience. They must also work to ensure that they remain abreast of changes and additions being made to the product while it is being developed and to changes in the marketplace that occur while they are developing their documents.

During the *production and distribution* phase, writers work with production specialists, or do their own final production work, to prepare the final version of the document to be published and distributed to customers or potential customers. In the not-so-distant past, publishing and distributing almost always meant sending camera-ready pages to a printer, who would print the requested number of copies and send them to a standard distribution point specified by the writer's organization. Today, of course, there are many more options. Documents may be "published" on paper, diskettes, or CD-ROMs; they may even be distributed electronically over computer networks. They may be produced in pre-determined quantities, based on expected customer needs, or they may be produced "on demand," as customers request copies.

The final phase of the process is to conduct *post-mortem analysis* to determine how well the document's development went and to make plans for any needed improvement so that documents can be developed more effectively or more efficiently the next time.

However, documentation work generally is not completed when a document is published; there is usually a need for maintenance and updates. This need may arise because of deficiencies in the document or because of projected changes to the product the document describes. In either case, it is generally necessary to go through most, if not all, of the process again to produce the next update of the document.

Setting "Freeze Dates" for Documentation Input

If writers hope to meet their production and publishing dates, they must, by necessity, set a "freeze date," after which they can no longer accept new material or changes for inclusion in the document without jeopardizing the schedule. Ideally, this date should be late in the product-development cycle so as to include as many of the late-breaking product changes as possible in the document. On the other hand, setting the date too late in the cycle does not allow sufficient time for doing a high-quality job, and the resulting document, although technically as up-to-date as possible, may be burdened with errors impossible to notice and correct in an overly compressed production cycle. Obviously, a cutoff date must be established, but writers need to remain flexible to accommodate as many product changes as possible.

Deciding When and What to Test

Ideally, all parts of a document should be tested for accuracy, completeness, and usability when the product and the document are complete. Product-development schedules are not set up with that luxury, however, and writers often need to compromise. There is generally no time to test everything after the product and the document are complete, but some parts, the parts that are thought to be most stable, could be tested earlier in the cycle to save time at the end. If there is not enough time to test everything, writers must decide which parts of the document will be most critical to users and which parts could benefit most from testing. Those parts would then become the most likely candidates for testing; other parts might have to be tested during development of the next version of the document.

Choosing Appropriate Media

There is always the temptation to use the fanciest, the newest, the most elaborate media for documentation. However, while some customers might like to use new media for some applications, many people are satisfied, and comfortable, with traditional print documentation. Writers may not be doing these people a service by using new media. On the other hand, some documentation applications may benefit greatly from a new treatment. Writers need to make choices of media with the same care and consideration with which they make other decisions about presenting information to their audience.

Making Processes Effective

Because many organizations are "downsizing" these days, a good deal of attention has focused on the need to streamline processes, to make them more efficient, so that organizations can operate and compete more effectively. This certainly is true. However, we must be clear in our understanding of the differences between streamlining and simply cutting corners. If, for example, writers tried to make the process outlined above more efficient by cutting out the first three steps and began writing at the very onset, they could save time and other resources at the beginning of the process, but they might pay an even larger price later when the lack of planning could necessitate a great deal of reworking.

Writers need to give thought to how they implement the information-development process. If they narrowly decide that each step in the process must be completely defined, implemented, and studied before they can consider the next step, then they will, of necessity, stretch out the process longer than may be necessary or prudent. In some instances, informal treatment of steps may be just as effective as more elaborate treatments.

If, for example, a single document needs to be produced and that document is similar to one already in existence, setting objectives may involve little more than jotting down the strengths and weaknesses of that document so that the strengths can be capitalized on and the weaknesses avoided. The response to those objectives may be little more than the stated resolve to meet the objectives. On the other hand, a radically new and complex set of documents may well require time, thought, and creativity in setting objectives and in responding to them with good, solid design.

For information on approaches to improving existing processes and developing new approaches, see, for example, "Technical Communication in the Computer Industry: An Information Development Process to Teach, Measure, and Ensure Quality," by Roger A. Grice; *Technical Writing: Theory and Practice,* edited by Bertie E. Fearing and W. Keats Sparrow (1989); *Perspectives on Software Documentation: Inquiries and Innovations,* edited by Thomas T. Barker (1991); and *Techniques for Technical Communicator,* edited by Carol M. Barnum and Saul Carliner (1993). For a description of the tasks that needed to be performed throughout an entire process, see *Designing, Writing, and Producing Computer Documentation* by Lynn Denton and Jody Kelly (1993).

AN EXAMPLE—DESIGNING A TECHNICAL REPORT

Many people equate technical communication with producing computer documentation. Although it is true that many technical communicators produce computer documentation for a large portion of their careers, it is certainly not the only focus of the profession. The process described in this essay applies equally well to other forms of technical communication, so, as an example, let's consider how someone creating a technical report—say, a report describing the results and implication of a research project—might follow the process described in this essay.

During *analysis,* the writer would consider the audience for the report—their background and interests, their disposition toward the subject and the writer, and their involvement, current or potential, with the subject matter. The writer would also make the best media choice for the report. Printed text, often with accompanying graphics, might be the easiest and most obvious choice, but audiotapes and videotapes as part of supporting evidence might be of great use. Multimedia presentations might create a suitably strong impact.

When setting *objectives*, the writer must consider what he or she hopes to accomplish. Is the purpose of the report merely to report on results? Or are there other purposes that must be served: obtaining additional funding, advancing a career as a result of significant findings, acceptance of the results for publication? Merely reporting results accurately may not be sufficient if a larger goal is to be met.

Writers set *specifications* to plan and describe how they will meet their stated, or unstated, objectives. In the case of the research report, they must devise strategies for making the information compelling to the intended audience. The specifications should respond to each and every objective; nothing should be left to chance. If, for example, the main objective is to obtain additional funding, the specifications would include strategies for stressing the importance of findings and possibilities for further investigation, rather than presenting results as *fait accompli*. Specifications for the report might define organization and structure, as well as the style and layout to be followed.

During the *development*, the writer follows through on commitments made in the specifications. In the case of the research report, development would include presenting the research finding in a way that highlights those features that best help achieve the stated objectives. During the report's development, the writer should continually think of the goals to be met and the strategies planned for meeting them, or the finished report that results may not be suitable for the intended purposes. If, for example, it becomes obvious that the report will not be a strong instrument for obtaining additional funding, the writer must rethink either the specifications or the way that the specifications are being met and make required changes and adjustments before the report is developed too far in the wrong direction.

During *verification*, the writer must ensure that the completed report is really suitable. Verifying the report might consist of the writer reading it with a critical eye or having colleagues read it to assess its effectiveness. Depending on the situation, it might even be possible to have someone from the intended final audience review the report before it is issued formally.

Production and distribution are often considered the more mundane aspects of technical communication and are often given less attention than they deserve. This can be a serious mistake. If the research report being considered will be used to request additional funding, it must certainly give the impression that serious, dedicated work has gone into the report as well as the research. If the report will be used to request additional funding, the writer must ensure that all those involved in making the funding decision receive a copy of the report; to slight a decision maker, even inadvertently, could have dire consequences.

During the *post-mortem analysis*, the writer must analyze what went right and what went wrong. If the report contributed to a favorable funding decision, what lessons can be learned and applied in the future? If the report was not successful, what lessons can be learned so that the next attempt is successful? This analysis should not be an occasion of "crying over spilled milk." Nor should it be overly focused on self-congratulation. Rather, it should be a sincere, honest assessment of how best to do a job.

The Importance of Collaborative Relationships

Successful technical writers do not work alone. The success of their efforts depends heavily on their ability to work effectively with others. Technical writers need to form two types of collaborative relationships:

- With other members of product-development teams: engineers, programmers, marketing and sales representatives, product planners, and usability experts
- With other members of the information-development team, other technical writers, editors, graphic designers, information planners, and production specialists

Of course, technical writers who work as one-person documentation groups must play many roles in the course of a document's development and production; at various times they will fill each of the information-development roles.

Collaboration in technical writing is an important topic; many people have written about it. For more information about collaborative writing, see the special issue of *Technical Communication*, edited by Deborah S. Bosley and Meg Morgan (1991); the special issue of *Technical Communication Quarterly*, edited by Rebecca E. Burnett and Ann Hill Duin (1993); and *Collaborative Writing in Industry: Investigations in Theory and Practice*, edited by Mary M. Lay and William M. Karis (1991).

IMPLICATIONS: WHAT TO TEACH AND HOW TO TEACH IT

How should teachers of technical writing best prepare students for careers as technical writers? I believe that the answer is to consider the many varied aspects of the job and to give students experience, or at least awareness, of what they will face in their professional work.

For example, many of the class assignments teachers give students are spelled out in great detail; teachers may feel that **they** are not doing their jobs well if the assignments are sketchy or vague. Teachers generally would not even consider changing the parameters of an assignment once students have started to work on it; educational structures are not set up to accommodate this sort of change easily. This clean and highly structured environment deprives students of valuable learning—of acquiring skills and a flexible attitude toward their work that they will need later in their careers.

School assignments always have an answer, often a "right" one. If this is not the case, students (with some justification) complain. Somewhere during the education process the expectation has been raised that all problems are solvable, that there is a teacher's "answer book" with the answers and keys to success. Is this realistic? No, it is not. But given the structures and environments in which educators so often work, breaking this pattern can be a real challenge, often one with little, if any, reward.

Technical writing courses and assignments generally emphasize the writing aspect of the technical writer's job. Certainly that is important, and it is at the core of the profession. But do teachers of technical communication overemphasize this one skill to the detriment of other, equally important, ones? Teachers need to understand and teach the full range of knowledge, skills, attitudes, and activities that students will need when they enter the workplace.

Technical writers are called on to do many things, and to do them well; the range is very wide, and it is constantly changing and evolving. Those who teach need to keep up with the pace of change. They need to be on the leading edge, helping to define the profession by preparing students to be full participants in it; they must not stay behind and force students to look elsewhere for the professional development they need.

REFERENCES

Barker, T.T. (Ed.). (1991). *Perspectives on software documentation: Inquiries and innovation.* Amityville, NY: Baywood.

Barnum, C.M. & Carliner, S. (Eds.). (1993). *Techniques for technical communicators.* New York: Macmillan.

Bosley, D.S. & Morgan, M. (Eds.). (1991). [Special issue on collaborative writing]. *Technical Communication, 38.*

Burnett, R.E. & Duin, A.H. (Eds.). (1993). [Special issue on collaboration]. *Technical Communication Quarterly, 2.*

Carliner, S. (1992). What you should get from a professionally oriented master's degree program in technical communication. *Technical Communication, 39,* 189–199.

Denton, L. & Kelly, J. (1993). *Designing, writing, and producing computer documentation.* New York: McGraw-Hill.

Fearing, B.E. & Sparrow, W.K. (Eds.). (1989). *Technical writing: Theory and practice.* New York: Modern Language Association of America.

Grice, R.A. (1987). *Technical communication in the computer industry: An information-development process to track, measure, and ensure quality.* Doctoral dissertation, Rensselaer Polytechnic Institute.

Heckel, P. (1984). *Elements of friendly software design.* New York: Warner.

Lay, M.M. & Karis, W.M. (Eds.) (1991). *Collaborative writing in industry: Investigations in theory and practice.* Amityville, NY: Baywood.

14

TECHNICAL EDITING

Elizabeth R. Turpin

Ferris State University

Judith Gunn Bronson

Stem Line Publishing Services, Inc.

INTRODUCTION

Technical editing is an art and a skill with which a document is improved so that it better serves the needs of its defined users. The concept of "technical" applies to the depth of expertise at which the material is being presented, as well as to the subject matter. That is, technical editing is practiced not only in subject areas such as computer science, medicine, agriculture, insurance, environmental law, finance, and polymer chemistry, but also on occasion in areas such as painting or music. For example, a book on the restoration of the Sistine Chapel ceiling would involve technical editing. Technical editors work on a wide array of documents: corporate and government reports, monographs, textbooks, proposals, talks for professional audiences, marketing and advertising pieces, sales literature, instructional and service support manuals, operational guides, installation instructions, laboratory protocols, clinical trial reports, case studies, new drug applications, journal articles, patient education literature, analytical and statistical reports, and CD-ROM video productions (see also Zook, 1983, pp. 20–26). In all subject areas and with all types of documents, the hallmark of technical editing is a focus on the user's needs and a stress on accuracy, precision, and usability (see Woolston et al., 1988).

Whatever their job description and extent of authority and autonomy, technical editors have one or more responsibilities. These can be grouped as content or substantive editing; copyediting (usually including proofreading); project management or coordination; satisfaction of compliance, usability, quality, legal, and ethical requirements; and production oversight (see Stainton, 1991; Eisenberg, 1992). Some of these are new editorial roles. To these are added a greater demand for expertise in media such as CD-ROM, tools such as desktop and on-line publishing, and use of images and even video rather than written words alone. Increasing the challenges to the technical editor's skills today are changes in the sophistication of the users of technical documents and in their applications of the information.

Diverse and difficult as these changes may seem, they are beneficial for the technical editor. Not only are they keeping the work environment interesting, but they are expanding the professional opportunities and increasing the status of the technical editor. Colleges and universities are adding editing courses, even programs, to their technical communication offerings, and students are choosing technical editing as a career. This essay summarizes the traditional roles of the technical editor, examines the changing roles and new professional opportunities, and offers suggestions concerning the skills students need to acquire to work in the technical editing field (see Mandell, 1995).

TRADITIONAL EDITORIAL ROLES

Substantive/Content Editing

Technical substantive editors work with authors to help assure that the focus, organization, depth of coverage, language, and supporting material of a document serve the intended users well and that any constraints (such as format or maximum length) are observed. Initially, the technical editor and the author agree on what Van Buren and Buehler (1980) describe as the appropriate "level of edit" for the document. Audience and purpose are significant in identifying problems that affect the document as a whole, such as deficiencies in its organization, progression, and level of information. These are corrected first. The editing process then deals with elements of style and presentation in relation to the users, including individual paragraph development and the use of format and headings for clarity. Without making unnecessary changes, the substantive editor also checks the document for economy of language and effectiveness of expression.

As a document expands or contracts during development, the substantive editor constantly tests logical levels of order and the relationships in both the text and the supporting materials that affect interpretation (see Dragga & Gong, 1989). One technique is to approach editing as what Berthoff calls an "audit of meaning" (see Wells, 1988). As Wells has written, the rhetoric of a text can "shape meanings by controlling the relations among ... findings, establishing patterns through selection and ordering" (p. 152). By upholding standards of review and revision, the substantive editor can help maintain both the logic of the content and the tone of a document so that it will be appropriate to the authorial purpose and the users' needs.

Copyediting and Proofreading

After a document has been revised for content and organizational development, the technical editor considers its accuracy in grammar, punctuation, usage (including correct terminology and freedom from trite expressions), and conformance with document specifications and appropriate style guides, making necessary changes while taking care not to change the original meaning (see also Judd, 1990; and Plotnik, 1982). The copyeditor must maintain a library of subject-area resources, including the most recent editions of works such as *Scientific Style and Format: The CBE Manual for Authors, Editors, and Publishers* (1994), the *Chicago Manual of Style* (1993), the *Publication Manual of the American Psychological Association* (1994), and the *New York Public Library Writer's Guide to Style and Usage* (1994). The copyeditor is also expected to develop a style sheet, and perhaps one or more checklists, for each document. The technical copyeditor also checks details such as callouts (text references to illustrations or attachments) to see that they correspond to the actual entry, verifies entries in tables and figures against the text, and makes certain that bibliographic entries are accurate (Eichorn and Yankauer, 1987, pp. 1011–1012). In checking formulas and equations, the copyeditor is alert for possible omissions or discrepancies. The copyeditor may also confirm the accuracy of changes from manuscript or disk to proof. The professional copyeditor organizes all these tasks so they can be completed with maximum thoroughness and efficiency.

The quality of the final document depends to a significant extent on the care taken with the copyediting and proofing (see, for example, Howell, 1983; Frank & Treichler, 1988). Readers notice inconsistencies, keyboarding mistakes, and grammatical errors, and their willingness to accept the accuracy and usefulness of the entire document declines if its author appears careless. Moreover, the consequences of even small mistakes can be significant, even calamitous. Writers and editors, as well as companies, may be held legally liable for the adverse effects of an error. A mistake in reporting the temperature at which a laboratory test was conducted could make it impossible to obtain the same results, perhaps leading to questions about misconduct. An error in a drug dosage could result in serious illness or even death. A misplaced decimal in a financial document could result in years of litigation and a cost to the firm of millions of dollars, and a missing minus sign in an accountant's report has caused a large mutual fund to cancel its announced dividend to shareholders. Technical copyediting is not a simple task. It requires rigorous training.

Document Coordination

The document coordinator identifies the type and amount of editing needed, as well as the time and staff requirements, in order to help schedule and budget for the project (see Stratton, 1989). If there are special requirements, such as unusual compliance elements or extensive illustrations, the document coordinator will assign appropriate staff and resources. The coordinator may also assume the responsibilities for document design, for ensuring that the document fits the specifications, and for checking to see that the format is appropriate and that the tables, figures, and other elements are properly placed. The document coordinator may also have the responsibility for establishing or approving a specification sheet for the project.

Production Editing

The production editor can have a variety of roles that ensure that the instructions from the editorial and design personnel are carried out by the printer and that the progress of copy through typesetting, printing, and binding is as efficient as possible (see Rude, 1991). The production editor can also be responsible for supervising the proofreading and for checking the quality of the paper and printing, page layout, color separations, and imposition and gathering. Giving the final okay to print is generally the responsibility of a technical editor, perhaps with appropriate signoff by others on a project team.

TECHNICAL EDITING IN TRANSITION

The far-reaching developments in communications technology have dramatically affected technical editors, creating new tools to exploit, new media to master, and greater responsibilities to bear. The spectacular growth of computer industry documentation, the appearance of desktop and on-line publishing, the introduction of multimedia, the creation of the Internet, the development of ways to produce multiple documents from single datasets using Standardized General Markup Language (SGML), and the growing stress on quality and global competitiveness are some of the most striking illustrations of the new environment. Traditional methods of handling documents now are often bypassed because of time constraints, and editors may need to deal with documents entirely on the computer screen and to transmit copy, including photography, electronically. Despite the significant cost, "commercial scientific publishers are feeling the pressure to enter the electronic arena" (Stix, 1994, pp. 109–110), and some professional journals exist only on the Internet. Even documents that eventually will be printed may see paper only as the final step. Secondary information publishers such as the Institute for Scientific Information are investing in electronic means of information dissemination as traditional publications come to be seen as too slow (Trolley & Potter, 1994, p. 97).

NEW RESPONSIBILITIES AND TOOLS OF THE TECHNICAL EDITOR

Although these developments have not changed the basic purposes of editing, they have changed the methods and responsibilities of editors (see also Farkas, 1987). During the early development of computer documentation, user needs were poorly defined, and, with pressures to get products on the store shelves quickly, the manuals were proverbially unsuccessful. As products and users came into better focus, writers were expected to do more of their own editing. Today, editors often pay more attention to teaching writers how to edit their own work and to testing the usability of document drafts (Soderston, 1985) than to traditional editing tasks. Those who formerly served as substantive editors may find themselves in the role of documentation managers, with responsibility for projects and writers rather than for manuscripts (see, for example, Kirsch, 1995). Those who formerly were publications managers—serving as liaisons with internal or out-of-house production facilities—may now manage in-house desktop publishing operations, being responsible for the final quality control procedures that formerly were assumed by the printers. Editors now must pay attention to the rapid changes in the electronic communications industry (Hibbard, 1990, pp. 13–21).

Even when editors are still doing traditional tasks, their work lives have changed. Editors today work less with writers one on one and more in editorial groups and other collaborative relationships (Lay & Karis, 1991; also Grice in this collection). Some organizations use local area network (LAN) groups to standardize routine aspects of copyediting. Groups of editors and authors can then work on the same document simultaneously and pass it around electronically with the revisions indicated by software that shows both the original and the changes. A lead editor (file manager) becomes the ultimate controller for the manuscript. In such a team environment, each member is expected to fulfill his or her responsibilities completely, and team members who are ill-prepared with basic skills will soon find themselves unemployed.

Mastery of the new electronic tools can be daunting to editors, but it has many benefits. Most technical editors use basic software programs for general grammar/style assists and spelling checks (although these tools cannot replace the meticulous live editor). Document tracking is simpler and less hazardous provided a standard procedure is followed. Copymarking through generic coding for type font, size of headings, table formats, and other mechanical elements is far easier and has more consistent results than marking each instance on the hard copy for the compositor. Accuracy in coding mathematical and other symbols is much greater with today's software tools. The use of SGML, which is part of a movement toward standardized handling of copy, makes blocks of material easier to package for production in many different formats. Where SGML is in demand, the technical editor must become proficient in its use and in editing for the various possible outputs (Garson & Schmidt, 1994, p. 92). Additional opportunities are developing rapidly in non-print media—CD-ROM, audio, and video—all of which have specialized requirements for editing and coordination (see also Shelton, 1993; Rainey in this collection).

Even though no one is likely to yearn for the old ways of producing documents after mastering the new computer tools, these tools have created some new problems in document control. Authors may want to undo editing changes made on-line—even reinsert misspellings! In the field of secondary information distribution, the problems of maintaining control over information archival and retrieval are only now being perceived. Intellectual property issues remain unresolved. Further, the distribution of products worldwide imposes demands for accurate perceptions of the needs of users in other situations and cultures (see also Fine, 1991, pp. 259–275).

QUALITY CONTROL AND THE TECHNICAL EDITOR

The growing stress on quality is reflected in the rapid spread of the ISO 9000 and TQM (total quality management) movement. Indeed, various quality protocols increasingly are a requirement of doing business with certain clients. For example, organizations that develop documents for the government often must comply with military (milspecs) or other specifications in addition to quality assessment audit regulations (Weiss, 1993, pp. 234–238). Correction of errors contributes to the satisfaction of user needs. This effort also saves money: The cost of quality is the cost of repairing mistakes, and failure is expensive. For example, inadequate technical documents may lead to large numbers of calls to the company's help lines, to costly equipment damage, and even to personal injury. Moreover, there may be legal liability for problems resulting from inadequate documents, such as wording and design of safety labels and instructions that do not comply with the hazard alert message standard (ANSI Z535) issued by the American National Standards Institute (Kemnitz, 1991, pp. 68–73).

Quality (conformance with designated standards) has always been an important responsibility of technical editors. Today, in the face of complex electronic methods of document development and dissemination, editors are often quality gatekeepers (see also *Proceedings*, 1991). They may also be responsible for compliance tasks such as securing copyright or copyright clearance, resolving legal questions on authorship, or satisfying proprietary restraints, as well as for monitoring ethical issues such as proper attribution of earlier work and avoidance of duplicate publication of research data (see Kirsch, 1995).

With the many changes in the technology of publication discussed in the previous section, some familiar errors have taken on new forms or become harder to find. Typographic and spelling errors or incorrect numbers that may be conspicuous on hard copy are more difficult to detect on the computer screen, and software cannot be expected to identify misused words. (The words "its" and "it's" are almost routinely misused, but a spell checker is unlikely to recognize incorrect usage.)

Mechanical errors are not the only problems that have plagued computer-based documents. The lack of a seasoned review by an objective, user-oriented technical editor has often resulted in documents that are rejected by the reader/user, who thus must acquire the necessary knowledge by calls to help lines.

Another area that has been neglected is document design (Schriver, 1993). The sudden move to desktop publishing shifted responsibility for page makeup and design layout to writers or editors with no training in these skills. Sometimes, the results have been merely annoying, such as the use of far too many typefaces on a single page. Other times, the results have been injurious, such as the placement of safety warnings in obscure sites or the printing of critical information in nearly illegible type.

Increasingly, company management is recognizing that doing a job right the first time is cheaper. Support for quality management efforts is growing. Usability testing and intelligent document design are being recognized as integral parts, not only of a successful publication, but of a successful product. The result has been greater professional development for technical editors and other documentation specialists as the mainstream role of their work has become clear (Gerich, 1994; Reilly, 1993; Winsor, 1996).

EDUCATION AND PROFESSIONAL OPPORTUNITIES FOR TECHNICAL EDITORS

To fill all their roles well, technical editors need knowledge, training, and experience, as well as certain personal attributes (see also Barnum & Carliner, 1993; Coggin & Porter, 1993). Some skills are required for all types of editing. For example, all editors must be meticulous readers with superior error-recognition capabilities, a passion for consistency, and an ability to be aware of both the overall structure of a document and its details. Mastery of language and its various aspects (grammar, syntax, usage) is essential, as is a grounding in design principles and measures to enhance document usability (see also Schriver, 1993).

Fortunately, technical editing has been attracting significant interest as a formal academic subject. Courses in rhetoric, language skills, content and design analysis, and desktop publishing enable students to gain strong skills for the workplace. The newer demands of multimedia and specialized knowledge such as SGML and quality auditing are also being incorporated into academic programs.

Training for a career as a substantive editor imposes additional demands. Such editors must be able to work collaboratively with authors and to understand the logic of presenting information in various situations in relation to an audience's needs (Schriver, 1989; Dragga, 1989; Michener, 1989). They must have sufficient knowledge of the subject matter to help the author develop an effective, logical organization and to resolve ambiguities and inconsistencies. In other words, substantive editors will need training in the technical field(s) in which they wish to work.

Because technical editors often carry considerable responsibility for document coordination, they also need to learn to be good managers. They must be able to work smoothly as a member of a team, sequence the work they do with that of others, and meet deadlines without compromising the quality of the product.

Professional acceptance of technical editing's importance and its greater visibility have helped to define its functions. Technical editors serving on product usability teams, in quality circles and audits, and as quality representatives on projects will continue to improve the position of technical editing (Weiss, 1993, pp. 234–238). Specialty areas such as medical editing have also grown with the development of professional organizations such as the American Medical Writers Association. The Society for Technical Communication and specialized groups such as the Council of Biology Editors have had a significant impact on editorial and communication policy, and the Board of Life Sciences' (BELS) certification program for editors is gaining considerable momentum (Phillips, 1993, pp. 56–58). In addition, as academic programs and industry interact more extensively in program and role development, technical editing should show additional growth in opportunity, responsibility, and prestige.

Technical writers, editors, and managers have an open challenge. With electronic capabilities expanding in a communications-oriented society, education and cooperation between academia and industry should maximize the values of all phases of the economy. The training of technical editors and writers will be significant, especially in the rhetoric of meeting user needs. That "user" is becoming even more fragmented, knowledgeable, and varied as a result of the information explosion. The jobs of all those associated with communicating—whether in print, on computer screens, or with complex multimedia operating across many platforms—are becoming increasingly sophisticated. Academia and industry must collaborate to produce skilled professionals prepared to succeed as technical editors in years to come.

REFERENCES

Barnum, C.M. & Carliner, S. (1993). *Techniques for technical communicators.* New York: Macmillan.

Coggin, W.O. & Porter, L.R. (1993). *Editing for the technical professions.* New York: Macmillan.

Dragga, S. & Gong, G. (1989). *Editing: The design of rhetoric.* Amityville, NY: Baywood.

Eichorn, P. & Yankauer, A. (1987). Do authors check their references? A survey of accuracy of references in three public health journals. *American Journal of Public Health, 77,* 1011–1012.

Eisenberg, A. (1992). *Guide to technical editing.* New York: Oxford, 1992.

Farkas, D.K. (1987). Online editing and document review. *Journal of Technical Writing and Communication 34,* 180–183.

Fine, M.G. (1991). New voices in the workplace: Research directions in multicultural communication. *Journal of Business Communication, 18,* 259–275.

Frank, F.W. & Treichler, P.A. (1988). *Language, gender, and professional writing.* New York, Modern Language Association.

Garson, L. & Schmidt, M.A. (1994). The use and importance of standard generalized markup language (SGML) to scientific and technical publishing. *CBE Views, 17,* 91–93.

Gerich, C. (1994). How technical editors enrich the revision process. *Technical Communication, 41,* 59–70.

Hibbard, J.L. (1990). Document processing by computer: Some generic models. *Technical Communication, 37,* 13–21.

Howell, J.B. (1983). *Style manuals in the English-speaking world: A guide.* Phoenix, AZ: Oryx.

Judd, K. (1990). *Copyediting: A practical guide.* (2nd Ed.). Los Altos, CA: Crisp.

Kemnitz, C. How to write effective hazard alert messages. *Technical Communication, 38,* 68–73.

Kirsch, J. (1995). *Kirsch's handbook of publishing laws.* Los Angeles, CA: Acrobat.

Lay, M.M. & Karis, W.M. (Eds.). (1991). Part 1: Theoretical overview of the collaborative process. In *collaborative writing in industry: Investigations in theory and practice.* New York: Baywood.

Mandell, J. (1995). *Book editors talk to writers.* New York: Wiley.

Michener, J.A. (1989). *James A. Michener's writer's handbook: Explorations in writing and publishing.*

Phillips, K.F. (1993). The BELS program: Certification for manuscript editors in the life sciences. *AMWA Journal, 8* (2), 56–58.

Plotnik, A. (1982). *The elements of editing: A modern guide for editors and journalists.* New York, Macmillan.

Proceedings: The first conference on quality in documentation. (1991). Waterloo, Ontario: University of Waterloo, Centre for Professional Writing.

Reilly, A.D. (1993). Professional recognition and respect through quality. *Technical Communication, 40,* 231–233.

Rude, C.D. (1991). *Technical editing.* Belmont, CA: Wadsworth.

Schriver, K.A. (1989). Evaluating text quality: The continuum from text-focused to reader-focused methods. *IEEE Transactions on Professional Communication, 32,* 238–255.

Schriver, K.A. (1993). Quality in document design: Issues and controversies. *Technical Communication, 40,* 239–257.

Shelton, S.M. (1993). Multimedia. *Technical Communication, 40,* 694–704.

Soderston, C. (1985). The usability edit: A new level. *Technical Communication, 32,* 16–18.

Stainton, E.M. (1991). *The fine art of copyediting.* New York: Columbia University Press.

Stix, G. (1994). The speed of write. *Scientific American, 271,* 106–111.

Stratton, C.R. (1989). Collaborative writing in the workplace. *IEEE Transactions on Professional Communication, 32,* 178–182.

Trolley, J.H. & Potter, P.M. (1994). Critical issues today in electronic information dissemination. *CBE Views, 17,* 97–98.

Van Buren, R. & Buehler, M.F. (1980). *The levels of edit.* (2nd Ed.). Pasadena, CA: JPL Publication.

Weiss, E.H. (1993). The technical communicator and ISO 9000. *Technical Communication, 40,* 234–238.

Wells, S. (1988). Auditing the meaning of the MOVE report. In L.Z. Smith (Ed.), *Audits of meaning: A festschrift in honor of Ann E. Berthoff* (pp. 151–160). Portsmouth, NH: Boynton/Cook.

Winsor, D. (1996). *Writing like an engineer: A rhetorical education.* Mahwah, NJ: Erlbaum.

Woolston, D.C., Robinson, P.A. & Kutzbach, G. (1988). *Effective writing strategies for engineers and scientists.* Chelsea, MI: Lewis Publishers.

Zook, L.M. (1983). Technical editors look at technical editing. *Technical Communication, 30,* 20–26.

15

VISUAL COMMUNICATION: THE EXPANDING ROLE OF TECHNICAL COMMUNICATORS

Kenneth T. Rainey

Southern College of Technology

INTRODUCTION

Visual communication is becoming a primary task for most technical communicators. The discrete skills involved in communication—writing, editing, designing, producing—are collapsing in on one other so that, in many cases, communicator, editor, designer, and producer are the same individual (see Caffarelli & Straughan, 1992, p. 7; Vaughan, 1993, p. 10). Moreover, new technologies confront technical communicators with challenging opportunities in design and production of documents and of their visual components.

The paper-oriented graphic artist employed pen and paper, rule and scale, to produce the visual components of printed materials. Visual communicators today accomplish almost all visual design with keyboard and mouse on a computer screen (see Search, 1993a). But the role of visual communicator encompasses far more than providing illustrations. The technical communicator now has become an information architect who orders, designs, and presents information visually and by means of visual connections. While the graphic artist provides illustrations that support, clarify, or emphasize verbal communication, the information architect formulates the entire design of a document. The design of the page, screen, or document is an act of visual communication, and the readability and the accessibility of information are the tasks of the technical communicator. And these tasks cannot be confined to print media. Soderson observed, as early as 1992, that "the attention of educators in communication skills must expand to the new [electronic multi-] media in order to develop principles for effective presentation" (p. 43). She called for students to be introduced "to additional genres, to forms of visual presentation, to extracting and articulating natural hierarchical relationships between ideas and chunking them visually, to enabling selective use by a variety of audiences for a variety of purposes" (p. 44). Finally, citing Wittgenstein, she incisively observed that "the essential and skillful application of rhetorical principles to communication forms the substance rather than being separable and arbitrary decoration" (p. 46). Thus, "visual communication" has become central to the role of technical communicator as information architect.

In this essay, I describe developing technologies and identify the knowledge that technical communicators increasingly need to operate in the new environment. Then, I discuss the implications these developments have for technical communicators. Finally, I suggest elements of visual communication instruction for technical communicators as information architects.

DEVELOPING TECHNOLOGIES

In the midst of the realignment of functions served by technical communicators and of rapidly developing technology, technical communication professionals must remember that their primary focus is on the transfer of accurate information from those who have it to those who require it. This responsibility requires technical communicators both to understand the principles of effective communication and to possess basic skills in design and production of visuals.

Before I discuss the ways in which responsibilities for and demands on visual communication change the role of the technical communicator, I will first describe technologies that are driving these changes.

Since the early 1980s, when workshops and offices began to employ desktop publishing (DTP), computer processing of information has become standard. In the 1990s, as William J. Mitchell (1994) notes, computerized recording, transmission, and processing of information is exploding into every area of communication (p. 70). In addition, engineers continue to develop new methods of organizing and searching sources, of presenting information, and of making available vast amounts of data. By the next century, new technologies for developing, storing, and transferring information will supplant DTP as the standard technology.

With the power of microprocessors doubling about every 18 months (Seabrook, 1994, p. 60) and thousands of programmers and designers working to exploit that power, it is impossible to predict what the technological landscape will look like by the time this discussion appears in print. So I will, instead, focus on the current state of technology and on some of its implications for technical communicators.

Clearly, interactive communication will replace, in the near future, the largely one-way communication now in place. Reconfiguration of communication avenues into two-way interaction between sender and receiver makes available a broad range of communication devices and techniques. These devices and techniques, in turn, require redesign of information databases if users are to access the information both efficiently and effectively.

Technical Formats

At present, two basic methods exist for encoding information: *analog* and *digital* technologies. *Analog technology* is the form by which sound and video systems have traditionally operated; it identifies "a continuous electrical signal that can vary in frequency and amplitude" (Shelton, 1993a, p. 700). In video, analog signals are transformed into what appears on the screen.

Digital technology—the technology of computers—employs binary code (0s and 1s) or electrical impulses that are either "off" or "on," unlike the continuous analog signals. The difference from analog technology might be compared to the difference between a watch with a second hand that sweeps smoothly around the dial (analog) and a digital watch with a second hand that jumps from second to second (digital).

Optical technology refers to the laser encoding and decoding of digital information. That is, the information has been encoded in a digital format (0s and 1s/off and on) and the signals are "read" by a laser. The most common device for this process is the compact disc (CD). CD-ROM technology continues to expand the sources and availability of information and will continue to be a primary medium of information storage and transfer for the foreseeable future.

Interactive Technology

In order to understand the future possibilities of communication technology, of new communication techniques, and of design and production of visual communication, technical communicators must understand what is meant by *interactive technology*. As Caffarelli and Straughan (1992) note, "the most common definition of interactivity is still limited to the ability to extract from information sources a specific answer to a specific question" (p. 22). This limitation will change with more sophisticated technology and with more creative methods of integrating the various devices for transmitting and organizing information. These integrative and organizational developments are represented by the words *multimedia* and *hypertext*.

Multimedia refers to a broad range of computer hardware and software—combining sound, color, moving images—and computer programs for simulating reality (lighting/shadowing, surface textures, and three dimensions) (see Fetterman & Gupta, 1993; Shelton, 1993a, p. 694; Vaughan, 1993; and Wodaski, 1992).

Hypertext identifies the organization of information in much the way the human brain organizes itself: that is, "the information we acquire day-by-day organizes itself, modifying the information already there, and being incorporated into the total body of our knowledge" (Caffarelli & Straughan, 1992, p. 23). Thus, to coincide with users' typical search methods, sources of information must be organized in a way that encourages intuitive (i.e., "creative" or "associative") exploration and accessibility. For example, hypertext includes coded "buttons" on key words in the text that link an idea to associated ideas; this feature allows users to branch out to related ideas and topics, so that they can follow their own non-linear pathways through the information (see Search, 1993b).

Integration of Technologies and Services

Mergers among cable television networks, telephone companies, and production studios now are actively pursued and, perhaps, by the end of the century will create a fully integrated information system (see O'Malley, 1993). Integration of analog, digital, and optical means of recording and transmitting information will emerge as the standard. In addition, voice-activated software will complicate the methods by which technical communicators create and transfer information while increasing the speed and the ease with which users access information. Moreover, the new systems will connect every computer terminal with many other communication sources (television and computer and telephone will likely meld into a single system; see O'Malley, 1993).

Undoubtedly, in the 21st century engineers will refine other sophisticated technical systems that will offer opportunity and pose challenges to technical communicators, particularly in visual communication. For example, a standard for *high-density television (HDTV)* for the United States has been agreed upon (see Bowes & Elliott, 1993). In addition, *holograms* (three-dimensional photographs recorded by laser beams) and *virtual reality* (a form of *artificial intelligence*) will provide entertainment, instruction, and training, as well as marketing information, with machines that approach the problem-solving and decision-making capabilities of the human brain (see Larijani, 1994).

Implications for Technical Communicators

These new technologies and integrated services will challenge technical communicators in several ways. First, technical communicators will need to understand the principles of effective communication as they apply to each of the new media. Second, technical communicators will have to be able to use sophisticated, complex hardware and software in designing and producing information that effectively and efficiently engages the users to interact with the information or services they desire. Third, they will have to employ their most versatile skills in designing and adapting communication to the demands and opportunities of new interactive media. These decisions may become the technical communicators' chief functions and involve at least the following three dimensions:

- Sorting, organizing, selecting, and encoding information
- Creating accessibility
- Revising and updating information

Communicators who understand how users search for information will need to construct databases to coincide with users' conceptual frameworks and intellectual schemata. Technical communicators are particularly suited to understand how to analyze audiences and to organize textual and visual information to suit users' associative search techniques and to meet users' expectations. Organization of information that allows users to construct their own information pathways will also benefit from technical communicators' abilities to understand principles of accuracy, accessibility, clarity, conciseness, and completeness.

Creating Accessibility

Technical communicators already understand the importance of making the use of complicated computer technology as easy and unintimidating as possible. With the advent of new technologies, technical communicators will need to design gateways into the information and create links among the nodes (locations) of information in ways that make it most usable (see Brooks, 1993; Grice & Ridgway, 1993; and Humphreys, 1993). The "human-computer interface" and associated human factors will be crucial to effective access.

REVISING AND UPDATING INFORMATION

As information changes, technical communicators who already understand the processes of revising—addition, deletion, rearrangement, and expansion—will be able to assist in keeping the information databases current.

IMPLICATIONS FOR INSTRUCTION

From this consideration of technical developments and their effects on communication, the following implications for instruction in visual communication seem fundamental. (For an extensive bibliography, see Lamb, 1991.)

Teaching the Basics

Technical communicators as visual communicators should know the basics (see Dragga, 1992; Kostelnick, 1989; Martin, 1989; and Welch, Hall, & Couture, 1987):

- How to keep audience and purpose central in their attempts to communicate visually
- How to explore the subject matter through research, including library, clinical, field, and expert sources

Teaching the Principles of Visual Communication

If technical communicators are to possess skills and knowledge necessary to function in the emerging environment of interactive communication, they must understand the principles underlying decisions about effective visual communication. Communicators can make some reasonably conclusive decisions based on research; they must make other, more subjective, decisions based on aesthetics and on rhetorical principles as they apply to visual communication (see Barton & Barton, 1985; and Kostelnick, 1989). In creating effective visual presentations, communicators must consider selection, design, position, production, and cost.

Principles of Selection

Principles of selection center on appropriateness of visuals in terms of subject matter, purpose, and audience:

- Whether the information can or should be communicated visually
- What visuals appropriately communicate the information
- The audience's knowledge, language, and visual and aural capabilities (see Cochran, Albrecht, & Green, 1989)

Principles of Design

Principles of design include aesthetic judgments as well as more practical decisions. Aesthetic judgments involve the following:

- Clarity
- Balance and symmetry
- Unity and coherence

Design principles also involve practical decisions about the use of such enhancing characteristics as the following:

- Color (see Gage, 1993; Keller & Keller, 1993, pp. 26–33; Keyes, 1993; Trummel et al., 1991)
- Typeface (font, size, and style; see Keyes, 1993)
- Width of lines
- Use of boxes and other highlighting devices (for a discussion of effective highlighting for on-line documents, see Fisher & Tan, 1989)

- Clear and appropriate labeling, indexing, and linkages
- Judicious use of white space (for a discussion of allocation of white space, see Gribbons, 1988)

For on-line and video information, the communicator must consider other dimensions of the design process (see Horton, 1991):

- Scripting or storyboarding that reveals the text to be displayed; the motions and sequences of text and images; and the sound used to introduce, conclude, and provide background accompaniment (see Benford, 1993; Gurewich & Gurewich, 1994; Shelton, 1993b)
- Animation, three-dimensional images, and motion pictures
- Wipes and fades to bring images and text on and off the screen in a variety of ways
- Textures to simulate realism
- Light sources to highlight and cast shadows for broadcast quality dimensionality

Principles of Position

Technical communicators should understand how to position visuals to effectively utilize the dimensions and capabilities of the selected medium. These decisions about position enhance the communication by attracting attention to it and by emphasizing important information. Visuals rarely exist apart from text; thus, principles of position, in short, merge with most of the decisions that communicators must make in designing a document (see Wise, 1993). These include the following:

- The size of the visuals in relation to other page layout components
- The physical relation of visuals to the text and to other visuals
- Their placement above or below the midpoint of a page and between the margins
- Their relation to the margins and to the edges of the paper (extending into the margins or bleeding to the edge of the paper)
- Their use to guide the eye along the page
- In a sequence of visuals, the logical and perceptual connections among them

In addition, decisions about position of visual communication on monitors take into account these factors:

- The size of the monitor (or the size of the projected image)

- The available space for substantive information
- The effect of programmatic information in menu bars, boxes, and windows

Principles of Production

Technical communicators should understand how various visuals are produced. If they produce the visuals themselves, they must understand the technology of production; they must have the budget to support the project and the time required to plan, to create, and to produce the final product. If technical communicators function as members of a team, they must understand at least the possibilities and the limitations of technology. Production includes the following tasks:

- Decisions about the capabilities of the available technology
    - What the available hardware and software can do (see Keller & Keller, 1993, pp. 14–19)
    - Compatibility of output equipment (see Caffarelli & Straughan, 1992, pp. 34–48)
- Decisions about production for print materials
    - The quality, weight, surface texture, color, and opaqueness of the paper
    - The selection of screens for blacks and grays and inks for colors
- Decisions about scanning (the process for transforming images into digital format)
    - The available scanning technology—hardware and software (see Blatner & Roth, 1993; also see Mitchell [1994] for ethical dimensions of this technology)
    - The possibilities of different graphic file formats for storing and transferring digital images (TIFF, PIX PICT, EPS, etc.)
- Decisions about time
    - To create the scenes one by one
    - To connect the scenes into a coherent whole

- To "render" the instructions, that is, to allow the hardware and software to process all of the algorithms that the designer has told the software to use

Considerations of Cost

Underlying all of the decisions about selection, design, position, and production are the cost and budget for specific projects. Typeset production costs more than photocopying, for example; use of color, three-dimensions, and animation can increase costs significantly. The technical communicator should be aware of the possible trade-offs between quality, ornamentation, and the cost of creating and producing a presentation.

Integrating Visual Communication Instruction

The pervasiveness of visual communication demands that instructors integrate visual communication education into all phases of technical communication instruction, not relegate it to one unit of study disconnected from the rest of a course (see Barton & Barton, 1985, p. 142).

Teaching Developing Technologies

Finally, instructors must assure that technical communicators of the 21st century have some knowledge of the technologies that facilitate interactive communication, including multimedia and hypertext. The technical communicator will not necessarily have to become a technician but will have to understand the capabilities and the limitations of the technology as well as the advantages and disadvantages of the various forms of visual communication that technology enables them to produce.

CONCLUSION

The role of visual communicator thus encompasses the total spectrum of communication:

- Possibilities and limitations of technology
- Principles of effective transfer of information
- Principles of visual imaging of information
- Constraints of cost versus quality and elaborateness of presentation

Such an extensive network of knowledge and skills seems beyond the capacities of any single individual. Yet, I suggest, a considerable acquaintance with all of these areas will characterize successful, effective information architects of the 21st century. The more of these areas that they master, the more essential they will be to business and industry and the more secure they will be as professionals.

REFERENCES

Barton, B.F. & Barton, M.S. (1985). Toward a rhetoric of visuals for the computer era. *Technical Writing Teacher, 12* (2), 126–145.

Benford, T. (1993). *PC sound, music, and MIDI: From mystery to mastery.* New York: MIS.

Blatner, D. & Roth, S. (1993). *Read world scanning and halftones: The definitive guide to scanning and halftones from the desktop.* Berkeley, CA: Peachpit.

Bowes, J.E. & Elliott, S.D. (1993). Standards for and development of a high-definition television system in the *U.S. Technical Communication, 40* (4), 705–714.

Brooks, R.M. (1993). Principles for effective hypermedia design. *Technical Communication, 40* (3), 422–428.

Caffarelli, F. & Straughan, D. (1992). *Publish yourself on CD-ROM: Mastering CDs for multimedia.* New York: Random House Electronic Publishing.

Cochran, J.L., Albrecht, S.A. & Green, Y.A. (1989). Guidelines for evaluating graphical designs. *Technical Communication, 36* (1), 25–32.

Dragga, S. (1992). Evaluating pictorial illustrations. *Technical Communication Quarterly, 1* (2), 47–62.

Fetterman, R.L. & Gupta, S.K. (1993). *Mainstream multimedia: Applying multimedia in business.* New York: Van Nostrand.

Fisher, D.L. & Tan, K.C. (1989). Visual displays: The highlighting paradox. *Human Factors, 31* (1), 17–30.

Gage, J. (1993). *Color and culture: Practice and meaning from antiquity to abstraction.* Boston: Little.

Gribbons, W.M. (1988). White space allocation: Implications for document design. *Proceedings.* International Technical Communication Conference. VC-1 — VC-43.

Grice, R.A. & Ridgway, L.S. (1993). Usability and hypermedia: Toward a set of usability criteria and measures. *Technical Communication, 40* (3), 429–437.

Gurewich, O. & Gurewich, N. (1994). *Easy multimedia sound and video for the PC crowd.* New York: Windcrest.

Horton, W. (1991). *Illustrating computer documentation: The art of presenting information graphically on paper and online.* New York: Wiley.

Humphreys, D.S. (1993). Making your hypertext interface usable. *Technical Communication, 40* (4), 754–761.

Keller, P.R. & Keller, M.M. (1993). *Visual cues: Practical data visualization.* Piscataway: IEEE Press.

Keyes, E. (1993). Typography, color, and information structure. *Technical Communication, 40* (4), 638–654.

Kostelnick, C. (1989). Visual rhetoric: A reader-oriented approach to graphics and design. *Technical Writing Teacher 16* (1), 77–88.

Lamb, A.C. (1991). *Emerging technologies and instruction: Hypertext, hypermedia, and interactive multimedia: A selected bibliography.* Englewood Cliffs, NJ: Educational Technology Publications.

Larijani, L.C. (1994). *The virtual reality primer.* New York: McGraw.

Martin, M. (1989). The semiology of documents. *IEEE Transactions on Professional Communication, 32* (3), 171–177.

Mitchell, W.J. (1994). When is seeing believing? *Scientific American, 270* (2), 68–73.

O'Malley, P.G. (1993). Information delivery systems: The future is here. *Technical Communication, 40* (4), 619–628.

Seabrook, J. (1994, 10 January). E-mail from Bill. *The New Yorker,* 48–61.

Search, P. (1993a). Computer graphics: Changing the language of visual communication. *Technical Communication 40* (4), 629–637.

Search, P. (1993b). HyperGlyphs: Using design and language to define hypermedia navigation. *Technical Communication, 40* (3), 414–21.

Shelton, S.M. (1993a). Multimedia. *Technical Communication, 40* (4), 694–704.

Shelton, S.M. (1993b). Script design for information film and video. *Technical Communication, 40* (4), 655–663.

Trummel, P., et al. (1991). Issues in graphic and visual communication: Special section on color. *IEEE Transactions on Professional Communication, 34* (3), 151–185.

Vaughan, T. (1993). *Multimedia: Making it work.* Berkeley: Osborne McGraw-Hill.

Welch, M., Hall, D. & Couture, B. (1987). Designing graphic aids for professional writing. In The Association of Teachers of Technical Writing (Ed.), *Professional writing: Toward a college curriculum* (pp. 169–216).

Wise, M.L. (1993). Using graphics in software documentation. *Technical Communication, 40* (4), 677–681.

Wodaski, R. (1992). *Multimedia madness!* Carmel: Sams Publishing.

PROGRAM DESIGN

16

DEVELOPING PROGRAMS IN TECHNICAL COMMUNICATION: A PRAGMATIC VIEW

M. Jimmie Killingsworth

Texas A&M University

There is a pleasure in the pathless wood.

—Byron, *Childe Harold*

WHERE WE ARE GOING: THE PRAGMATIST'S CASE AGAINST STANDARDIZATION IN AN EMERGING DISCIPLINE

When it comes to program design and most other issues in technical communication, I am a pragmatist. Pragmatism is a philosophy that, in problem solving and evaluation, favors the specific and the local over the abstract and the global. It prefers explanations grounded in historical understanding to rationalizations based on allegedly ideal or universal knowledge. It is what Richard Rorty (1979) would call an edifying or critical theory rather than a systematic way of knowing, and it looks upon what Dewey (1929) called "the quest for certainty"—the effort to find final solutions that claim to be 100% reliable and applicable in every case—with profound skepticism.

My aim in this introductory essay to the section on program design is briefly to take a pragmatic view of the development of programs in technical communication. I will argue that whatever principles of curricular development and whatever professional standards we put forward at this time are likely to be little more than practical reactions to historical contingencies and market demands. I will not say that we should cease to argue over principles and standards or stop making models for good programs, thereby allowing a kind of anarchy to prevail among the various programs, only that we should accept the reality of continual changes and dislocations, especially in hard economic times, both in the academic world and in industry. I will also contend that we should respect the local and specific solutions that our colleagues at different institutions create out of diverse and uncertain resources and that, in program design as in the other topics discussed in this volume, we should recognize our position as an "emerging discipline," to use Stephen North's (1987) term for composition, a field of study that, though mongrel in comparison to disciplines like geometry and astronomy, has a more venerable pedigree than our own in technical communication.

I like to think of the mission of program architects and evaluators in technical communication as analogous to that of government planners in "developing countries." Looking on mature and tradition-bound disciplines like physics and history, or even century-old upstarts like psychology and civil engineering, we are likely to suffer the same kinds of jealousies and frustrations that some citizens of "third-world countries" allegedly experience when they compare their standard of living to that of developed nations. But we may take some comfort in realizing that a lack of development can also mean the chance to avoid the mistakes of previous developments, much as planners in developing countries, recognizing that the large-scale industrialization of the first world has brought environmental poverty as well as monetary wealth, have a chance to circumvent the one while seeking the other, to take ecologically wise steps that would never have occurred to the rough pioneers of first-world development.

In this sense, to be a developing country, or an emerging discipline, means to be young, with the world lying before us as a set of options and opportunities, and to have the energy and health (if not always the money) to respond with enthusiasm and imagination. The guiding philosophy of youth (at least in its joyous, romantic mode) is not idealism, despite the clichés, but pragmatism, an outlook that remains open to change and takes pleasure in a multitude of paths or even, to use Byron's famous metaphor, a "pathless wood." Like Lester Faigley (1992), who sees the rapidly shifting theoretical perspectives and pedagogical directions of rhetoric and composition not as a sign of disorder or confusion but as an indication of activity and health, I see programs in technical communication as more robust than ever and would resist any attempt to rush toward standardization or artificial rigor (as in rigor mortis). The pragmatic attitude I recommend urges us to maintain, even to celebrate, our diversity and flexibility as an emerging discipline.

WHERE WE COME FROM: ENGLISH, ENGINEERING, AND INDUSTRY AS FORBEARS OF TECHNICAL COMMUNICATION

Using spatial rather than temporal metaphors (like youth and age), Michael Gilbertson and I have suggested that technical communication is not a discipline at all (or even a "discourse community") but rather a "field" of practice, a space of work that has opened in the interstices among several academic disciplines and professional communities of knowledge (Killingsworth & Gilbertson, 1992, pp. 183–184). In this way of thinking, the development of curricula and programs in technical communication is part of the history of the specialization of knowledge in a technological culture. As an academic and professional field, technical communication appeared in the twentieth century as an extension of applied science and engineering into territory once claimed by the humanities and the arts (the representation and interpretation of the world through the creation of written and illustrated texts). Sometimes in collusion and sometimes in competition with engineers interested in communication, humanists and communication specialists have tried to reclaim the territory or at least exert our influence over it through the instruction of first engineers and then specialists in technical communication.

Engineering itself grew up in the 19th century, the great era of professionalization in Western mercantile-capitalist nations. Engineers—initially as individual innovators, then as members of a profession and practitioners of a discipline—reinterpreted scientific methods and knowledge to allow for greater efficiency in the transfer of information between the theoretically oriented academy and the practically oriented realm of industry and the marketplace. With the increased pace of technological development after each of the world wars, the engineering disciplines diversified, and the need for special kinds of communication also arose, as government (especially the military) joined industry in promoting and supporting academic research at unprecedented levels. Hence the increasing demand in the last two generations for technical information that could be communicated and applied across various discourse communities and interest groups (Killingsworth & Gilbertson, 1992, Chapters 7 and 8).

As part of the effort to meet this demand, the first curricular developments in technical communication emerged in the early 20th century from a collaboration of engineering and English departments at state universities (Connors, 1982; Grego, 1987). Engineering professors, responding to recommendations from their contacts in industry, called upon their counterparts in English to help give technical students more supervised practice in writing on technical topics in genres they would use on the job. As best they could, English professors strove to meet these demands by creating the first courses and textbooks dedicated exclusively to technical writing, much as, a half century earlier, English departments had developed composition classes that answered the demand for a more literate professional work force (Berlin, 1987; Halloran, 1990; Killingsworth, 1993). Like composition, then, technical communication emerged as part of the increasing vocational specialization of American education at the turn of the century.

As this process of academic development unfolded, a similar process was at work in industry, where technical employees with special talents as communicators began to specialize as technical writers and editors. The growth of the defense industry in the 1940s and 1950s provided the first impetus. New speed and quality were required to develop massive project proposals in a hurry and then to write effective instructional materials to carry the projects out. New audiences for technical information appeared everywhere—ranging from the ordinary soldier operating advanced weapon systems to the householder installing and operating the new appliances and home technologies. The process accelerated again in the 1980s as home computers and related products hit the market.

At each stage, "technical writer" appeared more frequently as a job description, though in actual practice the duties of these workers varied from basic clerical work to integrated involvement in product and system design. Whatever the work, however, the process of professionalization and specialization had begun, and a number of universities that already had technical writing courses in place began to consider more elaborate and specialized programs for training professional technical communicators. In some places, like the University of Washington, technical communication appeared as a specialized branch of engineering. At other places, like Rensselaer or New Mexico Tech (where I taught at the time), it became the formalized emphasis of a communications or humanities department that had never offered a traditional English degree and had always given much of its time and energy to teaching technical writing. In departments of

English (in places like Texas A&M, where I now teach), technical or professional writing often became a secondary concentration or fall-back position for students wary of majoring in literature. When, in tight economic conditions, literary work came to seem rather esoteric and impractical (especially to parents financing all or part of the education), the appeal of the professional writing concentration became ever stronger.

WHAT WE HAVE BECOME: ENGINEERING, ENGLISH—AND US?

Thus, considered collectively, programs tend to show the marks of the evolution of technical communication as an extension of engineering and English or communication studies, with regular inputs from industry. The engineering emphasis appears dominant in some programs, while the humanities influence appears dominant in others. In some programs, there may also be signs of the influence of local industries—more courses in computer documentation, for example, in places that tend to supply students to the computer industry.

Looking at the curricula of the various programs, we can identify elements that represent clear instances of the engineering and English or communication heritage. The engineering influence is most obvious in requirements for blocks of technical courses or specific courses on computer use and graphics, as well as in program orientation courses that often include speeches by representatives from industry, in internships and cooperative education requirements, and in electives from management or business. The influence of established programs in English and communication appears in requirements for courses in literature, rhetoric, linguistics, general writing (like freshman and advanced composition), speech, journalism, media studies, and graphic arts. In many technical communication programs, courses from established engineering and English or communication curricula make up the bulk of the requirements.

Yet, even in the most makeshift programs, we can discern elements of technical communication as a field in its own right. These elements tend to be foregrounded in graduate programs (see Geonetta, Allen, Curtis, & Staples, 1993). They include not only variations on the basic *technical writing* course (which from the start has tended to be organized around key genres like reports and proposals and specific techniques like the use of headings and graphics, as Connors' [1992] history indicates), but also field-specific variations of courses taught in other fields, such as *technical editing* (as opposed to the general editing course taught in journalism or in publications programs), *research methods* (similar in aim to those taught in composition or social science programs, but different in content), and *theory and history of technical communication* (more than just a requirement in rhetorical or communication theory). Some highly specialized courses in technical communication, which attempt to define totally new aims and contents, have also begun to appear in recent years. Progressive programs may now include whole courses in *document design, user testing,* and *technology transfer,* for example.

THE PATHS THAT LIE BEFORE US: KEEPING THE CHANNELS OPEN

Any claim that we make for disciplinary status suggests that this field of practice we call our own has a significant measure of methodological or practical autonomy from its parent disciplines of engineering and literary or communication studies. But, even as the unique elements of technical communication emerge, engineering and English continue to evolve on their own and continue to make contributions to the emerging field. In engineering, for example, concepts related to total quality management as well as new technological innovations for the workplace have been influential. From the English side, literary and rhetorical scholars have contributed a new emphasis on theory and cultural studies that has proved extremely influential among researchers and teachers in technical communication, while compositionists have provided some very interesting innovations in research methodology and pedagogy. The ferment produced by the interaction of these changes within the same academic department has yielded a surprising and exciting effervescence.

To take only one example, consider a recent study by Davida Charney published in Jack Selzer's (1993) collection of methodologically diverse analyses of a single essay by biologists Stephen Jay Gould and Richard Lewontin. Charney designed a project that used the methods of talk-aloud protocols to gather the reactions of model readers of the Gould and Lewontin paper—graduate students and faculty in biological science. She then used rhetorical theory, cognitivist formulations of reading habits, and reader response theory drawn from literary studies to evaluate the responses of the readers and the kinds of effects the prose produced. Charney's essay gives us a fresh and fascinating combination of usability engineering and literary criticism. The result is a kind of hybrid discourse study that opens broad and inviting prospects for research and practice.

Innovations are coming from industry, too. In a comprehensive and suggestive metastudy of the literature on industrial roles for technical communicators, Donald Zimmerman and Marilee Long (1992) show that technical communicators still spend most of their time writing and editing, but other demands on their time continue to grow as the technological and social context of their work evolves. Zimmerman and Long stress, for example, the need for interactive communication and collaborative work that continues to appear in industry studies. They also note the increase in the number of women in the profession and imply that a number of the more subtle shifts in workplace style are dialectically related to this gender shift—a point that Charles Sides (1994) confronts more directly in a separate paper.

Like the article by Zimmerman and Long, the papers that follow give specific models for program development. The caveat I offer here merely asks you to consider such advice within the context of social and historical change and to weigh the models discussed against the local needs and resources of your own program. We ought to keep the paths open to influences from English, engineering, and industry. We should avoid rigidity in our self-conceptions and aim for curricular flexibility and strategic responsiveness. In our hurry to become a recognized discipline, we should not, that is, become overdisciplined.

REFERENCES

Berlin, J. (1987). *Rhetoric and reality: Writing instruction in American colleges, 1890–1985.* Carbondale, IL: Southern Illinois University Press.

Charney, D. (1993). A study in rhetorical reading: How evolutionists read "The Spandrels of San Marco." In J. Selzer (Ed.), *Understanding scientific prose* (pp. 203–213). Madison, WI: University of Wisconsin Press.

Connors, R.J. (1982). The rise of technical writing instruction in America. *Journal of Technical Writing and Communication, 12,* 329–352.

Dewey, J. (1929). *The quest for certainty.* New York: Putnam.

Faigley, L. (1992). *Fragments of rationality: Postmodernity and the subject of composition.* Pittsburgh, PA: University of Pittsburgh Press.

Geonetta, S.C., Allen, J., Curtis, D. & Staples, K. (1993). *Academic programs in technical communication.* (4th Ed.). Washington, DC: Society for Technical Communication.

Grego, R.C. (1987). Science, late nineteenth-century rhetoric, and the beginnings of technical writing instruction in America. *Journal of Technical Writing and Communication,* 63–78.

Halloran, S.M. (1990). From rhetoric to composition: The teaching of writing in America to 1900. In J.J. Murphy (Ed.), *A short history of writing instruction from ancient Greece to twentieth-century America* (pp. 151–182). Davis, CA: Hermagoras.

Killingsworth, M.J. (1993). Process and product, orality and literacy: An essay in composition and culture. *College Composition and Communication, 44,* 26–39.

Killingsworth, M.J. & Gilbertson, M. (1992). *Signs, genres, and communities in technical communication.* Amityville, NY: Baywood.

North, S. (1987). *The making of knowledge in composition: Portrait of an emerging field.* Portsmouth, NH: Boynton/Cook.

Rorty, R. (1979). *Philosophy and the mirror of nature.* Princeton, PA: Princeton University Press.

Selzer, J. (Ed.). (1993). *Understanding scientific prose.* Madison, WI: University of Wisconsin Press.

Sides, C.H. (1994). Community consensus and change in technical communication. In C.H. Sides (Ed.), *Technical communications: Essays in theory* (pp. 1–13). Minneapolis, MN: Association of Teachers of Technical Writing.

Zimmerman, D.E. & Long, M. (1992). Exploring the technical communicator's roles: Implications for program design. *Technical Communication Quarterly,* 301–317.

17

DESIGNING FOUR-YEAR PROGRAMS IN TECHNICAL COMMUNICATION

Sam C. Geonetta

University of Cincinnati

INTRODUCTION

The bachelor's degree forms the foundation of technical communication education in the United States. The 4th edition of *Academic Programs in Technical Communication* lists 44 Bachelor of Arts and 22 Bachelor of Science degrees in 58 different colleges and universities. They comprise 48% of the degree programs in technical communication (see Table 17.1) (Geonetta, Allen, Curtis, & Staples, in press).

TYPE OF PROGRAM	*NUMBER OF SCHOOLS OFFERING*
Ph.D.	11
MA	29
MS	15
Other Master's**	4
BA	44
BS	22
AA	8
AAS	4
Minor	28
Certificate	37
Other non-degree***	3

Number of Schools Responding to the Survey:	140
Number of Formal Programs of Study:	206*
Number of Schools Offering Coursework Only:	39

*There are more programs than there are schools responding because several schools offer multiple programs. For example, one school might offer a BA and an MA; each of these is counted as a separate "program."

**There are four programs in this category: Master of Special Studies, Master of Professional Communication, Master of Technical and Professional Writing, and Master of Technical and Scientific Communication.

***There are three programs in this category: Concentration, Option, and Emphasis.

Table 17.1 Degrees in Technical Communication[1]

Program growth has been clear and steady: in 1981 Pearsall, Sullivan, and McDowell reported 1 undergraduate program, while Kelley, Masse, Pearsall, and Sullivan (1985) reported 37 in 1985. As more bachelor's degree graduates move into the workplace, as more doctoral programs place faculty, and as the demand for technical communicators increases, the growth of four-year programs will continue. Articles found in the Annual Bibliography published by the Association of Teachers of Technical Writing in any given year show that how these programs develop in form and content is a central question in technical communication education. Discussion and analysis is devoted not only to how a program should be developed, but also to why it should be developed. The "why" is significant as a rationale for giving disciplinary identity to technical communication, especially because most practicing technical communicators today have not come from technical communication programs (Society for Technical Communication, 1992, p. 4). This essay develops reasons for establishing a bachelor's degree in technical communication and discusses the design of four-year programs in technical communication.

1. This information is current as of March 1993 when the survey results were forwarded to the national office of the Society for Technical Communication.

RATIONALE FOR A BACHELOR'S DEGREE IN TECHNICAL COMMUNICATION

Information products and services add about 45% in value to the United States Gross National Product (GNP). A third of the $5.5 trillion GNP is in information and ideas. The Department of Commerce reported a 20% growth in on-line information services, with a database market alone of nearly $5-7 billion worldwide (Dordick & Wang, 1993, pp. 1–7). With the commensurate growth of technology and science in the workplace—the Department of Labor estimates that the greatest number of jobs between 1990 and 2005 will be for technicians and related supporting occupations—much of the information will be technical in nature (*Occupational Outlook Handbook,* 1992, p. 9). Further growth is anticipated as society turns to science and engineering to solve its problems, and as more technology comes into the hands of end users. Hines (1994) argues that no segment of society will be immune from this phenomenon: from farmers to office workers, the incursions of the information society will change the way we do business (12). The *Occupational Outlook Handbook* relates this growth in technology and information to opportunities for technical communicators: "opportunities will be good for technical writers because of the more limited number of writers who can handle technical material" (1992, p. 172).

To meet the demand for new information and to solve the problems of disseminating the available, growing pool of information, the use of communication technologies, such as computer networks and multimedia systems, will spread. The technical communicator will be a principal agent in determining how effectively and efficiently information is disseminated and used and in how communication technology affects this information and its use.

Another need for the abilities of the technical communicator is in educating significant segments of society in the use and potential of new technologies. Entry-level technologists and scientists need to be educated in the use of new technologies, and those already in the field need the most current technical information to function effectively (Otala, 1993). Technical communicators are in the best position to communicate the latest information and ideas to those coming through the educational system. Technical communicators will also assist scientists and engineers when they are called on by their colleagues and the public to explain their ideas to decision makers and to articulate their ideas to the public that pays for and uses technology.

DESIGNING THE BACHELOR'S DEGREE PROGRAM IN TECHNICAL COMMUNICATION

The design of the four-year program in technical communication is a complex issue. "Technical communication" does not appear to have the departmental/institutional identity associated with well-established disciplines such as mathematics or journalism. Neither does it seem to have the same institutional clout to achieve the independent departmental status so often associated with an established discipline such as English or psychology. Few four-year degrees exist in independent departments of technical communication; most are housed in departments of English, where technical communication or technical writing is an "option," "concentration," or "emphasis." Some exist in such diverse departments as mass communication, language, literature, and communication, humanities, and general studies, as well as in a College of Engineering and a Division of Humanities. The degree is even difficult to discern by name: the cited 66 bachelor's degrees are offered under 25 different names, 10 of which have neither the word "technical" nor "scientific" in them (Geonetta et al., in press).

An examination of the Society for Technical Communication 1992 profile of its members illustrates this diversity. While 33% of those responding to the survey majored in English and 18% in technical communication, the remaining members report degrees in "other" (28%), education (10%), journalism (9%) and sociology (1%), among 13 college majors listed (p. 4). Still, those designing a four-year degree program can draw on sound sources. Many offer specific guidance about current demands and current thinking about what such a program should include.[2] These sources define the state of the profession through surveys of practitioners and observations of professional technical communication educators. They allow curricula to be defined by the current needs articulated by business and industry. The limits of these sources preclude their exclusive use and lead to other sources that offer broader advice. Anderson has asserted that too much attention to the specifics of the technical communicator's job in technical communication education is as undesirable as too general a preparation (1984, p. 6). He warns that practitioners present a biased view of technical communication because they seem to think that what they do represents what all technical communicators do (1988, p. 163). Marilyn Cooper (1991) has also addressed the issue of a too-prescriptive program design. At the 1990 Annual Meeting of the Council for Programs in Technical and Scientific Communication, she discussed "Model(s) for Educating Professional Communicators." Noting that she was "worried that you would expect me to come up with a definitive model or models, complete with curricular requirements....", she observed,

> my reluctance to talk about definitive model programs for educating anyone stems from my belief that all successful programs are site-specific, and what works at one university with one group of students and faculty at one time probably won't work at another university with other students and faculty at other times. (p. 3)

2 Heather Keeler (1990) offers an insightful review of an array of these articles. In a more current article with a slightly different emphasis, Zimmerman and Long (1993) offer an analysis of several of the same articles, with the addition of those published after Keeler's appeared.

Another avenue for those who design four-year degrees is to project the future professional needs of their students based on apparent trends in the practice of technical communication. As Corey and Gilbertson (1986) have concluded: "Of necessity, most industries live in the present; curriculum designers must live in the future" (p. 27). Attention to trends allows for current needs in a curriculum but also provides for areas of development. For example, McKown and Nauda (1993) define "The Brave New World of Professional Communication," highlighting the potential of multimedia/video compression technology, color document processing, display technology, and computer-based training, among others, for the practice of technical communication (p. 1; see also Brand, 1987; Tynan, 1993). Barclay, Pinelli, Keene, Kennedy, and Glassman (1991) as well as Thrush (1993), articulate the implications of the international workplace for curriculum development. Coonrod (1993) offers further food for thought for the program designer with her discussion of the growing significance of product liability, while Otala's (1993) work on "Studying for the Future" makes it clear that training and development, especially for engineers and other technically oriented professionals, offer fertile ground for technical communicators. By drawing on a variety of sources, one can determine some important characteristics for a four-year degree in technical communication. Anderson (1988) offers some direction with a model that defines technical communication in terms of the practitioners' common aims, their characteristic activities, and the contexts in which they work. Keeler (1990) reviews the survey literature on current demands and current thinking about the technical communication curriculum and concludes that certain attributes appear more frequently than others in the research results: Technical communicators must be

> total communicators with good writing, speaking, and human interaction skills. They must work collaboratively, as team players with other professionals, and they require project coordination skills that carry them through projects from initial planning to final production and evaluation. More important than specific technical expertise is a balance between a basic understanding of technical and engineering concepts. (p. 47)

Zimmerman and Long's (1993) review concludes with a model curriculum. They suggest that a

> bachelor's degree curriculum in technical communication should provide graduates with a liberal education, with knowledge of technical communication principles, with basic technical communication skills, with skills in interpersonal communication and management, and with a knowledge of a technical, scientific, or specialized subject outside of technical communication. (p. 307)

Directors of several undergraduate programs who caucused at the 1988 meeting of the Council for Programs in Technical and Scientific Communication drew similar conclusions. Lay (1988) reports that participants agreed that while writing courses formed the core of most programs, courses in oral communication, graphics, and specialized skills such as interviewing should be added. Furthermore, flexibility should also be a part of any curriculum with "Special Topics" courses in task-oriented or temporary subjects such as "alternative media" or "uses of technology in communication" (p. 34). Participants also gave high priority to technical courses within undergraduate programs, with courses in math, science, and computer science as "givens," and with advanced technical courses highly desirable (p. 33; See also Corey & Gilbertson, 1986, pp. 20–21, 23–24; Samson, 1988, p. 137).

At the Society for Technical Communication's academic-industry workshop in January 1993, several representatives from the academy and business met with the STC board to define broad curricular concerns.[3] Hayhoe, Kunz, Southard, and Stohrer (1993) conclude that

> The ideal curriculum in information product development includes writing, transferable lifelong learning skills, software tools, communication theory, the history and impact of technology on culture and human lives, and internships or practica which sharpen the students' focus on tasks they will perform in industry. (p. 4)

CONCLUSION

The four-year degree program in technical communication presents a formidable challenge to those who undertake its design. Its end is to produce professional communicators who can collect, analyze, and present information and ideas on relatively complex subjects, as well as assist others, such as engineers and scientists, who must also communicate with specific audiences.

The curriculum should strengthen writing, presentation, interpersonal, and visual communication skills to a high degree. It should offer education in the use of such technical tools of technical communication as the

---

3 Participants from industry included: Don Barnett of Hewlett-Packard Corporation, Charlie Brenninger of E.I. du Pont de Nemours and Co., Beth Ann Cyrus of IBM Corporation, Stephen Murphy of Digital Equipment Corporation, and Mike Rogers of SunSoft. Participants from academia included: Paul Anderson of Miami University, Sam Geonetta of the University of Cincinnati, Bob Krull of Rensselaer Polytechnic Institute, Kenneth Rainey of Southern College of Technology, and Tom Williams of the University of Washington.

computer and supporting peripherals. Management skills should also be a part of the curriculum. A sound foundation in professionalism, characterized by an exposure to key thinkers about and key theories of communication, is necessary. Cognate work in mathematics, science, and/or a technical area beyond the basic level provides subject matter and a way of thinking about it that is likely to be a part of the student's life as a practicing professional. Yet, given even these demands, the curriculum should be flexible to meet the changing demands of the technical communicator's profession: The program should be such that its key outcome is that its students "learn how to learn" in order to develop the kind of adaptability required to help them prosper in a dynamic field.

REFERENCES

Anderson, P.V. (1984). Introduction. *Technical Communication, 31*, 4–8.

Anderson, P.V. (1988). What technical and scientific communicators do: A comprehensive model for developing academic programs. *IEEE Transactions on Professional Communication, PC-27* (3), 161–167.

Barclay, R., Pinelli, T.E., Keene, M.L., Kennedy, J.M. & Glassman, M. (1991). Technical communication in the international workplace: Some implications for curriculum development. *Technical Communication, 38*, 324–335.

Brand, S. (1987). *The media lab.* New York: Viking Penguin.

Bowsher, J.E. (1991). *Educating America: Lessons learned in the nation's corporations.* New York: Wiley.

Coonrod, K. (1993). Why should technical communicators care about product liability? *Intercom, 38*, 3, 5.

Cooper, M. (1991). Model(s) for educating professional communicators. In J. Zappen (Ed.), *The Council for Programs in Technical and Scientific Communication Proceedings: 1990* (pp. 1–13). Troy, NY: Rensselaer Polytechnic Institute.

Corey, J. & Gilbertson, M. (1987). Quality in bachelor's degree programs. In S.C. Geonetta (Ed.), *The Council for Programs in Technical and Scientific Communication Proceedings: 1986* (pp. 18–29). Rolla, MO: University of Missouri-Rolla.

Dordick, H.S. & Wang, G. (1993). *The information society: A retrospective view.* Newbury Park, CA: Sage.

Geonetta, S.C., Allen, J., Curtis, D. & Staples, K. (in press). *Academic programs in technical communication.* (4th Ed.). Washington, DC: Society for Technical Communication.

Green, M.M. & Nolan, T.D. (1984). A systematic analysis of the technical communicator's job: A guide for educators. *Technical Communication, 31*, 9–12.

Hayhoe, G., Kunz, L., Southard, S. & Stohrer, F. (1993, May 31) Growing to fit the future: An STC white paper on academic programs in technical communication. Unpublished manuscript.

Hines, A. (1994). Jobs and infotech: Work in the information society. *The Futurist,* 10–15.

Keeler, H. (1990). Portrait of a technical communicator: A bibliographic review of current research. *Technical Communication, 37,* 41–50.

Kelley, P.M., Masse, R.E., Pearsall, T.E. & Sullivan, F.J. (1985). *Academic programs in technical communication.* (3rd Ed.). Washington, DC: Society for Technical Communication.

Lay, M. (1988). Report from the Undergraduate Caucus at the CPTSC October, 1988 Conference, in Minneapolis. In L.S. Hayes (Ed.), *The Council for Programs in Technical and Scientific Communication Proceedings: 1988* (pp. 31–35). St. Paul, MN: University of Minnesota.

McKown, R.R. & Nauda, A. (1993). The brave new world of professional communication. *IEEE Professional Communication Society Newsletter, 37,* 1–4.

Occupational Outlook Handbook. (1993). Washington, DC: Bureau of Labor Statistics.

Otala, L. (1993, October). Studying for the future. *ASEE Prism,* 23–29.

Pearsall, T.E., Sullivan, F.J. & McDowell, E.E. (1981). *Academic programs in technical communication.* (2nd Ed.). Washington, DC: Society for Technical Communication.

Samson, D.C. (1988). Humanities education and technical communication. *Proceedings, 35th International Technical Communication Conference* (pp. RET-134 – RET-137). Arlington, VA: Society for Technical Communication.

Society for Technical Communication. (1992). Profile 92: STC special report. *Intercom, 37,* [insert].

Storms, C.G. (1984). Programs in technical communication. *Technical Communication, 31,* 13–20.

Thrush, E.A. (1993). Bridging the gaps: Technical communication in an international and multicultural society. *Technical Communication Quarterly, 2,* 271–283.

Tynan, D. (1993, July). Multimedia goes on the job just in time. *Newmedia,* 36–46.

Zimmerman, D. & Long, M. (1993). Exploring the technical communicator's roles: Implications for program design. *Technical Communication Quarterly, 2,* 301–317.

18

TWO-YEAR COLLEGE TECHNICAL COMMUNICATION PROGRAMS: TOWARD THE FUTURE

Katherine Staples

Austin Community College

Being educated puts one almost on a level with the commercial classes.

—Oscar Wilde

INTRODUCTION

Jane has just completed updates for the on-line help system she has been assigned to. She is on her way to a team meeting. As a student intern, Jane, 34, a single parent, has made the last step away from a dead-end secretarial position and into technical communication. It took her years of part-time study at night, active STC membership, and a technical communication portfolio—as well as an associate's degree.

After a full workday, Barry, a high school history teacher, is moving steadily through rush hour traffic to his evening classes in documentation and desktop publishing. An advanced degreed career changer, Barry, 42, is taking specialized courses to build the technical skills and communication knowledge that will qualify him for an entry-level documentation position. He does not plan to complete a degree.

Sonia, a 19-year-old full-time student, is completing research for her part of a collaborative report in a technical communication service course. A full-time student, she is taking the course to fulfill a requirement of the AAS degree in electronics she is completing. Sonia is considering transfer to a local university's engineering program after she has worked in industry for a few years.

These nontraditional students are typical of those who enroll in two-year college technical communication courses. Their ages, college attendance patterns, and educational goals are more diverse than those of the 18- to 22-year-old students who enroll full time in many four-year programs. Two-year programs in technical communication can meet diverse needs of students like these, providing quality curriculum that responds rapidly and thoughtfully to regional employment and demographic trends. This essay describes the context, features, and problems of the two-year college technical communication program, defining its potential and showing its need to develop linkages with other academic programs in technical communication.

THE TWO-YEAR COLLEGE: HISTORY AND MISSION

Even before the Morrill Acts of 1862 and 1877 had been passed to found land-grant universities, the precursors of two-year colleges had begun to fill some of their educational functions. The "land-grant agricultural and mechanical colleges ... were to make college education available in the later nineteenth century to a hugely increased percentage of the population, ... to broaden and specialize the college curriculum in many ways" (Connors, 1982, p. 230). However, private academies with elements of secondary and postsecondary curriculum, providing terminal education, vocational study, and transfer credit, were operating as early as 1835 (Boggs & Cater, 1994, p. 218). Designed to serve the needs of specialized groups—African Americans, women, teachers—these academies were the academic forerunners of the "junior college" that provided transfer opportunities by offering curriculum parallel to that of local public universities (Boggs & Cater, 1994, p. 220). The growth of these academies, the social and curricular changes in higher education after the Civil War, and the educational needs of large numbers of immigrants led to the development of the junior college movement in the early part of this century.

Social and economic changes have always shaped the two-year college. The high unemployment rate of the Great Depression and a corresponding demand for vocational education further expanded its numbers and function. However, the GI Bill of 1944, like the original Morrill Act, was to reshape all of American higher education, providing more democratic access and more curricular options than ever before as a new influx of servicemen entered and expanded the college and university population, changing its demographics and its purposes (Boggs & Cater, 1994, pp. 221–222).

This kind of democratic educational access was to be reflected in later federal educational initiatives. In its 1947 report, President Truman's Commission on Higher Education stated that "The Commission does not subscribe to the belief that higher education should be confined to an intellectual elite, much less a small elite drawn from families in the higher income brackets," recommending an accessible education through grade 14 (Boggs & Cater, 1994, p. 222). The community college, designed to serve a broader range of purposes than the junior one, was an important part of the Commission's plan. With the tremendous postwar population growth of the 1940s, the numbers of two-year colleges again expanded as part of educational master plans to meet the educational need for transfer and career education in the 1960s (Boggs & Cater, 1994, p. 223).

With varying combinations of district, state, and federal support, today's two-year college offers a wider range of educational services than other post secondary institutions. These college offerings vary in emphasis from region to region and college to college, but typically include the following:

- Collegiate courses that allow students to transfer to colleges or universities
- Occupational or career programs geared to local employment opportunities.
- Remedial courses that prepare students for college-level work
- A wide variety of cultural, recreational, and professional noncredit offerings. (Griffith & Connor, 1994, p. 19)

From its earliest history, the two-year college has been democratic in intent, adapting to meet diverse populations and social change by providing evolving, often specialized, educational services (Lorenzo, 1994). Today the two-year college's educational services must meet and support a diverse and mobile population caught in the escalating change of an information society. Today's learners face downsizing, "dumbing down" of existing work roles, increased entry-level performance standards, and the need to keep up with and understand technological change—on and off the job. Technical communication students of all ages are coming to traditional and nontraditional two-year classrooms to meet all of these challenges. The two-year college's historic mission—open access, rapid response to social and economic change, and development of strong applied curriculum—makes it potentially well suited to the needs of such students. In this context, the focus on "community" can mean a productive educational collaboration with regional employers to develop innovative curriculum and to incorporate technical change.

TWO-YEAR COLLEGE OFFERINGS

Two-year colleges can provide a number of different kinds of technical communication offerings. The Associate and Certificate are terminal degree credentials, with potential for transfer to four-year programs. However, the two-year college can also provide noncredit technical communication courses that have tremendous potential for partnership with industry.

The Associate Credential

Despite a seeming disciplinary isolation from other program types, the Associate degree curriculum of two-year technical communication programs reflects current developments in both industry and education. Like academic programs in technical communication at other levels, two-year college AA and AAS programs are diverse in their emphases and goals. However, some common elements appear.

In general, associate programs require the hour equivalent of two years of full-time study, including state required general education hours (in mathematics, written and oral communication, and social science) in addition to between 4 and 12 courses in technical communication. Specialized technical communication courses are offered on topics ranging from technical reports to technical editing to document design or on-line documentation. Most programs require or emphasize coursework in oral and visual communication and "share with four-year and graduate programs an interdisciplinary strategy that combines courses in communication; training in a business, technical, or scientific field; and, in some programs, a communication internship in industry" (Storms, 1984, p. 14). Required supporting coursework typically calls for between 12 and 21 semester hours in one or more technical or applied areas, such as CAD/CAM, computer science, engineering, or electronics. Like the curriculum of other undergraduate technical communications programs, that of the two-year college emphasizes problem solving and learning to learn through a study of both liberal arts and technology.

Rock Valley College, for example, offers a technical or business concentration and an internship in addition to specialized technical communication courses (Bloomstrand, 1981, pp. E5–E6). Rock Valley's nationally acclaimed Advanced Technology Center supports a wide range of technical instruction through collaboration with industry. Cincinnati Technical and Community College's Technical Writing and Editing program offers a core of 13 courses emphasizing technical writing and document design—as well as strong computer skills with a variety of hardware and software products. The program requires a co-op or coursework/portfolio equivalent. Austin Community College's Department of Technical Communications offers 8 specialized technical communication courses, including an internship, requires a technical minor and a visual communication component, and encourages active student participation in the local chapter of STC. Located in areas with strong supporting industry, these Associate programs have active advisory committees, and all are housed in colleges with well-established technical/vocational instruction in a wide range of areas.

Evaluating Curricular Success

A review of recent academic and industry discussions of model technical communication curriculum suggests that such associate programs may be moving in the right curricular directions. Zimmerman and Long (1993) define a model four-year curriculum as a combination of communication courses, whether writing, editing, or product-specific, which focus on audience analysis and problem solving (p. 313, p. 315). They also emphasize the importance of study in one or more scientific or technical areas (p. 315). Likewise, Southard & Reeves (1994) outline a model curriculum that combines audience awareness and rhetoric, technical skills, logical and creative thinking, decision making, and a developing professionalism (p. 2). Most agree on the importance of collaborative skills, a commitment to lifelong learning, and an awareness of workplace diversity and change (Hayhoe, Stohrer, Kunz, & Southard, 1994; Keeler, 1990; Southard & Reeves, 1995).

The two-year Associate curricula described in the 1993 (Geonetta, Allen, Curtis, & Staples, in press) survey reflect these long-range educational goals, particularly in their emphasis on experiential learning and on educational collaboration with advisory committees reflecting a range of professional interests and points of view. These programs also tie courses in written, spoken, and visual communication to courses that teach technical skills and knowledge.

Given the limited duration of an Associate degree and the two-year college's mandate to serve the educational needs of regional constituents, two-year college programs may be, as Sullivan (in press) suggests, limited in scope as in length, but, as Pam Ecker, (1995) affirms, nonetheless global in educational mission. Like programs of other lengths, they must seek the right curricular balance to prepare thoughtful, responsible communicators with technical expertise and decision-making ability.

Transfer

While two-year programs attempt to prepare graduating students for entry-level technical communication positions, they must also provide opportunities for transfer because a BA or BS degree is becoming an increasingly important entry-level credential for technical communicators. *Profile 1992* indicates that 56% of STC members surveyed had obtained a Bachelor's degree as the highest level of education, while 30% held Master's degrees (Stolgitis, 1988, p. 4). An Associate degree can be a valuable step toward a professionally important higher credential.

The Two-Year College Certificate

Certificate offerings in two-year colleges reflect the diversity in scope and focus that Sherry Little describes in her essay in this collection. However, in general, two-year college credit certificates require no more than the hour equivalent of one year of full-time study. Because the certificate credential requires no general education courses, it can provide a specialized technical communication emphasis. It is therefore a useful credential for degreed career changers and for those already employed in the profession seeking a new direction inside it. Typical two-year college certificate specializations include electronic or desktop publishing and on-line documentation. Within the credential description, some certificates in technical communication, at Cincinnati and Austin, for example, can be tailored to meet the interests and career needs of individual students.

Lifelong Learning

Outside the college credit classroom, the two-year college—like the public university—can provide other important educational services. About 94%

of public community colleges offer at least one course based on job-related skills to public or private employers (Griffith and Connor, 1994, p. 91). In technical communication, such courses can provide valuable opportunities for academics, for students, and for practicing professionals. Richland College in Dallas, for example, provides a technical communication certificate made up entirely of advanced noncredit courses developed in collaboration with practicing professionals (Hart & Glick-Smith, 1994, p. 404), and Austin Community College has begun a series of similar noncredit offerings taught by area professionals in addition to high level technical communication workshops cosponsored with the local STC chapter.

Such noncredit courses serve a wide range of purposes. They allow technical communicators the opportunity for professional development, bringing business and academia together to redefine the nature of corporate training (Hart & Glick-Smith, 1994, pp. 402–403). Here, specific skills can be taught in the social context of decision making and a common view of service (Meister, 1994, p. 23). An institutional commitment to lifelong learning addresses more than the constant workplace need to learn and apply evolving technology. It also addresses the social purposes that companies, educational institutions, and technology can serve to make coherent meaning in the face of constant change and escalating amounts of information (Tebeaux, 1988, p. 45). To these critical ends, lifelong learning offers practicing professionals the opportunity to teach, and it gives academics the opportunity to experience, first-hand, the culture and processes of different technical communication workplaces. All of the benefits of noncredit collaboration strengthen and enrich a credit curriculum.

TWO-YEAR TECHNICAL COMMUNICATION PROGRAMS: WHERE ARE THEY?

For all their potential, despite some successes, two-year college programs in technical communication are surprisingly unrepresented in program surveys. Sam Geonetta's 1993 survey identified 11 two-year college technical communication programs, a growth in numbers from the 4 listed in 1981 (Pearsall, Sullivan, & McDowell, 1981) and 6 in 1985 (Kelley, Masse, Pearsall, & Sullivan, 1985). This rate of growth is strikingly lower than that of other technical communication program types, which grew from a combined total of 19 in the 1976 program directory to one of 205 in 1993. Clearly, this remarkable programmatic growth parallels the development of technical communication as a profession and as an academic discipline. However, the two-year technical communication programs listed in these surveys may not, in fact, reflect all two-year programmatic activity. Pickett and Angelo (1986) listed 21 programs offering a total 15 Associate degrees and 10 certificates (p. 129). Of these 21, 13 programs were still listed in their 1994–1995 institutional catalogs. Of the 13, only 6 are listed in the 1993 directory.

Where are they? Some simply disappear. As Dale Sullivan (in press) points out, two-year college technical communication programs can certainly develop high-level curriculum that responds to technical change and that meets local needs. However, because the existence of these programs depends on state regulation and local industry, they survive only as area need, in-house funding, and state education boards allow. Two-year programs must therefore adapt rapidly to current trends and schedule to suit student needs. They must somehow document nontraditional student success by traditional means to satisfy state requirements. Most significant, in hard times they must compete internally for resources against other, more established departments in more traditional disciplines—or vanish.

Two-year college technical communication faculty likewise have a low profile in academic organizations. Because two-year colleges typically require a heavy teaching load and reward service and teaching excellence rather than research and publication (Vaughan, 1994, pp. 217–218), two-year college instructors tend to be consumers, not producers, of research. And because academic organizations often recognize excellence in scholarship rather than leadership in teaching or administration, active two-year college representatives in such groups as ATTW and CPTSC are few. Two-year college technical communication programs can develop, grow, and live or die outside the knowledge, influence, and community of national organizations for technical communication programs and faculty. This invisibility may further explain the absence of two-year programs from surveys of programs.

Lack of membership in a wider disciplinary community also means lack of disciplinary identity, which McGrath and Spear (1991) consider a grave risk for the status and professionalism of two-year faculty. A nontraditional, emerging discipline, technical communication embraces so many seeming paradoxes—workplace with academy, technologies with humanities, sciences with arts, basic research with practical application—that it is hard to locate in any one academic department. Disciplinary identity, like departmental location, becomes key in each two-year program's struggle for resources, promotion, and even control over its own curriculum.

MEASURING SUCCESS: STUDENT POPULATIONS

Like the multidisciplinarity of technical communication, the two-year college's access and range of educational options pose another critical problem of self-definition for its academic programs. Measuring student success is a difficult task.

America's nearly 1,000 two-year colleges serve a diverse population of some 10 million students, 6 million in college credit courses (Griffith & Connor, 1994, p. 3). However, the nontraditional ages and diverse goals of students make their success hard to identify. If success is measured by the standards applied to four-year colleges—by tallying graduates, transfers, or rates of completion within a limited number of years—two-year colleges fail because students often reflect no predictable pattern of attendance or completion and are therefore difficult to track (Griffith & Connor, 1994, p. 129). Although some 93% of surveyed two-year colleges offered at least one technical communication course as of 1986 (Pickett & Angelo, 1986, p. 127), and two-year technical communication programs have been in existence since the early 1980s, there is little national evidence of completion or success—the kind of validation required for funding and programmatic expansion.

Likewise, surveys of educational achievement of practicing professionals reflect little or no contribution from two-year colleges. STC's *Profile 1988* shows that 6% of those surveyed listed "some college" and 5% a "two-year college or technical school" as highest level of education (Stolgitis, 1992, p. 4) However, *Profile 1992* provides no indicator of educational level between a high school diploma and a bachelor's degree (Stolgitis, 1992, p. 4). The two-year transfer function for traditional university liberal arts courses is declining, while the transfer rate from two-year career programs (such as technical communication) is increasing (McGrath & Spear, 1991, pp. 38–39). This trend is likewise not reflected in available technical communication surveys—academic or professional.

How to record successful participation in two-year college programs if participation leads—after only a course or two—to transfer or to fulfilling other, more limited, educational goals? Do these goals serve the learner, the community, or the regional profession itself? This problem of documenting the nature and success of educational contribution presents real difficulty for two-year programs attempting to justify funds, equipment, or state accreditation. As Eaton (1994) points out,

> [w]ith more and more of these [part-time and non-degree] students in higher education, a collegiate community college offering quality college-level studies that are structured to meet nontraditional needs can provide valuable leadership for the country. Models showing an effective marriage between collegiate programs and the needs of ... nontraditional students are badly needed—and the community college is the richest site for their development (p. 123).

No such model currently exists. If two-year college technical communication programs are to document and define their contribution to education, they urgently need one.

ACADEMIC COLLABORATION: COMMON GOALS

Two-year college technical communication programs share important goals with programs at other levels, most notably, supporting student success, adding to the body of technical communication knowledge and theory, and redefining the relationship between workplace and academy.

Transfer and Articulation

With the estimated 1995 costs of four years of college ranging from $39,324 for a public institution and $86,513 for a private one (Cash, 1991, p. 26), the two-year college is increasingly meeting a practical need, as students consider less expensive ways to earn transfer credits or to alternate study with work before attending college full time. Because we can assume that a lower division service course in technical writing will be a popular transfer offering, better coordination between two-year and four-year institutions will support strong transfer curriculum, even for those two-year colleges that offer courses but not programs in technical communication.

Better coordination between academic programs can also make articulation an easier alternative for students who need a more affordable means to pursue the BA or BS which most entry-level positions in technical communication require. Without membership in a national disciplinary community or an administrative network of programs, two-year colleges will find it difficult to establish the kinds of transfer and articulation agreements that can serve the long-term educational needs of their technical communication students.

Research Partnerships

Better collaboration between academic programs at every level also provides possibilities for research partnerships. Two-year colleges are well adapted to the "scholarship of *application*," which asks,

> "How can knowledge be responsibly applied to consequential problems?" "How can it be helpful to individuals as well as institutions?" And further, "Can social problems themselves define an agenda for scholarly investigation?" (Boyer, 1990, p. 21)

Such questions address the issues that underlie the balance of curriculum that educates—rather than trains—the future responsible technical communicator. These questions are also at the heart of technical communication research in such areas as collaboration, gender, and the rhetoric of technology.

Two-year colleges are ideally suited to the "scholarship of teaching," the study of "transforming and extending knowledge" (Boyer, 1990, p. 24) as integral to the work of the technical communicator as to the effective faculty member. Barchilon and Kelly (1995) describe such a study conducted in a collaboration between Arizona State University and South Mountain Community College. This NSF-funded project developed and piloted a flexible technical communication education model to prepare students for a changing workplace. The model focused on curriculum to foster excellence, flexibility, teamwork, multidisciplinarity, research skills, lifelong learning, conceptual ability, and appreciation for diversity. This study—and others like it—has wide implications for academia and workplace cooperation as well as research partnerships for two-year and university collaborators. Federal, state, and industry funding initiatives to support career education are receptive to such research projects and partnerships.

The inclusive scope and methodologies of technical communication research can surely find places for the contribution of two-year college scholarship and partnerships for two-year college scholars. Such partnerships can make an active contribution to technical communication research and can also help to establish two-year college technical communication faculty and programs in a disciplinary community.

CONCLUSION

The person who sets out to establish a two-year college technical communication program confronts special challenges. As Dale Sullivan (in press) points out, successful two-year college programs must be located in areas with strong supporting industry. Local employment surveys and interest from representatives of industry document the regional constituency that a two-year program is funded to support. However, this kind of community outreach is only the beginning. The successful two-year college program must rely on outreach of all kinds to develop, revise, and validate curriculum, to place students, to recruit faculty, to develop new kinds of instruction and instructional resources, and to locate partners in faculty development and research. Without such linkages, a two-year college technical communication program risks isolation, insularity, and failure.

Establishing constructive workplace partnerships is a critical and continuing process that needs to begin with a program's early planning stages (Bosley, 1995, pp. 614–615). Advisory committees can take an active interest in a program from its beginnings, providing time, resources, and innovative curricular suggestions. However, committee members must reflect a wide range of interests and points of view, recognizing that a technical communication curriculum must be dynamic, larger than the needs of any one company or technology, supporting students as decision makers in their careers, their professional roles, and their personal lives.

Colleges and member companies must also value the functions of advisory committees as a primary linkage between academia and industry. Such committees can create an open forum that can blur organizational boundaries—values, structure, and immediate interests—between member companies and between companies and college to define a new role for technical communication education (Bosley, 1995, pp. 611–613).

Links with local professional organizations are also valuable. These can provide essential opportunities for student networking and leadership, for staff development, and for recruiting enthusiastic adjunct faculty with specialized skills and knowledge. Such linkages can also provide opportunities for a wide range of other educational partnerships.

The two-year college technical communication program must also reach out inside the college itself. Other academic departments offer multidisciplinary partnerships and collegial recognition and support. However, advisors, administrators, librarians, noncredit staff, and admissions and placement officers all need to learn about the program's nontraditional goals and curriculum. Only by understanding technical communication as a discipline and as a profession can they support faculty and students. In some two-year institutions, these areas may work independently from one another. In too many, technical communication will be a new and unexpected discipline, one that must be actively and regularly promoted in-house.

However, the most valuable kind of outreach for the two-year program is also the most rewarding: establishing linkages with other academic programs at every level. Colleagues from other technical communication departments provide a network of support and antecedents, a source of curricular models and administrative possibilities richer for the diversity of program types and emphases. At conventions and through professional organizations, two-year technical communication programs have much to gain and much to offer.

The technical communication program located in a two-year college has an institutional commitment to serve diverse constituencies of learners and to evolve responsibly to meet social change. This mission makes it future-oriented and democratic, well suited to the kinds of productive workplace partnerships and curricular evolution that technical communication encourages. In addition, the two-year college program can provide a wide range of instruction for nontraditional learners—entering the profession and already working inside it. Only by maintaining strong and positive linkages in the community and region, inside the college, and especially with other technical communication programs, can the two-year college program realize its potential for quality education and for democratic access in an emerging academic discipline.

REFERENCES

Barchilon, M.G. & Kelly, D.G. (1995). A flexible technical communication model for the year 2000. *Technical Communication, 42* (4), 611–619.

Bloomstrand, D. (1981). Community college programs: Preparing the entry-level technical writer. *Proceedings, 8th International Technical Communication Conference* (pp. E6–E7). Washington, DC: Society for Technical Communication.

Boggs, G.R. & Cater, J.L. (1994). The historical development of academic programs in community colleges. In G.A. Baker (Ed.), *A handbook on the community college in America* (pp. 218–226). Westport, CT: Greenwood Press.

Bosley, D. (1995). Collaborative partnerships: Academia and industry working together. *Technical Communication, 42* (4), 611–619.

Boyer, E.L. (1990). *Scholarship reconsidered: Priorities of the professoriate.* Princeton, PA: Carnegie Foundation.

Cash, J.G. (1991). *College funding made easy.* White Hall, VA: Betterway.

Connors, R.J. (1982). The rise of technical writing instruction in America. *Journal of Technical Writing and Communication, 12* (4), 329–352.

Eaton, J.S. (1994). *Strengthening collegiate education in community colleges.* San Francisco, CA: Jossey-Bass.

Ecker, P. (1995). E-mail correspondence.

Geonetta, S.C., Allen, J., Curtis, D. & Staples, K. (in press). *Academic programs in technical communication.* (4th Ed.). Washington, DC: Society for Technical Communication.

Griffith, M. & Connor, A. (1994). *Democracy's open door: the community college in America's future.* Portsmouth, NH: Boynton/Cook.

Hammer, M. & Champy, J. (1993). *Reengineering the corporation: A manifesto for business revolution.* New York: Harper.

Hart, H. & Glick-Smith, J. (1994). Training in technical communication: Ideas for a partnership between the academy and the workplace. *Technical Communication, 41* (3), 399–415.

Hayhoe, G., Stohrer, F., Kunz, L. & Southard, S. (1994). The evolution of academic programs in technical communication. *Technical Communication, 41* (1), 14–19.

Keeler, H. (1990). Portrait of a technical communicator: A bibliographic review of current research. *Technical Communication, 37* (1), 41–50.

Kelley, P.M., Masse, R.E., Pearsall, T.E. & Sullivan, F.J. (1985). *Academic programs in technical communication.* (3rd Ed.). Washington, DC: Society for Technical Communication.

Lorenzo, A.L. (1994). The mission and functions of the community college: An overview. In G.A. Baker (Ed.), *A handbook on the community college in America* (pp. 111–122). Westport, CT: Greenwood Press.

McGrath, D. & Spear, M.B. (1991). *The academic crisis of the community college.* Albany, NY: SUNY.

Meister, J.C. (1994). *Corporate quality universities: Lessons in building a world-class work force.* New York: Irwin.

Pearsall, T.E., Sullivan, F.J. & McDowell, E.E. (1981). *Academic programs in technical communication.* (2nd Ed.). Washington, DC: Society for Technical Communication.

Pickett, N.A. & Angelo, F. (1986). Technical communication in the two-year college: A survey. *Teaching English in the Two-Year College, 13* (2), 126–134.

Southard, S. & Reeves, R. (1994). Educating future technical communicators. *The E&R Link, 3* (1), 2–3.

Southard, S. & Reeves, R. (1995). Education in action: Time to find the solutions. *The E&R Link, 3* (2), 6–7, 9.

Stolgitis, W.C. (1988). *Profile 88.* STC Special Report. Washington, DC: Society for Technical Communication.

Stolgitis, W.C. (1992). *Profile 92.* STC Special Report. Arlington, VA: Society for Technical Communication.

Storms, C. G. (1984). Programs in technical communication. *Technical Communication, 31* (4), 13–20.

Sullivan, D. (in press). Technical communication in a two-year college environment. *Programs that work.* Arlington, VA: Society for Technical Communication.

Tebeaux, E. (1988). Teaching professional communication in the information age: Problems in sustaining relevance. *Journal of Business and Technical Communication, 2* (2), 44–58.

Vaughan, G.B. (1994). Scholarship and teaching: Crafting the art. In M. Reynolds (Ed.), *Two-year college English: Essays for a new century* (pp. 212–221). Urbana, IL: NCTE.

Zimmerman, D. & Long, M. (1993). Exploring the technical communicator's roles: Implications for program design. *Technical Communication Quarterly, 2* (3), 301–317.

19

DESIGNING CERTIFICATE PROGRAMS IN TECHNICAL COMMUNICATION

Sherry Burgus Little

San Diego State University

INTRODUCTION

Two words characterize the development of certificate programs in technical communication in the United States: growth and diversity. The four editions of *Academic Programs in Technical Communication* have chronicled the dramatic growth of technical communication programs in the last 20 years. The first edition, published in 1976, reported 19 institutions with programs; the second, published in 1981, reported 28 institutions (Pearsall, Sullivan, & McDowell, 1981); the third, published in 1985, reported 56 institutions (Kelley, Masse, & Sullivan, 1985); and the fourth, to be published soon by the Society for Technical Communication reporting figures gathered during 1993, lists 101 institutions with a total of 205 programs in technical communication (Geonetta et al., in press). The number of programs almost tripled between 1976 and 1985; the number of programs between 1981 and 1985 almost doubled (Kelley, Masse, & Sullivan, 1986). Between 1985 and 1993, the number of programs has more than doubled once again. In this same period, the number of certificate programs reported has more than doubled as well, growing from 16 programs in 1985 to 37 programs in 1993.

Such growth reflects the demand by industry and business for people skilled in writing technical and scientific documents. More importantly, however, such growth reflects the recent theorizing about the place of writing in the university. As I have argued elsewhere (Little, 1994), questions about the history and structure of writing programs (Little, 1993a; Russell, 1991, pp. 3–34) are reconceptualizing the traditional associations of writing programs with English departments, as evidenced by the recent increase in the number of separate writing programs, for example, at Colgate University (Howard, 1993; Jamieson & Howard, 1993), San Diego State University (Little, 1991, 1993a; Rose, 1993), the University of Arkansas at Little Rock, and the University of Texas at Austin. Separate departments of technical communication exist as well at the University of Washington, Metropolitan College (Denver), and Clarkson College (Potsdam, NY).

The emphasis on writing across the disciplines in recent years focuses the attention of writing program scholars and teachers on discourses from many disciplines rather than privileging one text (such as the literary) over another (such as the scientific), resulting in the questioning of the shape and content of writing classes at all levels. The study of technical communication has emerged as a specialized discipline within this expanded view of rhetoric and writing studies, influencing theoretical conceptions of the relationship between academic and nonacademic writing. Under its large and hard-to-define umbrella, technical communication includes a broad range of writing. Many have tried to develop a workable definition that encompasses all its aspects.[1] It is this almost indefinable quality of technical communication that further complicates designing technical communication programs, encouraging the diversity that all programs, but especially certificate ones, exhibit.

---

[1] For a discussion of the different attempts to define or not define technical communication, see my "The Generation of Scientific and Technical Literature," in Southard's *History/Rhetoric of Scientific and Technical Communication*, forthcoming from Association of Teachers of Technical Writing.

RATIONALE FOR DESIGNING CERTIFICATE PROGRAMS IN TECHNICAL COMMUNICATION

The growth of all programs in technical communication is paralleled by the growth of certificate programs, and one might ask why such programs are developed, why a certificate program as opposed to other types of programs. Designing a certificate program in the academic setting has many advantages over designing other types of programs. The most obvious is that such programs are easy to implement. In most institutions, proposing a degree involves a staggering amount of paperwork and numerous procedures. A chain of approvals needs to be won from committees and administrators at all levels and frequently beyond the local institution itself to centralized administrations, boards of trustees, state-level educational approving agencies, and even state legislators. Such approval processes are time-consuming, sometimes taking years before a degree comes into existence. Conversely, a certificate program can be put into place quickly. Although it too must go through a careful approval process, this process rarely extends beyond the local institutional level.

Technical communication, as an interdisciplinary field, relies on knowledge already addressed by courses in a number of fields. Certificate programs can use many courses that already exist as part of other programs. Hard economic times constrain designing a new program that demands adding new courses. Because existing courses can provide much of the technical information that technical communicators need, such as in computer technology, graphics, science, engineering, and business, certificate programs can be developed needing few new courses, an advantage that allows them to be placed in operation with greater speed than other programs.

Many institutions already offer courses in technical writing, frequently to satisfy writing competency requirements. Sometimes these already existing technical writing classes can become the core of a certificate program, allowing a coherent program to be developed without needing many new resources such as faculty, staff, or equipment, a distinct advantage during times of budget crisis and resulting constraints on program development.

Because certificate programs entail fewer hours to complete, students can earn certificates quickly, an advantage that appeals especially to the returning student who may already have a degree and wishes to move quickly into another career field. Certificate programs, because of their structure and design, can also be more flexible to local needs. They can be modified easily and quickly, adapting to changing demands, because they are generally monitored and scrutinized less closely than other kinds of programs. Because of their flexibility—their content is rarely mandated by degree requirements or educational legislation—they can be individualized for students, adapting to diverse backgrounds and goals. Because technical communication is a dynamic field, with expanding roles and responsibilities for technical communicators that can change drastically and as quickly as the accompanying technology with which technical communicators work, the flexibility of certificate programs to modification duplicates the changing dynamics of the profession itself.

Some of these advantages, of course, can be sources for concern. The certificate's flexibility and lesser degree of monitoring and scrutiny could result in questions about its quality. Without the application of standards, either legislated or mandated by educational codes as they are for degrees, certificates may not gain much acceptance as credentials for hiring or promotion, especially beyond the regional area the institution serves. Additionally, this lack of standardization results in great diversity among programs. A study of descriptions of certificate programs in the draft copy of the forthcoming edition of the *Academic Programs in Technical Communication* shows this diversity in the design of certificate programs, although such diversity is true of other kinds of programs as well. Donald Cunningham remarked in 1985 that he was not sure that such "variety of programs is a good thing or not," although he did suggest a number of reasons for the "array of curricula" academic institutions have developed. A closer look at the descriptions of certificate programs can detail the diversity in their structure, design, and purpose.

Diversity in Technical Communication Certificate Programs

Studying the design and purpose of certificate programs in technical communication reveals a wide range of choices. Some programs serve those who wish to acquire entry-level knowledge, while others serve professional technical communicators who wish to upgrade their knowledge of the field. Some are designed for experts in the technical communication field, while others are designed for working professionals in technical and scientific fields who do writing as part of their job, but are not thought of as professional technical communicators.

Some of the programs are offered at the graduate level, and some are at the undergraduate level. Some of the certificate programs span both levels, with graduate and undergraduate students enrolling in the same courses to complete the certificate, the students receiving either undergraduate or graduate credit depending on their status. In some programs, the courses students take are the same as those taken by students who are enrolled in a degree program, either at the associate's, bachelor's, or master's levels.

The level of preparation for students in certificate programs consequently varies widely and reflects the design and purpose of the different programs. Some certificate programs require work experience and competencies in fields of graphics and computers. Others require knowledge in a technical field, or in marketing, management, advertising, human behavior, or interpersonal communication, while others merely encourage it.

Reviewing the number of units required to complete the certificate reveals tremendous differences. Some programs are extremely thorough, requiring as many units as an undergraduate major, while others require as few as three or four courses. Certificates listed in the draft copy for the forthcoming *Academic Programs in Technical Communication* require as few as 9 units up to as many as 40. Several institutions offer more than one kind of certificate, with requirements varying according to the type of certificate and the level of students. Generally, a little over 50% (18) of the 37 institutions offering certificates require between 15 to 20 units of credit, with the largest number (a total of 7) requiring 15 units of credit to complete the certificate.

Studying the descriptions of the courses required for the certificate as detailed in the data gathered in 1993 for the fourth edition of the *Academic Programs in Technical Communication* shows the expected diversity in course requirements that the variety in the design and purpose of certificate programs portends. In an early study of all types of technical communication programs, C. Gilbert Storms (1984) identified three components shared by most programs: courses in technical or professional writing, courses in technical areas, and experiential activities such as internships. This commonality is not present in the certificate programs described in the *Academic Programs in Technical Communication* information.

Professional writing courses were required by almost all of those institutions (32 of the 37) reporting certificate programs.[2] Other required courses illustrate a wide diversity. Courses in composition, speech, linguistics, grammar, psychology, science, computers, business ethics, and cognitive science were some of those listed as requirements by a few institutions. A slightly larger number of institutions required courses in applied art (such as graphics), word processing, and desktop publishing. About 25% reported a large group of electives from which students can choose, representing such areas as computers, art, management, creative writing, business skills, human behavior, interpersonal communication, intercultural communication, or organizational communication.

Next to requirements in professional writing, the widest agreement occurred in Storm's (1984) third component, experiential activities, with

---

2. Figures provided here are necessarily incomplete. Some institutions listed in the *Academic Programs in Technical Communication* did not provide descriptions of their program requirements. One reported that the program was individualized according to the needs of the students, and several reported that the courses were the same as those required for the Associate's, Bachelor's, or Master's degree.

approximately 32% of the programs requiring internships. In another study of internships, a survey of all technical communication programs revealed that 75% offered internships, with 44% requiring them (Little, 1993b). Fewer certificate programs require this important component of technical communication programs than do other kinds of programs. The internship can be a critical link in designing successful technical communication programs at any level (Little, 1994) and can help resolve a central issue vital to a debate not only in designing technical communication programs at any level or in the more general field of rhetoric and writing studies, but also to "a larger debate in American higher education" (Miller, 1989, p. 18). This debate, of course, is on the issue of *training* opposed to *education*, or, in other words, the conflict between theory and practice, a conflict familiar to most designers of writing programs in general and critical to designers of technical communication programs in particular. This issue is especially critical to the developers of certificate programs because of the certificate's closer association with the "vocationalism" decried by most opponents to the practical in higher education.

THE ISSUE OF THE THEORETICAL AND THE PRACTICAL IN DESIGNING TECHNICAL COMMUNICATION CERTIFICATE PROGRAMS

Designing certificate programs in technical communication crystallizes the debate about keeping a balance between theory and practice. The growing popularity of these programs challenges designers to translate the abstract ideas of the university into the concrete realities of the workplace to ensure the program's relevance. After all, one of the marks of a program's success is that its students get and keep jobs. However, there is as much danger in privileging knowledge without its connection to workplace reality as there is in preparing technical communicators for today's jobs while ignoring the needs of the future. Students in all technical communication programs need opportunities to master theoretical principles as well as current skills and techniques. A healthy balance must exist between the theoretical and the practical when designing certificate programs in technical communication and when assessing the needs of the industrial and business community and the academic community.

Industrial and Business Community Needs

Designers of certificate programs in technical communication must know the needs of the industrial and business community that will be hiring the students who complete the certificate. The success of a program relies heavily on the links that designers of such programs can develop with industry and businesses outside the academic environment. One method of forming such links is through the use of advisory committees or corporate advisory boards, a group formed of representatives from industry and business. Although little has been written about advisory committees, some information about establishing them and maintaining them exists (Bosley, 1991; Brockmann, 1982; Deming, 1991; Little, 1985), and there is no denying that such a committee can give strong support in designing programs and help in establishing internships and providing employment opportunities for students.

Another method of creating a tie is through needs assessment studies. Studies of practitioners (Little & McLaren, 1987; Green & Nolan, 1984; Buchholz, 1989) can supplement advice from advisory committees and provide important information about what industry and businesses need. However, programs should not become training grounds for today's jobs. In this dynamic and changing profession, technical communicators of the future will need more than the skills and techniques used by technical communicators in their current jobs. Both Miller (1989) and Anderson (1984) address the careful use that must be made of information about the practical, as do other scholars in technical communication studies such as Dobrin (1983, 1985).

Academic Community Needs

When designing certificate programs, developers must, of course, justify the use of university and departmental resources for such programs. I have already discussed the advantages certificate programs have in being able to use existing courses. Rather than having to develop and budget what may be a prohibitive number of new resources such as new courses that must be staffed, certificate program developers need to create cooperation among the departments offering the existing courses that can be used in the program. The close ties that must be developed with the industrial and business community are equally important to develop within the academic community as well. Critical to creating this cooperation is identifying the needs within the academic community that will be supplying the clientele for the program. Programs might be thought of as an attractive alternative career for English majors or as a way for creative writers to support their habit. As valid as these justifications may be, technical communication programs appeal to people in many fields. For example, at San Diego State University people enrolled in the certificate program come from many different fields such as engineering, religious studies, classics, nursing, and geology, as well as English.

The faculty needed to give a program continuity and permanence depends greatly on the program itself. If existing courses become part of the program, very few new faculty need be added; most of these would be specialists in the teaching of technical communication. Some certificate programs, such as the one offered at UCLA, are taught by local practitioners with experience in teaching as well as writing. Two important prerequisites exist for successful programs: some permanent faculty committed to the program need to be assigned, and faculty who teach in the program should have experience as both practitioners and academics.

The importance of these prerequisites is central to the debate about the place of technology in a college liberal arts curriculum. Despite the existence of a few programs outside departments of English, most programs are housed in English departments. A study by William Rivers in 1985 and the study of the *Academic Programs in Technical Communication* corroborate this fact. In many ways, this site is an uneasy home for technical communication, and any developer of a technical communication program, especially of certificate programs, needs to remain critically aware that if the program is perceived as one primarily concerned with training students to get jobs, the program may find widespread resistance and hostility. Faculty developing technical communication certificate programs walk a tightrope, balancing the opposing forces that such programs represent: the place of practice in relationship to theory.

Linking the Theoretical and the Practical

Identifying and taking advantage of existing resources helps developers keep a healthy balance when designing and directing successful certificate programs. All successful curriculum planning must link short-term goals with long-term planning for the future, and experienced program administrators know this as a continuing concern of healthy technical communication certificate programs.

Many professional organizations create forums for ongoing discussions at issue in designing and maintaining successful certificate programs. The Council for Programs in Technical and Scientific Communication (CPTSC) publishes proceedings from its annual meetings at which such issues are debated. CPTSC is also developing a self-study program, modeled after the self-study of the Council of Writing Program Administration, that will prove a valuable aid in the continual development and assessment technical communication programs demand. The Association of Teachers of Writing (ATTW) not only publishes the *Technical Communication Quarterly*, formerly *The Technical Writing Teacher*, but also publishes anthology series as well as reflective books such as this one. These resources chronicle the conversation fostered by the issues of curriculum development and assessment, and many other topics as well. Attending ATTW's annual meetings at the Conference on College Composition and Communication is a necessary scholarly activity that faculty in technical communication enjoy, creating essential ties and links among teachers and directors of technical communication programs. However, both ATTW and CPTSC, despite welcoming corporate memberships and participation of practitioners in their activities, represent mostly the academic side of the conversation.

The Society for Technical Communication (STC), the world's largest professional organization dedicated to the advancement of the theory and practice of technical communication, attempts to create a forum for both practitioners and academics in the field of technical communication. The proceedings from its annual conferences and its quarterly publication *Technical Communication* reflect the sometimes adversarial relationship between practitioner and academic in the conversation about the education of the technical communicator.

Additional resources, such as the *IEEE Transactions on Professional Communication*, the *Journal of Business and Technical Communication* (Sage Publications), and the *Journal of Technical Writing and Communication* (Baywood Publishing Company), provide opportunities to contribute and listen to the ongoing conversation. Yet, despite much good faith effort, the field of technical communication lacks a solid bridge in its professional forums between the theoretical and practical. In some of the conversation, in fact, downright hostility exists between those who are characterized as fuzzy-headed academics and those who really know. Such a break in conversation is illustrated by Kathy Sayers' (1994) report on designing a certificate program in the Winter 1994 newsletter of the Professional Interest Committee (PIC) on Education and Research, a group within the organizational structure of STC. The report claims that no needs assessments exist to guide developers of programs and then describes the use of the DACUM method in their own survey, ironically the same method described by Green and Nolan (1984) in their article published by STC's own journal, *Technical Communication.* Evidence that such bridges must and can be built exists from both practitioners and academics, as illustrated by Carol Barnum's (1983) report on faculty internships, Scott Sanders' (1983) study of technical writing in academe and industry, and the dedicated commitment of practitioners serving on advisory committees or corporate advisory boards (Bosley, 1991; Deming, 1991; Little, 1985).

In the words of Katherine Staples (1994), "The certificate program reflects the center of this debate and is precisely the point at which industry and academic goals and interests have the opportunity to meet and make high level alliances." Certainly, active professional participation is crucial to those identified with the discipline of technical communication, and the growth of these professional organizations and resources reflect the growth of the profession and its educational programs.

Linking the theoretical and the practical is an issue familiar not only to curriculum planning in general, but also to anyone associated with the conflicts facing composition studies itself, a conflict in the words of John Schilb (1991), "between its populism and its service ethos" (p. 96). This "is-ought" controversy (Johnson, 1991) has been addressed by a number of scholars in technical communication. Carolyn Miller suggests ways to reconcile these "related oppositions" (1989, p. 21) in teaching the "rhetoric of 'the world of work'" (p. 24) and in identifying the humanistic concerns of technical writing.

Experiential learning theorists, like David Kolb (1984), advance a partial solution when they report the growing acceptance of "the critical linkages that can be developed between the classroom and the 'real world'" (p. 4) where the workplace can be used to stress "the role of formal education in lifelong learning and the development of individuals to their full potential as citizens, family members, and human beings" (p. 4). Experiential learning theory sees education as a lifelong experience, not one that occurs only in the classroom, and it gives experience a central role as a way of knowing. One application of experiential learning theory is the internship, a learning strategy providing a bridge that can link the theoretical to the practical by combining experience, perception, cognition, and behavior. Kolb writes that this relationship of learning and knowing creates a "dialectic conflict in the Hegelian sense that although the results of either process cannot be entirely explained in terms of the other, these opposite processes merge toward a higher truth that encompasses and transcends them" (p. 107).[3]

Despite the strong identification of certificate programs with a degree of "vocationalism"—students of successful programs do get jobs—designers of such programs see the need for ensuring that these programs are part of a coherent writing program. As students perform the important role of making technology available to the user, their introduction and education into this world of communication questions critically such issues as ethics, the history of science and technology, and the implications of information as a product rather than a means—all humanistic concerns. As technical communication continues its growth and no doubt its diversity in an increasingly complex world, meeting the challenge of keeping a balance between its theory and its practice in designing and directing all technical communication programs will remain a central concern and a subject of continuing debate. Because of the certificate program's associa-

---

3. For more detail on the application of experiential learning theory as a means of bridging the gap between theory and practice in technical communication programs, see my "The Technical Communication Internship" (Little, 1993).

tion with the concept of "vocationalism," its design and development crystallizes the issues in this debate.

REFERENCES

Anderson, P.V. (1988). What technical and scientific communicators do: A comprehensive model for developing academic programs. *IEEE Transactions on Professional Communication PC-27.3*: 161–167.

Barnum, C.M. (1983). English professors as technical writers: Experience is the best teacher. *ADE Bulletin, 76*, 175–179.

Bosley, D.S. (1991). Articulating goals for a university/corporate advisory board. In *Proceedings*. 18th Annual Conference of the Council for Programs in Technical and Scientific Communication (pp. 56–65). Cincinnati, OH: CPTSC, 1991.

Brockmann, R.J. (1982). Advisory boards in technical communications programs and classes. *Technical Writing Teacher, 9*, 137–146.

Buchholz, W.J. (1989). The Boston study: Analysis of a major metropolitan business- and technical-communication market. *Journal of Business and Technical Communication, 3* (1), 5–35.

Cunningham, D. (1985). The education of technical communicators. [Keynote address]. 3rd Annual Education Workshop of the Kachina Chapter of the Society for Technical Communication. Socorro, NM.

Deming, L. (1991). New Mexico Tech's technical communication program: Introducing a corporate board. *Proceedings*. 18th Annual Meeting of the Council for Programs in Technical and Scientific Communication (pp. 55–58). Cincinnati, OH: CPTSC.

Dobrin, D. (1983). What's technical about technical writing? In P.V. Anderson, R. J. Brockmann & C.R. Miller (Eds.), *New essays in technical and scientific communication: Research, theory, and practice* (pp. 227–250). Farmingdale, NY: Baywood.

Dobrin, D. (1985). What's the purpose of teaching technical communication? *Technical Writing Teacher, 12* (2), 145–160.

Geonetta, S.C., Allen, J., Curtis, D. & Staples, K. (in press). *Academic programs in technical communication.* (4th Ed.) Washington, DC: Society for Technical Communication.

Green, M.M. & Nolan, T.D. (1984). A systematic analysis of the technical communicator's job: A guide for educators. *Technical Communication, 31* (4), 9–12.

Howard, R.M. (1993). Power revisited: Or, how we became a department. *WPA: Writing Program Administration, 16* (3), 37–49.

Jamieson, S. & Howard, R.M. (1993). From feminized to feminist: The maturation of a writing department. Conference on College Composition and Communication, San Diego, CA.

Johnson, B. (1991). The "is/ought" tension in technical and scientific communication program development. *Proceedings.* 18th Annual Conference of the Council for Programs in Technical and Scientific Communication (pp. 51–54). Cincinnati, OH: CPTSC.

Kelley, P.M., Masse, R.E., Pearsall, T.E. & Sullivan, F.J. (1985). *Academic programs in technical communication.* (3rd Ed.). Washington, DC: Society for Technical Communication.

Kelley, P.M., Masse, R.E. & Sullivan, F.J. (1986). Academic programs in technical communication: Status and trends. *Proceedings.* 33rd International Technical Communication Conference. Washington, DC: Society for Technical Communication.

Kolb, D.A. (1984). *Experiential learning: Experience as the source of learning and development.* Englewood Cliffs, NJ: Prentice-Hall.

Little, S.B. (1985). Industry and education working together: The use of advisory committees. *Proceedings.* 12th Annual Meeting of the Council for Programs in Technical and Scientific Communication. Oxford, OH: CPTSC, 1985.

Little, S.B. (1991). A home of their own: Writing programs as separate entities. Council of Writing Program Administration. Saratoga Springs, NY.

Little, S.B. (1993a). Separate writing departments: An historical overview. Conference on College Composition and Communication. San Diego, CA.

Little, S.B. (1993b). The technical communication internship: An application of experiential learning theory. *Journal of Business and Technical Communication,* 7 (4), 423–451.

Little, S.B. (1994). Developing a technical communication program: The role of the WPA. *WPA: Writing Program Administration, 17* (3), 21–33.

Little, S.B. & McLaren, M. (1987). Profile of technical writers in San Diego County: Results of a pilot study. *Journal of Technical Writing and Communication, 1* (1), 9–23.

Miller, C.R. (1979). A humanistic rationale for technical writing. *College English, 40,* 610–617.

Miller, C.R. (1989). What's practical about technical writing? In B.E. Fearing & W. K. Sparrow (Eds.), *Technical writing, theory and practice* (p. 14–24). New York: MLA.

Pearsall, T.E., Sullivan, F.J. & McDowell, E.E. (1981). *Academic programs in technical communication.* (2nd Ed.). Washington, DC: Society for Technical Communication.

Rose, S.K. (1993). Metaphors for composing a department of writing. Conference on College Composition and Communication. San Diego, CA.

Rivers, W.E. (1985). The current status of business and technical writing courses in English departments. *ADE Bulletin, 82,* 50–54.

Russell, D.K. (1991). *Writing in the academic disciplines, 1870–1990: A curricular history.* Carbondale, IL: Southern Illinois University Press.

Sanders, S.P. (1983). *Technical writing in academe and in industry: A study undertaken preliminary to the proposal of a bachelor of science degree program in technical communications to be offered by the Humanities Department.* New Mexico Institute of Mining and Technology. ERIC: ED 227 499 RIE.

Sayers, K. (1994). Developing a certificate program in technical communication. *E&R PIC Link, 3* (1), 4–5, 6.

Schilb, J. (1991). The conflict between "theory" and "practice." *Rhetoric Review, 10* (1), 91–97.

Staples, K. (1994, August 7). Personal correspondence.

Storms, C.G. (1984). Programs in technical communication. *Technical Communication, 31* (4), 13–20.

20

THE TECHNICAL COMMUNICATION SERVICE COURSE SERVES

Nell Ann Pickett

Hinds Community College

INTRODUCTION

Service courses in technical communication are designed for students majoring in technical, technological, and professional areas. These courses are designed to develop students' writing, speaking, and graphic skills related to their majors. Most postsecondary institutions across the nation offer one or more service courses in technical communication, enrolling hundreds of thousands of students each year.

Service courses in technical communication must be distinguished from technical communication *programs*. The objective of such programs is to prepare a person to become a professional technical communicator or technical editor. As of 1994, there are 205 formal programs of study in two-year colleges, four-year colleges, and universities across the country offering degrees or certificates or both in technical communication (Geonetta,

Allen, Curtis, & Staples, 1995, p. vi). Technical communication programs range in scope from certificate programs (participants often returning to college to retool for a career change or career advancement) to undergraduate programs with associate and bachelor's degrees to graduate programs offering master's degrees or doctorates.

EVOLUTION OF THE TECHNICAL COMMUNICATION SERVICE COURSE

Technical writing evolved from engineering writing, which developed following the two Morrill Acts, in 1862 and 1877, respectively, that provided for land-grant colleges. These were the agricultural and mechanical (A&M) colleges that made higher education available to a large segment of the population.

Engineering writing, or technical writing as it was sometimes called, developed in the first half of the 20th century, primarily in the land-grant colleges, as a service course. According to Connors (1982), "the first genuine technical writing textbook written for use in college courses" was *The Theory and Practice of Technical Writing,* published in 1911 by Samuel Chandler Earle of Tufts College. Connors maintains that this man "more than any other, deserves the title of Father of Technical Writing Instruction" (p. 332). (For a thorough examination of the development of engineering writing, see Kynell, 1996.)

In the second half of the 20th century, the technical writing service course has continued to develop and flourish, with most colleges and universities offering one or more such courses. The impetus for this phenomenal growth was the unprecedented technological advancements accompanying the last half of World War II plus the postwar influx of ex-military personnel into higher education, primarily as students but also as teachers.

Service courses in technical communication emphasize process explanations, instructions, descriptions, analyses through classification and cause-effect, various kinds of reports, feasibility studies, proposals, business correspondence, job application materials, data interpretation, graphics and visuals, and page layout and document design (Pickett, 1990). The emphases differ according to such factors as course level, prerequisites, and numbers of students.

To illustrate, here are thumbnail sketches of technical communication service courses at five institutions across the country.

- Agricultural Technical Institute, Ohio State University. College enrollment: 750. Sections yearly: 6 to 7. The college offers 20 majors; students in 14 majors take technical writing and the others, business writing.

- Hinds Community College. College enrollment: 13,000. Sections yearly: 18 to 20. Two-semester sequence fulfills for technical majors the English composition requirement for the Associate in Applied Science degree.
- Armstrong State College. College enrollment: 5,500. Sections yearly: 3 to 4. One course, upper division elective.
- Brigham Young University. College Enrollment: 28,000. Sections yearly: 100+. Two junior-level courses: one for students in engineering, physical sciences, and biological sciences; the other for students in social sciences. The university requires all juniors to take one of five advanced writing courses keyed to specific majors.
- Texas A&M University. College enrollment: 42,000. Sections yearly: 150+. Two courses: a sophomore-level introduction and a junior/senior-level preparation for workplace needs. In addition, the university offers an undergraduate minor and certificate in professional writing and an MA and Ph.D. in English with Concentration in Rhetoric and Composition.

Personal Perspective

Technical communication, for many students, makes writing sensible and palatable. For that reason, my professional career as a teacher, particularly from 1967, has been interrelated with technical communication. Several years before then, before I was aware of such a thing as technical writing or technical communication (or tech prep), I organized a high school course in applied English.

My first experience in teaching technical communication was with a group of high school "shop" students in the late 1950s. These were high school males. These young men—adroit at using routers and bench saws, instinctively knowing how to chop cotton while aspiring to be tractor drivers—experienced difficulties with English.

So why not set up a practical-application course in English that would serve as their English requirement? That's what we did. In the last two years of my three at Rolling Fork High School, students in the spring term had their choice of English classes—the conventional grammar and literature units or applied English. In applied English—or shop English, as students called it—all reading and writing assignments centered around what students were doing in shop, typically their favorite class. The teacher of this hands-on class and I worked together in planning the writing and reading assignments for English in this rural, Mississippi Delta community where cotton was king. The textbooks were the big Sears and Roebuck catalog, brochures from farm implement companies, and the wealth of materials from the U.S. Department of Agriculture that the county agent provided. Students learned how to write sets of instructions, order parts, describe machinery parts and problems, and keep daily logs of their activities in shop. (This latter activity was as much for me as for students; I learned new vocabulary and formed ideas for writing activities while students wrote daily.)

My more formal introduction to technical writing occurred in the fall of 1967 when, in my second year at Hinds Community College, I was assigned to teach the course. The 1967 course description in the college catalog was identical to that in the 1962-63 catalog when Hinds first offered the course:

> *English 92—Technical Writing.* A course for students pursuing a technical program. The course is designed to aid the student in developing proficiency in letter writing, report writing, technical descriptions and with other forms of writing related to his special field. Three hours per week. Credit, three semester hours. (Hinds Community College, 1962, p. 61)

I was handed the *Manual of Technical Writing* by W. O. Sypherd (University of Delaware), Alvin M. Fountain (North Carolina State College of Agriculture and Engineering), and V. E. Gibbens (Purdue University). This 1957 book was a revision and extension of *The Engineer's Manual of English* (1943, 1933).

Colleague Ann Laster, also assigned to teach technical writing, and I realized during the first week of class that this book would not work for our students. The book was designed for junior- and senior-level students nearing completion of requirements for a baccalaureate degree. Our students were in two-year technical programs: agricultural management, aircraft maintenance, drafting and design, electronics, mechanics, and refrigeration and air conditioning.

Unable to find an appropriate textbook, Ann Laster and I began to visit industries, businesses, and government agencies; we talked with technical instructors; we studied textbooks they used; we interviewed graduates of the technical programs about on-the-job communication skills. Then we set about devising our own units of study and producing lots of handouts for our students. With a grant of $500 from the college, in the summer of 1968 we wrote a 241-page, 8 1/2 x 11-inch, spiral bound textbook/workbook, *Effective Communication for the Technical Student.* Printed by vocational students in the college's Offset Printing Department, the book was then sold through the campus bookstore for $4.95 until 1970 when it was published by what is now Harper Collins as *Writing and Reading in Technical English.* With the second edition in 1975 came the name change to *Technical English: Writing, Reading. and Speaking,* which continues with the seventh edition.

Just as Ann Laster and I taught ourselves how to write a book (with lots of help, of course), we also taught ourselves how to teach technical writing in the same way that many teachers of service courses have—by doing it. Today, thanks to the development of technical communication as a profession and as an academic discipline, opportunities to prepare the teachers of service courses are plentiful.

PREPARING FACULTY TO TEACH THE SERVICE COURSE

Opportunities for learning to teach technical communication service courses are provided primarily by summer institutes (short courses), by NCTE and CCCC, by ATTW, STC, and IEEE, by publications, and by preparation in graduate programs.

Summer Institutes

Summer institutes, begun in the 1960s by universities to provide concentrated short courses for business and industry personnel, also attracted teachers of technical communication service courses. Popular on through the 1970s to the mid-1980s, summer institutes—typically three to five days in length—were offered by such institutions as Rensselaer Polytechnic Institute, Massachusetts Institute of Technology, the universities of Michigan, Washington, and Minnesota, and Colorado State University.

The oldest surviving summer institute designed specifically for teachers of the technical communication service course was founded in 1981 by a regional organization, the Southeastern Conference on English in the Two-Year College (renamed in 1996, Two-Year College English Association–Southeast). Begun by Nell Ann Pickett (Hinds Community College, Mississippi) and Dixie Hickman (then from the University of Southern Mississippi, now of Communication Resources, Atlanta, Georgia), the institute attracts teachers from two-year and four-year colleges, from universities, and from high schools (including those in tech prep programs). Most participants in the week-long institute are in one of two groups: those new to technical communication who want to retool composition skills for teaching technical communication and those who have been teaching technical communication for several years and want to fine-tune their skills and update their professional knowledge. Over the Institute's 15 years, very few of the participants have had any previous courses—undergraduate or graduate—in technical communication.

NCTE and CCCC

From the late 1960s to the present, NCTE and CCCC have provided learning opportunities through workshops, program sessions, and publications.

Since the early 1970s, the NCTE Committee on Technical and Scientific Communication has sponsored multiday workshops in conjunction with the annual convention. These study groups/workshops have typically had maximum enrollments. Enthusiasm for the Association of Teachers of Technical Writing and its journal *The Technical Writing Teacher* (now *Technical Communication Quarterly*) grew.

The CCCC Committee on Technical Communication also sponsors workshops in conjunction with its annual convention. These workshops, the series of panels offered each year at the NCTE and CCCC conventions, and the Studies in Technical Communication Series (selected papers presented at CCCC and NCTE conventions) provide major learning opportunities for technical communication teachers.

ATTW, STC, and IEEE

The Association of Teachers of Technical Writing (ATTW), since its founding at the 1973 CCCC convention in New Orleans, has provided continuous, significant help for teachers of technical communication service courses. Its journal *Technical Communication Quarterly (TCQ)* and semiannual *ATTW Bulletin*, its Best Article in *TCQ* Annual Award, its some twenty books and monographs, its annual meeting in conjunction with the CCCC convention, and its Society of Fellows—all have had a major impact in leading the entire discipline of technical communication.

The Society for Technical Communication (STC) and The Institute of Electrical and Electronics Engineers, Inc. (IEEE)—predating ATTW—were founded as professional organizations to enhance the practice of their constituencies in business, industrial, corporate, and government workplaces. STC, with a sizable academic membership, improves and advances the theory and practice of technical communication through its quarterly journal *Technical Communication*, newsletter *Intercom* (10 issues a year), books, seminars, workshops, international symposia, and annual conference. The Professional Communication Society, an organization within IEEE, publishes the quarterly journal *IEEE Transactions on Professional Communication* as well as other materials. The society is dedicated to improving the communication of technical information.

PLANNING AND IMPLEMENTING THE SERVICE COURSE IN TECHNICAL COMMUNICATION

When ideas are tossed about whether an institution should offer a service course in technical communication, a number of questions emerge. Some concern curricular matters that the institution must deal with; others concern the person who teaches the course. But foremost in the thinking of some is the question, "Doesn't English composition do all this?" Therefore, this section thus discusses first curricular concerns, then staffing ones.

Curricular Concerns

College personnel proposing a technical communication service course present their rationale something like this.

The proposed course in technical communication will:

- Improve speaking, writing, and graphics skills of students majoring in technical, scientific, and professional areas
- Better prepare students to become successful practitioners of their occupation or profession
- Help to fulfill employers' expectation that prospective employees have communication skills to support their technical expertise

It is essential that the person or committee making the course proposal has done the necessary homework: involving the affected departments in planning, checking with college officers in preparing the proposal, preparing a cost analysis for initiating and maintaining the course, conferring with appropriate officials for course description for college publications, enlisting the support of outside agencies, advisory groups, and prospective employers.

Typical questions that a college curriculum committee expects answered are listed in Figure 20.1.

The answers to these questions shape the development of the course, its emphasis and content, budgeting process, teacher qualifications, and interdepartmental relationships. However, the context for the course, its academic location, numbers of students, and academic partners are also important. The examples in Figure 20.2 illustrate varying circumstances for offering a technical communication course at four hypothetical institutions.

Although all four institutions are planning service courses in technical communication, the circumstances will guide the responses to the curriculum concerns listed in Figure 20.1.

Staffing Concerns

When an institution decides to offer a technical communication service course, a basic question is this: who will teach it?

1. Why is a service course needed?
2. What is the purpose of the course?
3. Which department or division will offer it?
4. What course content—communication and technical—will be emphasized?
5. Which majors will take the course?
6. Will the course be required, recommended, listed in the student's curriculum?
7. Which departments will be affected?
8. What are the service course prerequisites?
9. Can the service course be taken in lieu of composition?
10. Who will teach the service course? What qualifications are required?
11. Will the service course transfer?
12. In hard times, will the service course survive?

Figure 20.1. Curricular concerns.

John S. Harris (1992), in his enormously helpful *Teaching Technical Writing: A Pragmatic Approach*, writes:

> The ideal teacher of technical writing knows everything about writing, everything about technical subjects, and everything about teaching. Unfortunately, few people have this combination of knowledge. The administrator of the technical writing program thus has to make do with what is available. A few people are now being especially trained to teach technical writing, but their numbers are still few. The choices are usually people from sciences and engineering, technical writers with industrial experience, and retread English teachers. (p. 4.1)

Although other departments or schools (business, technology, engineering, agriculture) sometimes house the service course in technical communication, most often it is taught by the English department. Harris makes this very wise observation:

> Not all English teachers ... are suited to become teachers of technical writing. Those who view literature as the only true gospel, those who view science and technology as threatening, those who see themselves as too free spirited to conform to any organizational strictures, and those who are physically and intellectually lazy are probably constitutionally incapable of becoming good technical writing teachers. But those who are congenitally—even

Institution A is planning a required junior-level technical communication course for all students in the college of technology. The course is to be offered each semester and summer term by the English department in the college of arts and sciences. Anticipated enrollment: 1,200 students each year.

Institution B wants to offer an elective course in technical communication for students in vocational programs. Most of the students are in a one- to two-year certificate program; some are working toward successful completion of the GED. The course will be offered once a year and team-taught by trades and English department instructors. Anticipated enrollment: 15-20 students a year.

Institution C plans to offer a technical communication course as a preferred elective for students in the business division, which houses eight departments. The service course, to be offered each quarter by the business department, will be managed by a business department teacher with presentations from professionals. Anticipated enrollment: 400-500 students a year.

Institution D has offered for many years through the English department a service course in technical communication open to all students. Now the institution plans for each school within the university to offer technical communication courses tailored to the needs of its own students.

Figure 20.2. Examples of various approaches to the technical communication service course.

> pathologically—curious, those who are flexible and inventive, those who can respect science and technology, and those whose fundamental world view is pragmatic can be made into good technical writing teachers, even though the subject matter is quite new to them. (pp. 4.2–4.3)

Those new to teaching technical communication, volunteers or enlisted composition teachers, must typically help the department find answers to instructional and teaching questions such as the ones listed in Figure 20.3.

CONTINUING CHALLENGES

Challenges to the technical communication service course continue. In the foreseeable future, many service courses will continue to be taught by persons without benefit of graduate education in technical communication. However, opportunities for self-teaching continue to expand through an increasing number of articles and books, presentations and workshops at professional conferences, and other services from professional organizations. Many courses will continue to be taught in classrooms without

1. What qualifies faculty to teach technical communication? What special technical expertise and communication is needed?
2. If several sections of the service course are offered, should students be grouped in classes homogeneously (by major) or heterogeneously (mixture of majors)?
3. Which textbook and instructional materials should be used?
4. What are sources of timely workplace materials for use in the course? What workplace communication practices should shape instruction?
5. What major assignments should the service course include and what is the rationale for their inclusion?
6. On what bases should student-written reports be evaluated, particularly relative to one-the-job communication?
7. How can the service course earn the cooperation and support of technical faculty?
8. How can advisory committees, cooperative education personnel, employment personnel, and the like contribute to instruction?

Figure 20. 3. Teaching concerns.

sufficient access to computers and software packages for word processing, graphics, and desktop publishing. However, inventive teachers will continue to turn limited electronic capabilities into exciting, inventive writing possibilities for students. The importance of service courses may also be minimized by the increasing number of undergraduate and graduate programs in technical communication. Or the technical communication service course may become theory-inflated, with less attention to workplace applications. However, the balance of theory, research, and application will continue to sort itself out. Such possible tensions are healthy for the discipline.

I see a bright future for service courses in technical communication and for those who teach them. Current attention to writing at all levels, writing-across-the curriculum programs, and monetary respect for workplace communication skills—all heighten the significance and the responsibility of technical communication service courses.

As James W. Souther (1989) writes, "Technical communication emerged in the 1980s as a discipline possessing both professional maturity and academic sophistication" (p. 2). In the mid-1990s and into the 21st century, technical communication is teamed with technology. There is respect for writing in the workplace; clear, unencumbered writing is a desirable commodity. A new generation of technical communication teachers is emerging that is well grounded in theory, research, and electronic technology, that comes to the classroom well prepared in the discipline of technical communication.

REFERENCES

Connors, R.J. (1982). The rise of technical writing instruction in America. *Journal of Technical Writing and Communication, 12,* 329–351.

Geonetta, S.C., Allen, J., Curtis, D. & Staples, K. (1995). *Academic programs in technical communication.* (4th Ed.). Washington, DC: Society for Technical Communication.

Harris, J.S. (1992). *Teaching technical writing: A pragmatic approach.* (Rev. Ed.). University of Minnesota: ATTW.

Hinds Community College. (1962). *Catalog 1962-63.* Raymond, MS: Hinds Community College.

Kynell, T.C. (1994). *Bridging technology and humanism: The evolution of technical writing in America, 1850–1950.* Doctoral dissertation, Michigan Technological University.

Pickett, N.A. (1990). Teaching technical communication in two-year colleges: The courses and the teachers. *Technical Writing Teacher, 17,* 76–85.

Pickett, N.A. & Laster, A.A. (in press). *Technical English: Writing, reading, and speaking.* (7th Ed.). New York: HarperCollins. (Rev. Ed. of *Writing and reading in technical English.* [1st Ed.], 1970).

Souther, J.W. (1989). Teaching technical writing: A retrospective appraisal. In B.E. Fearing & W. K. Sparrow (Eds.), *Technical writing: Theory and practice* (pp. 2–13). New York: MLA.

21

DESIGNING A RESEARCH PROGRAM IN SCIENTIFIC AND TECHNICAL COMMUNICATION: SETTING STANDARDS AND DEFINING THE AGENDA

Billie Wahlstrom

University of Minnesota

INTRODUCTION

Research in the field of technical communication has reached a critical point in its evolution. Voices from both the academy and workplace have questioned the quality of research in technical communication as well as methodologies employed (Blakeslee, et al. 1996; Carliner, 1994; Gross, 1994). Technical communication practitioners and academics have been criticized both for focusing on the trivial and for lacking rigor when they examine questions of substance. Those who work in this maturing discipline need to examine these criticisms and address the ones that are valid. In fact, if technical communication is to thrive as a discipline, a strong research agenda is essential. Technical communication has achieved maturity as a discipline, has created an academic infrastructure (a critical mass of academic programs, researchers, and practicing professionals), and has the professional apparatus (scholarly and professional journals; local, regional, national, and international scholarly and professional organizations) necessary for it to define, conduct, and distribute first-class research.

Generally speaking, an expanded vision of technical communication as a discipline has not been matched by the development of a comprehensive disciplinary research agenda. Although academics and practicing professionals no longer narrowly define the field as the study of making effective manuals, the technical communication research agenda has not expanded to include complex issues of language and representation in a technological society. On one hand, educators must remain concerned with creating effective messages in whatever media are available, and today that includes multimedia, hypertext, and electronic forums as well as print. On the other, educators must extend their interests in the rhetorical dimensions of the efficacy and ethics of public discourse in a technological age.

Instead of leading "to the discovery of hitherto unknown novel facts" (Lakatos, 1978, p. 5) in coherent, discipline-defined areas, technical communication research is often designed to generate a publication, to obtain tenure, or to meet departmental salary increase criteria rather than to develop practical solutions to real communication problems, to explore the impact of science and technology on civic life, or to create new knowledge for its own sake. Moreover, the methodologies employed in disciplinary research have come into question, both in terms of those chosen and the rigor with which they are employed (Carliner, 1994; Doheny-Farina, 1993; Goubil-Gambrell, 1992; Gross, 1994; Kirsch, 1992). If technical communication is to be a robust discipline, research institutions in the field must address these concerns, defining the parameters of and setting high standards for research—for theory building, hypothesis testing, analysis, and enacting of theory into practice.

THE CURRENT STATE OF RESEARCH IN TECHNICAL COMMUNICATION

What has opened technical communication research to criticism is actually a complex set of factors tied to the age of the discipline and the era in which it is practiced. Political realities and disciplinary issues have had great impact on research programs. Although there are many places to look for evidence of this impact, examining a few of these issues illustrates the problem.

Preparing Practitioners

Currently, there are seven Ph.D. granting institutions producing trained scholars and researchers in technical communication. Each year, approximately 400,000 students take technical communication courses, usually technical writing. With only a handful of Ph.D.-granting institutions functioning, and with most of those being less than five years old, a small percentage of people teaching technical communication courses have extensive discipline-specific training. Moreover, most technical writing courses are taught in English departments that do not have technical communication programs and often have only one or two technical writing teachers who are seen as outside the department's main mission—the teaching of literature. As a consequence, technical communication teachers have little institutional support for developing and maintaining their own scholarly and research agendas because tenure and promotion will be determined by colleagues who understand and value primarily belletristic writing.

At many other universities, technical writing courses are taught not by faculty but by Ph.D. students in the English department whose areas of interest are not technical communication, composition, or writing across the curriculum, but literature, literary theory, or creative writing. As a result, many have little concern for or training in technical communication research and cannot convey to their students the research base supporting the pedagogy they enact in the classroom.

These staffing decisions and departmental hiring patterns are not without consequence throughout the discipline. Students, especially those in engineering and computer science, who take technical writing classes from people who are not themselves experts in the field later find themselves called upon to do technical writing on the job. These students do not have the research tools that enable them to examine issues they face, nor do they have the exposure to research methodologies or resources that allows them to find answers to questions that arise in the workplace. This is not to suggest that the questions they come up with are not worth answering, but both the questions asked and the answers given demonstrate a lack of awareness of research that has been done and is being done in technical communication. This results, as Saul Carliner (1994) has reported, in researchers who have tried to claim literature reviews as original research.

This problem is demonstrated by the kinds of questions asked about practical problems on a Listserv for technical communicators (Techwr-L).

In late 1994, for example, technical communicators on the list asked the following questions:

- What is the most efficient packaging and choice of documentation that will be updated frequently? Should be ring binders and film-wrapped packs accompany updates? Should material be on CDs with updates sent out on diskettes? Should documentation be perfect bound so people can't misplace pages and then updated every year or so? Should other options be used? What are the relative costs, advantages, disadvantages, legal and recycling considerations of such choices?
- What cost savings, if any, accompany the use of online help? Are there real dollar savings for cost or for time? Put another way, to what extent does documentation provide a value-added component to a project?
- What do technical communicators do in the course of a day? What kinds of jobs and media do they use?

These are nontrivial questions, raised in good faith, but they show a lack of awareness of current research and available resources, and little understanding of technical communication as a profession. This is not surprising because many current technical writers were not originally hired as technical communicators and have come to their current jobs almost accidentally. Consequently, many didn't receive the specialized education that technical communication majors receive. Lacking an awareness of technical communication as a discipline is not just a problem of engineers and others who have ended up doing technical communication without the training. It is also a result of companies not realizing the advantages of hiring trained communicators.

Disorder in the Ranks

At this stage in the history of technical communication, more people call themselves technical communicators and technical communication teachers than have the training and background needed to do so. Only about 20% of technical communicators who belong to the Society for Technical Communication hold degrees in technical communication. That's not surprising because it wasn't too long ago that all technical communication teachers were retreads, that no one teaching technical communication had academic credentials in the discipline. Before the development of degree programs, people interested in business or technical communication were largely self-taught. This first generation of teachers and practitioners is only now beginning to retire.

Times have changed, and the need for well-trained technical communicators is growing, but discipline-specific education is available. There are more than 100 certificate, B.S., B.A., M.S., and M.A. programs nationally educating students in scientific and technical communication. Moreover, many of these master's degree programs have been around for decades, graduating significant numbers of competent practitioners into the workforce and providing a pool of teachers at the community-college level. That's one reason why it's disconcerting to find substantial numbers of people being hired to teach technical communication without the proper education. Quality control in technical communication programs is a serious issue, and there is no national accreditation program in our field, despite years of discussion at the Council of Programs in Technical and Scientific Communication (CPTSC), the national council of technical program chairs and directors.

Without an accreditation or evaluation mechanism in place, too many schools are still offering education only in technical writing. They send out graduates who are poorly equipped to handle the variety of media they must use and who lack the research background necessary to answer workplace questions. Students graduate as technical communicators but having had only a small core of classes in technical writing and perhaps an additional course in newsletter or proposal design. And while such graduates can obtain jobs as entry-level practitioners, they are not trained to keep themselves current or to carry out necessary research in their workplace.

The mere existence of Ph.D.-granting institutions graduating scholars and researchers into the field of technical communication is unlikely to solve this problem soon. No unified vision of the discipline has emerged from those institutions, although there are signs that one is developing. Departmental administrators have yet to agree on a standard name for the degrees they offer. In English or chemistry, for example, one gets a Ph.D. in English or chemistry and has an area of expertise, say, organic chemistry or medieval literature. This is not the case in technical communication. Of the seven universities offering Ph.D.s in the field, only the University of Minnesota (Rhetoric/STC), Michigan Technological University (Rhetoric and Technical Communication), and Texas Tech University (Technical Communication and Rhetoric) have the words *technical communication* in their degree titles. The others have named their Ph.D. degrees in other ways:

- Carnegie Mellon University (Rhetoric)
- Iowa State University (Rhetoric and Professional Communication)
- New Mexico State (Rhetoric and Professional Communication)
- Rensselaer (Communication and Rhetoric)
- Washington State University (Rhetoric and Composition)

Looking at where these degrees are housed indicates that technical communication has not yet settled on a home department in an existing discipline nor has it created its own department:

- Carnegie Mellon (English Department)
- Iowa State University (English Department)
- Michigan Technological University (Humanities Department)
- New Mexico State (English Department)
- Rensselaer (Department of Language, Literature, and Communication)
- Texas Tech University (English Department)
- University of Minnesota (Rhetoric Department)
- Washington State University (English Department)

Institutionally, scholars and administrators have not described technical communication's scholarly domain in a consistent way, and each program has had to work within its individual institution to explain itself. This problem is reflected in the Rhetoric Department's experience at the University of Minnesota when it added an M.A. and Ph.D. to its existing undergraduate and M.S. programs. The graduate school placed the M.S. under the supervision of the Social Science Council and the M.A. and Ph.D. under the supervision of the Humanities Council. This decision on the part of the graduate school was made despite the fact that both degrees share a common theoretical and research base and have the same faculty.

Moreover, technical communication teachers and researchers have not yet fully defined what mix of scholarly interests is needed to create the model department. Within existing Ph.D. programs, various levels of interdisciplinarity are to be found. All programs have faculty trained in writing with an emphasis on some aspect of workplace writing (collaboration, impact of technology). Most program faculty include scholars trained in other areas such as literature, composition, speech communication, graphic arts or document design, publications management, and rhetoric. A few have among their faculty scholars trained in psychology, American studies, mass communication, education, foreign language, history of science, video production, and philosophy. How all these disciplines interact with technical communication is only now being worked out, and we have not settled comfortably on what constitutes the preferred methodologies of our domain.

Despite these issues of disciplinary definition, graduates of these advanced degree programs are much different from those coming out of traditional English degrees. Nevertheless, they do not represent a significant portion of the faculty teaching or the faculty teaching B.S., B.A., M.A. and M.S. programs. Many of these positions are filled by scholars whose primary training is in literature or composition. Research in technical communication intersects with that in literature and composition, but it is not coextensive with it. Textual analysis, critical studies, and composition theory all have their place in technical communication, which is by its nature interdisciplinary, but scholars in these areas often do not have the background or interests of scholars trained in technical communication. Therefore, when they assign research to their students and as they conduct it themselves, they often do not center their research concerns on technical communication.

Additionally, because most technical communication programs exist in humanities, rhetoric, or English departments, technical communication scholars and researchers in the academy have often been isolated. To get tenure, such faculty must generate publications that make sense to their departmental colleagues. To be promoted, they must publish in mainstream disciplinary publications. If they try to publish in technical communication, they are considered to be working outside the mainstream. Although technical communication scholars may never find easy acceptance of their research and publications in their departmental homes, their cases will be much strengthened if technical communication develops a strong scholarly reputation.

DEFINING THE RESEARCH AGENDA

Technical communication needs a clearly articulated and carefully defined national research agenda. However, this doesn't mean that national organizations should determine what questions scholars and practitioners should address. Yet the importance of research done well should be a subject of discussion at our national organizations—ATTW, CPTSC, STC, and the Technical Communication Committees of CCCC and NCTE. To some extent, those of us who are members of these organizations are beginning to describe the parameters of our research agenda, and that is a positive move. This emerging consensus is reflected by the fact that all Ph.D. programs have the word *Rhetoric* in their degree title:

- Carnegie Mellon University, Ph.D. in Rhetoric
- Iowa State University, Ph.D. in Rhetoric and Professional Communication
- Michigan Technological University, Ph.D. in Rhetoric and Technical Communication
- New Mexico State, Ph.D. in Rhetoric and Professional Communication
- Rensselaer, Ph.D. in Communication and Rhetoric

- Texas Tech University, Ph.D. in Technical Communication and Rhetoric
- University of Minnesota, Ph.D. in Rhetoric/Scientific and Technical Communication
- Washington State University, Ph.D. in Rhetoric and Composition

Research in technical communication has been, since its inception, pragmatically oriented, designed to solve the problems of practicing professionals. It grows from the rhetorical traditions (Aristotle, 1990, p. 153) that emphasize effective communication. Given the increased complexity of communication in a technological age and the need for effective messages, research will have to continue in that direction.

Yet if programs hope to develop a disciplinary research agenda to sustain and nurture faculty and students, educators must look at more than practical problems. Technical communication, created to provide specific practical solutions to communication questions growing out of World War II, can only be sustained if it can reconceive its original mission in light of today's complex technological era. It is technical communication's tie to rhetoric that provides a central vision to support research programs. Rhetoric is not just about being a good (effective) communicator; it is also about being a good (moral and ethical) communicator. As Cicero said in *De Oratore*, if we only teach the skills associated with effective communication, we will have put "weapons in the hands of madmen" (p. 55). If technical communication is to flourish as a discipline, the ethical and moral dimensions of rhetoric must be recognized in the research agenda (Wolf, 1992). Scholars, practitioners, and administrators must nurture a commitment, as Alan Gross has put it, to the "renewal of rhetorical practice in the interest of emancipatory reason" (1994, p. 86). The discipline's particular focus must be on science and technology's impact on civic life and on ways to bring debate about the issues of science and technology to our existing and emerging communication forums.

Tailoring a Research Agenda to a Particular Program

In a sense, a research agenda is both a promise and a contract. For a department, it is a contract with upper-level administrators guaranteeing that funds will be spent in a more or less predictable fashion on activities for which there is a need and for which there is reasonable hope that something specific can be accomplished. College administrators need departmental research agendas to justify college-level expenditures to central administration. A productive department can use its agenda therefore as a way of leveraging resources and positions.

But a research agenda is more than a contract promising work for pay. It is also a promise or vision that unifies the activities within a department and is consonant with the mission of the college and university. It is a disciplinary and departmentally defined space in which excellence is recognized, authorized, and rewarded. Departments must develop a vision of what research in the department adds up to. The profession's inability to articulate a unifying vision has hurt individual faculty members as they have sought to justify their research in inhospitable departments, and it has hurt technical communication's development of a coherent and rigorous research agenda. The expectations of the discipline have not been clear, resulting in what Saul Carliner (1994) has called the "trivial nature of most research questions," the failure to ask "compelling questions," and our unwillingness to "seek and acknowledge feedback" in our research projects (Blakeslee, et al. 1996, p. 131).

The biggest problem in developing a research program on the departmental level is one of scope. A lot of compelling questions and a variety of methodologies actually exist, and technical communication teachers need to show students how to read and appreciate them; yet, departments and faculty cannot duplicate the entire discipline's concern. A department's research agenda should fit into the national agenda, broadly speaking, but be tailored to local strengths. If we agree that rhetoric informs the national research agenda in technical communication, then a department will have to carve out areas of practical problems to address as well as a particular area of civic discourse to examine.

A major research program cannot be built on scattered efforts. It requires a focus congruent with national goals and tailored to fit local strengths and needs. As technical communication develops, research programs are developing their individual areas of expertise. Schools are becoming known for particular strengths. For example, Rensselaer has special strengths in visual communication and graphics. Carnegie Mellon has long been strong in quantitative and experimental methodology. Michigan Tech's research program grows out of its long-standing leadership in the areas of composition, writing across the curriculum, and computer literacy; it favors qualitative methodologies—those of cultural studies, textual and critical theories. Minnesota has strengths in rhetorical theory, pedagogy, and communication technologies. None of these institutions has tried to take on all of these areas, and all are working to build on strength.

Methodologies

Departmental research programs should determine what methodologies will be privileged in the department, but students should be trained to read, understand, and evaluate many. If the profession is to develop research programs nationally that address both practical problems and the nature of ethical public discourse in a technological era, then we cannot be limited to the methodology of the social sciences or the humanities. Contemporary problems in technical communication are complex and need to be examined from both empirical and humanistic perspectives (Goubil-Gambrell, 1992). Gross' (1994) objection that technical communication researchers do not practice rigorous *methods* in social science approaches has validity, as does the objection that they do not bring rhetorical or humanistic perspectives to many problems of communication at all.

In actuality, it doesn't matter what methodologies are privileged at technical communication research programs as long as students are required to develop an understanding and appreciation of multiple methods and the rigor with which these methods must be applied. Many questions in technical communication cannot be answered by social empirical or case approaches alone; they require triangularization or a multioffense methodological approach. This is especially true if teachers and scholars are committed to both the practical and the ethical dimensions of rhetorical study that underpin technical communication. For example, I have a graduate student who is interested in what media and format should be used to teach young children about the Holocaust. Her father is a Holocaust survivor, and she is concerned that the stories of survivors be preserved and presented in such a way that young children can learn from them and not be frightened away from the subject. This problem has both qualitative and empirical dimensions. It raises questions of message design and media selection as well as questions about theories of representation and the ethical uses of technology. Research programs have to provide methodological training to allow these questions to be answered carefully and thoroughly.

DIRECTIONS IN TECHNICAL COMMUNICATION RESEARCH

Departmental administrators, directors of graduate study, and individual faculty members need to design research programs that ask Carliner's (1994) "compelling questions" and that explore ways to empower the public and foster democratic debate on matters of science and technology (Harding, 1991). Below, I've suggested a few of the areas in which research needs to be done with both of these ideas in mind. Although there are many other areas in which research is needed, these three areas require immediate attention: pedagogy, document design, and communication technologies. Research here will help technical communication programs meet their obligations to students, to practicing professionals in the workplace, and to the citizens of the United States.

Pedagogy and Curriculum

Research on curriculum and pedagogical practices in the field of technical communication is greatly needed. In order to assure that technical communication students are able to approach the complex communication problems they will need to study, teachers need to do classroom research themselves. They need to research the content both of programs and of individual courses, and they need to teach appropriate research techniques to students. Educators have to instill in students an understanding and appreciation of the need for rigorous research. These are some of the pressing questions that need to be addressed:

- What does a technical communicator need to know to do his or her work, and how can that best be taught? How are current programs doing?
- How should courses be designed and sequenced?
- What should the specific content of individual courses be?
- What are the canonical works of the field, and how should they be determined?
- What communication technologies are most useful in teaching what kinds of material?
- What historical and contemporary understandings of their discipline must technical communication students have?
- How can students gain the ethical understandings they need, and what are those understandings?
- How can teaching in technical communication programs better promote the ideals of democratic participation in public discourse on issues of science and technology?
- How can the findings of classroom researchers concerning technical communication curriculum and pedagogy be used to increase the ability of citizens to read, understand, and act responsibly on technical and scientific issues?

Document Design

Research is badly needed in the area of document design. Just as research in pedagogy and curriculum helps a department meet its obligations to its students, research can help a department repay the profession as a whole by supporting the work of professionals in the field. And given the rate of change in communication practices in the workplace, this area of scholarly inquiry will be generating questions for a long time. Some of those most pressing include the following:

- What are the guidelines for effective display of online, hypertext, and multimedia information?
- How can readability of online, hypertext, and multimedia information be enhanced?
- How can documents be designed to facilitate technological literacy?
- What is the nature of ethical design?
- What rhetorical strategies are most effective in designing documents (such as homepages on the World Wide Web) for display on the Internet?
- How can research on document design best reach people in the field?
- How do laws governing intellectual property as well as other standards (ANSI and ISO, for example) affect document design?

Communication Technologies

New technologies are emerging at a staggering rate, and it is up to research programs to examine both their effective use and their impact on civic life. In particular, new technologies raise questions about literacy, "cybersociety," access, and the role of technology in fostering democratic participation and change. The questions below suggest some of these research needs:

- How is the Internet changing social interaction?
- How can emerging technologies be used to foster democratic change?
- To what extent does the technical communicator serve the needs of users or those of manufacturers in rendering new technologies usable?
- How do race, class, and gender affect new communication technologies and what is the impact of these technologies on these social variables?
- How are issues of literacy, knowledge, and power affected by new technologies?
- What are the international and cross-cultural dimensions of cyberspace?
- What are the legal and ethical dimensions of new communication technologies? How are such things as privacy, property, and piracy handled?

- What are the standards to be used for media selection given today's media and mixed media?
- What is the best way to use MOOs (Multi-Object Oriented Domains) and educational modules on the World Wide Web?
- What makes for the most effective online learning environment?
- What should technical communication teachers be teaching the leaders of business, industry, and academe who will manage MOOs, MUDs (Multi-User Domains), Listservs, e-mail, and other electronic forums? What do they need to know about the technology, its management, and issues of access and literacy surrounding it?

DEFINING PROGRAM NEEDS AND RESOURCES

Developing a sound research program has costs attached to it. Releasing faculty to do research and rewarding them for success, providing facilities and resources—all are real costs attached to a research program. To develop a sound one, a department must perform a conscientious audit of all available resources. These may constrain the types of research that can be supported by a particular program. Below, I have listed a few of the most critical resources.

Computing

Among those resources to consider first are those provided by the university as a whole. Computing facilities have to be available to support many kinds of technical communication research. A university-wide information infrastructure must exist so that faculty and students can reach the Internet if departmental research is going to focus on cyberspace communication. Adequate mainframe support or powerful workstations need to be available if faculty are going to work with CAD or other aspects of design, and ample storage in the gigabyte range must be available to support multimedia teaching and research.

Library

To develop a sound research agenda in any area of inquiry, adequate library holdings must support that area. A library doesn't have to have major holdings in all areas, but it must have adequate holdings in some. In some cases, library holdings can and should direct research conducted in the department. For example, technical communication programs housed in engineering schools can focus on communication within engineering fields, on issues of growing professionalism. Departments housed in colleges of agriculture can research risk communication in connection with food or ground water contamination.

Laboratories

Some faculty and departmental research agendas require the presence of laboratories. For technical communication research, these are seldom the $500,000+ facilities that one finds in the sciences. Nevertheless, they are expensive in terms of what is generally found in the humanities. If technical communication departments cannot afford their own labs—as undoubtedly will be the case for technical communication programs seeking to support research in virtual reality, interactive video used for distance education, or document design and publications management—then they will have to develop cooperative plans with other units. However technical communication programs solve their laboratory needs, they must first begin by acknowledging that these facilities must be available if some research programs are contemplated.

Departmental Resources

In addition to laboratory support, resources are needed at the faculty level if a department is to develop a research agenda. First of all, there must be enough faculty and staff to allow research to go forward without damage to the department's teaching mission. Second, departmental resources need to be used to support faculty and staff research. These resources include travel funds, computer hardware and software, support for research assistants, and space.

Even with the financial support for research, a department cannot hope to develop a research program unless it has a vision that includes research. Some departments are good at teaching and have no desire to change their focus. This isn't a bad thing and should be respected. An administrator who thinks a research agenda can be forced on faculty will be unhappy with the result. Major research institutions that require research for promotion, tenure, and merit increases will have less trouble getting faculty to develop research projects, but without a departmental commitment and vision, research in the department will lack synergy and the result is likely to be isolated pockets of individual effort.

Because the questions we address are complex, departments must structure their research programs so that they draw upon the resources of the whole university, and so that students see research in technical communication as connected to a larger domain of knowledge. Much of the interesting research that has a bearing on technical communication is done outside the field, in such areas as cognitive psychology, history of science, critical studies, business, education, and vocational technology. Departmental research efforts that do not consider the work done in these disciplines are bound to be naive and incomplete. To mitigate against that, departments need to bring together graduate faculty from many departments around a solid core of technical communication trained faculty as they design research programs.

Departments with technical communication programs must link their research and teaching agendas. When research and teaching are not linked, departments develop a two-tier system—researchers and teachers. The result of such a system is that the department's teaching mission lacks access to the research results, and researchers don't think about getting their ideas out to practitioners or to citizens (Fonow and Cook, 1991). A second reason for linking research and teaching missions lies in the department's external relations. Information developed by researchers needs to reach practicing professionals outside the academy. One way to link teaching and research is to make use of advisory boards made up of representatives of companies that hire graduates. These advisory boards can suggest research questions, provide advice on curriculum, and serve as a conduit for research to move from the academy to the workplace.

Creating an Evaluation Process

In order to ensure quality in a technical communication research program, an evaluation mechanism with internal and external components must be built into departmental procedures. Advisory boards, external review, and departmental research committees are all necessary in some combination so that accountability is defined and maintained. Carliner's recent practitioner's plea underscores the need for quality control: The value of information is linked to the quality of the research that creates it, and "we have no widely accepted definition(s) of quality in our field" (1994, p. 617). In the absence of such definitions for the field as a whole, each program has the responsibility of developing its own control mechanisms.

The internal structures to ensure quality should include a departmental emphasis on focus. Individual faculty research should contribute to the departmental mission. Research need not be practical, but must address meaningful questions that have a component dealing with civic discourse, that contribute in some fashion to the common good. Last, just as a department's research program has review mechanisms attached to it, so should each individual research project have both internal and external review mechanisms built in. At the least, research being done in the department should be read with care by the department's administrator and the researcher's colleagues.

Designing, creating, and maintaining first-rate research programs is not just a responsibility of the department; it is also a responsibility of the discipline as a whole. Over the next several years, major professional organizations in technical communication need to sponsor forums focusing on defining research in the field, on strengthening research programs in industry and the academy. Administrators of the existing Ph.D. programs should participate in discussions about the status of research in their institutions and how they might offer leadership in the profession. All of us—teachers, researchers, and practitioners—need to reexamine the idea of research in our circle of influence with an eye to establishing quality measures. In this way, we can all begin to strengthen research in technical communication and to articulate the goals of good research for the discipline as a whole. By thinking more about how to foster research in the ethical dimensions of rhetoric as well as in its practical ones, we can shape research programs that allow us to meet our responsibility to the public good.

REFERENCES

Aristotle. *Rhetoric.* (Book I). (Trans. W. R. Roberts). (1990). In P. Bizzell & B. Herzbergieds (Eds.), *The rhetorical tradition: Readings from classic times to the present* (pp. 151–160). Boston, MA: Bedford.

Blakeslee, A.M., Cole, C.M. & Confrey, T. (1996). Evaluating qualitative inquiry in technical and scientific communication: Toward a practical and dialogic validity. *Technical Communication Quarterly, 5,* 125–149.

Carliner, S. (1994). A call to research. *Technical Communication, 41,* 615–619.

Cicero. *De Oratore. Ill. XIV,* 55.

Doheny-Farina, S. (1993). Research as rhetoric: Confronting the methodological and ethical problems of research on writing in nonacademic settings. In R. Spilka (Ed.), *Writing in the workplace: New research perspectives* (pp. 253–267). Carbondale, IL: Southern Illinois University Press.

Fonow, M.M. & Cook, J.A. (1991). *Beyond methodology: Feminist scholarship as lived research.* Bloomington, IN: Indiana University Press.

Goubil-Gambrell, P. (1992). A practitioner's guide to research methods. *Technical Communication, 39,* 582–591.

Gross, A. (1994). Review: Theory, method, practice. *College English,* 56, 828–840.

Harding, S. (1991). *Whose science? Whose knowledge? Thinking from women's lives.* New York: Columbia University Press.

Kirsch, G. (1992). Methodological pluralism: Epistemological issues. In G. Kirsch & P. Sullivan (Eds.), *Methods and methodologies in composition research* (pp. 247–269).Carbondale, IL: Southern Illinois University Press.

Lakatos, I. (1978). *The methodology of scientific research programs.* J. Worrall & G. Currie (Eds.). New York: Cambridge University Press.

Wolf, M. (1992). *A thrice told tale: Feminism, postmodernism, and ethnographic responsibility.* Stanford, CA: Stanford University Press.

22

EVALUATING TECHNICAL COMMUNICATION PROGRAMS: COLLABORATING FOR QUALITY

Meg Morgan

University of North Carolina at Charlotte

INTRODUCTION

When teachers discuss collaboration in technical communication, they speak of it in highly theoretical terms (Thralls & Blyler, 1993, pp. 3–34) and as a practice for their classrooms (Morgan, 1993b, pp. 230–242). Administrators, too, can speak of collaboration as they embark on the process of evaluating programs in technical communication. Just as a collaborative pedagogy is inclusive, placing responsibility for learning on the students, so an approach to program evaluation that is truly collaborative involves all the "stakeholders" in the program, exhorts them to speak and contribute, empowers them to make needed changes, and places responsibility for the quality of the program on the very people who live in it.

In this essay, I argue for a collaborative approach to evaluating technical communication programs and also for some of the assumptions that the term "collaboration" carries with it. I weave traditional notions of program evaluation into my discussion, call up issues of quality improvement articulated in Total Quality Management theory, and present a model of evaluation for technical communication programs that is collaborative and potentially comprehensive.

DEFINITIONS OF EVALUATION

Traditional definitions of evaluation do not necessarily evoke the need for collaboration. Usually, these definitions include some mention of the "systematic" nature of evaluation, the fact that evaluation's primary activity is the collection of information, usually from a variety of sources and often to help program administrators make decisions (Patton, 1982, p. 15). There is usually some mention of the fact that a quality issue is at stake in an evaluation: Evaluation is often carried out to assess whether a program is effectively meeting its goals and objectives. In addition, a program evaluation may be carried out "to determine whether a human service is needed and likely to be used, whether it is sufficiently intense to meet the need identified, whether the service is offered as planned, and whether the human service actually does help people in need" (Posavac & Carey, 1985, p. 5).

This final statement about the purpose of evaluation suggests that there may be several reasons why a program is evaluated in the first place. Administrators and teachers often see program evaluation through a two-dimensional lens: Program evaluation is either formative or summative. If the program evaluation occurs before the end of a program, the evaluation is considered formative, that is, to make improvements in the program so that it will more effectively meets its goals. This probably represents one end of a spectrum of reasons for program evaluation—the program is in no danger of being abolished, and its administrators want to satisfy the requirements for quality for such internal audiences as students, faculty, and administrators. A summative evaluation occurs at the end of the program or program cycle to see if the program has met its goals. Such an evaluation involves a judgment about program effectiveness, often for an external audience—a licensing body, an accrediting agency, a state agency. Sometimes, through a summative evaluation, one program is compared to other, similar programs (Wolf, 1990, p. 20). Program evaluation in a university is almost always formative, finding out how the program is doing and using what is learned through the evaluation to make changes to improve performance. Even external reviews of programs by state or national accrediting agencies are formative—mainly because university programs are not easily abolished. While many program evaluations are aimed at improvement, they can also be used to make financial decisions about a program and to serve political ends. Program evaluation by external agencies can have an adverse effect on program funding, can force curriculum changes to conform to the goals of the external agency, and can, in the case of state institutions, mark the "intrusion of state agencies into curricular and teaching matters" (Bogue & Saunders, 1992, p. 4).

Within these two types of evaluation, there may be other reasons why program evaluations are performed. Programs are often evaluated to determine the relationship between cost and benefits, to identify needs for staff and program development, to help administrators make decisions, and to examine "unintended effects of programs" (Posavac & Carey, 1985, p. 11). Program evaluation has some public relations benefit—a high-quality program (a quality that is determined through an evaluation) certainly can attract students and garner university and community support. Finally, some program evaluation is done for "enlightenment" (DeRoche, 1987, p. 4), to examine how a program works and to understand how and why it succeeds or fails (p. 4).

In addition, preprogram needs assessment is often seen as a kind of program evaluation (Posavac & Carey, 1985, pp. 13–14), and I have argued elsewhere (Morgan, 1989) that the process of program evaluation for both improvement and outcome assessment should begin when new programs are put in place.

Program evaluation is controversial. Many people oppose it because of the way programs have been assessed in the past, because program evaluation may lead to eliminating a program for reasons that have nothing to do with its effectiveness, and because of what can be seen as the conservative influence in program evaluation—a "frenzy for evaluation" that reflects an "antiintellectual, antiuniversity, anti-Ivy League, and antiliberal animus. Evaluation is one way to apply conservative, businesslike realism in order to abolish programs" (Myers, 1981, p. 3). On the other hand, done in a collaborative, inclusive way, program evaluation can also meet humanitarian goals—"individual growth and well-being" and "the achievement of collective goals" (Braskamp, 1989, p. 44). The issue of quality, achieved through and documented by a collaborative evaluation process, may, in fact, be boiled down to one criterion: how well the university cares for its students (Bogue & Saunders, 1992, p. 218).

THE COLLABORATIVE EVALUATION PROCESS

Like a collaborative pedagogy, a collaborative program evaluation emphasizes and values process as it moves toward a final product. In a collaborative pedagogy, students learn that each group member has value, that each has a job to perform, but that all members must understand the nature of the task and how their roles interact and transform the task and the group. At the end of a group project, students evaluate the group process (Bosley, 1990, pp. 160–162; Morgan, Allen & Atkinson, 1989, pp. 83–94). In a collaborative pedagogy, the group requires time to come to a full understanding of what the process is and how it works. All of this is also true for the process of program evaluation; it is an ongoing process, taking time to evolve, to retreat, to reassert itself, and to reflect upon itself. The least effective methods of evaluation are those imposed from without, one-shot deals that require little or no investment from the participants in the program and do little more than produce uncertainty—uncertainty evoked by the possibility of change (Sell, 1989, p. 29). Making the evaluation process explicit and collaborative can reduce that uncertainty and also ensure that the results of the evaluation will be "owned" by those involved in the process.

There are several ways the evaluation process can proceed, but most of them include the following steps or activities (Davis, 1989, pp. 14, 16–17; Guba & Lincoln, 1989, p. 42):

1. The evaluation leader or leaders must identify all stakeholders (also called users, customers, or clients) in the program in order to include all or a representative number of them in the process. For a program in technical communication, these stakeholders might be students, program faculty, faculty in the department that houses the program, college and university administrators, program alumni, and members of relevant communities outside the university, such as employers or professional organizations.
2. Leaders should solicit "claims, concerns, and issues" (Guba & Lincoln, 1989, p. 42) from all stakeholders. In addition, evaluation leaders should also begin any evaluation process with a consideration of the mission and goals of the program, program standards, values, and tacit belief systems, discussion as to the purpose of the evaluation, and related issues. No evaluation is value-free, but articulating assumptions can be liberating. There are probably several ways this might be done. Large groups might be asked to comment using a mailed questionnaire; small groups (such as administrators and faculty) might be interviewed.
3. Once issues have been identified that cannot be resolved through negotiation or already gathered data, both the evaluation leaders and

the stakeholders must decide how concerns and issues can be clarified or resolved. Some concerns are easy to dispel and some issues are easy to resolve because they may emanate from misunderstandings or lack of information. Clarifying issues may involve collecting new data, and if this is the case, the stakeholders should decide on the best way to collect the data to resolve the issue.

4. Using the new data, all stakeholders should try to resolve issues.

The successful outcome of this process—a usable report or proposal—depends on the involvement of the stakeholders and the articulation of concerns that *they* have identified. Involving all stakeholders increases the possibility that findings from the evaluation will be accepted and used. The leader of the evaluation—as an important stakeholder—must also articulate concerns and raise issues. Together, the stakeholders and evaluation leader must draw conclusions about their inquiry so that those responsible for making change can do so. In this way, the stakeholders are agents of change in ways they could not be in a "top-down" evaluation process. Having some control over the outcomes—the changes wrought by the evaluation—may not only alleviate uncertainty but also may create a climate in which change is welcomed.

PROGRAM GOALS

Even the mission and goals of a program and the roles they play in the collaborative evaluation process should be the subject for debate. In fact, the role of goals in program evaluation is an ongoing debate among researchers and practitioners in program evaluation. On one hand, goals are necessary because they set "standards of care and service" (Posavac & Carey, 1985, p. 155). Goals encourage stakeholders to "look carefully and critically at their plans" (p. 159). They enable stakeholders to set limits, to act as measures of achievement, and even provide motivation for stakeholders. They help stakeholders "monitor performance" (p. 159). If a program is driven by goals, then goals must be accompanied by ways to reach them and by criteria to evaluate whether they have been reached (Patton, 1982, p. 106). In addition, goals are not value-free. A program's goals reveal much about that program and, at times, the goals themselves should undergo scrutiny.

Whether a program should establish goals—a practice I once thought beyond question—has now come into question. Goals, for example, may be set so artificially low that achieving them is not really a measure of program quality (Posavac & Carey, 1985, p. 160). An airline that I regularly fly has consistently met its on-time arrival goals, even when the airplane leaves the runway 20 or 30 minutes late. Apparently, the goal for arrival takes into consideration late departures. Sometimes there may be a disjunction between the goals of the program and its success or between one set of goals and another. This is the case when the operation is successful but the patient dies anyway. Sometimes goals are "latent," deliberately unarticulated or imposed on a program by external agencies (Myers, 1981, p. 113). Sometimes goals outlive their usefulness or are no longer relevant, yet are followed without question. Goals themselves must be constantly evaluated and not become "an internal set of specifications that are beyond question" (Wolf, 1990, p. 15).

As wedded as I am personally to using goals to begin an evaluation, there are alternatives to goal setting. The evaluation process that I explained above suggests that program evaluation may begin by identifying concerns or issues that the stakeholders want to explore (Davis, 1989, p. 11). In addition, stakeholders might focus on questions they would like to answer or have answered, on problems they have identified, on the unmet needs of other stakeholders, and on the gaps between theory and practice—what the program is supposed to do and what actually occurs (Patton, 1982, pp. 111–112).

PROGRAM RESEARCH METHODS

One of the most animated debates in the arena of research methods is the debate between the "positivists" and the "naturalists." Unfortunately, this debate often creates a duality where there should be none: "positivists" are those who see reality as externally verifiable, and this verification is usually achieved through a quantitative methodology—usually a true experiment that decontextualizes the empirical situation. "Naturalists," on the other hand, are those who see reality as socially constructed and who use research methods that are qualitative and contextualized. (See articles by Guba & Lincoln, 1989; Larson, 1993; Hayes, 1993.) I should be squarely on the side of the naturalists—I've done "naturalistic" research, I've argued for a collaborative pedagogy, and I am here arguing for a collaborative effort in program evaluation. Yet I am not going to argue for a totally naturalistic approach. Instead, I am going to argue for a multimodal approach to research methods in program evaluation. The choice of research designs—from ethnography to true experiment—must depend on the research questions raised. If determining the effects of a certain teacher intervention becomes a focus of the program, one of the best ways to measure these effects is through a true experiment. If the stakeholders want to examine the effects of the program on the neighboring workplace community, a true experiment is not possible—a survey might be better.

And if the stakeholders want to know the relationship between the pedagogical practices of the program and quality of the student writing in that program, stakeholders might have to observe the teaching practices by sitting in classes and by examining in depth student processes and products. Stakeholders should not be locked into one way of gathering information—both qualitative and quantitative methods are valuable in generating answers.

The above examples reveal a bias on my part—that technical communication programs are not simple entities; multiple questions can be asked, and there can be multiple ways to answer them. The examples also reveal another phenomenon about technical communication programs: Parts of the program are interconnected. An investigation into effects of a program on the neighboring workplace community may produce some unintended insight into the quality of the program's teaching or the quality of the student products. A statement that absolutely denies the value of quantitative methods—experimental especially— is just as limited as one that admits only quantitative data—a position that dominated the field of program evaluation until quite recently (Guba & Lincoln, 1989, pp. 22–26).

THE COLLABORATIVE TEAM

The premise for this essay is that program evaluation must be a collaborative effort involving all stakeholders. There are three kinds of stakeholders (Guba & Lincoln, 1989, pp. 40–41):

- Agents are those people who are "involved in producing, using and implementing" a program. In technical communication, they would certainly include program administrators and teachers.
- Beneficiaries are those who benefit, either directly or indirectly, from a program. For example, students are direct beneficiaries of a program in technical communication, but employers are indirect beneficiaries when they hire students.
- Victims are those who feel the "negative effects of the outcome" of program evaluation. If an evaluation identifies incompetent teaching or administration, the person so identified would be the victim of that evaluation.

In a collaborative effort, all types of stakeholders must be part of the process, including the victims or potential victims, which is one of the more interesting and perhaps disconcerting aspects of collaborative evaluation. Victims or potential victims are often left out of the evaluation process for several reasons: Confrontation between the victims and the other stakeholders may disrupt the process, especially in the clarification of goals and values; victims or potential victims may be more aware of problems in the program; victims or potential victims may challenge those in authority; victims or potential victims may see themselves as potential scapegoats in the process and may be unwilling to participate even if asked.

A positive outcome of a collaborative effort in technical communication program evaluation is a building of community around that program: Marginalized members of the community can be unmarginalized, victims can be unvictimized. To create community requires that members understand and accept (even if they don't agree with) the values and assumptions of that community and enact its behaviors. The process of evaluation is a process of questioning and negotiating those values, assumptions, and behaviors. It really is a process of understanding what the stakeholders expect from the program and what the program expects from the stakeholders, but it is also a process of how the stakeholders affect the program and how the program affects the stakeholders (Bogue & Saunders, 1992, p. 98). In some ways, the process of evaluation can effect "caring... and without caring there will be no quality, for there will be no standards" (p. 23).

ISSUES OF QUALITY AND A MODEL FOR PROGRAM EVALUATION

Quality has been an increasingly important issue in American corporate cultures. Often this concern for quality is expressed through principles of Total Quality Management (TQM) from which those involved in program evaluation in technical communication can learn. The basic principles of TQM that I think are particularly relevant for program evaluation are the following:

- Leaders demonstrate a vision of the program. This principle goes beyond simply articulating a vision, but calls upon leaders to act in ways that reify that vision for other employees.
- A "continuous analysis" will improve the company's product and service. In TQM, this process of ongoing analysis invokes the principle called *kaizen*—"day-to-day, week-by-week discovery of small slips that make the process increasingly more efficient, more economical, and more dependable" (Schmidt & Finnigan, 1992, p. 40). In technical communication, the product is the curriculum, and the service is the way it is taught. The notion of improvement must become part of "day-to-day" consciousness, even though it might not be efficient or economical.

- Companies must "empower and liberate employees," a mandate that requires that all teachers, staff, and administrators be involved in the process of evaluation. It also requires a commitment to improving the quality of each employee's performance through education, "training and coaching" (Schmidt & Finnigan, 1992, p. 44).
- Companies and employees pay attention to the needs of the customers (or, using the terms of this essay, "stakeholders") and consider the customer "anyone to whom you give your work" (Brocka & Brocka, 1992, p. 36). Customers are multiple: students, faculty, administrators, and the profession—the people at the other end of the service these programs provide.

In previous parts of this essay, I have discussed how the evaluation process calls for creating a vision by negotiating concerns and issues. I have also discussed the need to see evaluation as an ongoing process and especially the need to involve all stakeholders. In this section, I propose a model for technical communication program evaluation that is collaborative, ongoing, and focused on the needs of the stakeholder. This model schematizes the relationships of the components of any program in technical communication and the stakeholders of that program. The model, created with the principles of collaboration and TQM, should operate within a mission statement, which is the product of collaboration among groups of stakeholders—faculty, students, and members of the university and workplace communities. A mission statement can help identify stakeholders of a program and focus the model. For example, the mission statement for the program in technical communication at UNC–Charlotte says that the program will serve two communities: the academic community and the workplace one. It will serve the academic community by training undergraduate and graduate students to communicate technical information and the workplace community by being responsive to its educational, research, and consulting needs. The model I am using as an example is based on a matrix that connects the components of a technical communication program and the program's stakeholders as determined by the mission statement. Although I am creating a model based on a specific program in technical communication, it is flexible enough so that it can be adapted to any program; it identifies program components (faculty, curriculum, and others) and asks program evaluators to consider how these components interact with the stakeholders of the program. A fully developed model also incorporates specific goals, criteria, and means to determine if goals have been met. The model tries to answer this question for our program: How do the components of our program in technical/professional communication (faculty, students, materials/equipment, and curriculum) create a quality program for its stakeholders?

The model, based on this question, looks like this:

		Components		
	Faculty	*Students*	*Materials/Equipment*	*Curriculum*
Major Stakeholders				
Students	Quality student advising	Study groups	Textbooks, handouts, computers, software	Career preparation
Faculty	Peer observation	Student feedback	Computers	Innovation
University	Enhance university image	Community influence	Experiment with state-of-the-art software/ hardware	Writing across curriculum
Community	Consulting Outreach	Interns/ Co-op	Research into state-of-the-art Equipment Testing	Adjunct faculty
Profession	Research	Graduate school	Computers as tools for learning	Curriculum models

The number of cells in the model depends on the number of components in the program and the number of stakeholders to be included in the evaluation. The model above identifies four components and five stakeholders, for a total of 20 cells. (This configuration might not be required for another program.) The model can also accommodate any kind of goal and can include any number of items in each cell. Setting goals for each cell would be an outcome of the collaborative evaluation process I described earlier. In each of the cells created by connecting one component with one customer or user, the program developer creates a goal, criteria, and a way to measure achievement of the goal. Take, for example, the cell created by asking the question: How does the Component "Faculty" create a quality technical communication program for the stakeholder "Students"?

The phrase in the model names "Quality student advising" as the goal to be achieved. Once the goal has been established, articulated criteria are needed to mark successful goal achievement and to measure whether goals have been achieved. The criteria and measurements used to achieve the goal might be articulated as follows:

- **Criterion #1:** Students will be advised when they enter the program.
- **Measurement #1:** Each student must complete an application and have it signed by a faculty member in technical communication before registering for a course.

- **Criterion #2:** Students will be advised when they appear to be in potential danger, such as receiving a grade of "C" or lower in a required course.
- **Measurement #2:** Student accounts will be flagged and students will not be able to register until they have been advised and the advisor has lifted the flag.

At any time in the course of the program, the goals may be changed. For example, the goal "Quality student advising" might be changed to "Quality student learning," with the resulting criteria and measurement changes:

- **Criterion #1:** Students know how to write a user manual.
- **Measurement #1:** Students must design and write a user manual that receives a grade of "C" or better.
- **Criterion #2:** Students know how to produce documents on a computer.
- **Measurement #2:** Students must show that they can use at least two software packages (WordPerfect and Pagemaker, for example) to produce a technical document.
- **Criterion #3:** Students can communicate orally to a variety of situations and audiences.
- **Measurement #3:** Student must pass a test of oral communication skills in at least two different situations (persuasive and instructive) and before two audiences (hostile and indifferent). At least one presentation must be videotaped.

Many technical communication teachers design these or similar activities, yet seldom position these activities in context of program assessment. The information can be collected in any number of ways: end-of-program evaluation, portfolios, or final course certification.

Using another cell as an example, in response to the question: How does the component "Curriculum" create a quality program for the stakeholder "Profession?" the goal to indicate a quality program might be stated as:

- **Goal:** The curriculum provides new models for teaching and course development to the profession.

Achieving such a goal will demonstrate quality if the program developers believe that a quality program has a responsibility to announce itself to the field so that others can imitate it.

- **Criterion #1:** Articles are published or presentations are made at professional meetings.
- **Measurement #4:** Faculty will publish articles and/or make presentations about the curriculum over the next three years.

Some might argue that a strictly numerical presentation is limiting and reductive. I agree to some extent. When stated so coldly, the numbers do look mechanical. Yet, teachers and administrators in technical communication often perform these acts—writing and presenting—anyway: they want their programs to serve as models for other schools. Yet their presentations and articles are never framed as a way to assess the quality of a program, and they only get "counted" toward tenure or promotion of *individual* faculty. This model allows faculty and administrators to see certain professional activities in a new context.

The goals, criteria, and measures are created collaboratively by the program developers; they also can be changed if they prove unworkable. It may not be possible, for example, to flag a student's account. Or there might be some question about the quality of the faculty presentations. If the marker cannot be used confidently to measure quality, it may and should be dropped. With this model, the process of evaluation is ongoing. Program stakeholders might set annual goals or five-year ones. Regular review of the goals, criteria, and measurement would become part of a collaborative evaluation process.

CONCLUSION

The demands for accountability in these times of retrenchment require increasing attention to evaluating programs in technical communication, regardless of past performance or quality. I have argued that program evaluation must be done collaboratively with all the stakeholders taking an active part. If program stakeholders adopt this perspective, then program evaluation is more than just assessing student written or oral communication skills, which is only one small slice of the program evaluation pie. To effectively assess the impact technical communication programs make on all their stakeholders, we must assess programs more broadly. The pursuit of quality is a lifelong process.

REFERENCES

Bogue, E.G. & Saunders, R.L. (1992). *The evidence for quality: Strengthening the tests of academic and administrative effectiveness.* San Francisco, CA: Jossey-Bass.

Bosley, D. (1990). Individual evaluations in a collaborative report project. *Technical Communication, 37,* 160–162.

Braskamp, L.A. (1989). So, what's the use? In P. J. Gray (Ed.), *Achieving assessment goals using evaluation techniques* (pp. 43–50). San Francisco, CA: Jossey-Bass.

Brocka, B. & Brocka, M.S. (1992). *Quality management: Implementing the best ideas of the masters.* Homewood, IL: Business One Irvin.

Davis, B.G. (1989). Demystifying assessment: Learning from the field of evaluation. In P. J. Gray (Ed.), *Achieving assessment goals using evaluation techniques* (pp. 5–20). San Francisco, CA: Jossey-Bass.

DeRoche, E.F. (1987). *An administrator's guide for evaluating programs and personnel: An effective schools approach.* (2nd Ed.). Boston, MA: Allyn and Bacon.

Guba, E.G. & Lincoln, Y.S. (1989). *Fourth generation evaluation.* Newbury Park, CA: Sage.

Hayes, J.R. (1993). Taking criticism seriously. *Research in the Teaching of English, 27,* 305–315.

Larson, R.L. (1993). Competing paradigms for research and evaluation in the teaching of English. *Research in the Teaching of English, 27,* 283–292.

Morgan, M. (1993a). Starting at the beginning: Program assessment as part of program design. In J.A. Zappen (Ed.), *Proceedings of the Council for Programs in Technical and Scientific Communication* (pp.89–95). Cincinnati, OH.

Morgan, M. (1993b). The group writing task: A schema for collaborative assignment making. In N. R. Blyler & C. Thralls (Eds.), *Professional communication: The social perspective* (pp. 230–242). Newbury Park, CA: Sage.

Morgan, M., Allen, N. & Atkinson, D. (1989). Evaluating collaborative assignments. In R. L. & A. M. Scott (Eds.), *Collaborative technical writing: Theory and practice* (pp. 83–94). Minneapolis, MN: Association of Teachers of Technical Writing.

Myers, W.R. (1981). *The evaluation enterprise.* San Francisco, CA: Jossey-Bass.

Patton, M.Q. (1982). *Practical evaluation.* Newbury Park, CA: Sage.

Posavac, E.J. & Carey, R.G. (1985). *Program evaluation: Methods and case studies.* Englewood Cliffs, NJ: Prentice-Hall.

Schmidt, W.H. & Finnigan, J.P. (1992). *The race without a finish line.* San Francisco, CA: Jossey-Bass.

Sell, G.R. (1989). An organizational perspective for the effective practice of assessment. In P. J. Gray (Ed.), *Achieving assessment goals using evaluation techniques* (pp. 21–41) San Francisco, CA: Jossey-Bass.

Thralls, C. & Blyler, N.R. (1993). The social perspective and professional communication: Diversity and directions in research. In N.R.Blyler & C. Thralls (Ed.), *Professional communication: The social perspective* (pp. 3–34). Newbury Park, CA: Sage.

Wolf, R.M. (1990). *Evaluation in education: Foundations of competency assessment and program review.* (3d Ed.). New York: Praeger.

ABOUT THE CONTRIBUTORS

Stephen A. Bernhardt teaches professional communication in the MA and PhD programs at New Mexico State University in Las Cruces. His recent publications have appeared in *Technical Communication Quarterly*, *The Journal of Computer Documentation*, and *Written Communication*.

Judith Gunn Bronson is CEO of Stem Line Publishing Services, Inc., which provides book and journal development, professional journal management, editing, and writing in the biosciences. She has worked as a technical writer for Parke, Davis & Co. and as a technical editor for the University of Minnesota Medical School.

Rebecca E. Burnett, an Associate Professor in the Department of English at Iowa State University, focuses much of her research on the decision-making processes of classroom and workplace teams.

Mary Coney, Professor, teaches rhetorical theory, style, writing for publication, and advanced technical writing in the Department of Technical Communication at the University of Washington. Her research findings are published in *IEEE Transactions on Professional Communications*, *ASEE Journal of Engineering Education*, *Technical Communication Quarterly*, *Journal of Technical Writing and Communication*, and *Journal of Advanced Composition*.

Ann Hill Duin, an Associate Professor and Director of Graduate Studies in the Department of Rhetoric at the University of Minnesota, designs and studies technological systems that link diverse collaborators throughout the globe.

Sam Geonetta is a Professor of Communication and Department Head of Humanities at the University of Cincinnati. His teaching and research focus on effective technical and professional presentations, as well as on the use of electronic media, from personal computers to satellite conferencing.

Roger A. Grice, who retired from the IBM Corporation after a career as an information developer, is currently an information consultant and teacher. He is an Adjunct Professor of Technical Communication at Rensselaer Polytechnic Institute's Department of Language, Literature, and Communication and an instructor of electrical engineering at the State University of New York College at New Paltz.

Teresa M. Harrison is an Associate Professor of Communication in the Department of Language, Literature, and Communication at Rensselaer Polytechnic Institute. Her research and teaching specialties include organizational communication, communication theory, and computer-mediated communication.

Susan M. Katz is an Assistant Professor of English at North Carolina State University where she teaches technical and professional communication. She earned her PhD in Communication and Rhetoric from Rensselaer Polytechnic Institute. Her research focuses on issues of socialization, expertise, and authority in organizational contexts.

M. Jimmie Killingsworth is a Professor of English at Texas A&M University. He has published widely in technical communication journals and is currently series editor for the *ATTW Contemporary Studies in Technical Communication* book series with Ablex Publishing Corporation. He received his PhD from the University of Tennessee.

Linda LaDuc, who earned her PhD at Rensselaer Polytechnic Institute, directs Business Writing Programs in the School of Management at the University of Massachusetts in Amherst. Her research and teaching areas include organizational communication, proposal writing, rhetoric and leadership, gender issues in professional communication, and international business writing.

Sherry Burgus Little is a Professor of rhetoric and writing studies at San Diego State University, where she directs the technical and scientific communication program and teaches courses in the rhetoric graduate program. She is working on a book on ethics and technical communication.

Paul R. Meyer has taught rhetoric and professional communication at Texas A&M University and New Mexico State University. His work has been published in *Text, Rhetoric Review*, and elsewhere. He is currently a member of the professional staff of the Texas Higher Education Coordinating Board, the agency that regulates and sets policy for public higher education in Texas.

Meg Morgan is an Associate Professor at the University of North Carolina at Charlotte, where she is Director of Rhetoric and Writing and where for six years she directed the Technical Communication Program. Her articles have appeared in *The Journal of Business Communication, The Journal of Advanced Composition, Technical Communication,* and *The Bulletin of the Association for Business Communication.*

Cezar M. Ornatowski is an Associate Professor of Rhetoric and Writing Studies at San Diego State University, where he teaches courses in technical communication, modern rhetoric, science and technology, and Renaissance literature. His articles have appeared in numerous journals, and his major research interest include rhetoric of science and technology and discourse and political change in Central/Eastern Europe and Russia.

Nell Ann Pickett is a Professor of English at Hinds Community College in Raymond Mississippi, where she teaches technical communication, British Literature, and world literature. The author/coauthor of five books on writing and of numerous articles, she has just completed a seven-year stint as editor of *Teaching English in the Two-Year College.*

Kenneth T. Rainey teaches communication graphics, multimedia, and document design at Southern College of Technology in Marietta, Georgia. He has published articles in major technical communication journals and holds a PhD from Ohio State University.

Janice C. Redish is President of Redish & Associates, Inc. in Bethesda, Maryland. After directing the Document Design Center at the American Institute for Research for many years, she became an independent consultant, helping clients create documents and other products that are easy for people to understand and use. She earned her PhD in Linguistics from Harvard University.

Scott P. Sanders is an Associate Professor of English at the University of Mexico, where he teaches courses in professional writing and editing and directs the department's internship program. His articles on professional writing and editing have appeared in numerous journals.

Stuart A. Selber is an Assistant Professor in the Technical Communication and Rhetoric program at Texas Tech University. His articles have appeared in numerous journals, and he edited a book titled *Computers and Technical Communication: Pedagogical and Programmatic Perspectives,* 1997, for Ablex Publishing Corporation series *ATTW Contemporary Studies in Technical Communication.*

Henrietta Nickels Shirk is an Associate Professor of Technical Communication in the Department of English at the University of North Texas. Her articles have appeared in *The Journal of Technical Writing and Communication*, *The Technical Writing Teacher*, and *Technical Communication*.

Katherine Staples if founder and Department Head of Technical Communications at Austin Community College. She is active in STC and CPTSC, and her research interests include technical communication program design and adult learning. She received her PhD from the University of Texas.

Mahalingam Subbiah is an Associate Professor of English at Weber State University, where he teaches technical writing, literature, and composition. His work has appeared in *Technical Communication* and *IEEE Transactions on Professional Communication*. His current research interests include the relationship between culture and communication.

Emily A. Thrush is an Associate Professor at the University of Memphis where she teaches courses in both professional/technical writing and the teaching of English as a second language.

Elizabeth R. Turpin is a Professor in the Department of Languages and Literature at Ferris State University, where she teaches courses in technical communication and literature. She has been a writer and technical editor in academia and industry for half a century.

Billie Wahlstrom is a Professor and Head of the Rhetoric Department at the University of Minnesota. Her primary areas of research are on the impact of new technologies on communication practices and gender and technology. She is coeditor of *Technical Communication Quarterly*.

Christianna I. White, a PhD student in Rhetoric and Professional Communication in the Department of English at Iowa State University, is currently working to situate vantage theory within a larger theoretical frame created by the intersections of rhetoric, discourse analysis, and social–cognitive theory.

Author Index

Subject Index